RE-READING
GREGORY OF
NAZIANZUS

RE-READING
GREGORY OF NAZIANZUS

ESSAYS ON HISTORY, THEOLOGY,
AND CULTURE

EDITED BY

Christopher A. Beeley

The Catholic University of America Press
Washington, D.C.

Library of Congress Cataloging-in-Publication Data
Re-reading Gregory of Nazianzus : essays on history, theology, and culture /
edited by Christopher A. Beeley.
p. cm. — (CUA studies in early Christianity)
Includes bibliographical references and index.
ISBN 978-0-8132-1991-2 (alk. paper)
1. Gregory, of Nazianzus, Saint.   I. Beeley, Christopher A.
BR65.G66R47 2012
270.2092—dc23   2012004268

CONTENTS

ABBREVIATIONS

ACO *Acta Conciliorum Oecumenicorum.* 1st series, 4 vols. Edited by Eduard Schwartz and Johannes Straub. Berlin: Walter De Gruyter, 1914–1982. 2nd series, 3 vols. Edited by Rudolf Riedlinger. Berlin: Walter De Gruyter, 1984–2008.

ACW Ancient Christian Writers. 63 vols. New York: Paulist Press, 1946–.

ANF *The Ante-Nicene Fathers: The Writings of the Fathers Down to A.D. 325.* 10 vols. Edited by Alexander Roberts and James Donaldson. Revised by A. Cleveland Coxe. Edinburgh: T. and T. Clark, 1867–1872. Reprint, Peabody, Mass.: Hendrickson, 1995.

CCSG Corpus Christianorum, Series Graeca. 60 vols. Turnhout: Brepols, 1977–.

CPG *Clavis Patrum Graecorum.* 6 vols. Edited by Maurice Geerard. Corpus Christianorum. Turnhout: Brepols, 1974–1998.

CSEL Corpus Scriptorum Ecclesiasticorum Latinorum. 97 vols. Vienna: C. Gerodi, etc., 1866–.

CTh *Theodosian Code.* Edited by Paul Krüger, Theodore Mommsen, and Paul Meyer, *Theodosiani Libri XVI cum Constitutionibus sirmondianis.* 3rd ed., 3 vols. Hildesheim: Weidmann, 2002–2005.

FC The Fathers of the Church. 122 vols. Washington, D.C.: The Catholic University of America Press, 1947–.

GCS Die griechischen christlichen Schrifsteller der ersten drei Jahrhunderte. 53 vols. Leipzig: J. C. Hinrichs, 1897–1969. New series. 14 vols. Berlin: Walter De Gruyter, 1995–.

GNO *Gregorii Nysseni Opera.* Edited by Werner Jaeger, et al. Leiden: Brill, 1952–.

Hahn *Bibliotek der Symbole und Glaubensregeln der alten Kirche.* Edited by A. Hahn. Revised by G.L. Hahn. Hildesheim: Georg Olms, 1962.

LCL Loeb Classical Library. 516 vols. London: Heinemann; Cambridge, Mass.: Harvard University Press, 1912–.

LSJ *A Greek-English Lexicon.* Compiled by Henry George Liddell, Robert Scott, and Henry Stuart Jones, with Roderick McKenzie. 9th ed. Oxford: Clarendon, 1940.

Mansi *Sacrorum Conciliorum Nova et Amplissima Collectio.* 31 vols. Edited by J. D. Mansi. Florence: Expensis Antonii Zatta, 1759–1798.

NPNF *A Select Library of Nicene and Post-Nicene Fathers of the Christian Church.* Series 1–2, 14 vols. Edited by Philip Schaff and Henry Wace. Edinburgh: T. and T. Clark, 1886–1890. Reprint, Peabody, Mass.: Hendrickson, 1994.

PG Patrologiae Cursus Completus Series Graeca. 161 vols. Edited by J. P. Migne, et al. Paris: Garnier, 1857–1912.

PTS Patristische Texte und Studien. 66 vols. Berlin: Walter de Gruyter, 1964–.

SC Sources Chrétiennes. 529 vols. Paris: Cerf, 1941–.

Christopher A. Beeley

GREGORY OF NAZIANZUS
Past, Present, and Future

The past forty years have seen nothing short of a revolution in the study of St. Gregory of Nazianzus. Long honored with the title "the Theologian," conferred by the Council of Chalcedon in 451, Gregory is now widely recognized as the veritable architect of Eastern Orthodox Christianity, a source of great importance for the historiography of late antique and early medieval Christianity, a reservoir of information about classical antiquity, and a major theologian and literary figure in his own right. As he attracts new scholarship in several academic disciplines, Gregory Nazianzen is rapidly emerging as a subject of historical and ecclesiastical importance comparable only to Augustine in the West among the major figures of the high patristic period.

Until fairly recently the study of early Christian theologians concentrated on other figures: St. Augustine, the other two "Cappadocian Fathers," Basil of Caesarea and Gregory of Nyssa, and the much-maligned Origen of Alexandria. The extent of Gregory's neglect can be seen in the fact that the full set of his forty-five *Orations* (hardly a giant corpus on its own) appeared in English translation only in 2003.

This new period of Gregorian research has been motivated especially by the critical editing of Gregory's corpus, which until recently was available only in the nineteenth-century edition of Armand Benjamin Caillau printed in Migne's *Patrologia Graeca*. Following Paul Gallay's edition of Gregory's *Letters* in the mid-1960s, the critical editing of Gregory's works began in earnest in the 1970s in the Sources Chrétiennes series. French, Belgian, and later Italian scholars spearheaded the editing of Gregory's forty-five *Orations,* and that work is now almost complete. The editing of Gregory's hundreds of *Poems,* however, is still in its early stages, under the supervision primarily of Italian and German scholars. Together with this editorial work, important studies of Gregory's life and work have appeared by Jean Bernardi, Frederick Norris, Heinz Althaus, Donald Winslow, Francesco Trisoglio, Claudio Moreschini, Neil McLynn, Susanna Elm, John McGuckin, Brian Daley, and Christopher Beeley, among others.

Among English-speaking scholars, the one person who has done more than any other to inspire and accelerate the current wave of Gregorian research is Frederick W. Norris. Professor Norris' 1970 Yale dissertation, "Gregory Nazianzen's Doctrine of Jesus Christ," remained the standard treatment of Gregory's Christology for over thirty years, informing even the most recent synoptic studies of fourth-century theology. After taking his Ph.D., Fred Norris spent several years teaching in Tennessee and, from 1972 to 1977, working as a research associate and eventually as director of the Institut zur Erforschung des Urchristentums in Tübingen, Germany, and a lecturer at the University of Tübingen. After his return to the United States in 1977, Norris spent the rest of his teaching career in the southern end of the beautiful Blue Ridge Mountains, based at Emmanuel School of Religion (now Emmanuel Christian Seminary) in Johnson City, Tennessee, a graduate seminary in the American Stone-Campbell movement affiliated with the Churches of Christ and the Christian Church (Disciples of Christ). Thanks to his long tenure there, Emmanuel retains a strong emphasis on the study of patristic traditions. In the 1990s Norris expanded his work in patristics and church history to include the fields of world Christianity and global Christian missions, a project that involved serving as chair of the Consultation on American Born Churches for the Faith and Order group of the National Council of Churches.

In addition to his Lord and his family, Fred Norris has devoted his adult life to the study and teaching of early Christianity. Over the years he has written several books and numerous articles on a wide variety of subjects in early and modern Christianity, with a special focus on the Christian East. His work has covered topics as diverse as the biblical canon and the nature of apostolic tradition, late-antique Christian Antioch, individual figures such as Origen,

Paul of Samosata, and Eusebius of Caesarea, the debates over Arianism, Christian deification, the ninth-century Timothy of Baghdad, head of the East-Syrian Church, Black American preaching, and contemporary ministerial vocation and Christian mission. He has also been extremely active as an editor. Among his many projects, he served as associate editor and author of over 130 articles for the *Encyclopedia of Early Christianity,* which remains the leading single-volume reference work on the early church and is now in its second edition. Professor Norris has won research fellowships in multiple countries, and he has served the field of patristics and early Christian studies in several administrative capacities as well, being honored with the presidency of the North American Patristic Society in 1993–94.

After spending nearly fifteen years working on other subjects, Norris returned to his first scholarly love, Gregory of Nazianzus. Beginning in the 1980s, he published a series of important articles on Gregory, focusing on basic historical questions and topics in theological method. Norris' articles include studies of the identity of Gregory's opponents in the *Theological Orations* and the complicated manuscript tradition of the series, as well as Gregory's rhetoric, argumentation, and use of Scripture and his understanding of theological language, which, as Norris observed, takes a different turn from the position held by the brothers Basil of Caesarea and Gregory of Nyssa. Norris' crowning achievement was his 1991 commentary on the *Theological Orations,* entitled with a phrase taken from the second oration of the series: *Faith Gives Fullness to Reasoning.* Countless students have had occasion to consult this work, which remains the standard commentary on one of the most important texts of the patristic period. Among the many insights that it provides into Gregory's work, perhaps the greatest contribution of Norris' commentary is the new vista that it offers into Gregory's understanding of how Christian theology, Greek philosophy, and the practice of rhetoric interrelate at a deep level. Norris has convincingly shown that Gregory worked deliberately and by professional training as a "philosophical rhetor" in the tradition of Second Sophistic rhetoric, as exemplified by the likes of Hermogenes of Tarsus. That is to say, Gregory had a fundamentally integrative understanding of Christian theology, philosophy, and rhetoric, which may surprise those who harbor the long-standing myth that philosophy and theology stand in opposition to rhetoric, a fantasy that has long been reinforced by a selective and unsophisticated reading of Plato's *Gorgias.* Norris found support for his new reading of Gregory from the likes of Gregory's twelfth-century commentator Elias of Crete. By drawing our attention to Gregory's real intellectual style and milieu, Norris has made Gregory accessible to many modern readers who previously had little informed access to the work of this major early theologian.

As a fitting tribute to Frederick Norris' career as a scholar and a churchman, we offer this collection of pathbreaking studies of Gregory Nazianzen. The array of topics included here abundantly demonstrates Gregory's richness as a scholarly and ecclesiastical resource, much as Norris has endeavored to show us over the last four decades.

In the theological sphere, Brian Daley gives an insightful account of Gregory's theological system as presented in his didactic *Poemata arcana,* a series of poems modeled on Origen's *De principiis.* As Daley shows, Gregory's choice of Homeric vocabulary and meter reveals much about his poetic mind and temperament. Basing herself in Gregory's Festal *Orations* and his three *Orations* "On Peace," Verna Harrison has written an important study of the "grammatical" character of Gregory's Trinitarian theology, and particularly its social dimension, which has been neglected in recent conversations about differing models of the Trinity among patristic and modern theologians. We have two pieces as well on Gregory's biblical interpretation: a general study of the Origenian, Christological, and rhetorical character of Gregory's exegesis by Ben Fulford, and Brian Matz's analysis of Gregory's use of Scripture in *Oration* 14 "On the Love of the Poor" in particular. Looking at the background of Gregory's theology, Everett Ferguson gives an illuminating account of the Alexandrian sources of Gregory's baptismal theology; William Tabbernee analyzes Gregory's characterizations of Montanism in his polemical defense of the divinity of the Holy Spirit, and the possible sources of Gregory's knowledge of Montanism; and Claudio Moreschini examines Gregory's views toward Greek philosophy and his appropriation of certain Cynic ideas.

Taking us into matters of historiography, Suzanne Abrams Rebillard demonstrates Gregory's deliberate and artful emulation of the classical historians Herodotus and Thucydides in his poetic self-presentation as a Christian priest. Again drawing on Gregory's poetry, Andrew Hofer gives a moving description of Gregory's literary treatment of his attempted stoning at the Easter Vigil of 380, as a species of autobiographical Christology that shows a connection with the pagan *rhetor* Libanius. Two particular episodes in Gregory's life receive new studies as well. Vasiliki Limberis draws our attention to Gregory Nazianzen's and Gregory of Nyssa's unpleasant dealings with their challenging colleague Bishop Helladius of Caesarea; while Neil McLynn provides a new analysis of Gregory's poem "To Hellenius" in order to shed light on Gregory's theological endeavors, his disputed consecration as bishop of Sasima, and his complicated relationship with Basil.

In a third group of essays, we have several pieces that deal with Gregory's enormous legacy in later Eastern traditions. Paul Blowers, Norris' successor at Emmanuel, has written an intriguing study of the way in which Maximus Confessor reworked Gregory's notion of the providential "play" of the Logos. Andrea Sterk gives us a new glimpse into the role that Gregory played in the Eastern mission to the Slavs, as seen in the work of Constantine the Philosopher, also known as St. Cyril, apostle to the Slavs. Drawing from the ninth-century illustrated manuscript of Gregory's *Orations* presented to Emperor Basil I, Susanna Elm reveals the use of Gregory as an imperial and priestly model by Photius and the Macedonian emperors. And Andrew Louth offers a new look at the Byzantine commentaries on a particularly problematic notion in Gregory's work, namely his remarks on Jesus' statement that "the Father is greater than I." As Louth argues, the practice of commentary illustrates the extremely high authority that Gregory came to acquire in many regions during the Byzantine period through the hymnody of the church as well as its formal theological reflection.

John McGuckin brings the volume to a close with an appropriate final *logos:* a highly scientific and deadly serious analysis of the humor in Gregory's first two *Theological Orations*—an aspect of Gregory's work that was first made evident by the delivery of one of Gregory's sermons in church by none other than Professor Norris himself. As McGuckin notes, there are both amusing and painful comparisons to be made with the humor of our honoree. Yet it is also fully in keeping with the character of the Christian Gospel that Gregory's work, like that of his devotee Fred Norris, contained plenty of wit, humor, and real joy alongside the more serious aspects of scholarly and theological work.

This collection of new studies represents the cutting edge of Gregorian research in the early twenty-first century. We offer this work as a tribute to one who has done so much to recover for modern readers the magisterial and multifold achievement of St. Gregory the Theologian.

Frederick Norris

PART I ❧ THEOLOGY

Brian E. Daley, SJ

---

1. Systematic Theology in Homeric Dress

Poemata arcana

In the American academic world today, it is customary to distinguish between "systematic" theology and theology in its historical or scriptural forms. Whatever one thinks of the validity of such distinctions—and from a Christian perspective, at least, they raise serious questions—one must recognize that the project of forming one's religious understanding of God, the world, and the human journey into a single, coherent whole began long before Barth or Tillich, or even Thomas Aquinas. From Varro to academic Platonists, scholars and thinkers in antiquity showed a perennial instinct not just for research and speculation, but also for tying together the strands and wisps of previous human learning into an organic body. Augustine, in his *Enchiridion,* attempted this for our understanding of the Christian Gospel, and the great *summas* of the twelfth and thirteenth centuries adapted this systematizing instinct to the technical discourse and the intellectual cut-and-thrust of the new universities. Gregory of Nyssa, too, in the 380s, attempted something of the sort in his fascinating but enigmatic *Catechetical Discourse,* at once an echo of earlier Christian apologies (and Athanasius's treatise *On the Incarnation*) and his own, more ambitious attempt to show, in one short treatise, the persuasiveness and inner consistency of Christian faith and practice, despite the apparent foolishness of the message. What I want to suggest here is that his family friend Gregory of Nazianzus undertook this same synthetic task at roughly the same time, but from his own theological perspective and in his own characteristically artistic way: not in an oration or even a set of orations, but in the set of eight medium-length poems, written in Homeric dialect and the classical hexameters of epic and didactic verse, that together have come to be known as the *Poemata arcana* or TA ΑΠΟΡΡΗΤΑ: "poems on ineffable mysteries."[1]

Writing didactic poems on technical, scientific, and even theological subjects was not a new pastime for learned Greeks in the late fourth century. The language, grammatical forms, and galloping meter of the Homeric epics had been used to convey moral and religious messages by Hesiod at the beginning of the eighth century before the Christian era and for speculations on nature by the pre-Socratic philosophers Parmenides and Empedocles. The third-century BCE scholar Aratus of Soloi wrote a long poem on the constellations, the *Phaenomena,* in the same style, and later philosophical theologians—the third-century BCE Stoic Cleanthes, in his *Hymn to Zeus,* or the authors of the collection of *Orphic Hymns*, which may have been put together as late as the third century of our own era—sang the praises of all the major gods, all the hidden divine forces in the universe, in dactylic hexameters. In a more narrative style, the Homeric hymns and their highly refined echoes by Callimachus, the third-century Alexandrian, retold traditional Greek religious myths in the same poetic form. The Latin tradition of didactic poetry, written also in hexameter, began with Lucretius's *De rerum natura* in the early first century before Christ, and was continued elegantly by Virgil in his *Georgics* a few decades later. The Latin Christian writer

<hr/>

1. These poems have recently appeared in a critical edition: Claudio Moreschini, ed., *Gregory of Nazianzus: Poemata Arcana,* textual introduction by Claudio Moreschini, English translation, introduction, and commentary by Donald A. Sykes, English translation of textual introduction by Leofranc Holford-Strevens, Oxford Theological Monographs (Oxford: Oxford University Press, 1997). Previously, the most readily available Greek text was the eighteenth-century Maurist Benedictine edition of A. B. Caillau, reprinted in Migne's *Patrologia Graeca* 37 (Paris: 1858). Although these eight poems clearly form a unified set in the manuscripts, Caillau's edition included another poem of Gregory's on the subject of Providence as no. 6, because of its similarity of subject to no. 5, even though it is written in the iambic meter rather than dactylic hexameter. The title TA ΑΠΟΡΡΗΤΑ is given to these poems, along with six others (in the PG numbering: *Carm.* 1.2.9, 14, 15 and 16 [as one work], 17 [including also *Carm.* 2.1.2], 31, and 33), in a collection, with prose paraphrases made by the ninth- and tenth-century Byzantine scholar Nicetas David. Some early manuscripts further divide *Poems* 4 and 8, and the eighth-century commentator Cosmas of Jerusalem refers to the whole collection by the title Περὶ ἀρχῶν ("On First Principles"). In this article, I have used the superb new edition of Moreschini and have benefited greatly from Sykes's excellent translation and notes. There is also a fine recent translation of these and other poems into English by Peter Gilbert, *On God and Man: The Theological Poetry of St. Gregory of Nazianzus* (Crestwood: St. Vladimir's Seminary Press, 2001).

Juvencus, a Spanish contemporary of the Emperor Constantine, wrote a biblical epic paraphrasing the four Gospels around 330, an effort that was followed in the mid-fifth century, in Greek, by Nonnos of Panopolis's hexameter versification of the Gospel of John, in twenty-four books, and in the sixth century by Arator's Latin epic based on the *Acts of the Apostles*. Augustine of Hippo composed what was probably the first non-biblical Christian didactic poem in Latin: his early *Psalmus contra Partem Donati* (394), a narrative of the origins of the Donatist sect written not in classical epic meter, but in an accentual rhythm and simple language apparently intended for congregational singing.

Greek Christian didactic poetry began, in fact, probably in the 360s, with the work of the grammarian Apollinarius of Laodicaea, father of the bishop of the same name who came to be regarded as the first Christological heretic. In response to the Emperor Julian's decree of June 17, 362, banning Christians from teaching Greek literature in the schools, the elder Apollinarius is said to have written an epic in twenty-four books on the "antiquities of the Hebrews" from the beginning of Genesis to the time of Saul, as well as other Biblical paraphrases in dramatic and comic meters;[2] the fifth-century Christian historian Sozomen assures us that it was only contemporary prejudice in favor of earlier authors that prevented these works from being regarded as equal to the best classical literature in style and dramatic power.[3]

This same desire, born out of the challenge posed by Julian's edict to the growing class of cultivated Christian Hellenists to create a new body of literature, Christian and orthodox in content but fully conforming to classical Greek forms and standards, seems to have been one of Gregory of Nazianzus's main motives in composing his own poetic corpus of some 19,000 extant lines.[4] This

2. Socrates, *Historia Ecclesia* 3.16; Sozomen, *Historia Ecclesia* 5.19. The still-extant paraphrase of the 150 biblical psalms in Homeric hexameters, attributed to Apollinarius (Apollinarius, *Metaphrases in Psalmen*, ed. Arthur Ludwich [Leipzig: Teubner, 1912]), is now generally agreed to be by an unknown author writing shortly after the Council of Chalcedon who echoes phrases from Gregory's *Poemata arcana* as well as from Nonnos of Panopolis: see Joseph Golega, *Der Homerische Psalter: Studien über die dem Apolinarios von Laodikeia zugeschriebene Psalmenparaphrase*, Studia Patristica et Byzantina 6 (Ettal: Buch- und Kunstverlag Ettal, 1960), esp. 2–3, 169–75.

3. Sozomen, *Historia Ecclesia* 5.19.

4. According to Jerome, *De viribus illustris* 117, and the *Souda* 1.496, Gregory wrote a total of some 30,000 lines of poetry. In his poem "On his Own Verses" (*Carm.* 2.1.39), Gregory gives four reasons for writing his poetry: to "put constraints on my prolixity, that I may write, but never write too much"; to provide a "pleasant potion" and a persuasive view of Christian teaching for young readers and lovers of poetry; to prove to the "Sophists" or literary professionals that Christians could write Greek literature as

enormous literary productivity seems mainly to have been the work of Gregory's last years, after he had retired from being bishop of the Nicene community
in Constantinople in the early summer of 381 and had returned to his ances-
tral estate of Karbala, in rural Cappadocia. Gregory's poetry includes works of
widely varying length and content: long, dramatic narratives of his own earlier
life and experiences, written either in Homeric epic language and meter or in
the Attic iambic form used for dramatic dialogue; treatises on the virtues or the
ascetic life; and what we might term "occasional verse"—soliloquies, prayers,
epigrams, verse letters, epitaphs—many of them in the more complicated meters and dialects of Greek lyric poetry. Among the most celebrated of these
compositions, in the world of Byzantine connoisseurs and copyists, were the
eight "mystery-poems" or *Arcana* we are discussing here: eight dense, solemn
works in the sophisticated style of classical Greek didactic poetry, which together present us with a coherent overview of the core of Christian doctrine, as
seen through the lens of Gregory's peculiar version of the Cappadocian theological project. More than any of his forty-four orations or his 249 letters, they
seem intended to offer us a comprehensive view of Christian faith as an organic
whole.

As I have already mentioned, synthetic prose summaries of a particular approach to philosophical or theological doctrine were not a new idea in
fourth-century Greek culture, and most of those that still exist, in fact, tend to
follow the same general outline. One of the most complete syntheses that has
come down to us is the textbook of school Platonism or *Didaskalikos,* attributed in the manuscripts to an otherwise unknown Alcinous, which has often
been identified, in modern times, as the lost *Eisagoge* of the second-century
Middle Platonist Albinus. This manual, which presents itself as an introduction to the Platonic tradition of philosophy as the means for "freeing and
turning around the soul" in its quest for wisdom,[5] begins with a brief sketch of
the rudiments of epistemology and logic and concludes with a summary treatment of ethics and politics. In its central chapters, however, it deals with the
origin and constitution of the world we live in: the "first principles" of reality,
namely matter (§8), intelligible forms (9), and the transcendent "primary in-

---

well as pagans; and to console himself in the midst of illness and advancing age. See my translation in Brian Daley, *Gregory of Nazianzus: The Early Church Fathers* (London: Routledge, 2006), 164.

5. Alcinous, *The Handbook of Platonism,* trans. John Dillon (Oxford: Clarendon Press, 1993), 3.

tellect" we call God (10); and the created or composed world of sensible be-ings, including the human person. The human soul, which is intended to be in control of its body, is created by the "primal God" (23.1), and is immortal (25) and self-determining (26), not programmed in its choices by the fate that sets the rules of the universe (26). Choosing and embodying the good is the heart of human virtue, and the key to real happiness (27), which consists in gradu-ally attaining "likeness to God." (28)

A similar handbook, digesting the central teachings of fourth-century neo-Platonism, is Sallustius's *On the Gods and the Universe,*[6] probably the work of Flavius Sallustius, consul in 363 and a friend and protégé of the Emperor Ju-lian. Although the work does not mention Christians, it may well have been inspired by Julian's program to reorganize the teachings and practices of tra-ditional philosophical paganism in ways that would compare favorably with Christian catechesis and charitable activity. Arguing that real piety has to be grounded in philosophical sophistication (1), Sallustius—like Alcinous—pres-ents the divine being as changeless, impassible, and incorporeal (1–2); myths and traditional conceptions of the gods must be interpreted allegorically against this philosophical background. The "first cause" is unique and above knowledge (5); the gods known to humanity come forth from it in an intelli-gible order (6) and exercise their influence in an eternal, ordered universe (7). The soul is naturally immortal (8) and uses the body as its instrument, acting freely in a world framed but not wholly determined by fate, and guided by di-vine providence (9). Evil, in this universe, is not a substance, but a privation of being and order (12), caused by erroneous human activity. The soul becomes virtuous by following reason (10); prayer and sacrifices express the soul's yearn-ings, although they do not change the minds of the gods (14–16). The universe will never be destroyed by the gods, but although souls may move on to inhabit other human bodies after death (20), they can, through virtue and reason, puri-fy themselves from all corporeality and come to dwell with the gods (21).

Even more clearly than Alcinous' handbook, Sallustius's treatise presents the reader with an ordered view of the divine being, the universe and its natu-ral laws, the human person, the heart of virtue and religion, and the future we can look forward to—with a systematic summary of the pagan counterparts of

---

6. Sallustius, *Concerning the Gods and the Universe,* ed., trans. Arthur Darby Nock (Cambridge: Cambridge University Press, 1926).

what Christians would call theology, the doctrine of creation, anthropology, ethics, prayer and the sacraments, and eschatology. Anthony Meredith recently offered the persuasive suggestion that Gregory of Nyssa's *Catechetical Discourse,* composed perhaps twenty years after Sallustius's handbook, may well be loosely modeled on its structure and be intended to offer educated Christian readers, still smarting from the challenge of Julian's decree to their sense of worth as Greek intellectuals, an alternative that put the Christian "myth" of salvation through Jesus' death and resurrection into a coherent and intelligible form that does justice to what reasonable people seek to know about God, the world, and ourselves.[7]

Gregory of Nazianzus's *Poemata arcana,* probably written during the first two years after the theologian's retirement from the throne of Constantinople in 381,[8] is thus almost exactly contemporary with his namesake's synthetic essay.[9] The cultural and religious context of both works, then, was identical; so it is more than likely that a strong sense of the need, in the wake of Julian's cultural and religious challenge, to present a cohesive panorama of Christian doctrine in terms likely to impress cultivated believers and pagans as attractive, engaging, and spiritually profound would have lain behind this Gregory's effort, too. The result, however, is utterly different in his hands, and thoroughly revealing of the different interests and styles of the two Cappadocian theologians. While Gregory of Nyssa attempts to retell the Christian narrative of redemption in a way that would appear philosophically compelling to Platonists, Gregory of Nazianzus draws instead on his well-honed literary virtuosity and his love of classical poetic and rhetorical forms; equally important, his conceptual model for the collection is not a handbook of Middle Platonic or neo-Platonic philosophy, but the great Christian synthetic work of his own chosen theological forebear, Origen's *De principiis,* which provides these eight

7. See Anthony Meredith, unpublished paper delivered at the International Conference on Patristic Studies, Oxford, 2003.

8. For the dating of the poems, see Sykes's argument in Moreschini, ed., *Poemata Arcana,* 66–67. For a survey and chronology of the events of Gregory's life, see Daley, *Gregory of Nazianzus,* 3–26 and the literature cited there.

9. Relatively little is known about the details and chronology of Gregory of Nyssa's life, so that the dating of his works is almost entirely conjectural. For two attempts at it, see Jean Daniélou, "La chronologie des oeuvres de Grégoire de Nysse," *Studia Patristica* 7 (TU 92; Berlin: Universitätsverlag, 1966): 159–69; and Gerhard May, "Die Chronologie des Lebens und der Werke des Gregor von Nyssa," in *Écriture et culture philosophique dans la pensée de Grégoire de Nysse,* edited by Marguerit Harl, 51–66 (Leiden: Brill, 1971).

poems with the thematic frame on which Gregory weaves his own distinctive doctrinal fabric.

As is now well recognized, Origen's work has an unusual (though, in antiquity, not unique) structure, which we must recognize if we are to grasp its full meaning.[10] Origen sketches out what he understands as the basic contents of the apostolic teaching or "rule of piety" in the treatise, not once but twice. *De principiis* 1.1 to 2.3 offers the reader a relatively straightforward account of what Origen understands to be the basic doctrines necessary for progress in the Christian life, buttressed with the scriptural grounds for asserting them: God as an incorporeal, spiritual being, who is Father, Son, and Holy Spirit; the role of each of the persons of the Trinity in the divine economy; God's work of creation; the nature of rational creatures, capable of turning from God because of their freedom; the goal of creation's history, which is the restoration of all created intelligences to union with God in knowledge and love, through enlightenment and purgative suffering; the nature of embodiment and the purpose of the material world; the role of the material world and bodies in the final state of creatures, in which "God will be all in all" (1 Cor 15:28).[11] Having finished this survey in *princ.* 2.3, Origen takes up the same sequence of key doctrines again in the second part of the work (*princ.* 2.4–3.6), now elaborating on his argument with a noticeably anti-Gnostic twist, to emphasize the unity of both testaments, the origin of the material world in the providence of the one God, the freedom of the created mind to determine its own fate, and the involvement of the body in final salvation. In the third part of the work (book 4), he turns to the related problem of how to interpret the generally accepted body of Christian Scripture—as a whole and in its particular texts—in light of this broad doctrinal structure, which is itself built up from Scripture's inspired teaching. Finally, in the work's last chapter, Origen briefly summarizes the whole structure of Christian doctrine a third time: now under the rubric of God's unique incorporeality, in which the believer is called to share to an increasing degree. As we participate knowingly, through faith, in the ut-

---

10. For a detailed analysis of the structure and purpose of this work, see Daley, "Origen's *De Principiis:* A Guide to the Principles of Christian Scriptural Interpretation," in *Nova et Vetera: Patristic Studies in Honor of Thomas Patrick Halton,* edited by John Petruccione, 3–21 (Washington, D.C.: The Catholic University of America Press, 1998).

11. Origen outlines this series of doctrines, as the common fund of teaching shared by all Christians, in the preface to *de Principiis* 7.

terly incorporeal life of God, our present life—and even our understanding
of the text of Scripture—is gradually set free from the limitations imposed by
our present existence as embodied intelligences.

When one compares the content and structure of Gregory's *Poemata arcana* to that of the *De principiis*, the similarity strikes one as unmistakable,
even though the presentation and coloring of the content are, just as unmis-
takably, Gregory's own. The first poem, which deals with the characteristics
of the ineffable divine substance, is itself entitled "On First Principles"—a title that the earliest Byzantine commentator on the poems gives to the entire
collection.[12] The title apparently refers to the fact that this divine substance,
as the poem makes clear, the ἀρχή or Mystery at the origin of all things, is ir-
reducibly manifold in its singularity: Father, Son, and Holy Spirit. *Poem 2*,
"On the Son," is an extended reflection on the eternal, immaterial generation of Son from Father (lines 13–21), and on the enduring paradoxes of the
Son's incarnation for our sakes (61–80). *Poem 3*, "On the Spirit," closely parallels Gregory's fifth *Theological Oration* (*Or.* 31) in acknowledging the difficulty of finding a clear statement of the divine and hypostatic identity of the
Spirit in Scripture, and goes on to reflect on the mutual inherence of Father,
Son, and Spirit as "three lights" (71), exercising "a bright-shining single rule"
(79) and sharing "one strength, one thought, one glory, one might" (87–88).
Poem 4, "On the Universe," offers a survey of the beings that constitute the
visible and invisible cosmos, and emphasizes, against all forms of ontological
dualism, that everything in the world—even the matter and form that are its
metaphysical principles—have a beginning in time, and are the creation of the
one and only God. Before the created universe, God existed without tempo-
ral succession, contemplating his own beauty and "gazing on the forms of the
world that would later come to be, but which were present to God" (68–69).
In *Poem 5*, "On Providence," Gregory rejects two widespread ancient ways of
explaining the unrolling of events in history—pure chance and fatalism—and
argues, with a sharp glance at those who believe in astrology, that it is God the
Word who "steers all these things," above and below (34–36). *Poem 6*, "On
Rational Natures," paints a panorama of the world of angels and demons: created intelligences that naturally find moral change harder than we do (53–55),
but that are still capable of turning away from their proper end. Lucifer's fall,

---

12. See above, n. 1.

which came from aspiring to "the royal honor of the great God" (57), led him to envy human creatures and ultimately to "drive them out of Paradise" (65); Christ has refrained from simply annihilating him and his cohorts, but has limited his powers, and Gregory holds out the possibility that someday even the stubborn Lucifer will "pay his penalties," his rebel "substance" consumed by the purging fire of judgment (92–93). In *Poem* 7, "On the Soul," Gregory summarizes the view of human nature he shares with the other Cappadocians: the soul is "a breath of God," mingled with earth, "a light hidden in a cave" (1–3), divine and immortal as an image of God, and created to mingle mind and matter as "the godlike king of earthly affairs" (60). Gregory goes on to tell the story of the fall, in terms similar to those of his oration "On the Theophany" (*Or.* 38): the first pair were tricked into tasting prematurely of the fruit of "perfect discrimination between good and evil" (108–9), something beneficial to those who are "full-grown," but dangerous for complete beginners (109–10). *Poem* 8, "On the Testaments and the Appearance of Christ," then takes up the rest of the narrative of salvation: God's gift of laws to humanity, grounded in the plan of his Word (4–7); the decision of the Word to "empty himself of the glory of his immortal Father" (39–40) and to become the son of a virgin: "a strange son, born without father, yet no stranger, for it is from my stock that the immortal one, now mortal, came" (41–42). Echoing Gregory of Nyssa's *Catechetical Oration,* the poet speaks of the "veiled" appearance of this "new and different Adam" (53), which led the "seemingly wise serpent" to assault him, only to encounter God (56–57). After summing up the Gospel story in terms that again remind us of his Christmas Oration—the humble birth of Christ, his circumcision and baptism, his work as mediator, his gift of the Spirit to all peoples—Gregory concludes this poem on the divine economy, as Gregory of Nyssa concludes his *Catechetical Oration,* with a brief reflection on baptism, as the way in which—like Israel on the first Pasch—he receives "the best of seals, flowing from God, coming from Christ the giver of light" (92–93). This gift, offered now to all humanity like the air and the open sky, allows Gregory to lift his gaze and "move my feet on the path back towards life" (95).

Anyone familiar with Gregory's other works will recognize, even in this brief summary of the *Poemata arcana,* themes and colorings that occur throughout his orations and letters: his central focus on the Trinity, conceived in precise terms of shared being and distinctive relationships, not to be conceived as any material generation, but imagined most accurately as self-communicating light; his emphasis on the Word as the agent of both creation and the economy of redemption, and on the paradoxical human presence of the Word among us, as the stunning culmination of that history; his stress on our own need to be purified and led by God's Spirit, if we are to have any understanding of God and God's works (*Poem* 1.9–13, 22–24, 35–39); his allusions to the present human condition as a laborious yet hopeful pilgrimage: "We journey on our upward path; for we hasten towards a rational, heavenly nature, even though we are bound to earth" (*Poem* 5.70–71); his hint of a promise of divinization, as the work of the Holy Spirit "who is God to me, by whom I know God, who is God in that other world, and who makes me God in this one" (*Poem* 3.3–4). All these are familiar touches; what is new is their compression, their poetic form, and their organic arrangement in a theological scheme carefully constructed to match and evoke the structure of Origen's masterpiece, as if it (not Platonic handbooks) served best as the paradigm for Christian doctrinal synthesis.

As modern readers we may be puzzled by the fact that Gregory chose to build his own synthesis in Homeric vocabulary and meter, to proclaim the Christian Gospel—as Herbert or Milton would later do—in the voice of a religious poet rather than that of a preacher or a polemicist. Was it simply a show of linguistic virtuosity, a demonstration that this Christian bishop, at least—despite his allegedly rustic origins[13]—could equal the most accomplished of his Hellenic contemporaries in singing with the accents of classical wisdom and piety? Or was it that the poet, for classical tradition, was understood to speak in more than simply assertive human tones, to be an inspired prophet as well as a verbal artisan? As Gregory presents it here, in any case, the structure of doctrine that Origen had called the "rule of piety"[14] has been elaborated into an elegant and subtle work of art, a colorful and harmonious landscape of Cappadocian orthodoxy, formed in terms calculated to move and purify the heart, as well as to satisfy the mind. As such, Gregory's "mystery poems" remain a unique theological accomplishment.

13. See, e.g., *Or.* 26.4; *Or.* 38.6; *Or.* 42.2, 20–24; *De vita sua* 592–99.
14. See e.g., Origen, *princ.* 1.5.4; 3.1.17; 3.5.3; 4.3.14.

Verna E. F. Harrison

2. Illumined from All Sides by the Trinity

Neglected Themes in Gregory's
Trinitarian Theology

In recent studies Michel Barnes and Lewis Ayres have drawn attention to a broad consensus among fourth-century defenders of Nicaea, in particular the Cappadocians and Augustine. They have highlighted how these theologians argue for the full divinity of the Son and the Holy Spirit and their equality with the Father on the grounds that the activity of the three persons in the created world is one, and hence their nature is one. Thus, when Scripture speaks of one of them acting, the other two must be present and active, too, and together they produce a single activity.[1] Ayres concludes from this that the textbook contrast between Augustinian and Cappadocian—or Eastern and Western—understandings of the Trinity is misleading, and further that there is a fundamental disconnect between the classic Trinitarian faith of the pro-Nicene fathers and the kinds of social Trinitarianism popular among many of today's theologians.[2] Much of this contemporary reflection has been sparked by Karl Rahner.[3] He asserted that the Trinity must be understood in accord with biblical texts that speak of each divine person acting in specific

1. Michel Barnes, "One Nature, One Power: Consensus Doctrine in Pro-Nicene Polemic," *Studia Patristica* 29 (1997): 205–23, at 220, and other articles; Lewis Ayres, *Nicaea and Its Legacy: An Approach to Fourth-Century Trinitarian Theology* (Oxford: Oxford University Press, 2004), 279–301.

2. Ayres, *Nicaea and Its Legacy,* 301; see also 384–429.

3. Karl Rahner, *The Trinity,* trans. Joseph Donceel (London: Burns and Oates, 1970).

ways and with the *lex orandi* of Christians throughout the centuries, who in prayer and worship have encountered each of them personally *and* all three together as one God. Rahner's question is still crucial, as are the pro-Nicene fathers' views. The issue is not *whether* pro-Nicenes understand the divine activity *ad extra* as one, but *how*. Do Father, Son, and Spirit each contribute to their common activity in a distinctive way capable of manifesting each of them personally in the created world, or are their roles in divine activity indistinguishable and interchangeable?

Much more study is needed to see in detail how the pro-Nicenes understand the unity or triunity of divine activity. Ayres focuses on Gregory of Nyssa, whose spirituality emphasizes divine perfections such as goodness, purity, wisdom, justice, and all the virtues, which he sees as inhering in the divine nature *per se*.[4] Thus, for him each perfection is one, and together they comprise a unity.[5] However, Ayres devotes much less attention to Gregory Nazianzen,[6] whose spirituality is profoundly Trinitarian and whose theological method and understanding of the Trinity differ significantly from those of the Nyssen and of Augustine. The present short chapter cannot explore this in depth, but will discuss a few key texts in Nazianzen's writings that address the issue of divine self-manifestation and activity in the created world.

Christopher Beeley has suggested in a fine book that Gregory does not articulate his Trinitarian theology most fully in the five *Theological Orations,* where he uses logical puzzles and argumentation to debate his Eunomian opponents on their own ground. Beeley looks to the other orations Gregory wrote throughout his career, which contain many carefully wrought confessions of faith in the Trinity, for expressions of his own theology. These passages occur in the context of liturgy, prayer, pastoral care, and praise. Beeley claims, I believe rightly, that they provide the best foundation and context for rightly understanding passages in the *Theological Orations,* whose meaning is obscure and whose interpretation has proven controversial.[7] I would add that of the "other" orations, those Gregory preached on the major church feasts of

4. Ayres, *Nicaea and Its Legacy,* 298, cites Gregory of Nyssa, *Against Eunomius* 1.19 and other texts.

5. Gregory of Nyssa, *Beatitudes,* 4.5.

6. Ayres, *Nicea and Its Legacy,* devotes a chapter each to Gregory of Nyssa (344–63) and Augustine (364–83), but only pages 244 to 251 to Nazianzen.

7. Christopher A. Beeley, *Gregory of Nazianzus on the Trinity and the Knowledge of God: In Your Light We Shall See Light,* Oxford Studies in Historical Theology (Oxford and New York: Oxford University Press, 2008).

Easter, Christmas, Epiphany, and Pentecost are among the most important.[8] His three orations on peace, numbers 6, 22, and 23, in which he uses Trinitarian theology to address divisions in his congregations, together with *Oration* 42, his farewell address at the Council of Constantinople, are also important. We will study key Trinitarian passages from some of these orations below.

Many things could be said regarding Gregory's immensely creative, multifaceted, and foundational thought about how God is Trinity, beyond what can be said here.[9] After discussing the influence of rhetoric on Gregory's theological method, we will consider how he anticipates some major themes in contemporary Trinitarian theology. First we will focus on God as both one and three, and divine activity, by which God is known and encountered in the created world, as both one and three. Then we will discuss movement among the divine persons and human community as an image of the Holy Trinity.

Rhetoric and Antimony

Gregory makes creative use of his considerable literary, philosophical, and rhetorical talent and training as he makes various attempts to express what he can of the mysteries of the Trinity, Jesus Christ, and the human person. Though always mindful that the divine mystery is largely incomprehensible and ineffable, he is aware of his gift for *logoi,* words and discourse. His theological writings are didactic and sometimes polemical, but they are above all doxological. He uses logical argumentation to articulate theology, but also prayer and praise, poetry and rhetorical prose. Immersed as he is in the literary forms of the Second Sophistic, in many texts he employs the balanced clauses and antithetical structures of rhetorical Greek to speak of the Trinity and other topics.[10] During his long education in Athens he absorbed these structures

8. *Or.* 1, 38, 39, 40, 41, and 45, which I have translated into contemporary English in Verna E. F. Harrison, *Gregory of Nazianzus: Festal Orations,* Popular Patristics Series (Crestwood, N.Y.: St. Vladimir's, 2008). Renderings of texts cited from *Or.* 39 and 40 are taken from this work. Other translations in this essay are my own as well, unless otherwise noted.

9. See, e.g., Daley, *Gregory of Nazianzus,* 41–50; John A. McGuckin, "Perceiving the Light from Light in Light (Oration 31.3): The Trinitarian Theology of St. Gregory the Theologian," *Greek Orthodox Theological Review* 39 (1994): 7–32; Beeley, *Gregory of Nazianzus on the Trinity,* chap. 4; and Beeley, "Divine Causality and the Monarchy of God the Father in Gregory of Nazianzus," *Harvard Theological Review* 100, no. 2 (2007): 199–214.

10. See McGuckin, "The Vision of God in St. Gregory Nazianzen," *Studia Patristica* 32 (1997): 145–52, at 147.

into his mind so thoroughly that they molded his way of thinking. He was thus able to transform them from literary ornament to theological method.

Balance and symmetry were prized in many aspects of Greek culture, including everything from art to law, ethics to medicine.[11] The μέν/δέ construction that plays a large role in Greek language and literature, especially in Late Antique rhetorical Greek, expresses this sense of balance. Gregory transforms a common figure of speech, antithesis, into a new "logic" or "grammar" for speaking about the Trinity and other theological topics. He often uses it to juxtapose and balance two different truth claims so as to affirm both together in such a way that they reinforce each other instead of conflicting. Thus, he does not start from unity of essence in God and argue to threeness of persons, nor does he start from three persons and argue to one essence. Instead he begins by declaring that the divinity is simultaneously one in three and three in one. Vladimir Lossky, who quotes him extensively, is right to emphasize antimony as a structural element in Gregory's Trinitarian theology.[12] Because of this, he does not use divine unity to rule out multiplicity in divine activity. Rather, he affirms both unity and trinity in God's being and in the activities through which God is manifest to the created world. He does not develop a theology of "appropriation" because his theological "grammar" differs from that of Augustine, and indeed from Basil and Gregory of Nyssa. We will examine some examples of his way of thinking and speaking below.

Lossky, however, is mistaken in identifying antinomy as exclusively apophatic.[13] Some of Gregory's antinomies are in fact neither/nor statements, rejecting the opposite errors of Sabellianism and Arianism, or "Jewish" unitarianism and "pagan" polytheism within Christian theology. Yet such double negations establish the context for affirming the mean between the extremes. For example, in *Oration* 38.8 he says:

When I say "God," I mean Father and Son and Holy Spirit. The divinity is not diffused beyond these, lest we introduce a crowd of gods, nor is it limited to fewer than these, lest we be

---

11. G. E. R. Lloyd, *Polarity and Analogy: Two Types of Argumentation in Greek Thought* (Cambridge: Cambridge University Press, 1966), 15–171; and Richard Garner, *Law and Society in Classical Athens* (New York: St. Martin's, 1987), 75–83.

12. Vladimir Lossky, *The Mystical Theology of the Eastern Church,* trans. members of the Fellowship of Saint Alban and Saint Sergius (Cambridge: James Clarke, 1957), 44–66.

13. Lossky, *Mystical Theology,* 42–43.

condemned to a poverty of divinity, either Judaizing because of the monarchy or Hellenizing because of the abundance. For the evil is alike in both cases, though it is found in opposites.

Similarly, in *Oration* 39.11 he says, "Let both the contraction of Sabellius and the division of Arius be equally far from us, the evils that are diametrically opposed yet equal in impiety."[14] However, more often his antinomies are double affirmations, both/and statements intended to combine theological affirmations while recognizing the mystery between them that holds them together. Thus, he affirms that in being and activity God is both one and three, and that Christ is fully divine and fully human. His antinomic theology is an eloquent and flexible method for expressing the emphatic doctrinal affirmations that Gregory loves to make while acknowledging the apophatic context that surrounds them.

God As One and Three

In one of his earlier discourses he speaks of divine attributes as both singular and plural, describing the Trinity as follows:

Lives and life, lights and light, goods and good, glories and glory; true and truth and Spirit of truth, holy ones and holiness itself; each one is God if contemplated alone, with the intellect dividing undivided entities; the three [are contemplated] as one God through their identity of movement (κινήσεως) and of nature (φύσεως) when apprehended with each other. (*Or.* 23.11)

This text shows how Gregory's understanding of the Trinity differs from that of the later, exclusively Western "Athanasian" Creed, which is grounded in Augustine's theology and objects to naming divine attributes in the plural.[15] Yet Gregory's plurals are all combined with singulars. As he names the divine characteristics of three distinct persons, he takes care to affirm their oneness also. He notes that in contemplation, that is, in prayer or theological reflection, which for him are surely interconnected, one can perceive each of the persons as God, but also all three together as one God. Though the human mind can think of the persons as separate, in reality, he declares, they are inseparable in nature and movement, by which he surely means being and activ-

---

14. See also *Or.* 2.36–37, 40.42, and 42.16.

15. Jaroslav Pelikan and Valerie Hotchkiss, *Creeds and Confessions of Faith in the Christian Tradition* (New Haven: Yale University Press, 2003), 1:675–77.

ity. Yet this does not mean the hypostases are indistinguishable. When Gregory names "true and truth and Spirit of truth," he refers to them in the standard sequential order that all three of the Cappadocians identify in divine activity *ad extra:* from the Father, through the Son, in the Holy Spirit.[16] This pattern of self-manifestation follows the same sequence as the relations of origin by which the divine persons are distinguished and related to each other. So they are not indistinguishable or interchangeable in their common activity, which itself has a threefold structure that reveals them as distinct persons in the created world.

In *Oration* 39, *On Epiphany,* his discussion of the Trinity begins with a simultaneous affirmation of oneness and threeness.

When I speak of God, be struck from all sides by the lightning flash (περιαστράφθητε) of one light and also three; three in regard to the individualities (ἰδιότητα), that is hypostases, if one prefers to call them this, or persons, for we will not struggle with our comrades about the names as long as the syllables convey the same idea; but one if one speaks of the essence, that is the divinity. For they are divided undividedly, if I may speak thus, and united in division. For the divinity is one in three, and the three are one, in whom the divinity is, or, to speak more precisely, who are the divinity. But we omit the excesses and omissions, neither making the union a fusion, nor the division a separation. Let both the contraction of Sabellius and the division of Arius be equally far from us, the evils that are diametrically opposed yet equal in impiety. For why is it necessary to either fuse God together wrongly or cut him up into inequalities? (*Or.* 39.11)

In this passage Gregory carries further the points he made in *Oration* 23.11. He specifies that the threeness pertains to the hypostases and the oneness to the essence. He identifies what he regards as correct Trinitarian terminology, while noting that consensus about concepts is more important than use of the same vocabulary. At the end he clarifies his position further by locating it as the mean between two opposing errors.

The intensity and immediacy of the image he uses to introduce this discussion are particularly significant. He invites his listeners to "be struck from all sides by the lightning flash" of the one divine light, yet also by three divine lights. This powerful image suggests that the divine persons surround Gregory's congregation as three overwhelming lights that are also one light enveloping them. Such language brings us very far from imagining a single indis-

---

16. Basil, *De spiritu sancto,* 18.47, SC 17:412; Gregory of Nyssa, *On Not Three Gods,* GNO 3.1.47–48.

tinguishable activity coming down from a Trinity isolated within itself from the created world. Gregory is saying that the three divine persons who are one God are present in the liturgical celebration of a great feast as intensely as sheets of lightning striking the ground all around the center of an extreme thunderstorm, and that he and his listeners stand at that storm's center. Browne and Swallow's translation of this phrase as "be illumined at once by one flash of light and by three"[17] does not convey this adequately. Gregory uses words carefully and does not attach prepositions to verbs without meaning, as some Late Antique writers may do. The preposition *peri* is important in this text, and it occurs again in another important Trinitarian passage in the sermon he preached the next day, *Oration 40, On Baptism.* Both of these texts may be alluding to Luke 2:9, which he quotes in *Oration* 39.14: "Therefore at his birth we kept festival, both I the leader of the feast, and you, and all that is in the world and above the world. With the star we ran, and with the Magi we worshipped (Mt 2:8–11), and with the shepherds we were surrounded by light (περιέλαμψεν), and with the angels we gave glory (Lk 2:9–14)."

Near the end of *Oration* 40, a long and eloquent exhortation to be baptized that Gregory preached in the Church of the Holy Apostles in Constantinople, newly restored to the Nicene faith, he makes a solemn confession of the Trinitarian faith he will entrust to those he baptizes. The context of festal celebration and union with Christ through baptism provides an appropriate setting for Gregory's extraordinary depiction of how he contemplates God as three and as one. Here he revisits the simultaneous affirmation of divine unity and plurality we read in *Oration* 23.11, but with greater clarity, detail, and intensity.

This I give you as a companion and protector for all your life, the one divinity and power, found in unity in the three, and gathering together the three as distinct; neither uneven in essences or natures, nor increased or decreased by superiorities or inferiorities; from every perspective equal, from every perspective the same, as the beauty and greatness of heaven is one; an infinite coalescence of three infinites; each God when considered in himself; as the Father so the Son, as the Son so the Holy Spirit; each preserving his properties. The three are God when known together, each God because of the consubstantiality, one God because of the monarchy. When I first know the one I am also illumined from all sides (περιλάμπομαι) by the three; when I first distinguish the three I am also carried back to the one. When I picture one

17. Trans. Browne and Swallow, NPNF 2.7.355.

of the three I consider this the whole, and my eyes are filled, and the greater part has escaped me. I cannot grasp the greatness of that one so as to grant something greater to the rest. When I bring the three together in contemplation, I see one torch and am unable to divide or measure the united light. (*Or.* 40.41)

Gregory speaks of how his spiritual gaze moves back and forth between God as one and the three persons, and between each divine person and all of them together, though he knows that most of what he contemplates escapes his grasp. He invites those he will lead into full communion with the church to follow him into an immensely rich Trinitarian spirituality in which each hypostasis can be known directly and appears as the whole of God, yet the three are also manifest as related to each other in a sequential order, and as being one God. Again Gregory uses a περί compound to speak of the hypostases as three lights surrounding him, adding that together they constitute one undivided light. And again Browne and Swallow, who render περιλάμπομαι simply as "I am illumined,"[18] miss the immediate and all-encompassing character of the triune presence by missing the preposition. This is the same verb used in Luke 2:9 to speak of the glory of the Lord shining all around the shepherds. Since God is infinite, this light cannot be measured quantitatively or divided into circumscribed parts, and by implication, nor can any one of the divine hypostases or the one divine nature as such. The language of contemplation and light shows further that this text refers not only to the Trinity in itself, but also to its self-manifestation and activity in the world in a way capable of being perceived by created beings like Gregory and his congregation.

The texts we have studied from *Orations* 23, 39, and 40 can help us understand a similar passage in *Oration* 31, the fifth *Theological Oration,* which boldly confesses the full divinity of the Holy Spirit and Gregory's doctrine of the Trinity. In §3 he summarizes his Trinitarian position in a way that adds precision and clarity to what he said earlier in *Oration* 23.11.

He "was the true light that illumines every human being coming into the world" (Jn 1:9)—the Father. He "was the true light that illumines every human being coming into the world"—the Son. He "was the true light that illumines every human being coming into the world"—the other Advocate (Jn 14:16, 26). Was and was and was, but was one. Light and light and light, but one light and one God. This is indeed what David perceived long ago when he said, "In your light we see light" (Ps 35:10). As for us, now we also have seen and we proclaim, from the

---

18. Trans. Browne and Swallow, NPNF 2.7.375.

light of the Father grasping the light of the Son in the light of the Spirit, a concise and simple theology of the Trinity.

Again Gregory speaks of the persons as three lights, yet one God. When he says "but one light," this statement is juxtaposed antithetically to the statements about threeness that precede it and must not be understood as negating or superseding them. The interpretation of Psalm 35:10 that follows makes this clear. Gregory proclaims that he receives light from the divine persons in the usual sequential order: from the Father's light he grasps the Son's light in the Spirit's light. This brings him into direct and distinct encounters with all three persons in a single act of contemplation. Though he looks most immediately toward the Son, who is the Father's Logos and revealer, he is illumined from all sides by the three. He finds himself in the center of their common self-revelatory activity, in which each of them participates in a unique way.

These texts show that Gregory perceives the Trinity in at least two different ways, both of which reveal God's activity, which comes down to the created world where he can see it. First, he sees both one light and three. This means that each of the divine persons is present to him and acts directly and immediately. The action of each is distinct, though they all act jointly, "as if among three suns conjoined to each other there were one commingling (σύγκρασις) of light" (*Or.* 31.14). The word σύγκρασις is a Stoic technical term that the Cappadocians borrowed and used theologically. It refers specifically to a kind of mixture in which the things blended—in this case the *activities* of the three divine persons, named as light—each retain their own identity and properties. This kind of blending contrasts with a fusion in which the distinct identity and properties of each are lost.[19]

Secondly, there is one divine activity to which each person contributes in a distinct way, which proceeds from the Father, through the Son, in the Holy Spirit. In *Oration* 23.11 and 31.3,14, Gregory places each of these patterns side by side. In *Oration* 40.41 he alludes to a variety of ways in which the Trinity is manifest to him. As described in *Oration* 31.3 above, the second way that God acts, from the Father, through the Son, in the Holy Spirit, unfolds from the relations of origin that distinguish the divine persons from each other and

19. On Gregory's use of Stoic mixture theory as modified by neo-Platonism, see Jean-Marie Mathieu, "Sur une correction inutile (Or. 28.8, lignes 8–9 Gallay)," in *Symposium Nazianzenum II: Louvain-la-Neuve, 25–28 août 1981,* edited by Justin Mossay, 52–59 (Paderborn: Schöningh, 1983).

also unite them to each other. This is the standard way in which the Cappadocians speak of divine activity. In the Holy Spirit, members of the church perceive the Son, Jesus Christ, who reveals the Father to them. As this experience of the Trinity deepens, through prayer, worship, and contemplation, Gregory and those he leads come to perceive all three divine persons together,[20] as described in *Oration* 23.11 and 31.3, and in other ways as well. Clearly, God is free to act in this world and to reveal himself to his saints in a variety of ways. Gregory places these descriptions of divine self-manifestation side by side to show that they are compatible with each other, and to point to the abundance of the Trinity's life.

Gregory also speaks of the divine persons sharing distinctively in common activities as recounted in Scripture. Father and Son collaborate with each other, and so do Son and Spirit:

For indeed Scripture says that [the Son] was given up (Rom 4:25; 1 Cor 11:3), but it is also written that he gave himself up (Gal 2:20; Eph 5:2, 25); and he was raised and taken up to heaven by the Father (Acts 17:31; Rom 4:24; Mk 16:19), but he also resurrected himself and ascended there again (Mt 22:6; Mk 16:9, 19). For one is the Father's good will, the other is his own power. (*Or.* 45.27)

Christ is born, the Spirit is his forerunner (Lk 1:31); Christ is baptized, the Spirit bears him witness (Mt 3:13–17; Lk 3:21–22); Christ is tempted, the Spirit leads him up (Mt 4:1; Lk 4:2); Christ performs miracles, the Spirit accompanies him (Mt 12:22, 12:28); Christ ascends, the Spirit fills his place (Acts 1:9, 2:3–4). (*Or.* 31.29)[21]

The distinct, yet collaborative activities of the divine persons are in the first place revealed in Scripture.

The Trinity and Its Human Image

Texts cited above have shown how Gregory encounters the Trinity as one and three together, and thinks of the divine persons' actions as both distinctive and united. This concept portrays the Trinity in a way that can serve as a model for community among human beings. However, before we can speak

---

20. See Beeley, *Gregory of Nazianzus on the Trinity,* 187–233.

21. Gregory of Nazianzus, *St. Gregory of Nazianzus: The Five Theological Orations and Two Letters to Cledonius,* trans. Frederick Williams and Lionel Wickham (Crestwood, N.Y.: St. Vladimir's Semiary Press, 2002), 139.

of how they provide a model for humans, we must ask how Gregory understands the divine persons as interacting with each other. Gregory does not discuss their interaction in psychological terms, as Ayres notes, which, in his view could risk being too anthropomorphic.[22] Yet Gregory does speak of movement and mutuality among them. Ayres and McGuckin agree that he anticipates the idea of Trinitarian perichoresis.[23]

In a number of texts, once Gregory speaks of distinct persons, he seeks to show them as relating to each other in such a way that they genuinely comprise a unity.[24] In other words, he speaks of God as "a nature that is in internal agreement with itself" (*Or.* 23.11),[25] though this God is a plurality of hypostases. In the third *Theological Oration,* he again stresses God's unity:

> Monarchy [in God] is what we value, yet not a monarchy restricted to one person;... but held together by equality of nature, agreement of will, identity of movement, and convergence to the one from whom they came—all of which is impossible for created nature. So though there is distinction in number, there is no division of the essence. Because of this, from the beginning a one is in movement to two and stops at three—that is, for us, the Father, the Son, and the Holy Spirit. Apart from passion, time, and body, one is parent of the "offspring" and originator of the "emanation" (*Or.* 29.2)

Here Gregory describes a movement that is atemporal, yet genuine. It begins from the Father in the begetting of the Son and the breathing forth of the Spirit. They come from him, so the unity expands into three, but in a reciprocal movement they also converge back toward him. The persons move toward each other, as it were, so as to hold their unity together. This movement originates in the Father, but the Son and Spirit join with him to support their unity. Gregory acknowledges that such equality, unanimity, and seamless collaboration are impossible for created beings, such as humans, to imitate. Nevertheless, in texts cited below he will declare that the angels, though they are also created, do imitate the divine unity-in-community, and he exhorts people in the church to do the same.

Gregory returns to the same theme in the fifth *Theological Oration:* "We

---

22. Ayres, *Nicaea and Its Legacy,* 408.

23. Ayres, *Nicaea and Its Legacy,* 246; McGuckin, "Trinitarian Theology," 28–29.

24. Beeley, "Divine Causality," 209.

25. Gregory of Nazianzus, *St. Gregory of Nazianzus: Select Orations,* trans. Martha Vinson (Washington, D.C.: The Catholic University of America Press, 2003), 139.

have one God because there is a single Godhead. Though there are three objects of belief, they are from the one and are carried back to it" (*Or.* 31.14). As Beeley has shown, the "one" here is the Father, whom Gregory names later in the paragraph as the "primal cause."[26] The text speaks of the Trinity's lack of inequality and division, then returns to the unity with which it began.

> For one [person] is not a greater God, nor is another less; one is not before, nor another after; they are not sundered in will, nor divided in power; nor can any of the properties present in divided beings be found there. To speak briefly, the divinity exists undivided in things divided; it is as if in three mutually connected suns there were a single commingling of light. Therefore, when we look toward the divinity, the primal cause, the sole sovereignty, the One appears to us; but when we look toward those in whom the divinity is, those who come from the primal cause atemporally and in equal glory, it is three that we worship. (*Or.* 31.14)

Again, there is a movement of the Son and the Spirit out from the Father, who is the primary and sovereign source of Godhead. In a human community such a relationship could cause inequality and division, but in God the persons remain fully equal and fully united. God's being is like three mutually connected suns that are together manifest in their activity, the shared light.

In the next paragraph, Gregory poses a question, then provides the answer. Since it believes in a Trinity, he asks, how does Christianity differ from Greek paganism, which believes that there are many gods, just as there are many human beings? In reply, Gregory notes the division and variability of humans, and thus of the nonexistent pagan gods who bear their image. Notice the contrast between humans and the Trinity, as described above.

> The individuals are widely separated from one another by time, passions, and capacity. We human beings are not merely composite; but also mutually opposed to each other and to ourselves. We do not remain exactly the same for one day, let alone a lifetime. In our bodies and in our souls we are ever fluctuating, ever changing. I do not know whether this is true of angels and of all that nature above, which comes next after the Trinity. They, though, are not composite, and by their nearness to the highest beauty are more firmly fixed in their relation to beauty than we are. (*Or.* 31.15)[27]

In regard to community, the angels hold an intermediate position between God and humans. Because of their closeness to God and their internal unity—

---

26. Beeley rightly emphasizes the primacy of the Father throughout Gregory's Trinitarian theology: see especially Beeley, *Gregory of Nazianzus on the Trinity*, chap. 4: 187–233.

27. Gregory of Nazianzus, *Five Theological Orations*, trans. Williams and Wickham, 128, modified.

a lack of component parts that cause instability—their community life is stable. Humans, on the other hand, are beset by both internal and interpersonal conflicts.

Gregory experienced interpersonal conflict especially during his turbulent ministry in Constantinople, where he preached the *Theological Orations*. The conflicts came to a head after his triumph, when he chaired the Second Ecumenical Council (381), but was pressured into resignation. So he contrasts the unanimity of the Trinity with conflicted human community again in *Oration* 42, his *Farewell Address* to the council. Yet he first praises his own congregation in the city, who were true to the Trinity in faith and, significantly, in conduct: "They are authentic worshippers of the Trinity.... They think as one, praise as one, are ruled by one doctrine in their relationships to each other, to us, and to the Trinity"[28] (*Or.* 42.15). Gregory's point is that authentic belief in the Trinity affects how people live together in community. The believing congregation's way of life is an imitation of the way the three persons conduct their life together. This concept has extraordinary implications for Christian ethics and pastoral care.[29] It also finds echoes in the discussions of contemporary theologians.

In *Oration* 42.15, there follows one of Gregory's extraordinary summaries of Trinitarian theology. After describing the three persons in their relations of origin, he speaks of their unity: "The unity [among them] is the Father, from whom and towards whom everything else is referred, not so as to be mixed together in confusion, but so as to be contained, without time or will or power intervening to divide them."[30] Once again, the Father is the source of divine unity, and with the Son and Spirit he also holds the Trinity together. As we have seen in other texts, he begets the Son and breathes forth the Spirit, and they turn back toward him. This reciprocity between the Father and the other two persons grounds their movements toward each other, according to Gregory. It is a small step from this rhythm of movement to an idea he does not express directly—that is, the Father gives his very being in love to his Son and Spirit, and they give themselves in love to him in return. This is the common-

---

28. See Daley, *Gregory of Nazianzus,* 147.

29. Beeley's book, which centers around Gregory's Trinitarian theology, shows how Gregory draws implications from it for pastoral care and ecclesial life.

30. Daley, *Gregory of Nazianzus,* 147.

place among modern theologians who think of the divine persons in "psycho-logical" terms. Yet the ethical conclusion Gregory draws, his concept of the Trinity as a model for human community, surely presupposes that he holds some such idea about the mutual relations of the Father, Son, and Holy Spirit.

Oration 42.15 continues by speaking of God's human creation and con-trasting it with the internal divine life Gregory has just described: "These three have caused us to exist in multiplicity, each of us being in constant ten-sion with ourselves and with everything else, but for them, whose nature is simple and whose existence is the same, the principal characteristic is unity."[31] Gregory has experienced this constant tension, within himself and between himself and others, in Constantinople, and he spends most of this long ora-tion describing and lamenting it. As he is about to depart, he has given up hope that the people of the capital could fashion their life together into an im-age of the Holy Trinity.

Toward a Peaceful Human Community

Gregory gives a more positive account of the Trinity as a model for hu-man communities in *Orations* 6, 22, and 23, the three *Orations on Peace,* in which he exhorts his congregations to end various conflicts. Near the end of *Oration* 23, as his parishioners shake hands with each other, he exclaims, "Be-hold the works of the Trinity, which alike we glorify and worship! This will make you more kind, as well as more orthodox" (*Or.* 23.13). Again, as we saw in *Oration* 42.15 above, he observes that adoration of the Trinity has ethical as well as doctrinal implications.

Orations 22 and 23 were preached in Constantinople, but the circum-stances that occasioned them are disputed; even in the manuscript tradition, it is unclear which of the two came first.[32] In *Oration* 22.14, Gregory explains that God is the source of "the good of concord," at every level.

This good has originated from the Holy Trinity, of whom nothing is so proper as the unity of nature and internal peace. It is shared by the angelic and divine powers, who are at peace toward God and toward each other. It extends even to the whole of creation, whose adorn-

31. Daley, *Gregory of Nazianzus,* 147.
32. Gregory of Nazianzus, *Select Orations,* trans. Vinson, 131n1; McGuckin, *Saint Gregory of Nazian-zus: An Intellectual Biography* (Crestwood, N.Y.: St. Vladimir's Seminary Press, 2001), 249–51, 262–64.

ment (κόσμος) is freedom from faction. In us it reigns, in the soul by the mutual implication and communion of virtues, and in the body by the harmony and balance of the members and parts with each other; of these, the first both is and is called beauty; the second, health.

Significantly, in this text the inner life of the Trinity is the source of concord and order throughout the creation, not only the highest example to be imitated. The angels, who are the closest creatures to God, are again examples of peace, though it is manifest as well in the order and cooperation among the good soul's virtues and the healthy body's parts. Indeed, as Beeley notes,[33] elsewhere Gregory speaks of the peace and order, the harmonious functioning, of the stars (*Or.* 7.7); the whole created world, including angels, stars, seasons and weather, night and day, air and water, wind and rain (*Or.* 32.8); and the church community (*Or.* 2.4). The disciples defer to one another, following Christ who defers to the Father and is a model for us (*Or.* 32.18). In this last example, the church's relationship with Christ introduces it to an encounter with the Trinity.

Gregory developed the idea of the Trinity as a model for human community early in his ministry when assisting his father at Nazianzus. He preached *Oration 6*, the *First Oration on Peace*, intending to heal a schism between Gregory the Elder and some local ascetics over Trinitarian doctrine. The younger Gregory, who had close ties with those on both sides, mediated a reconciliation in which both made concessions.[34] His oration celebrates, strengthens, and ratifies the agreement and in this context offers profound theological reflection on the value and meaning of peace and harmony in the human community. He praises the renewed concord of the congregation as linking them to God who is one and three: "Now, belonging to the One we have become one, and belonging to the Trinity we have come to be the same in nature and in soul and in honor" (*Or.* 6.4). This Trinitarian language follows the pattern noted in texts cited above, an antinomical juxtaposition of the unity and Trinity of God so as to affirm both equally. The connection of these divine characteristics with the unity and communal harmony of the congregation suggests

33. Beeley, *Gregory of Nazianzus on the Trinity*, 216n91.

34. See Neil McLynn, "Gregory the Peacemaker: A Study of Oration Six," *Kyoyo-Ronso* 101 (1996): 183–216; and Susanna Elm, "The Diagnostic Gaze: Gregory of Nazianzus' Theory of Orthodox Priesthood in his Orations 6 *De Pace* and 2 *Apologia de fuga sua*," in *Orthodoxie, Christianisme, Histoire*, edited by Susanna Elm, Éric Rebillard, and Antonella Romano, 83–100 (Rome: École française de Rome, 2000).

that a human community with this character imitates and thus belongs to, or indeed participates in, the unity in diversity of the Godhead.

Later in the same homily, Gregory makes this more explicit as he exhorts his audience to strengthen and preserve their newfound peace. He encourages them to follow the examples of God, and of angels who are illumined by God and thus like God live in unity, without division or conflict among themselves. He warns them to avoid the example and influence of the fallen angels, who broke their peace with God and who instigate conflicts among human beings. Gregory then returns to the example of the holy angels and shows how this harmonious community participates in the life of the Trinity, as do human communities that love peace and reject conflict. The angels who do not fall, he says,

remain in their own condition, which first is peace and absence of division, having received unity as a gift of the Holy Trinity, from which also comes their illumination. For it is one God and is believed to be such, no less because of its harmony (ὁμόνοιαν) than because of its sameness of essence. So those [people] belong to God and are close to divine realities who are shown as embracing the good of peace and rejecting the opposite, division. (*Or.* 6.13)

The harmony named here characterizes the Trinity as community, while the sameness of essence characterizes God as one. Gregory goes on to identify peace in human community as the image and likeness of God, thereby providing an early, groundbreaking example of a favorite theme among contemporary theologians: humankind as image of the Trinity.

Only one thing can constrain us to such benevolence and harmony (συμφωνίας), the imitation of God and of divine realities. Toward this alone it is prudent for the soul to look, having come into being according to the image of God, that it may preserve its nobility as far as possible through inclination toward the divine and, to the extent it is able, likeness to it. (*Or.* 6.14)

The divine perfection that people are invited to share here is harmony, whose model in God can only be the communal life of the Trinity. There follows a long description of peace and harmony throughout the creation, which is also an example to humankind, a theme we have seen him develop elsewhere, too. One wonders whether, in the *Orations on Peace,* Gregory hints at an idea Augustine will develop, that although humankind is the image of God in a special way, there exist "traces" of the Trinity throughout creation.[35]

35. See Eugene TeSelle, *Augustine the Theologian* (New York: Herder and Herder, 1970).

Conclusion

Gregory Nazianzen, who devoted his life to the Trinity and developed much of the early church's Trinitarian theology, anticipated themes that are of great interest in the current Trinitarian revival in systematic theology. First, he understood divine unity together with divine threefoldness. His antithetical method, based on ancient rhetorical patterns of speech, made this possible. So instead of starting from one position, such as absolute unity in God, and arguing to its conclusions, such as appropriation, he starts from both Unity and Trinity and looks for ways to affirm both together. This process enables him to affirm that God is manifest as Trinity in the created world in a variety of ways, so that we can know God as one and also know each of the divine persons. This conclusion supports the New Testament and ecclesial experience of God as Trinity, the experience that led early Christians to develop the doctrine in the first place and that makes it significant for people's lives throughout the ages.

Second, Gregory reflects on the interactions among the divine persons that are grounded in their relations of origin. Thus, the Son and Spirit move out from the Father who begets the one and breathes forth the other, and then they return back to the Father. Thus, divine unity is grounded in the Father's essence, which he shares with the other two, yet it is also grounded in the persons, the Father's movement toward the Son and Spirit and their movement back toward him.

Third, for Gregory, the Trinity provides a model for human community life, since humans are created in the image of God. Thus, the church's affirmation of the Trinity has implications for how people act as well as what they believe. Instability, discord, and division are inconsistent with faith in the Trinity. The Trinity has created the harmony and mutuality present in heaven and earth, the seasons, and the biosphere. The harmony among diverse creatures discloses hints of the Trinity itself. This is true above all of the angels, but humans, created in the divine image, are called to follow the same example in their life together, by preserving unity, by moving toward each other in self-giving, service, and love.

Augustine and Gregory of Nyssa rely on linear logic, arguing from the divine unity to unity of divine attributes and activities. We have seen that

Gregory Nazianzen uses a different "grammar" of theological reflection and consequently understands divine unity differently and arrives at different conclusions. Since Nazianzen was among the leading fourth-century advocates of the Nicene faith, there is significant diversity among "pro-Nicene" theologians.

Gregory Nazianzen's influence on the Byzantine and subsequent Eastern churches has been without parallel.[36] For centuries, his orations were read in church, and they are quoted extensively in the hymnography used in the Byzantine rite to this day. Such continual liturgical use imperceptibly forms the theology and spirituality of church members who may never read his orations. Although I cannot trace the history of his influence on Eastern theologians, it must be tremendous. In the twentieth century, as a result of ecumenical dialogue, their voice has been heard in the West and has made a large contribution to the current revival of Trinitarian theology in the Western systematics community. Hence the contrast between Eastern and Western Trinitarian theologies, limited and oversimplified as it is. Gregory has surely had a hidden impact on contemporary Trinitarian theological discussions.

36. On Gregory's influence, see the introduction to my article, Verna E. F. Harrison, "Gregory Nazianzen's Festal Spirituality: Anamnesis and Mimesis," *Philosophy and Theology* 18 (2006): 27–51.

Ben Fulford

3. Gregory of Nazianzus and Biblical Interpretation

Although sought after as a teacher of Scripture in his own day, Gregory of Nazianzus does not conform to our expectations of patristic exegesis and has attracted relatively little sustained attention as a biblical interpreter.[1] We have no formal hermeneutical treatise, no commentaries, and no proper exegetical homilies extant from him.[2] In what sense, then, if any might Gregory merit attention as a biblical interpreter? In what follows I do not attempt to examine every angle of Gregory's work as a biblical interpreter, but focus on three in particular to help answer this question.[3] First, Gregory carried forward an Origenian understanding of Scripture, but one focused on the pastor-rhetor's task

---

1. Jerome in several writings referred to Gregory as "my teacher in exegesis": *De Viribus Illustris* 117; *Ep.* 50:1; *In Isaiam* 3; all cited by McGuckin, *Saint Gregory of Nazianzus,* 265. On sustained studies of Gregory on Scripture, Kristoffel Demoen, *Pagan and Biblical Exempla in Gregory Nazianzen: A Study in Rhetoric and Hermeneutics,* Corpus Christianorum Lingua Patrum II (Turnholt: Brepols, 1996), is a rare exception focused on the use of biblical *paradeigmata.*

2. *Or.* 37 comes closest, but, though exegetical in form, seems more an example of bold speech before a Christian ruler than something like one of Origen or Chrysostom's homilies on a biblical book.

3. For such an overview, see Paul Gallay, "La Bible dans l'oeuvre de Grégoire de Nazianze le Théologien," in *Le monde grec ancient et la Bible,* vol. 1, edited by Claude Mondésert, 313–34 (Paris: Beauchesne, 1984); Frederick W. Norris, "Gregory Nazianzen: Constructing and Constructed by Scripture," in *The Bible through the Ages,* vol. 1, *The Bible in Greek Antiquity,* edited by Paul M. Blowers, 149–62 (Notre Dame, Ind.: University of Notre Dame Press, 1997); and Daley, "Walking Through the Word of God: Gregory of Nazianzus as a Biblical Interpreter," in *The Word Leaps the Gap: Essays on Scripture and Theology in Honor of Richard B. Hays,* edited by J. Ross Wagner, C. Kavin Rowe, and A. Katherine Grieb, 514–31 (Grand Rapids, Mich.: Eerdmans, 2008).

of persuasively and carefully conveying Scripture's pedagogy to diverse audiences. Second, he addressed one of the key hermeneutical questions of his day in formulating a hermeneutic of the biblical witness to Jesus Christ.[4] Third, his use of Scripture in the Orations exemplifies the practice of this understanding and hermeneutic and thus constitutes his main contribution to patristic biblical interpretation in the crafting of discourse that skillfully weaves exegesis, allusion, and quotation into a persuasive structure at once interpretative and applicative of biblical pedagogy, alerting us to the importance of this mode of biblical reading and defying simple categorization as literal, typological, and allegorical.[5]

The Distribution of the Word

One of Gregory's concerns in several of his orations is the formation of Christian teachers as those who deploy the teachings of Scripture in their speech. It is best exhibited in *Oration 2*, Gregory's defense of his flight after his ordination to the priesthood. A key part of his argument rests on the difficulty of pastoral ministry and the high demands it places on the skill and character of the pastor. Gregory turns to the subject of Scripture when he raises the question of "the distribution of the *logos* ... that divine and exalted *logos* which all now study."[6] It requires, he thinks, not a little of the Spirit to give to each in a timely manner his "daily portion and steward with judgment the truth of our doctrines" on a variety of subjects, from matter, soul, and intellect through to God's saving action and triune identity. The *logos* Gregory speaks of here is Jesus Christ, as he implies by the Christological allusions of his description of it in his praise of Basil, in *Oration 43*, as steward of this same *logos* that is the bread of angels "wherewith souls are fed and given to drink, who are hungry for God, and seek for a food which does not pass away or fail, but

4. Gregory makes an equally significant contribution to hermeneutical issues surrounding the question of the Spirit's divinity in *Or.* 31, but this is a topic for another time; see the discussion in Beeley, *Gregory of Nazianzus on the Trinity*, 180–86, and Tom A. Noble, "Gregory Nazianzen's Use of Scripture In Defence of the Deity of the Holy Spirit," *Tyndale Bulletin* 39 (1988): 101–23.

5. Here I am indebted to and seek to build upon the arguments of Frances Young, *Biblical Exegesis and the Formation of Christian Culture* (Cambridge: Cambridge University Press, 1997), in which she seeks to reconfigure approaches to patristic exegesis on such questions, and in which she presents Gregory of Nazianzus as illustrating the importance of intertextuality in patristic biblical exegesis.

6. *Or.* 2.35, SC 247:134.

abides forever."[7] This same *logos* is also Scripture, as Gregory clearly implies in *Oration* 4 when speaking of the Christian *logos* "existing in doctrines and in testimonies from above, both ancient and new, ancient in the predictions and illuminating movements of the divine nature, new in the latest theophany and in the wonders from it and concerning it."[8] Like Origen, Gregory conceives of Scripture as a truly theo-logical text, embodying textually the incarnate Word of God.[9] Its purpose is to nourish souls with Jesus Christ, and this purpose is served by the work of the pastor in teaching Scripture.

It is also a rhetorical task. Adequately to understand and present the truth of Scripture, especially the doctrine of the Trinity, Gregory argues, requires the Spirit "by whom alone God is conceived and explained and understood, for only by purity can we grasp the pure."[10] The distribution of the *logos*, then, requires adequate comprehension, explication, and understanding: the three parts into which Aristotle analyzed the rhetorical act. Christian pastors as teachers find themselves tossed among three dangers, he continues: in all likelihood either their intellect is not illumined, or their language is weak, or the listening of their audience is not purified, and so the truth will be lamed.[11] Gregory likens the teacher's task to that of a scribe, writing doctrine on the soul; it is easier to write on a fresh soul than to try to efface one script and superimpose another.[12] For Gregory, integral to this distribution are both the careful choice of what to distribute to those of varying capacities and the use of language to persuade others to accept it, help them retain and be formed by it, unconfused with other ideas.[13] Gregory's account of Basil as teacher underlines this rhetorical character and the transformative path on which it aims to lead the hearer: Basil's homilies on the Six Days of Creation, Gregory tells us, "persuaded me not to rest with the letter nor look only to things above, but to advance further and proceed further still from depth to depth, deep calling out to deep and finding light in light until I attain the summit."[14]

7. *Or.* 43.36, SC 384:204. The same identification is implied in *Or.* 45.16, PG 36:644C–45B.

8. *Or.* 4.110. Frederick Norris identifies the *logos* in *Or.* 45.16 as Scripture ("Constructed by Scripture," 159–60), and the passage is strongly suggestive of such an identification in the manner of Origen in *Treatise on the Passover*, 26.

9. See Henri Crouzel, *Origen,* trans. A. S. Worrall (Edinburgh: T. and T. Clark, 1989), 70.

10. *Or.* 2.39, SC 247:140.   11. *Or.* 2.39, SC 247:140, 142.

12. *Or.* 2.43, SC 247:146.   13. *Or.* 2.45, SC 247:148.

14. *Or.* 43.67, SC 384:272.

Scripture and the Formation of Christian Teachers

Such a task requires the proper formation of the teacher. In making this case, Gregory cites a Jewish practice, according to which not all of Scripture was entrusted to persons of every age, "since not all Scripture is graspable to everyone and those of greatest profundity would damage the multitude by their appearance."[15] Other parts are accessible to all in common: those "whose bodily component is not unseemly."[16] Scriptures in the former category were reserved for those over twenty-five years of age:

> Those whose mystical beauty, veiled by coarse covering, is the reward for hard labour and a shining life, shining and appearing to those of purified mind alone, since this age is capable—just—of transcending the body and ascending beautifully to the spirit from the letter.[17]

Gregory's concern is with those who style themselves as Christian philosophers before they have gained the required maturity in reading, and who scorn the value of the more accessible teachings: those for whom "the letter is nowhere, and all must be understood spiritually."[18] In language recalling Origen's descriptions of the somatic and pneumatic senses of Scripture, Gregory thus distinguishes between the appearance of difficult passages and what lies behind or beneath.[19] Here, purification of mind and luminosity of life are the conditions of understanding, a process in which, Gregory's two metaphors together suggest, both reader and the hidden beauty are active.

In *Oration* 4 Gregory's argument in favor of Christians teaching Greek language and literature includes the case for the superiority of Christian over pagan *paideia* and of Christian over pagan sacred literature. Both have stories that conceal deeper meanings, but whereas Homer, Hesiod, and the Orphic hymns conceal their theological and ethical lessons beneath tales of the gods' immoral behavior, the covering meaning in Christian Scripture is not unfitting to its depth, and that deeper meaning "is wonderful and exalted and exceedingly bright."[20] Scripture is like "a beautiful and unapproachable body, it

15. *Or.* 2.48, SC 247:152.   16. *Or.* 2.48, SC 247:152.
17. *Or.* 2.48, SC 247:152.   18. *Or.* 2.49, SC 247:154, 156.
19. Origen, *On First Principles* 4.2.4–6. For a good account of these senses in Origen's hermeneutics and exegetical practice, see Elizabeth Dively Lauro, *The Soul and Spirit of Scripture within Origen's Exegesis,* The Bible in Ancient Christianity 3 (Leiden: Brill, 2005).
20. *Or.* 4.118.17–21, PG 35:657B; SC 309:282.

is veiled in clothing that is not mean."[21] And whereas pagan myths fail to teach virtue with their destructive moral examples, Jesus' commandments teach a demanding degree of virtue. Gregory conveniently passes over the issue of biblical texts whose covering might be damaging to the immature, and that would require a more subtle argument. Jean Pépin and Kristoffel Demoen have therefore with some justice charged Gregory with inconsistency here in refusing to pagans the allegorical method he himself employs.[22] There are, however, many ways of seeking a "deeper sense" to a text that might broadly be called "allegorical." In any case, here Gregory indicates, recalling Origen's insistence on the edificatory value of Scripture's covering, that for him the covering or body of Scripture bears meaning that, in some cases, at least, teaches virtue.[23]

Origen's influence is evident again later in *Oration* 2, when Gregory returns to his point about the scriptural formation of the pastor:

Who [would take on himself the dress and name of a priest], whilst his heart has neither burnt with the holy and purified *logois* of God when the Scriptures were explained to him, nor yet been inscribed these threefold on the tables of his heart so as to have the mind of Christ, nor gone inside the invisible and dark treasures hidden from the multitude so as to espy the wealth in them and be able to enrich others, explaining spiritual things to those who are spiritual?[24]

Gregory's question indicates a progressive structure to the process of being formed by Scripture, beginning with hearing the exposition of the divine oracles of Scripture and their predictions of Christ (the allusion here is to Jesus' exposition of Jewish Scripture as speaking of him in Luke 24:27), proceeding to the threefold internalization of its teaching, then to the more independent exploration of its inner treasures, and finally to imparting those spiritual riches to those capable of receiving them.

The threefold inscription on the heart alludes to Proverbs 22:20–22 (LXX), the very text that Origen took up in his discussion of biblical interpretation in book 4 of *On First Principles*.[25] It seems likely that Gregory here alludes to Ori-

---

21. *Or.* 4.118.17–21, PG 35:657B; SC 309:282.

22. Demoen, *Pagan and Biblical Exempla*, 265; and Jean Pépin, *Mythe et allégorie: Les origins grecques et les contestations judeo-chrétiennes*, 2nd rev. ed. (Paris: Études Augustiniennes, 1976), 474.

23. Origen, *On First Principles* 4.2.8.

24. *Or.* 2.96, SC 247:214, 216. The content of the conditional clause at the beginning of the period must be supplied from the preceding *kolon*, which begins, "Or how could I take on the dress and name of a priest, before consecrating my hands with pious works?" *Or.* 2.95.8–9, SC 247:214.

25. As Kristoffel Demoen observes in *Pagan and Biblical Exempla*, 264–65.

gen's account, which explains the threefold inscription in terms of the edification of the simple soul by Scripture's flesh, of the slightly more advanced soul by its soul, and the perfect person by the spiritual law, the shadow of things to come.[26] Gregory, like Origen, correlated the components of the human person with different levels of spiritual maturity, and his argument here suggests, as in Origen, the possibility of progressing from level to level through these differentiated levels of biblical instruction.[27] Origen's illustrations of psychic and spiritual senses indicate that both involve going beyond the explicit, literal force of the text, and the latter involves identifying the heavenly realities, the good things to come—Jesus Christ and the Church—whose copy and shadow the Law displays in events, objects, and persons.[28] Gregory does not offer any explicit explication of the threefold inscription, but he does speak of an interpretive activity resembling this description of the spiritual sense later in *Oration* 2. The pastor should be able to recognize

the kinship and difference between types and truth, withdrawing from the former and adhering to the latter in order, by fleeing from the antiquity of the letter, to serve the newness of the Spirit and pass over entirely to grace from the law that is fulfilled spiritually in the abolition of the body.[29]

We may note here that as well as asserting that proper understanding involves leaving behind the literal force of the Law, Gregory also asserts its continuing spiritual force in ascetic practice and a fundamental connection between Old Testament realities and the truth they figured forth, as the root meanings of τύπος—an impression or imprint—suggest. Elsewhere in *Oration* 2 Gregory illustrates this connection in his appropriation of a traditional typology when stressing the demands of the spiritual combat priests must wage: "who is the Moses who triumphs by stretching out his hands on the mountain, so the cross may prevail by being figured forth and being revealed in advance."[30] Here, on a related occasion in the history of Israel, Moses' physical actions configure the cross by their shape, thus revealing it in advance; and by this pre-

26. Origen, *On First Principles* 4.2.4.
27. *Carm.* 1.2.34 (PG 37:963A).
28. As his examples from 1 Cor. 10:11, Heb 8:5, and Gal 4:21–24 indicate. The methodical implications of the illustration of the psychic sense from 1 Cor. 9:9–10 are more ambiguous.
29. *Or.* 2.97, SC 247:216.
30. *Or.* 2.88.4–5, PG 35:492B; SC 247:202.

figurement the cross itself is effective on Israel's behalf. Here the figural representation of the cross mediates its reality almost iconically. As Frances Young observes, it is this mimetic relationship, contributing to a sense of providential history, that makes a type.[31]

Traversing the Titles of Christ

Another of the competencies Gregory requires of Christian pastors and teachers in *Oration* 2 is to have traveled "by action and contemplation through the titles and powers of Christ, both the prior and more exalted as well as the humbler latter ones for which we are the reason."[32] Who, he asks, would present himself for priesthood who "hears these names and realities in vain and does not have communion with the Word or participate in him in respect of whom each of these [names] is and is called?"[33] This lived participation in the reality named diversely by Christ's titles is part, Gregory implies, of "learning to speak 'the wisdom of God hidden in a mystery,'" and we may also infer part of a proper understanding and internalization of the spiritual sense.[34] Gregory defended this practice and articulates the hermeneutic it involved against his Eunomian opponents in *Orations* 28, 29, and 30, thus contributing to one of the key hermeneutical debates of the fourth-century Trinitarian controversies: the interpretation of Christological texts.

In *Orations* 28 and 30, Gregory opposes any attempt to define comprehensively or to name the essence of God, arguing instead that biblical names for God denote imagistic, partial, and obscure perceptions of God's being as reflected in divine activity in creatures.[35] Theology here is a work of creative imagination, gathering these concepts together into a partial, composite image of the truth, rather than a direct mastery of the divine being in thought and language. Therefore the language of divine Fatherhood, Sonship, and generation must be understood in terms of the reality it denotes, and therefore the concepts involved must be pared of the connotations of time and corporeality.[36]

What, though, of Christological texts that seem more directly to assert

---

31. Young, *Biblical Exegesis,* 153.
33. *Or.* 2.98, SC 247:216.
35. *Or.* 28.3.11, 13; *Or.* 30.17–18.

32. *Or.* 2.98, SC 247:216.
34. *Or.* 2.99, SC 247:216.
36. *Or.* 29.3–5.

his inferiority to the Father, either comparatively or by force of his human finitude and frailty? Gregory articulates his hermeneutical response toward the end of *Oration* 29. The key to explaining these texts in the most pious way, Gregory asserts, is to attribute the more exalted names to the divinity "and the humbler ones to the composite One who was emptied and became flesh for my sake ... and was made human and was exalted" that we might learn to exist in a more exalted way and ascend with the divinity, ascending from visible to intellectual things.[37] For, Gregory adds, "the one who is now despised for your sake was once above you and he who is now man, was incomposite: what he was, he remained; what he was not, he assumed."[38] Hence we find in the case of Christ that for every lowly creaturely event, experience, or attribute ascribed to him, there is also a corresponding and contrasting index of his divinity. How, Gregory asks, "can you trip over what is seen, and not espy what is understood?"[39]—in other words, the story of the saving condescension of the Son in his incarnation, life, death, resurrection, and exaltation and his salvific uniting of himself to human form that provides the key to understanding the particular attributes he displays at any point along that trajectory.[40] In light of that story, we must understand the coincidence of humble and exalted descriptions of Christ in Scripture in terms of his identity as the incarnate Son, for because of his saving involvement in our human existence and the path it took, the divine Son is *in addition* the humiliated, suffering, hungry one who prays to the Father who sent him.[41] To use this hermeneutical key is to be able to move from what appears in Scripture to its meaning.

To drive this argument home, Gregory shows the strength of his hermeneutical point by alluding to a great list of scriptural descriptions of Christ, each period beginning with one of Christ's human weaknesses and juxtaposing it with two or three examples, linked variously by metaphorical or literal contrast, of his divine power. For example, "He hungered, but fed thousands, and is the living and heavenly bread."[42] Here Gregory alludes to Jesus'

---

37. *Or.* 29.18, SC 250:216.   38. *Or.* 29.19, SC 250:216.

39. *Or.* 29.19, SC 250:218.

40. Christopher Beeley has drawn attention to Gregory's Christological stress on unity, as well as to the narrative form of this scheme, in his *Gregory of Nazianzus on the Trinity*, 123, 128.

41. As Beeley again rightly notes, for Gregory the more exalted and the humbler statements about Christ in Scripture are "to refer to the same Son of God, though in different ways"; Beeley, *Gregory of Nazianzus on the Trinity*, 132.

42. *Or.* 29.20, SC 250:220.

extreme hunger after fasting in the desert after his baptism (Mt 4:2/Lk 4:2), and juxtaposes first the feeding miracles, then Jesus' metaphorical description of himself in John's Gospel as the living bread from heaven (Jn 6:41) so that, following the Johannine Jesus, the theme of miraculous food from God is appropriated to speak of a greater nourishment and the heavenly origin and saving power inherent in Christ. Carefully weighting each phrase to emphasize the contrast and its transposition to a higher place, Gregory makes brief allusions that effect with great economy an interpretation of the scriptural depiction of Christ around the theme of hunger and food.

The underlying conception of the meaning uncovered by Gregory's hermeneutic here is conveyed by another period in the passage: "He gives over his life, but he has authority to take it again, and the veil is taught—for things above are made manifest—the rocks are torn asunder and the dead rise early."[43] In each case, the intention is to bring out the *overall* force or intention of the total scriptural witness (the Gospels especially), over against a forced deductive exploitation of isolated passages: what Gregory goes on to call "profaning the letter and stealing the mind of the scriptures."[44] That mind, for Gregory, is the manifestation of saving, powerful divine reality in Jesus Christ's frail humanity. As Young has shown, Athanasius has a similar concern for the mind of Scripture in his anti-Arian writings, and similar concerns can be traced back to Irenaeus.[45] As Young argues for Athanasius, so also Gregory's exposition of that mind does not fit the main categories invoked in the study of patristic exegesis (literal, typological, and allegorical). Here the deeper sense is, in one respect, deeply historical: for Gregory, Scripture shows that in Jesus Christ heavenly reality has been disclosed in a human life.

This hermeneutic Gregory applies in more detail to some of the more difficult texts contested in the fourth-century doctrinal controversies over Christ. One of the better examples is his interpretation of Jesus' cry of dereliction, which Gregory argues does not express Jesus' abandonment by the Father or by his divinity, as though retracting from the suffering Christ from fear of death; rather "he images our condition. For we were first abandoned and overlooked, then assumed and saved by the sufferings of the impassible."[46] Once we know that Psalm 21 refers to Christ, we can read the cry against the

43. *Or.* 29.20, SC 250:222.
44. *Or.* 30.1, SC 250:226.
45. Young, *Biblical Exegesis,* chap. 2.
46. *Or.* 30.5, SC 250:234.

narrative of the saving action of the Logos in becoming human.[47] For Gregory, Christ becoming human for us extends to Jesus' dereliction on the cross as mimetically signifying that assumption of our condition. Indeed, one could argue that for Gregory Christ's *mimēsis* of our condition grounds the possibility of our transformation in imitation of him. Less felicitous are those cases where Gregory appears to distinguish what pertains to Christ's divine and human natures respectively, against the grain of his Christology.[48] Gregory's exegesis here also displays the use of the reading procedures learned in the elementary training of the late antique orator, clarifying the logical force of "until" or the range of ways in which someone can be said to be unable to do something.[49]

All this close analysis and application are in service of the commendation and facilitation of the kind of reading Gregory required of candidates for priesthood, and for this reason he closes the oration with an exposition of the meaning and mystical significance of the names of Christ.[50] The former are explained in terms of the Son's relation to the Father and his divine powers in creation and redemption; the latter in terms of the saving purpose and efficacy of his incarnate existence.[51] The listener is then exhorted, in language recalling *Oration* 2.98, to "walk through them divinely, as many as are exalted, and with the same attitude, as many as are bodily, or rather in an entirely divine manner, in order to become God by ascending from here below, through him who descended from above for us."[52] In action and contemplation, then, one is either to attend to the Christ's divine identity or imitate the divine virtues manifest in his incarnate life so as to be assimilated to God through participation in Christ.[53] The hermeneutic Gregory applies to his opponents' objections is implicit in this practice, and his exposition can now be seen to be entirely in order to clear obstacles that stand in the way of this kind of transformative appropriation of the mind of Scripture.

---

47. See Young, *Biblical Exegesis,* chap. 6, on the wider picture on reference in patristic exegesis.

48. As when Gregory distinguishes talk of Jesus' God and Jesus' Father in this way; *Or.* 30.8, SC 250:240, 242.

49. *Or.* 30.4 and *Or.* 30.10–11. On that grammatical training, see Young, *Biblical Exegesis,* 77.

50. *Or.* 30.16, SC 250:260.

51. *Or.* 30.20–21, SC 250:266, 268, 270, 272, 274.

52. *Or.* 30.21, SC 250:274.

53. See also Beeley, *Gregory of Nazianzus on the Trinity,* 149–51.

Scriptural Teaching in Rhetorical Mode

Young has shown that Gregory's allusions to Scripture in his orations, especially when understood in relation to ancient rhetorical theory on allusions, served to lend authority to Scripture by incorporating it into highly wrought rhetoric while claiming biblical authority for his purpose.[54] She illustrates this function of this intertextuality in patristic writings in five forms, the following four illustrated by Gregory: re-minting biblical language and transferring it to the description of an individual to lend weight to the delineation of their character; use of biblical maxims in moral reflections and in consolation; *synkrisis* or comparison of the subject of panegyric with biblical characters; the use of quotation and allusion in the form of festival panegyric. Here I turn to the last of these as exemplified by *Oration* 38, delivered on the festival of the Theophany and Nativity, January 4, 381.[55] Here Gregory's use of Scripture is also interpretative. Largely through allusion, he applies Scripture in relation to the Christianized purpose of the rhetorical form and according to the function of its different parts. He thus can be seen to carry out the understanding of biblical interpretation examined above in an alternative mode to commentary and exegetical homily.

Gregory's opening or *exordium* introduces the subject of the oration and of the feast: the coming of Christ as the appearing of God in human birth. The tone is set by the opening lines: "Christ is born, give glory; Christ from heaven, go and meet him."[56] This sense of the presence of the event of Christ's birth in its liturgical celebration and the imperative of a right response is carried through first with injunctions to worship Israel's God from Psalms 95 (LXX) and 2, the implication being that the God of Israel is manifest in Christ's birth, and so the Psalms apply also to its celebration.

Gregory's evocation of this event and its liturgical *anamnesis* are carried forward by relating them to the history of salvation:

Again the darkness is dissolved, again the light is established, again Egypt is punished with darkness, again Israel is illumined by the pillar. Let the people seated in the darkness of ignorance behold a great light of knowledge. The old things have passed away, behold all things

54. Young, *Biblical Exegesis,* chap. 5.
55. For the dates I follow McGuckin, *Saint Gregory of Nazianzus,* 336–40.
56. *Or.* 38.1, SC 358:104.

have become new. The letter withdraws, the spirit claims its due, the shadows run away, the truth draws near.[57]

Gregory thus alludes to Genesis 1:3–4, Exodus 10:21, and 13:21, and quotes and rewords Isaiah 9:2 to render Christ's birth—re-present in the festival—as the reiteration of the dissolution of darkness and the creation of light, the punishment of Egyptian idolatry with darkness, the pillar of fire that guided Israel through the wilderness to the Promised Land, and the fulfillment of prophecy.

The theme of light conquering darkness and dividing darkness from light as acts of judgment and deliverance connects these intertexts, and Gregory relates them all to Christ's birth, understood figuratively as the saving illumination of the knowledge of the God who appears through birth, destroying the darkness of demonic power and judging idolatry.[58] That birth gathers up and repeats these events so as to fulfill them; it is the newness of the spirit, the truth, that these shadows adumbrated. Gregory's formulations here emphasize both the concrete reality of figure and fulfillment and the greater luminosity of the latter, which shines back on its anticipations. The birth of Christ is thus an event in time whose reality somehow transcends the boundaries of its occurrence, and this quasi-eternal quality bears hermeneutical consequences: it brings into relief the spiritual sense of these Old Testament texts as their fulfillment.[59] By alluding to these events and this prophecy in this way, Gregory implies this interpretive work, inviting his listeners' recognition and response to see the festival in this way. His use of the present tense and his repetition of "again," along with the regularity of the form of the phrases, serve this end, performing the *anamnesis* and investing Christ's birth and its celebration with this sense of the recurrence and completion of primal and ancient events of great magnitude and the fulfillment of ancient oracles and promises.

Gregory shows a self-consciousness about his use of rhetorical form and art in the context of Christian liturgy: it is fitting, he argues, to worship the *Logos* by reveling in discourse and in divine law and narratives, above all those

57. *Or.* 38.2, SC 358:104, 106.

58. See *Or.* 38.3, SC 358:108; compare here Origen, *Homilies on Genesis,* Homily 1.1.

59. Gregory's oratory is not unique in this regard; see Young, *Biblical Exegesis,* 148–52, for a similar phenomenon in Ephrem the Syrian's *Hymns on Paradise,* though in Gregory the birth of Christ is not simply or atemporally fused with its prefigurations or its liturgical celebration, which cannot quite be described as entry into an *eternal* now. As in Ephrem, so in Gregory, however: history and typology are not simply linear.

concerning the festival.[60] Gregory's oratory will be the true and proper feast. After celebrating the divine being, one of the standard *topoi* of this form, Gregory turns to another key *topos:* the stories to which the feast relates. He begins with Creation and Fall as providing the context for the re-creation of humanity in Christ.[61] After the creation of spiritual and material worlds, the "artisan-Logos displays an even greater wisdom and beneficence in uniting them in the creation of humankind, one living being from both, I mean the invisible and visible natures."[62] So taking a body from already existing matter, he placed in it a breath from himself, which the story knows to be an intellectual soul and image of God.[63] Alluding to and interweaving the two creation accounts of Genesis 1:26–2:7 and echoing the attribution of the act of Creation to the *Logos* in John 1:1, Gregory treats the formation and in-breathing of Adam in effect as figurative language for the Word's crafting of the human person. The product is a mixed being, spiritual and bodily, ruling and contemplating the material realm (echoes of Gen 1:28), but a subject and initiate in the spiritual world and, in virtue of this double existence, constituted with an inherent tendency to deification through participation in divine illumination. Already Gregory has concisely communicated an interpretation of these texts and brought out their force for his hearers as identifying the roots of a fundamental tension in human nature: that between the infinite horizons of our desire to experience and enjoy spiritual reality and the finitude our frail flesh imposes upon it.

God placed Adam "in paradise," Gregory continues, and honored him with free will that he might choose and possess the good. While Gregory's exposition relies on the reality of Adam, his explanation of the details of the story is somewhat open-ended and includes symbolic exegesis. For example, Gregory leaves open the question of what paradise was, and hazards a symbolic interpretation of the plants in the garden and Adam's keeping of it (Gen 2:8, 2:9, and 2:15) by calling Adam the tiller of "immortal plants, perhaps divine conceptions at once most simple and more perfect." Such an interpretation seems rather different from the typology we saw earlier or the figural and pro-

60. *Or.* 38.6, SC 358:112.
61. As Peter C. Bouteneff points out in *Beginnings: Ancient Christian Readings of the Biblical Creation Narratives* (Grand Rapids, Mich.: Eerdmans, 2008), 147.
62. *Or.* 38.11, SC 358:124.
63. *Or.* 38.11, SC 358:124.

phetic connections in the *exordium* of this oration: the connection between
the elements of the story and their meaning does not rely on mimetic or providential connection, but is more like cracking a code.[64] Once cracked, the symbol can be seen to illumine its meaning: thoughts, like a plant, are capable of
slow organic growth with careful attention; the reality symbolically depicted
comes to be understood in terms connoted by the symbol.

The tree of the knowledge of good and evil is surely Gregory's key for this
line of interpretation, and Gregory takes it to signify contemplation, which
is beneficial if partaken of at the right time, but dangerous for the more simple who are still more avid in their desire, just as rich food is not good for
those still needing milk. His "contemplation" (θεωρία) seeks to offer a way of
reading the text with a number of theological gains. First, the commandment
thus understood evinces divine beneficence, not a jealous hoarding of divine
goods, as well as providing the means for human beings to exercise their free
will. Second, Adam's fall becomes more comprehensible, given his vulnerable
condition.

Gregory's term for his interpretation is the same as that used by the Antiochene tradition for the way in which some biblical narratives, understood
according to their sequence, look forward prophetically to others.[65] However,
Gregory uses it in a way more closely resembling Origen's idea of the interweaving of impossible elements in the narrative—like a tree of knowledge—
that point to its spiritual sense, as Peter Bouteneff points out.[66] Gregory thus
exceeds an Antiochene concern for θεωρία as the prophetic meaning of the
narrative iconically represented, yet without sacrificing the narrative coherence or an interest in the action narrated that Antiochene objectors to Alexandrian allegory sought to uphold.[67]

For Gregory, Adam is victim of the trap of a jealous Satan and a persuasive Eve, also understood as a victim here. He sins by forgetfulness of the divine command rather than blunt rebellion.[68] And his responsibility is ours:
"alas for my weakness, for that of my first father is mine."[69] Adam is not so

64. I have borrowed this use of "symbolic" from Young, *Biblical Exegesis*, 163ff.

65. See Young, *Biblical Exegesis*, 178–79.   66. Bouteneff, *Beginnings*, 151.

67. Young, *Biblical Exegesis*, 162ff.

68. As Bouteneff notes, pointing to the long tradition in which Gregory stood on this point; *Beginnings*, 149.

69. *Or.* 38.12, SC 358:130.

much a symbol here as a kind of concrete universal: the first human being with whom we have a profound solidarity, and who thus represents our condition to us—the tunics of skin symbolizing a new condition of embodiment, "the coarser flesh, mortal and rebellious."[70] Gregory's retelling of this story is thus interpretive in interesting ways, but as a retelling incorporating commentary, rather than commentary *tout court,* it brings the story alive while clearing away obstacles to understanding, so that the hearers may come to see the present moment and their own condition and salvation as consequent to it—indeed, may come to see themselves in the story, as Adam.

The significance of this retelling becomes clear when Gregory moves the story forward to the incarnation. Here he relates how humanity declined into increasing sin despite divine pedagogical measures, so that a greater remedy was needed—and provided: the *Logos* of God became man in every respect save sin, echoing John 1:14 and Hebrews 2:14ff and 4:15.[71] Here is Gregory's narrative of divine condescension for the sake of human salvation again. Gregory amplifies the identity of the *Logos* by citing biblical and creedal Christological titles and divine attributes: "the light from light, the source of life and immortality, the beautiful impress of the archetype, the unchanging seal, the incomparable image." Gregory stresses the Logos' equality, distinction-in-relation to, and perfect representation of the Father of the salvific power he therefore bears to make God known and bring life. The incarnation Gregory portrays in terms echoing his earlier retelling of the *Logos'* creation of Adam: "He came to his own image and bore flesh on account of the flesh and was mixed with an intellectual soul on account of my soul, purifying like with like." Where Gregory had portrayed himself in profound solidarity with Adam's fall, now he suggests a profound solidarity of Christ with him—and so with us.

As in *Oration* 29, the emphasis falls on the unity of Christ: "God advances with what he assumed, one from two opposites, flesh and Spirit, of which one deified, the other was deified." Here we have, implicitly, a second Adam, only of more wondrous constitution: "O new mixture! O amazing blending! He Who Is becomes and the uncreated is created and the uncontained is con-

---

70. *Or.* 38.12, SC 358:130. I adapt the term "concrete universal" from Paul Ricoeur, *The Symbolism of Evil,* trans. Emerson Buchanan (Boston: Beacon Press, 1969), 244.

71. *Or.* 38.13–25 (PG 36:325B); SC 358:132.

tained." Gregory's paradoxes recall those used in respect to human nature, and signal that divine generosity has excelled itself. The incarnation thus reverses the fall and "communicates a second communion, more wonderful than the first." The basic narrative is drawn from Scripture—the Johannine Prologue, 2 Corinthians 8:9 and Philippians 2:5–11 are all echoed or alluded to—as is much of the amplification. On this basis, Gregory communicates a sense of the consistency and continuity of divine action—and thus of the fittingness of the Incarnation—together with a sense of its excessive newness, which evokes wonder. Having presented the human predicament in Adam's story, he presents the new Adam in whom God is united to humanity.

On this basis Gregory can now address objections to his doctrine and in effect employ the hermeneutic for which he had argued in *Orations* 29 and 30. To that end, he takes up a series of striking biblical images and stories to make his point, including the parables of the lost sheep and the lost coin in Luke 15. Gregory glosses these as he appropriates them:

> Do you accuse God ... because he lit a lamp, his own flesh, and swept the house clean, cleansing the world from sin, and sought the drachma—the royal image confounded by the passions, and on finding the drachma called his friends, the powers and initiates of the mysteries of the economy, to share in his joy?[72]

Jesus' parable in Luke is a saying ostensibly to justify Jesus' practice of eating with sinners, and easily transmuted from an analogy to an extended metaphor about his saving work and the heavenly joy it evokes. Gregory concisely communicates an exegesis along these lines, explicating the details of the narrative symbolically in light of the story of salvation he has already woven from other scriptural material. By appropriating this story by way of allusion, he incorporates its narrative form in his rebuking rhetorical question, thus casting gainsayers as ingrates at the same time as vividly picturing the logic of his response to their objections: Christ's degrading involvement in lowly humanity is a gracious means to a compassionate end: our salvation.

It remains for Gregory to facilitate an appropriate attitude in reception of this spiritual teaching in his peroration. Here the instrumentality of different elements of the action in the infancy narratives are singled out for reverence, in effect providing various ways into the salvific significance of the Incarna-

---

72. *Or.* 38.14, SC 358:134, 136.

tion: "And be in awe at the registration, by which you were inscribed in heaven, and revere the birth, through which you were freed from the bonds of generation."[73] The second of these connects Christ's entry into the world of birth and death with his overcoming of that entire order; the first makes the connection between the literal census and inscription in heaven as a figure of inclusion in salvation (Lk 10:20). The manger opens the way for Gregory to speak about how one receives Christ: "reverence the manger, through which you, though irrational, were nourished by the Logos."[74] Given Gregory's account, it seems that it is precisely this kind of meditative reading of Scripture—as articulated in *Oration* 2 and defended in *Orations* 29 and 30—that provides the way to participation in the Incarnation. Such consumption recognizes Christ's identity: "Recognize, with the cattle, your creator—Isaiah commands it—and, like the ass, the manger of your Lord."[75] Gregory thus takes up the traditional interpretation of this prophecy (Is 1:3) and uses the force of its rebuke to supply a figure of faithful reading and set up a choice between two responses to the Incarnation: "Be either one of the pure animals, under the law and ruminating on the Logos and prepared for sacrifice, or one of the unclean and inedible and unsacrificeable and belonging to the Gentiles."[76] Here is something like a realization of a psychic sense—a meaning that seeks to inform a right disposition or discipline of the soul in relation to Christ—whose thrust, realized through framing the sense in terms of repeated imperatives, is to draw the hearer into the story to revere, be amazed, rejoice, and partake. In fact, such participation will involve one long involvement in the story of Christ, as Gregory suggests in a long, highly allusive, and suggestive passage that largely leaves it to the congregation to work out the paraenetic exegesis implied.[77]

Conclusion

Oration 38 thus illustrates how Gregory's account of the interpretation of Scripture and his Christological hermeneutic could be realized in rhetorical form and to a particular end, shaping the properly spiritual celebration of

73. *Or.* 38.17, SC 358:142.
75. *Or.* 38.17, SC 358:144.
77. *Or.* 38.18, SC 358:146.

74. *Or.* 38.17, SC 358:142.
76. *Or.* 38.17, SC 358:144.

Christ's nativity in a feasting on Christ himself, as the incarnate Logos present in the Gospel story. It also illustrates something of the interpretive and
performative character of his use of biblical allusion, and of the complexity of
exegetical procedures and tools involved beyond the categories of literal, allegorical, and typological and in a way that conforms neither to strictly Antiochene principles nor to what the Antiochenes rejected. In this way, I suggest,
it shows why Gregory is worthy of attention as a patristic biblical interpreter.

Brian J. Matz

4. Deciphering a Recipe for
Biblical Preaching in *Oration* 14

Everyone who studies the works of Gregory Nazianzen in this day eventually passes with no little amount of pleasure through the scholarship of Fred Norris. I have worked my way more than once through his helpful commentary on Gregory's *Theological Orations,* through his insightful connection between Wittgenstein and Gregory's own use of language, through his critique of Harnack in appreciating Gregory's careful use of secular literature, and in many other fields of Gregorian studies that our editor has outlined in his introduction.[1] Meeting Professor Norris for the first time at a meeting of the North American Patristic Society some years ago and hearing from him a humorous address based upon quotations from Gregory's corpus was every bit as exciting as has been my study of his scholarly output. So, it is with much fear and trepidation that I offer a little exercise of my own in Gregory studies. May

---

1. A full bibliography of Norris's works appears elsewhere in this volume. Here, I list a few texts that have been particularly helpful to my research: The introduction and commentary in Frederick W. Norris, *Faith Gives Fullness to Reasoning: The Five Theological Orations of Gregory Nazianzen,* introduction and commentary by Frederick W. Norris, trans. Lionel Wickham and Frederick Williams, Supplements to Vigiliae Christianae 13 (Leiden: E. J. Brill, 1991); "Of Thorns and Roses: The Logic of Belief in Gregory Nazianzen," *Church History* 53, no. 4 (1984): 455–64; "The Theologian and Technical Rhetoric: Gregory of Nazianzus and Hermogenes of Tarsus," in *Nova et Vetera: Patristic Studies in Honor of Thomas Patrick Halton,* edited by John Petruccione (Washington, D.C.: The Catholic University of America Press, 1998); and "Theology as Grammar: Gregory Nazianzen and Ludwig Wittgenstein," in *Arianism after Arius,* edited by Michel Barnes and Daniel Williams, 237–49 (Edinburgh: T. and T. Clark, 1993).

it be as helpful to Professor Norris and to its readers as Professor Norris has proven to be for so many of us.

This chapter argues that, despite the oration's title, *On Loving the Poor*, the evidence of Gregory's use of biblical literature in *Oration* 14 reveals his having begun his work on the homily with a biblical idea, rather than a social ideal, to which he added a heavy dose of illustrative biblical material. That such is not an obvious conclusion is due to the fact that no single surviving oration by Gregory is an exposition or commentary of a particular biblical text (though perhaps one may think of *Or.* 37 and 45 as having begun this way). Thus, it is not self-evident that this oration, which encourages love for the poor, was constructed with a biblical-soteriological purpose in mind. It would seem just as likely that a social justice ideal—that of care for the needs of the poor—was at least as important or more important.

On this last point, it should be acknowledged that we know something of the occasion for which the homily was preached. Basil of Caesarea's famous Basileia, a complex of buildings just beyond the city walls of Basil's bishopric of Caesarea intended for care of the dying, the poor, and weary travelers, either had been constructed or was in the process of being built. The building project was, as Gregory informs us in another of his orations, the result of a severe famine in Cappadocia.[2] Certainly, the Basileia was beneficial to the poor and leprous, but it was also of benefit to Basil's status within the region, as Gregory Nazianzen's encomium for Basil also suggests. Moreover, Peter Brown has argued this type of project also would have enshrined Basil in the classical role of public benefactor (εὐεργέτης).[3] Naturally, we should expect also that preaching about "the poor" and about the plight of the poor was part of the strategy preachers in late antiquity such as Gregory had for ensuring that philanthropic institutions like the Basileia moved from the drawing board to reality, and for ensuring that the contributions needed to sustain

---

2. See *Or.* 44.63. The Basileia is the principal subject of Daley, "Building a New City: The Cappadocian Fathers and the Rhetoric of Philanthropy," *Journal of Early Christian Studies* 7 (1999): 431–61. Interested readers should also consult Konstantina Mentzou-Meimari, "Eparkhiaka evagé idrymata mekhri tou telous tés eikonomakhias," *Byzantina* 11 (1982): 243–308, which provides a list of institutions for poor relief in and around Constantinople during late antiquity.

3. Peter Brown, *Poverty and Leadership in the Later Roman Empire*, the Menahem Stern Jerusalem Lectures (Hanover N.H.: University Press of New England, 2002), 33–44. Brown provides a fresh evaluation of Basil's own actions in light of a possible re-dating of the construction of the Basileias (from 368 to 370) on 41–42. Basil defends his Basileia and its benefit to the state in his *Ep.* 94.

them were forthcoming.[4] Having said this, however, this chapter argues that
the biblical idea of loving the poor for the sake of one's own salvation is of
far greater prominence in this oration than any particular concern to buttress
Basil's public works project in Caesarea. The Basileia certainly heightened
Gregory's concern to speak about the needs of the poor, but the arguments
of this oration defy too close an identification with Basil's particular project.[5]

Even so, it is best to see the social justice ideal as contributing still some
role to Gregory's "rule of faith" guiding his selection and use of biblical literature. Indeed, the socio-ethical realities on the ground often underscore the
significance of God's command to love the poor. Yet *Oration* 14 has far more
to say about soteriology than it does about social ethics. It is Gregory's pastoral concern for his flock that trumps every other concern expressed in the
oration. This having been said, the chapter begins with an overview of the 154
biblical citations found in this oration. Then it analyzes the function of these
citations in each of five parts, or movements, of the oration.

Survey of Biblical Citations in the Oration

As was just stated, the reader will encounter 154 biblical citations in this
oration. Included within that number are 126 unique citations of Scripture, either in the form of a direct quotation (60) or an allusion (66) that may be securely traced to one particular biblical text. That is to say, Gregory's oration
leaves us in little doubt as to which biblical text he is referring for each of these
citations. These 126 securely traced citations are listed in table 4-1. The number to the right of each verse is the section in Gregory's oration where that citation is located.

4. McGuckin, *Saint Gregory of Nazianzus*, 145, proposes seeing the oration as one Gregory delivered as a traveling rhetorician in the late 360s hoping to raise money for the Basileia. That some version
of this oration was delivered orally is suggested by a few places in the text where Gregory incorporated
comments indicative of a worship setting. For example, in §4, Gregory is explaining how Christ is an
example of humility. He wrote, "Humility is a fine thing; the examples are many and varied, but chief
among them is the Savior and Lord of all ... *he who purges the world from sin*" (ὁ τὸν κόσμον καθαίρων τῆς
ἁμαρτίας, *Or.* 14.4). The underlined portion expresses a contrast between the humility of Jesus' humanity
with his power as God to forgive humans of their sins. The contrast is unnecessary to create in order to
substantiate the point that Jesus was humble; indeed, Gregory had already given three reasons in support
of this. The statement here about Jesus' power as God is gratuitous. Perhaps Gregory sought to evoke an
"Amen!" from the audience.

5. See McGuckin, *Saint Gregory of Nazianzus,* 147.

TABLE 4-1.   Securely Traced Biblical Citations

Old Testament								
Genesis		3:11-12	11	**Ecclesiastes**	
2:7	14	10:11	14	7:3	13
3:15	21	11:7	30	11:2	22
4:26 LXX	2	31:40	18		
6:4-7	23			**Isaiah**	
10:8	23	**Psalms**		1:6	37
15:6	2	4:2	21	29:4	29
19:3	2	9:12	35	53:12	4
49:17	21	9:18	35	58:7	38
		10:12 (9:33)	35	58:8-9	38
Exodus		10:14 (9:35)	27		
16:13-35	1	11:4 (10:4)	35	**Jeremiah**	
		12:5 (11:6)	35	9:23	20
Numbers		35:3 (34:3)	37		
12:3	2	37:26 (36:26)	27	**Daniel**	
25:6-8	3	37:26 (36:26)	38	3:39 LXX	40
		38:5 (37:5)	37		
Deuteronomy		41:1 LXX (40:2)	38	**Hosea**	
22:1-4	28	78:25 (77:25)	1	14:9	30
		84:5-6 (83:6-7)	21	14:10 LXX	21
2 Samuel		112:5 (111:5)	38		
23:15-17	3	132:1 LXX (131:1)	2	**Amos**	
				6:4-7	24
1 Kings		**Proverbs**		8:5	24
17:9-24	4	3:28	38		
18:42	4	16:6 (LXX 15:27)	36	**Micah**	
19:14	3	17:5	36	2:9-10 LXX	21
		19:17	36		
Job		22:2	36	**Sirach**	
2:8-9 LXX	34			1:2-3	30

New Testament and Early Christian Literature					
Matthew		5:45	25	19:21	4
1:18-23	3	8:17	15	19:21	39
2:11	40	9:13	40	22:36-40	5
3:4	4	9:22	37	25:32-33	39
4:1-11	3	11:29	15	25:35	40
5:7	38	14:15-21	1	26:36	3
5:42	27	19:8	25		

TABLE 4-1. *(cont.)*

New Testament and Early Christian Literature							
Luke		**Romans**		**Ephesians**			
1:80	4	1:21-23	33	2:10	2		
6:35-38	5	8:17	14	4:11	27		
7:36	40	8:17	14				
10:30	37	8:17	23	**Philippians**			
12:20	18	9:3	2	2:7	4		
16:9	40	11:33-34	30				
16:22-25	34	12:5	8	**Colossians**			
19:8	4	12:8	38	3:1	21		
21:19	22	12:15	6				
				Titus			
John		**1 Corinthians**		2:14	15		
1:29	14	2:10	28				
5:14	37	3:6-7	27	**Hebrews**			
5:29	31	6:13	17	2:4	27		
10:11	15	6:15	37	4:12	21		
12:3	40	7:25-39	3				
12:6	39	12:8	32	**1 Peter**			
13:5	4	13:12	23	4:10	24		
14:2	5	13:13	2				
14:31	21			**1 John**			
19:38-39	40	**2 Corinthians**		4:8	2		
		11:2	3				
Acts				**Ps.-Clement**			
7:58-60	2	**Galatians**		Hom. 12.6			
		2:10	39				
		6:14	21				

In addition to the 126 citations listed above, the language of the oration in twenty-two additional places strongly suggests Gregory was either quoting, paraphrasing, or alluding to a biblical text, but the language is sufficiently generic that one cannot be sure to which biblical text that includes this language Gregory was referring. For example, this list includes those places in the oration where Gregory cited an event in Jesus' life that is found in more than Gospel text, and it is not clear to which Gospel text Gregory was referring. These twenty-two cases are listed in table 4-2.

Finally, one counts seven further places in the oration where a biblical al-

TABLE 4-2.   Generic Biblical Citations

Section	Gregory's Text	Scripture text possibilities
2	Rahab connected with virtue of hospitality	Jos 2:1–24; Heb 11:31
2	quote: "legions of angels"	Mt 26:53; Lk 22:50–51; Jn 18:10–11
2	Jesus connected with virtue of meekness	Is 42:2, 53:7; Mt 12:19
3	quote: "Zeal for thy house has consumed me"	Ps 69:9; Jn 2:17
3	Paul connected with virtue of mortification	1 Cor 9:27; Rom 11:17–25
4	Jesus connected with virtue of solitude/quiet	Mt 14:23; Jn 6:15
4	Jesus purges the world of sin	Jn 1:29; 1 Jn 1:7
5	quote: "the narrow way [and] gate"	Mt 7:13–14; Lk 13:24
6	examples of leprosy	Job 33:19–22; Pss. 38:3, 102:3–5
6	warring against the body	Rom 7:15–25
14	the leprous have put on Christ	2 Cor 4:16; Gal 3:27
14	the leprous have the guarantee of the Spirit	2 Cor 1:22, 5:5
14	the leprous are buried and raised with Christ	Rom 6:4; Col 2:12
15	quote: "the holy nation . . . chosen people"	Ex 19:5–6, 23:22; 1 Pet 2:9
15	humility of Jesus in taking on human flesh	1 Cor 5:6–7; Gal 5:9; Phil 2:8
15	poverty/pains of Jesus in taking on human flesh	Is 53:5; 2 Cor 8:9
15	quote: "the one that went astray . . . which is lost"	Ezek 34:4–16; Mt 18:12; Lk 15:4
20	quote: "glory in this . . . understanding [God]"	1 Cor 4:6; Jer 9:24
23	God is the treasure we ought to seek	Rom 8:14; Gal 3:26
23	the giants of old who terrorized human race	Dt 9:2; Num 13:32–33
37	we are called to be "white as snow"	Ps 51:7; Is 1:18
40	Pauline-style references to Gregory's audience	Rom 8:17; Eph 3:6

lusion may lurk,[6] but the literary context surrounding each of these allusions does not lend itself either to knowing if Gregory was making an allusion or, if so, what biblical passage he had in mind. Nevertheless, for the sake of completeness, granting for the moment that Gregory had intended the reader to identify his text with that of a biblical passage, the following table identifies these seven cases.

Taking into account all three groups of biblical citations, there are 154 places in this oration where Gregory quotes, paraphrases, or alludes to a text

6. I have not included one that Martha Vinson proposed, which is a biblical reference behind the words "mountains and deserts" in §11, for which she suggests Ezek 33:28, 35:15 or Heb 11:38. The context of none of these three texts matches that of the oration; moreover, the words are too commonplace even to narrow them down to one of these three biblical texts, even if the contexts did match.

TABLE 4-3. Possible Biblical Citations

Section	Gregory's Text	Scripture text possibilities
4	Jesus' face having been spit upon	Is 50:6; Mt 27:30; Mk 15:19[1]
5	God being mercy and truth	Ps 89:14
6	Humans are composed of clay	Gen 2:7; Rom 9:21
10	Reminder that we are flesh, just like the leprous	Job 10:11; Gen 6:3(?)[2]
19	The wise save themselves for the afterlife	Mt 6:20
30	Even the righteous not free from sin's corruption	Rom 3:5–7; Job 25:4
37	ἀφή and σημασίας: types of injuries	Lev 13:2[3]

1. The LXX of Is 50:6 is a closer match to the Greek of Gregory's text than the two Gospel references, thus it is quite possible this is a loose quotation. However, that fact alone is not sufficient to securely identify this reference to either Isaiah's prophesy or to the Gospel texts' recounting of the event.

2. Vinson has proposed the Genesis text, but since Gregory has been speaking of Job at some length by this point, it seems better to find this allusion better in that book rather than in Genesis.

3. These words describe skin conditions associated with leprosy in Lev 13:2, so this, among the others in this table, is most likely a biblical citation. However, although it is the only biblical citation where leprosy and these symptoms are linked, it cannot be ruled out that they were also widely known symptoms of leprosy in the fourth century.

FIGURE 4-1. Citations from the Old Testament

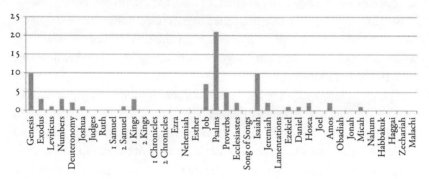

of Scripture. Figures 4-1 and 4-2 show the distribution of these biblical citations across the spectrum of biblical books, first with respect to the Old Testament and then with respect to the New Testament. These charts include the different possible texts listed in tables 4-2 and 4-3.

As these tables and figures show, Gregory possessed a command of a wide array of biblical literature. Once he set himself to the task of articulating the biblical idea of loving the poor, he cast his net widely in search of biblical phrases and stories that lent themselves to this idea. The average length of a

FIGURE 4-2.   Citations from the New Testament

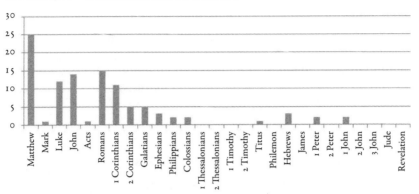

biblical quotation from among those listed above is four words; the median length is three.[7] This suggests that many of the quotations were taken from memory and not from having looked up the texts themselves. In light of this, the disproportionate quantity of citations from the Psalms and Gospels makes sense. The former would have comprised hymns sung in church and thus more frequently recited than other literature from the Old Testament. The latter would have been read on a more regular basis in church than other literature from the New Testament.

One citation where it seems certain Gregory looked up the text in order to record it, but where, strangely enough, he also misidentified its author, is found in §24. Here, Gregory recalled the teaching of the prophets Amos and Micah. Both prophets spoke out against the excesses of the rich in Israel. Gregory begins by referring to Amos, then lists five criticisms of the Israelite people he finds in Micah's text. However, none of the five are listed in Micah, but all are found in Amos 6:4–6. It would seem that Gregory thought he had shifted from talking about Amos' text to Micah's, but, in fact, he had continued with Amos' text. What is interesting about this example is that this list of five items is presented in the oration in the same sequence as found in Amos 6, and he even uses some of the text's own words. Thus, it would seem Gregory had troubled to look up the text in order to get both the list and some of the words cor-

7. This calculation is based upon a database I have constructed recording every biblical citation, and the Greek text of every quotation, in the homily.

rect. However, when he went to record the list in his oration, he was confused about the text's author. One wonders how he could have copied material from a text, only to go out of his way to indicate that it came from a different author. It would seem possible only if the oration had gone through more than one stage of composition and editing. Indeed, one may surmise a situation in which Gregory's first draft included the list of criticisms under Amos' name, joining it to his remarks from Amos' text earlier in the section. Then, at a later stage, Gregory or perhaps one of his students thought differently about the source of the material and so added the reference to Micah.

If some version of this oration was delivered orally, it would go some way toward explaining this previous problem, but it raises a new question: how many in Gregory's audience would have picked up on even half of the 154 biblical citations in this oration? It would seem improbable that any but the monks would have recognized much beyond the quotations and allusions from the Psalms and the Gospels, and perhaps also the ten citations of Isaiah, nearly all of which come from the messianic passages and so may have been known as standard proof texts for Jesus as the Messiah. Job's story of suffering and redemption is mentioned often in the oration, but Gregory never explained who Job was. Perhaps his story, too, was one Gregory could assume the audience knew well. Yet, the nearly 100 remaining biblical citations in all likelihood would have passed over the heads of the audience. In fact, of the 126 securely traced biblical citations identified in table 4-1, forty-three of them function rhetorically as proof texts and thirty-nine function as ornamental speech. That is to say, eighty-two of this group of 126 citations decorate the speech of Gregory's oration. They highlight the biblical idea of loving the poor, but they are not the texts upon which the argument to love the poor hinges. To Gregory's audience, they delightfully ornamented the speech, much as we, too, recognize that was their role in the overall construction of Gregory's argument. This understanding, as well as others with respect to Gregory's use of Scripture in *Oration* 14, is the subject of a more detailed analysis in the next part of this chapter.

From Biblical "Idea" to Oration

Most noteworthy about Gregory's use of Scripture in this oration is, figuratively speaking, the amount of water it carries. Put bluntly, the oration's argument is stated in biblical language. Gregory rarely expresses a thought without recourse to a biblical word or image. Today we would treat this as an example of plagiarism. Rather than using biblical material to *support* or to *reinforce* an argument he has already made with his own words, Gregory uses biblical words to make the arguments themselves. The oration's overall structure may conveniently be divided into five movements. In what follows, we consider the oration's development from a biblical "idea" upon which Gregory has set his course prior to drafting it to his explanation of this idea with biblical language in the oration in each of its five movements.

The first movement comprises §1–5. Here, Gregory argues there are many virtues to which Christians are called, but the greatest of the virtues is love, and the greatest expression of love is love for the poor. Yet, Gregory does not express this point with his own words until the very end of §5. Instead, the reader is treated to a laundry list of virtues, together with biblical exemplars that substantiate them. The list begins with Gregory saying what is good are "faith, hope and love, these three."[8] Connected to these three are twelve additional virtues, including hospitality, meekness, mortification of the body, and poverty. One or more Hebrew or Christian saints are identified as exemplars for each virtue. Noteworthy as well is that Gregory finds a way to include Jesus as an example of nearly every one of the virtues. Thus, Christians may look both to the lives of Hebrew or Christian saints *and* the life of Jesus for understanding the practice of the virtues to which they are called.[9]

The main point is that Gregory has not made any argument from his own words throughout the first movement of this oration. Instead, Gregory crafted the argument by weaving together one biblical quotation or allusion after another, ever conscious of the need to connect his human exemplars with the life and teachings of Jesus. The genius of Gregory in this first movement of the oration is found, then, not in his explanation of a point of view, but in his ability to draw connections between virtues and exemplars. Every virtue is introduced as καλὸν, and since he quoted 1 Cor 13:13 at the head of this list,

8. Καλὸν πίστις, ἐλπὶς, ἀγάπη, τὰ τρία ταῦτα (1 Cor 13:13); *Or.* 14.2.

9. In explaining the virtue of simplicity, Gregory gives as an exemplar the story of Peter consuming meager amounts of food. This is from *Hom.* 12.6 in the Pseudo-Clementine homilies. Not only is it interesting that Gregory treats this story as of equal weight in authority to the biblical exemplars, but it is also noteworthy that Gregory provides no background on this story. Thus, one suspects it was a commonplace for his audience.

Gregory's audience expects eventually to read about which one is πρώτην τῶν ἐντολῶν καὶ μεγίστην. That eventually comes in §5, where Gregory says ἀγάπη is best expressed in terms of φιλοπτωχίαν, σπλάγχνίαν, and συμπάθειαν. Even here the reader is not left bereft of a biblical proof text, for Gregory writes, "no other thing is more proper to God, whose mercy and truth go before."[10] Thus, the argument of the first movement of this oration—that Christians are to grow in virtue, that all virtues are a path leading to salvation, and that the greatest of the virtues is love of the poor—is made almost exclusively through a patchwork of biblical quotations and allusions. Gregory had a biblical "idea" in mind, but set out not only to express the idea but also to prove its verity by letting the Scripture do all the talking.

The second movement of the oration is §6–16, in which Gregory details the plight of those who suffer two afflictions, poverty and leprosy, the latter compounding the difficulties of the former. In this movement, Gregory grouped the biblical citations into two places, the beginning (§6) and toward the end (§14–15). The intervening paragraphs, §7–13, are a contemporary description of the lives of people who are poor and leprous. Much like today's televised infomercials for organizations that serve the poor, which seek to move our sympathies and our pocketbooks by showing graphic images of the struggles of poor people, Gregory, too, did not leave to his audience's imagination what the lives of the poor and leprous are like. He described the lurid and decrepit conditions in which they live. He expressed the anguish they feel when people spurn their requests for assistance. One expects that Gregory's audience intellectually understood what life was like for poor, sick people, but, like the infomercials today, that audience needed an emotional connection to their lives, as well.

Serving as bookends to this description are the arguments Gregory makes by way of biblical citations in §6 and 14–15. In §6, Gregory shifts from talking about the virtue of loving the poor to talking about how to love a particular group of poor people with a quotation from Romans 12:15, "Rejoice with those who rejoice and weep with those who weep." He lists the misfortunes that bring about poverty (e.g., widowhood, orphanhood, ruthless tax collectors), but then he suggests even greater pity ought to be extended to those whose problems of poverty, which are often chronic, are exacerbated by the

10. ὅτι μηδὲ οἰκειότερον ἄλλο τούτου Θεῷ, οὗ ἔλεος καὶ ἀλήθεια προπορεύονται, Or. 14.5, in Gregory of Nazianzus, *Select Orations,* trans. Vinson.

acute condition (relative to poverty alone) of leprosy. Gregory's biblical theology here comes to his aid in reflecting upon the mystery that is the human body and why God allows the bodies of some persons to experience such great pain in this life.

Initially it seems Gregory has in mind some Scripture texts that identify leprosy as a punishment visited upon some persons as a consequence of their sin. He refers to leprosy "as the threat against some people."[11] Yet Gregory's biblical theology suggests a different direction, one in which he puts into perspective all the trials that face humans as a consequence of their souls having been joined to bodies. He writes,

How I came to be joined to it, I do not know; nor how I am the image of God and concocted of clay at the same time, this body that both wars against me when it is healthy and when warred against brings me pain, that I both cherish as a fellow-servant and evade as my enemy.[12]

The imagery that the human body is both made of clay and at war with the body suggests allusions to Romans 9 (in parallel with Gen 2.7) and 7, respectively. This is then drawn by Gregory into a theological conclusion: that whether we suffer physical infirmities, such as leprosy, or we suffer the myriad indignities from being composed of a body, our ascent to God is only possible by a successful reigning in of the body. Such difficulties are the proving ground of virtue.

This ties us back to the biblical idea articulated in the first movement: the cultivation of virtues is the path of salvation, and the greatest virtue is love for the poor. Also similar to the first movement, in §§14–15 Gregory crafts his argument not with his own words, but almost exclusively with biblical quotations, imagery, and allusions. He argues that the leprous bear the same marks of humanity as everyone else. They are "formed of the same clay," (cf. Rom 9:21) and "knit together with bones and sinew just as we are, clothed in skin and flesh like everyone else" (cf. Job 10:11).[13] Gregory acknowledges Job,

11. ὡς ἡ κατά τινων ἀπειλὴ, *Or.* 14.6. Vinson is rather dynamic with her translation, making explicit the connection between leprosy and Scripture teaching. She translates this same phrase, "the visitation that Scripture threatens against certain individuals"; *Select Orations,* trans. Vinson.

12. ᾧ πῶς συνεζύγην, οὐκ οἶδα. καὶ πῶς εἰκών τέ εἰμι Θεοῦ, καὶ τῷ πηλῷ συμφύρομαι. ὃ καὶ εὐεκτοῦν πολεμεῖ, καὶ πηλῷ συμφύρομαι. ὃ καὶ εὐεκτοῦν πολεμεῖ, καὶ ἀνιᾷ πολεμούμενον. ὃ καὶ ὡς σύνδουλον ἀγαπῶ, καὶ ἀνιᾷ πολεμούμενον. ὃ καὶ ὡς σύνδουλον ἀγαπῶ, καὶ ὡς ἐχθρὸν ἀποστρέφομαι; *Or.* 14.6, Gregory of Nazianzus, *Select Orations,* trans. Vinson.

13. ἐκ τοῦ αὐτοῦ πηλοῦ ... οἱ νεύροις καὶ ὀστέοις ἐνειρμένοι παραπλησίως ἡμῖν, οἱ δέρμα καὶ κρέας ἐνδεδυμένοι πᾶσιν ὁμοίως...; *Or.* 14.14, Gregory of Nazianzus, *Select Orations,* trans. Vinson.

whose true humanity seemed to outstrip the devastation of his physical body. Then, in §15, Gregory turns his attention to his audience, whose obligation it is to care for the leprous. Here, too, biblical quotations and allusions abound to describe both the Christian community as God's chosen people and Christ, on account of his self-emptying (cf. Phil 2:6–8), as the exemplar for our compassion toward the poor and leprous.

In view of Gregory having grouped his biblical material together in the way that he did in the second movement, one senses a similar pattern here, as in the first movement. In both, the argument is to love the poor. In the first movement, this is grounded in a recitation of biblical virtues. In the second, it is grounded in the inherent dignity of leprous persons as fellow humans and in the obligation of Christians to live out their calling as people of faith, this latter point being one upon which Gregory expands in the next movement.

The third movement of the oration, §17–29, turns from the plight of the poor to the vagaries of the human condition, with particular attention paid to the disposition of Christian people. Continuing his argument of the second movement, here Gregory defends an obvious point: human life is full of ups and downs. Health and good fortune are cyclical. Thus, it is better to place one's trust in the love of God for its creation and in the heavenly home God has promised to people of faith. The aim is divinization, which has not only eternal benefits, but also earthly implications, including especially imitating the compassion and love of God for every person. Unsurprising, then, is the fact that, of the thirty-eight biblical citations in this movement, twenty-two are found in just three sections, §21, 23, and 27, which are precisely where this matter of divinization and imitating God's compassion is described. In the main, as in the earlier movements, Gregory relies upon the language of the biblical citations to make his theological arguments.

Consider this one illustration about divinization in this third movement. Gregory defines "wisdom" against the backdrop of cyclical patterns of fortune (§19). Wisdom teaches one to avoid misfortune through a life of piety and generosity toward others and, if misfortune does come, to view it as an opportunity for one's betterment. According to Gregory, one accesses wisdom by ascending to God (§21–22). Gregory recalls Jesus' words in John 14:31, "Rise, let us go from here," and then offers this interpretation,

He is not merely conducting his disciples of the moment from that specific place, as one might think, but he is drawing all his disciples as well away for all time from the earth and the things of earth to the heavens and the blessings of heaven.[14]

The context of John 14 is Jesus' teaching on the Holy Spirit as one who will come after Jesus' departure from the earth to lead and guide the disciples into further truth. Gregory recognizes that the words "Rise, let us go from here" are, in a literal sense, Jesus' shift from didactic mode to what they needed to do at that moment—leave the Upper Room and head to the Garden of Gethsemane. Yet, in a figurative sense, the words are a continuation of Jesus' teaching about his departure, and signify that Jesus' followers are called also, eventually, to follow him back to the presence of the Father. Thus, Gregory signals that he is aware of the literal, literary context, but that he prefers the figurative understanding, since it better fits the point of Jesus' instruction about what the Spirit will help the disciples to do: ascend to God.

Gregory then connects this ascent to God to Christianity's social ethics in terms of a loan transaction with the poor (§27). Here Gregory substitutes our actions for God's, depicting clearly θεοποιέω. Christian people "become" God to the poor and leprous when they care for their needs (cf. here Gregory's use of Mt 5:42, Ps 10:14, and possibly Ps 37:26). This lending idea is furthered when Gregory recalls 1 Corinthians 3:6–7, where Paul says that he watered and nurtured the seeds of faith earlier planted by Apollos. Gregory writes,

[Lend] your words and solicitously seeking repayment of the loan with interest in the form of the spiritual increment of the one you have benefitted. In this way, the beneficiary adds steadily to the deposit of your words and little by little makes grow in his own right the seeds of piety.[15]

Spending one's wealth to meet the needs of the poor creates a loan for the poor person to repay. Repayment of the loan is made with the spiritual growth of the poor person himself or herself. In other Christian writers of late antiquity, the idea of caring for the poor as the creation of a loan transaction is

---

14. οὐ τοὺς τότε μαθητὰς μόνον ἐξ ἐκείνου μόνου τοῦ τόπου μετατιθείς, ὡς ἂν οἰηθείη τις, ἀλλ᾽ ἀεὶ καὶ πάντας τοὺς ἑαυτοῦ μαθητὰς ἀπὸ γῆς καὶ τῶν περὶ γῆν εἰς οὐρανοὺς ἕλκων καὶ τὰ οὐράνια, Or. 14.21, Gregory of Nazianzus, Select Orations, trans. Vinson.

15. δανείζων τὸν λόγον, καὶ ἀπαιτῶν φιλοπόνως τὸ δάνειον μετὰ τόκου τῆς τοῦ ὠφελημένου προσθήκης. ἣν ἀεὶ τῷ λόγῳ προστίθησιν, αὔξων ἑαυτῷ κατὰ μικρὸν τὰ τῆς εὐσεβείας σπέρματα, Or. 14.21, Gregory of Nazianzus, Select Orations, trans. Vinson.

not new. However, in those other texts, repayment of the loan with interest is construed in terms of spiritual blessings and/or heavenly rewards accruing to the account of the person who showed philanthropy.[16] Here, though, Gregory says repayment of the loan is the philanthropist's joy at watching the poor person both grow in faith and sow their own seeds of piety. This is precisely the type of joy God experiences, as described by Jesus in several parables (cf. Lk 15). Thus, Gregory's description of this loan transaction transforms the Christian into the face of God for the poor.

The soteriological aspect to loving the poor yields to the socioethical aspects in the fourth movement, §30–34. Here Gregory attends both to the possible causes of injustice and the right response to injustice. The biblical evidence leads Gregory to conclude that he cannot know why God allows injustice and evil to persist. "Who really knows whether one man is punished for his misdeeds while another is exalted for praiseworthy behavior, or whether the opposite holds true."[17] Gregory then alludes to one and quotes from four other biblical texts as proof texts of this point. He alludes first to the biblical idea that no one is free of guilt, so righteous people should expect problems in this life equally as much as unrighteous people. Since he will quote both from Romans and from Job in the following sentences, perhaps he has here in mind either Romans 3:5–7 or Job 25:4. Following this, he quotes from four texts that extol the inscrutable wisdom and judgment of God: Sirach 1:2–3, Romans 11:33–34, Job 11:7 and Hosea 14:9 (14:10 in LXX). Since God's ways are inscrutable, and yet believed to be perfectly just and good, it stands to reason for Gregory that the injustices of the world are allowed by God for some reason one cannot now know (§31–32). This leads him to an articulation of what the Christian ought to believe about God:

[L]et us rather both believe that God is the Maker and Creator of all things ... and also include Providence, whose role it is to bind and keep this whole together.... And let us have faith that our [Maker] gives especial attention to our affairs even if our lives take an adverse turn quite unintelligible to us. (Or. 14.33)[18]

---

16. Interested readers should consider Basil of Caesarea, *Homily* 8.6; Pseudo-Basil, *Concerning Beneficence;* Pope Leo I, *Sermon* 17; and Origen, *On Psalm 36, Homily* 3.11.

17. Καὶ τίς οἶδεν, εἰ ὁ μὲν διὰ κακίαν κολάζεται, ὁ δὲ ὡς ἐπαινούμενος αἴρεται; *Or.* 14.30, Gregory of Nazianzus, *Select Orations,* trans. Vinson.

18. Ἀλλὰ καὶ Θεὸν εἶναι τὸν πάντων ποιητὴν καὶ δημιουργὸν πιστεύωμεν.... Καὶ Πρόνοιαν συνεισάγωμεν, τὴν τοῦδε τοῦ παντὸς συνεκτικήν τε καὶ συνδετικήν.... Καὶ τοῖς ἡμετέροις μάλιστα ἐπιστατεῖν

The point, then, is that why some people suffer from poverty and leprosy and why others experience financial success has nothing to do with righteousness or unrighteousness. To be sure, these things happen for good reasons, but what those reasons are cannot be understood this side of heaven. Once again, Job's story is held up as the perfect example. Thus, for Gregory, the best course of action is to love the poor and leprous by meeting their needs (§34).

The fifth and final movement of the oration is §35–40. Here, Gregory returns to the oration's opening theme: loving the poor is a *sine qua non* of Christian faith. Gregory drums one biblical quotation or allusion after another into the ears of his audience, quite literally overwhelming the audience with the conviction that God demands love for the poor from those who claim to have Christian faith. Little, if any, of this argument is made with Gregory's own words; the biblical quotations and allusions so dominate the text that he seems rather pleased to let the biblical texts do all the talking.

Gregory begins this final movement by proposing one final reason for loving the poor: it reminds both oneself and others of their inherent dignity. One runs afoul of God if he or she does not love what God loves, namely, the poor, the sick, and the needy. The biblical citations that fill the final paragraphs of this oration trumpet, in staccato fashion, both that the cries of the needy rise up to God and that God, in return, rises up to meet their needs. Nine proof texts are adduced in §35–36 (Lk 16:22–25, Pss 9:12, 9:18, 10:12, 11:4, 12:5, Prov 16:6, 17:5, 19:7, and 22:2) to demonstrate the poor are a central concern of God in Scripture. This is followed in §37 with ten biblical citations that together argue that philanthropy or almsgiving are not to be seen as penance for sin. Even those who might want to think of themselves as, at any given moment, free from sin still ought to be philanthropic in order to honor Christ for his having taken upon himself the burden of our sinful condition. So, in §38–39, Gregory scours the biblical text looking for proof texts on mercy and compassion as the proper disposition of Christian people. He includes twelve biblical citations in these paragraphs, eight of which are quotations. Then finally, in §40, Gregory fills these few sentences alone with no less than ten further biblical citations, which argue that, whereas during his earthly ministry Jesus was offered many gifts (e.g., those of the Magi, food at banquets, Mary's ointment, Joseph

---

δεξώμεθα τὸν ἡμέτερον … κἂν διὰ τῶν ἐναντίων ὁ βίος ἡμῖν διεξάγηται; *Or.* 14.33, Gregory of Nazianzus, *Select Orations*, trans. Vinson.

FIGURE 4-3

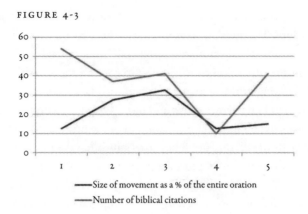

——Size of movement as a % of the entire oration
——Number of biblical citations

FIGURE 4-4

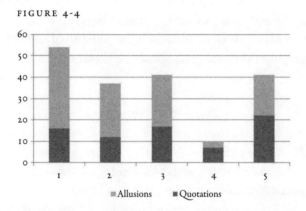

■Allusions   ■Quotations

of Arimathea's tomb), now the gifts Christ seeks are those that are given in his honor to the poor. In all, forty-one biblical citations fill the final paragraphs of the oration. Gregory employed them both to restate the biblical idea outlined in the first movement and to reinforce the benefits attendant to the Christian person for engaging in philanthropy toward the poor and the leprous.

Restating the above analysis, figures 4-3 and 4-4 depict not only the quantity of biblical citations in each of the five movements of the oration, but also the ways in which Gregory incorporated these sources. Figure 4-3, a line graph, tracks both the size of each movement as a percentage of the overall oration's length (based upon the number of paragraphs in each movement) and the number of biblical citations found in each movement. In both the first and fifth movements, the lines are at the greatest distance from one another. This reveals that the shortest movements of the oration have the highest concentration of biblical citations. The lines converge in movements two, three, and four, revealing a lower density of biblical citations in them. This line graph highlights what was noted in the discussion above—that Gregory let the biblical texts do almost all the talking in the first and fifth movements. Figure 4-4, a bar graph, reveals that, even in movements two and three, Gregory incorporated as many (or nearly as many) biblical citations as found in the first and fifth movements. So, even though the density of biblical citations is lower in these movements, the quantity of citations is still formidable. Finally, figure 4-4 also reveals just how much use Gregory made of biblical allusions in comparison to quotations. With the exception of movement four, they comprised half or much more than half of the total number of citations. This, too, confirms the argument of this paper—that Gregory constructed the oration principally around a biblical idea, to which he added as much biblical "color" as he could find without much concern to exposit the meaning of individual biblical texts.

Conclusion

This analysis of the use of biblical quotations and allusions in Gregory's *Oration* 14 lent itself to the conclusion that Gregory constructed the oration around a desire to articulate a biblical-soteriological idea—love for the poor acts as a guarantor of one's salvation—and then liberally sprinkled the text of the oration with biblical quotations and allusions that support this idea. Gregory's project in this oration was too grand to limit himself to an exposition of any one text. He wanted to argue that God *demands* love for the poor as a feature of genuine faith. To Gregory's mind, this is not a point that can be made from any one pericope or even one biblical book. God had made this point time and again throughout salvation history in ever more profound ways. Thus, there really was no way to establish this biblical idea without recourse to a laundry list of biblical evidence, be it in the form of proof texts, ornamental speech, or theological exposition. Thus, we have a recipe for Gregory's use of biblical literature in the construction of this, and perhaps other, orations: start with a grand project, a biblical idea that is rooted in the character of God, and then liberally sprinkle the text with as much biblical evidence as one can find. Finally, as much as possible, let Scripture do the talking.

5. Gregory's Baptismal Theology and the Alexandrian Tradition

Fred Norris has made major contributions to understanding the Trinitarian theology of Gregory of Nazianzus, and in tribute to him I want to give further consideration to Gregory's baptismal theology, for which he is a principal fourth-century source.[1] Gregory of Nazianzus shares much in common with his fellow Cappadocians Basil the Great and Gregory of Nyssa, but for this chapter I want to note his commonalities with the Alexandrians, principally Clement of Alexandria and Origen.[2] Gregory's indebtedness to Origen is well recognized,[3] and Fred noted Gregory's view of language was the same as Clement's and Origen's.[4]

In a passage that may be considered a systematized statement of Origen's scattered discussions, Gregory of Nazianzus distinguishes five kinds of baptism: the types of baptism in the crossing of the Red Sea and the washings in water of the law of Moses; the baptism of John, which was not only in water,

---

1. For a fuller treatment of baptism in Gregory of Nazianzus, including the ceremony of baptism, see Everett Ferguson, *Baptism in the Early Church: History, Theology, and Liturgy in the First Five Centuries* (Grand Rapids, Mich.: Eerdmans, 2009), 592–602.

2. Everett Ferguson, "Exhortations to Baptism in the Cappadocians," *Studia Patristica* 32 (1997):121–29 compares the similar sermons exhorting to enroll for baptism by these three Cappadocians. For their information on baptism in general, see Ferguson, *Baptism in the Early Church,* 582–91 for Basil, 603–16 for Gregory of Nyssa, 309–21 for Clement of Alexandria, and 400–28 for Origen.

3. Beeley, *Gregory of Nazianzus on the Trinity,* especially 271–74.

4. Norris, *Faith Gives Fullness to Reasoning,* 38. In the same book he notes Gregory's use of the Trin-

but was also accompanied by repentance; the perfect baptism of Jesus, which is in water and the Spirit; the baptism of blood in martyrdom, which cannot be defiled by later sin; and the baptism of tears, in which one baptizes his couch in tears of remorse for sins.[5] Later in the oration Gregory adds a "last baptism," the baptism of eschatological fire, longer lasting and more painful than one's penance for sins (*Or.* 39.19).[6]

Old Testament Connections

Gregory of Nazianzus elsewhere alludes to the Exodus typology, mentioning the parting of the sea, Pharaoh being drowned, and bread raining down from heaven.[7] Beginning with Paul in 1 Corinthians 10:1–2, this association was common in Christian authors. Origen had the fullest elaboration of the typology among early writers. Following Paul, he identified the sea with water or baptism and the cloud with the Holy Spirit, connecting them with the water and Spirit of John 3:5. The manna is spiritual food, and the rock is Christ; Christ's flesh is true nourishment, and his blood is true drink, with reference to John 6:55.[8] Gregory had the same interpretation: the sea is water, the cloud the Holy Spirit, the manna the bread of life, the drink the divine drink (*Or.* 39.7).

Gregory of Nazianzus appealed to the anointing of doorposts at the Exodus in order to protect the firstborn (Ex. 12:22–23, 29) and to the performance of circumcision on the eighth day (Gen. 17:12) in justification of baptizing infants in danger of death, even though they are unconscious of both sin and grace (*Or.* 40.28).

Origen expresses the view that those in the church were "circumcised by means of the grace of baptism."[9] This statement accords with the early Christian understanding that baptism was not itself the equivalent of circumcision,

---

itarian baptismal formula as an argument for the deity of the Son and Spirit (e.g., *Or.* 33.17) against Eunomius (54, 66–68).

5. *Or.* 39.17. Clement of Alexandria shares the imagery of being baptized a second time with tears in a comparison of penitence to baptism as a regeneration; *Quis Dives Salvus* 42.14–15.

6. Origen makes frequent reference to the eschatological baptism of fire; see Ferguson, *Baptism in the Early Church,* 408–10.

7. *Or.* 45.21.   8. *Hom. Ex.* 5.1, 5; *Hom. Num.* 7.2.

9. *Comm. Rom.* 2.12.4 and 2.13.2; cf. *Hom. Josh.* 5.5–6; Origen, *Origen: Commentary on the Epistle to the Romans Books 1–5,* trans. Thomas P. Scheck, Fathers of the Church 103 (Washington, D.C.: The Catholic University of America Press, 2001), 143.

but was the means through which (or the occasion at which) the spiritual circumcision was effected by the Holy Spirit on the human heart.[10]

The Baptism of Jesus

Jesus' baptism by John was commonly interpreted as purifying water and so providing for human purification.[11] Gregory of Nazianzus is representative of this interpretation: "Jesus submitted to be purified in the river Jordan for my purification, or rather, sanctifying the waters by his purification (for indeed he who takes away the sin of the world had no need of purification" (*Or.* 38.16; also 29.20).[12] Jesus came to the Jordan "to bury the whole of the old Adam in the water; and before this and for the sake of this, to sanctify Jordan; for as he is Spirit and flesh, so he consecrates us by Spirit and water" (*Or.* 39.15). By his baptism Jesus became a model for Christian baptism: "Christ is baptized: let us descend with him that we may also ascend with him" (*Or.* 39.15).

Clement of Alexandria stated the purifying effect of Jesus' baptism: "The Savior was baptized, although he did not need to be, in order that he might sanctify all water for those who are being regenerated."[13] More distinctive of Clement is his development of the meaning of Christian baptism as applying also to Jesus' baptism: by his baptism he was regenerated, perfected, and sanctified in his humanity; thus he became the pattern for us.[14]

Names of Baptism

Gregory of Nazianzus lists the names for baptism: "We call it gift, grace, baptism, enlightenment, anointing, clothing of immortality, bath of regenera-

---

10. Everett Ferguson, "Spiritual Circumcision in Early Christianity," *Scottish Journal of Theology* 41 (1988): 485–97; cf Jean Daniélou, "Circoncision et baptême," in *Theologie in Geschichte und Gegenwart: Michael Schmaus zum sechzigsten Geburtstag dargebracht von seinen Freunden und Schülern,* edited by Johann Auer and Hermann Volk, 755–76 (Munich: K. Zink, 1957) who makes the identification that for Origen circumcision is the figure of the sacrament of baptism (773).

11. Ferguson, *Baptism in the Early Church,* 113–15.

12. I quote, but occasionally modify, unless otherwise noted, the translation by Charles Gordon Browne and James Edward Swallow in *Nicene and Post-Nicene Fathers,* vol. 7, Second Series (Grand Rapids, Mich.: Eerdmans, 1955).

13. Clement of Alexandria, *Eclogae Prophetae* 7.2; translations from Clement are my own.

14. *Paed.* 1.6.25.3–6.1. For these descriptions of baptism, see below.

tion (Titus 3:5, παλιγγενεσία), seal, everything honorable" (*Or.* 40.4). This listing is remarkably similar to Clement of Alexandria. After speaking of our being regenerated on the pattern of Jesus (cited in the preceding paragraph), he says, "This work is variously called a grace gift, enlightenment, perfection, and bath" (*Paed.* 1.6.26.2).

Gregory of Nazianzus often refers to baptism as simply "the gift."[15] It is so named "because it is given to us in return for nothing on our part" (*Or.* 40.4). "What folly it is to put off the gift" (*Or.* 40.27). Hence, he exhorts, "Run to the gift" (*Or.* 40.11) and "Let us hasten to salvation. Let us arise to baptism. The Spirit is eager, the consecrator is ready, the gift is prepared" (*Or.* 40.44). Grace is an equally frequent word in connection with baptism.[16] Baptism is called grace "because it is conferred even on debtors" (*Or.* 40.4); this grace reaches to the depth of the soul (*Or.* 40.11). "He supports me by many means, one of which is grace which washes mortals" (*Poemata arcana* 8.86–87).[17] Here, the full phrase "grace of baptism" occurs (*Or.* 40.41). Lest there be misunderstanding, Gregory adds that there must be "the right disposition [to receive] grace" (*Or.* 40.27).

The phrase "grace of baptism" is common in Origen. For example, to come to the "grace of baptism" is to be baptized into Christ's death (Rom. 6:3).[18] One of Clement's names for baptism was "grace gift" (χάρισμα), because "in it the penalties belonging to our sins are removed" (*Paed.* 1.6.26.2).

By the time of Gregory of Nazianzus "enlightenment" or "illumination" (φώτισμα) was a common name for baptism.[19] The commemoration of the baptism of Jesus was "the Feast of the Holy Lights," at which occasion Gregory delivered his *Oration* 39, and a common name for a baptistery was the related word "place of enlightenment" (φωτιστήριον). Gregory begins his sermon "On Baptism" with an elaboration of baptism as enlightenment, including the statement: "Light is in a special sense the enlightenment of baptism ... which contains the great and marvelous mystery of our salvation" (*Or.* 40.6). The

15. *Or.* 40.11, 12, 16, 18, 21, 22, 23, 25 (plural), and other passages cited in the text.
16. *Or.* 40.12, 20, 24, 25, 26, 28, 34, 44, and other passages cited in the text.
17. Translations from this work are taken from Moreschini, ed., *Poemata Arcana*, here 47.
18. Origen, *Hom. Lev.* 2.4.6; other occurrences are *Hom. Lev.* 9.4.4; *Hom. Jos.* 15.7; *Hom. Ex.* 8.4–5; 10.4; 11.7; *Princ.* 1.3.2; *Comm. Rom.* 3.1.12.
19. Joseph Ysebaert, *Greek Baptismal Terminology: Its Origins and Early Development,* Graecitas Christianorum primaeva 1 (Nijmegen: Dekker and Van de Vegt, 1962), 158–78.

theme continues through the sermon.[20] In *Oration* 39.1 he says that the baptism of Christ brought enlightenment and purification.[21] The name "enlightenment" is appropriate because of the splendor of baptism (*Or.* 40.4).

Baptismal enlightenment was also a prominent theme in Clement of Alexandria. He defined enlightenment as "to know God" (*Paed.* 1.6.25.1) and explained, "When we are baptized we are enlightened" (*Paed.* 1.6.26.1). The name applies to baptism because by its holy, saving light we attain a clear vision of the divine (*Paed.* 1.6.26.2). Baptism enables one to see with spiritual eyesight "the divine, as the Holy Spirit flows down upon us from heaven" (*Paed.* 1.6.28.2). This illumination is related to the knowledge imparted in relation to baptism, especially the moral knowledge, for "the one grace of enlightenment is to be no longer the same as before one's washing" (*Paed.* 1.6.29–30).

I shall artificially separate Gregory of Nazianzus's designation "bath of regeneration" and treat "bath" here as a name for baptism and regeneration in the next unit on blessings accomplished in baptism. Baptism is called "laver" or "bath" (λουτρόν) "because it washes us" (*Or.* 40.4). He encourages his hearers, "Let the bath be not for your body only but also for the image of God in you" (*Or.* 40.32). "Common to all mankind is the baptism [λουτρόν] which gives salvation to mortals" (*Poemata arcana* 8.99).

The "bath [or washing] of regeneration" (παλιγγενεσία) was Origen's favorite phrase for baptism.[22] Origen treated the language of new birth from 1 Peter 1:23 (ἀναγέννησιν) and John 3:5 as equivalent to the regeneration of Titus 3:5. For instance, he says, "Through the bath of regeneration, in which they were born [ἐγεννήθησαν] they desire as newborn babes the pure spiritual milk [1 Peter 2:2]" (*Comm. Mt.* 13.27).[23] Origen marks the transition from the second century, when John 3:5 was the favorite baptismal text, to the fourth century, which saw increasing use of Titus 3:5.

Clement of Alexandria still preferred the language of John and Peter,[24] but he does use *palingenesia*.[25] And one of his names for baptism listed above

20. *Or.* 40.10, 34, 36.

21. Heinz Althaus, *Die Heilslehre des heiligen Gregor von Nazianz* (Münster: Aschendorff, 1972), 157–62, discusses Gregory's doctrine of baptism under these two headings—purification and enlightenment.

22. Ferguson, *Baptism in the Early Church*, 413.

23. See also *Comm. Jo.* 6.33.169; *Pasch.* 4.29–36; *Comm. Mt.* 15.23.

24. As *Prot.* 9.84.2; *Paed.* 1.12.98.2; *Q.D.S.* 23.2; *Ecl.* 5.7–8; *Exc. Thdot.* 80.2–3; see next section for the meaning of this usage.

25. Clement, *Q.D.S.* 42.15.

was bath (λουτρόν). Similar to Gregory, Clement explains that baptism is a bath because "through it we thoroughly cleanse ourselves of sins" (*Paed.* 1.6.26.2). "Bath" simply equals baptism in the statement that "those who fall into sins after the bath are disciplined" (*Str.* 4.24.154.3).

Gregory of Nazianzus referred to his sister Gorgonia's baptism by saying that she "obtained the blessing of cleansing and perfection, which we have all received from God as a common gift and foundation of our second life" (*Or.* 8.20). As we noted, perfection was one of the names Clement of Alexandria gave to baptism. "When we were regenerated [ἀναγεννηθέντες], we immediately received the perfection which we sought" (*Paed.* 1.26.25.1).[26] "Believing alone and being regenerated is perfection in life" (*Paed.* 1.6.27.2).

Gregory of Nazianzus' list of names for baptism includes a seal, which was a popular image for him.[27] This name was present from the early second century.[28] Gregory explains that baptism is a seal "because it preserves us and is an indication of dominion" (*Or.* 40.4), referring to two functions of a seal—that is, protection and conferring authority. Like his fellow Cappadocians, he uses the illustration of a seal or brand on a sheep: "A sheep that is sealed is not easily snared, but that which is unmarked is an easy prey to thieves."[29] In the same context Gregory uses sealing, signing, and anointing as equivalent: "Fortify yourself before death with the seal, secure yourself for the future with the best and strongest of all aids, being signed both in body and in soul with the anointing, as was Israel [Ex. 12:22]" (*Or.* 40.15).[30]

Although not included in Clement of Alexandria's list of its names, baptism as a seal was part of his terminology.[31] Baptism as "a seal of the Lord" is

26. Antonio Orbe, "Teologia bautismal de Clemente Alejandrino segun *Paed.* I, 26.3–27.2," *Gregorianum* 36 (1955): 410–48, considers Clement's emphasis on perfection as a refutation of Valentinian views that ecclesiastical baptism in water was imperfect in contrast to Gnostic baptism of the Spirit.

27. In reference to baptism, *Or.* 40.7, 10, 17, 18; 8.20.

28. G. H. W. Lampe, *The Seal of the Spirit: A Study in the Doctrine of Baptism and Confirmation in the New Testament and the Fathers*, 2nd ed. (London: SPCK, 1967); Ysebaert, *Greek Baptismal Terminology*, 204–26, 390–401.

29. *Or.* 40.15; Basil *Hom.* 13.4; Gregory of Nyssa *Bapt. diff.* (PG 46.417B).

30. Cf. *Poemata arcana* 8.87–95.

31. Harry A. Echle, *The Terminology of the Sacrament of Regeneration According to Clement of Alexandria*, Studies in Sacred Theology, Second Series 30 (Washington, D.C.: The Catholic University of America Press, 1949); Carlo Nardi, *Il battesimo in Clemente Alessandrino: Interpretazione di Eclogae propheticae 1–26*, Studia ephemeridis Augustinianum 19 (Rome: Institutum Patristicum Augustinianum, 1984), 115–16.

a "perfect protection."[32] His language of "the seal of knowledge" (*Str.* 1.5.31.5) relates to the theme of enlightenment and "the seal of righteousness" (*Str.* 6.12.104.1) to the subsequent life. A passage that may distinguish the seal from baptism by listing baptism, the blessed seal, the Son, and the Father (*Str.* 2.3.11.2) is either borrowing the expression from his opponents or (as is likely) is applying "seal" to the Holy Spirit given in baptism and so is not referring to a post-baptismal rite.

A distinctive feature in Gregory of Nazianzus is the designation of baptism as itself a metaphorical anointing (χρίσμα). This name makes it "priestly and royal, for such were they who were anointed" in Israel (*Or.* 40.4). This usage fits Gregory's omission of any reference to post-immersion rites, except clothing with a robe and entering the church accompanied by psalmody and lighted lamps to receive the Eucharist (*Or.* 40.46).

Origen frequently mentions an anointing in connection with baptism. A literal anointing is indicated by his statement, "All of us may be baptized in those visible waters and in a visible anointing, in accordance with the form handed down to the churches."[33] The washing and anointing of priests in Leviticus 7:36–37 is given a Christian application: "If the word of the law has washed you and made you clean, and the anointing and grace of your baptism remained uncontaminated."[34] It has been suggested that Origen may have known a pre-baptismal anointing instead of or in addition to a post-baptismal anointing,[35] but this is doubtful.[36]

By the time of Gregory of Nazianzus the terminology of "mystery" (μυστήριον) was beginning to attain in the Greek Church its later status as

32. *Q.D.S.* 42.4; cf. 39.1; *Ecl.* 12:9; *Exc. Thdot.* 80.3; 86.
33. Origen, *Comm. in Rom.* 5.8.3, trans. Thomas P. Scheck, FC 103.
34. Origen, *Hom. in Lev.* 6.5.2, trans. Gary Wayne Barkley, FC 83.
35. Paul F. Bradshaw, "Baptismal Practice in the Alexandrian Tradition: Eastern or Western?" in *Living Water, Sealing Spirit: Readings on Christian Initiation,* edited by Maxwell E. Johnson, 82–100 (Collegeville, Minn.: Liturgical Press, 1995), 96–97; Georg Kretschmar, "Die Geschichte des Taufgottesdienstes in der alten Kirche," in *Leiturgia: Handbuch des evangelischen Gottesdienstes,* vol. 5, edited by K. F. Müller and Walter Blankenburg, 67–169 (Kassel: Stauda, 1970), with reference to Basil; and Jean Daniélou, "Chrismation prébaptismale et divinité de l'Esprit chez Grégoire de Nysse," *Recherches de science religieuse* 56 (1968):177–98, with reference to Gregory of Nyssa, argued for a pre-baptismal anointing in Cappadocia. Reservations about this interpretation in Ferguson, *Baptism in the Early Church,* 584, 604–5.
36. Victor Saxer, *Les rites de l'initiation chrétienne du IIe au VIe siècle:Esquisse historique et signification d'après leurs principaux témoins,* Centro Italiano di Studi Sull'Alto Medioevo 7 (Spoleto: Centro Italiano di Studi Sull'Alto Medioevo, 1988), 182, 189, 191; excludes the hypothesis.

the comparable term to *sacramentum* in the Latin Church. Even though writers were no longer as reticent about employing the terminology of the Greek mystery religions as earlier writers had been, Gregory still had to explain that he was not dealing with the mysteries of pagan religion, which to him were nonsense (*Or.* 39.3–6). "Mystery" (or "sacrament") is, nevertheless, a common word for baptism without any sense of reservation.[37]

As part of his program of appealing to pagans and interpreting Christianity in terms of the Greek cultural tradition, Clement of Alexandria anticipated the fourth-century usage by making occasional use of "mystery" for Christian practices.[38] He uses Dionysiac ceremonies to phrase his invitation to receive Christian initiation (*Prot.* 12.120.1–2). Yet, initiation "in the holy mysteries" seems to refer primarily to entrance into heaven (*Prot.* 12.118.4). Since "seal" was a term for baptism, Clement's phrase "mystery of the seal, through which God is truly believed" (*Str.* 5.11.73.2) may have baptism in mind, but in context may refer to the triune name in which baptism was administered.

The Blessings of Baptism and What It Accomplishes

Gregory of Nazianzus began his *Oration* 40 "On Holy Baptism" by referring to "the benefits which accrue to us" from baptism, followed by a long list of the blessings associated with baptism (*Or.* 40.3).[39] As noted above, one of his names for baptism was "bath of regeneration" (*Or.* 40.4).[40] Although the passage from Titus 3:5 uses παλιγγενεσίας, Gregory's preferred term (apart from the phrase in Titus) was ἀναγέννησιν ("rebirth" from 1 Peter 1:23; John 3:5), as in "a regeneration, a remaking, a restoration to our former state" (*Or.* 40.8).[41] A striking development of the theme is the bringing together of three births—natural birth, birth of baptism, and birth of the resurrection—with the elab-

---

37. *Or.* 40.6, 25, 28, 43, 46.

38. Herbert G. Marsh, "The Use of ΜΥΣΤΗΡΙΟΝ in the Writings of Clement of Alexandria with Special Reference to His Sacramental Doctrine," *Journal of Theological Studies* 37 (1936): 64–80; Echle, "Sacramental Initiation as a Christian Mystery Initiation according to Clement of Alexandria," in *Vom christliche Mysterium: Gesammelte Arbeiten zum Gedächtnis von Odo Casel OSB,* edited by Anton Mayer, Johannes Quasten, and Burkhard Neunheuser, 54–65 (Düsseldorf: Patmos Verlag, 1951).

39. Comparable listings in Basil of Caesarea *Exh.* 5 and *Spir.* 15.36.

40. Ysebaert, *Greek Baptismal Terminology,* 89–154, studies the terms for "renewal, re-creation, and rebirth."

41. *Or.* 8.20, "regeneration from the Holy Spirit"; also 31.28; 39.2, "season of new birth."

oration that Christ honored all three—by breathing life into human beings (Gen. 2:7), by becoming incarnate and being baptized, and by his resurrection (*Or.* 40.2–3).[42]

Treating παλιγγενεσίας and ἀναγέννησιν as equivalent,[43] Origen parallels "receiving the forgiveness of sins" with the "bath of regeneration" (*Hom. Jer.* 16.5.2) and interprets "water" as "the bath of regeneration" (*Frg. Jer.* 26).

A closer parallel to Gregory of Nazianzus is supplied by Clement of Alexandria. Regeneration is Clement's favorite imagery for baptism, and his preferred term is ἀναγέννησιν.[44] Clement exhorts pagans "to become little children and be regenerated" (*Prot.* 9.84.2). "Regeneration is of water and Spirit [John 3:3, 3:5], as was all generation," referring to Creation and citing Genesis 1:2 (*Ecl.* 7–8). God made human beings from dirt, but gives them regeneration in water (*Paed.* 1.12.98.2).[45]

The name "bath" suggests the idea of washing, cleansing, and thus specifically forgiveness of sins, as stated above. Gregory of Nazianzus explains that Christian baptism is superior to the purifications of the Old Testament law, for the latter were a temporary cleansing of the body and did not provide a "complete removal of sin" (*Or.* 40.11). "Sin is buried with it [baptism] in the water" (*Or.* 40.4). Gregory affirms the power of baptism to bring "a purification of the sins of each individual and a cleansing from all the bruises and stains of sin" (*Or.* 40.7). "Baptized souls" are those "whose sins the bath has washed away" (*Or.* 40.35).[46] In describing a storm at sea when he and all on the ship despaired of life, while he was yet unbaptized, Gregory revealed his thoughts: "All of us feared a common death, but more terrifying for me was the hidden death. Those murderous waters were keeping me away from the purifying waters which divinize us."[47] Another way of expressing the idea was

42. Gregory of Nyssa more fully developed the analogy of Christ and Christians by bringing together the biblical designations of Christ as "firstborn" in relation to "creation" (Col. 1:15), "among many brethren" (Rom. 8:29), and "from the dead" (Col. 1:18) as corresponding to the three births of Christians in the body, in regeneration, and in the resurrection; see *Eun.* 3.2.45–54; *Ref. conf. Eun.* 79–81; *Hom. Cant.* 13; *Perf.* (*GNO* 8.1, 200.4–204.9).

43. *Pasch.* 4.29–36; *Comm. Mt.* 13.27; 15.23.

44. He does use *paligenesia* in *Q.D.S.* 42.14–15 (referred to above) in a comparison of penitence to baptism as a regeneration by being "baptized a second time with tears."

45. Other passages include *Prot.* 9.82.4; *Q.D.S.* 23.2; *Str.* 3.12.88.1; 4.25.160.2; *Exc. Thdot.* 76.3.

46. The theme of forgiveness is prominent: *Or.* 40.3, 7, 34; for cleansing or purification: *Or.* 40.13, 26; 17.32; 8.14.

47. *De vita sua* 162–69, trans. Meehan.

with the word salvation: "Common to all mankind is the baptism [λουτρόν] which gives salvation to mortals."[48]

The association of baptism with the forgiveness of sins went back to John the Baptist (Mk 1:4) and the beginning of the Christian movement (Acts 2:38). Hence, the common affirmations in Origen and Clement of Alexandria with Gregory are not significant in themselves, but are worth noting. Origen spoke of the grace of baptism cleansing from "all filth of flesh and spirit" (*Hom. Ex.* 11.7). He states the purpose of baptism, "You have come to Jesus and through the grace of baptism have attained the remission of sins."[49] This theme of forgiveness is frequent in Origen.[50]

For Clement of Alexandria, "Transgressions are forgiven … by the baptism that pertains to the Word. We thoroughly wash all sins away from ourselves and at once are no longer evil" (*Paed.* 1.6.29–30.1).[51] Or simply, "Baptism is for the forgiveness of sins" (*Paed.* 1.6.50.4).[52]

The major exception to the early church's teaching on the necessity of baptism to receive forgiveness of sins applies to the martyrs who had not yet been baptized, but were killed for confessing their faith in Jesus. The baptism "of blood" was the "fourth baptism" in Gregory of Nazianzus's listing of kinds of baptism given above (*Or.* 39.15 also refers to the "baptism of martyrdom").

Origen was an important figure in developing the theology of martyrdom.[53] The confession of faith before the authorities with subsequent martyrdom brought forgiveness of sins, as did baptism in water and Spirit, so martyrdom was with good reason called a baptism (*Comm. Mt.* 16.6). Martyrdom brought forgiveness of post-baptismal sins as well: "Because there is no forgiveness of sins without receiving baptism, and that according to the laws of the gospel it is impossible to be baptized again with water and the Spirit for forgiveness of sins, a baptism of martyrdom has been given us" (*Mart.* 30). The baptism in blood is superior to the baptism in water, for the person who experiences the former is not able to sin any more (*Hom. Jud.* 7.2).

48. *Poemata Arcana* 8.99, in Moreschini, ed., *Poemata Arcana*, trans. Sykes.

49. *Hom. Jos.* 15.7, trans. Barbara J. Bruce, FC 195

50. *Hom. Lc.* 27.5; 21.4; *Hom. Gen.* 13; *Hom. Jud.* 7.2; *Mart.* 30.

51. For Clement's characteristic association of the baptism with the Logos, see *Paed.* 1.6.50.4 (the context of the next quotation and *Prot.* 10.99.3). For baptism as washing or cleansing, see *Str.* 3.12.82.6; 7.14.86.4–5.

52. For forgiveness in baptism see *Str.* 4.24.154.3.

53. Ferguson, *Baptism in the Early Church*, 417–19, for Origen's teaching on martyrdom as a baptism.

For Gregory of Nazianzus, baptism made one a Christian (*Or.* 40.16), one of the "faithful" (*Or.* 40.11, 16). Origen said that baptism placed one in the church. "Those who are being regenerated [ἀναγεννώμενοι] through divine baptism are placed in Paradise, that is, in the church" (*Comm. Gen.* 3, on Gen. 2:15).

Baptism is an escape from slavery to sin and the Evil One (Gregory of Nazianzus, *Or.* 40.3). The "unclean and malignant spirit" is chased out of a person by baptism, for "he fears the water" (*Or.* 40.35). This motif in Origen was developed especially in the comparison of baptism to Israel's exodus from Egypt (alluded to above). The Egyptians were spiritual evils seeking to recall you to their service. "These attempt to follow, but you descend into the water and come out unimpaired, the filth of sin having been washed away. You ascend a new man [Eph. 2:15], prepared to sing a new song [Isa. 42:10]. But the Egyptians who follow you are drowned in the abyss."[54] The demonic forces are drowned in the water, and we are freed from the "Egyptian reproaches" (*Hom. Jos.* on Joshua 5:9). Clement of Alexandria seems to adopt Theodotus's view that baptism brings deliverance from the powers of evil (*Exc. Thdot.* 76–77).

The Divine Role in Baptism

Gregory of Nazianzus, like other early Christian authors, declared that baptism was a work of God, not of human beings.

Through these [the threefold God] I am raised to a new and different life, when in baptism [λουτρῷ, the bath] I spring again into light after the burial of death. For the threefold Godhead has made me shoot up as a bearer of light. No, I shall not deny you, dear cleansing power of baptism [three words added by translator]. If, being washed by Godhead, I should tear asunder that shining Godhead, ... relying on the hope of the divine grace [grace gift] in baptism [λουτρόν]. If he has cleansed me fully, then God is to me a single whole calling for my worship.[55]

Preaching in the context of the Trinitarian debates of the late fourth century, Gregory makes much of baptism in the name of the Trinity (*Or.* 40.41–42, 44–45).

The deity of the Holy Spirit was especially at issue, so Gregory affirms the role of the Spirit in baptism. Only that which is divine can give eternal salva-

54. *Hom. Ex.* 5.5, 7, trans. Ronald E. Heine, FC 71; cf. *Hom. Jud.* 7.2.
55. *Poemata Arcana* 3.44-52, in Moreschini, ed., trans. Sykes.

tion, and baptism is the work of the Holy Spirit as well as of the Father and the Son. "If [the Holy Spirit] is not to be worshipped, how can he deify me by baptism?" (*Or.* 31.28). "From the Spirit comes our regeneration [ἀναγέννησιν], and from the regeneration our new creation" (*Or.* 31.28; cf. 41.14).[56] Baptism consecrates a person by the Spirit (*Or.* 40.17, 43). The administrator of baptism does not confer grace, but is the instrument used by the Spirit, who is always ready to act (*Or.* 40.44).

Hence, Gregory emphasizes that baptism involves both Spirit and water. The Spirit transforms the soul through water (*Or.* 7.15). Human beings are both body and soul, "so the cleansing also is twofold, by water and the Spirit; the one received visibly in the body, the other concurring with it invisibly and apart from the body; the one typical, the other real and cleansing the depths" (*Or.* 40.8). Gregory thus gives primacy to the inner cleansing by the Spirit, of which the outward washing with water is a type; but he does not separate the two cleansings, for they are simultaneous.

The preceding quotation from Gregory closely approximates Origen's view.

The bath through water is a symbol of the purification of the soul, which is washed clean from all filth of evil, and is in itself the beginning and source of divine gifts to the one who surrenders to the divine power at the invocations of the worshipful Trinity.... The Spirit resided so manifestly in those being baptized, since the water prepared the way for the Spirit to those who sincerely approached. (*Comm. Jo.* 6.33.166–67)

The Spirit is "borne above the water" (Gen. 1:2) as at the Creation (*Comm. Jo.* 6.33.169). "The one who has died to sin and is truly baptized into the death of Christ, and is buried with him through baptism into death [Rom. 6:3–4], he is the one who is truly baptized in the Holy Spirit and with the water from above [John 3:5]."[57] For Origen, however, there is the recognition that the Spirit and the water did not always work together: there were those washed in the water, but not in the Spirit, and some catechumens who were not strangers to the Spirit.[58]

The invocation of the Trinity, along with the presence of water and the Spirit, was essential to baptism. Origen writes, "It should not be deemed a legitimate baptism unless it is in the name of the Trinity," citing Matthew 28:19.[59]

---

56. Also *Or.* 8.20, cited in n. 41.
58. Origen, *Hom. Num.* 3.1; *Hom. Ezech.* 6.5, 7.
59. Origen, *Comm. Rom.* 5.8.7, trans. Scheck.

57. Origen, *Comm. Rom.* 5.8.3, trans. Scheck.

"Baptism is not complete except when performed ... by the naming of the Father, Son, and Holy Spirit" (*Princ.* 1.3.2).

Clement of Alexandria, although not so explicitly, is also a witness to the importance given to the Trinity in baptism. References to baptism "into the name of the Father, Son, and Holy Spirit" as giving regeneration occur in the *Excerpts from Theodotus* 76.3 and 80.2–3. There are hints of the idea elsewhere. "The three days [Gen. 22:3–4, 12, 18] may be the mystery of the seal, through which God is truly believed" (*Str.* 5.11.73.2); since seal is a name for baptism, the association of "three" with truly believing may refer to the use of a confession of the threefold divine name.[60] The Holy Spirit is associated with water in the statement "We are protected by the power of God the Father and the blood of God the Son and the dew of the Holy Spirit" (*Q.D.S.* 34).

Human Response and Prerequisites to and Consequences of Baptism

Although baptism was a grace and a divine work, it had to be received by human beings. Hence, Christian authors before Augustine stressed free will in the reception of baptism. In his exhortation to catechumens not to wait for their deathbed to be baptized, Gregory of Nazianzus urges, "While you are still master of your thoughts, run to the gift; ... while your welfare is not yet in the power of others, but you yourself are still master of it." And he asks, "Why will you receive the blessing of force and not of free will; of necessity rather than of liberty?" (*Or.* 40.11, 12).

This emphasis on free choice accords with the great importance Gregory attached to the verbal confession of faith at baptism. In the context of the preceding quotations he contrasts the normal procedure with sickbed baptism, "while your tongue is not stammering or parched, or (to say no more) deprived of the power of pronouncing the sacramental [mystagogical] words" (*Or.* 40.11). He summarized the initiation process as "Having spoken, be baptized; and having been baptized, be saved" (*Or.* 40.26). He rehearsed what must be believed in a paraphrased Credo (*Or.* 40.45). Having discussed the use of the triune name in the baptismal ceremony, Gregory called on his hearers,

60. So too the reference to the seal, the Son, and the Father in *Str.* 2.3.11.2.

"Be baptized with this faith" (*Or.* 40.44). Baptism made a person one of the "faithful" (*Or.* 40.11, 16). The confession of faith meant that the enlightenment of baptism was a "pledge of the conscience to God [1 Pet. 3:21]" (*Or.* 40.3).

Free will was a fundamental conviction of Origen's theology.[61] That accords with the importance of instruction, faith, and repentance for his baptismal theology.[62] Those "who desire to receive holy baptism" are "first" to hear "the word of God."[63] Instruction included the Trinity and the resurrection (*Hom. Lev.* 5.10.3).

Origen defines faith: "Faith properly speaking is the acceptance with the whole soul of what is believed at baptism" (*Comm. Jo.* 10.43.298).[64] The confession of this faith was made in answer to questions (*Hom. Num.* 5.1). Repentance also was required. Origen says to catechumens: "Repent, so that baptism for the remission of sins will follow."[65] Baptism has its benefit from the intentional choice of the one being baptized. This benefit comes to the one who repents, but to one who does not approach baptism with repentance the result will be more serious judgment (*Comm. Jo.* 6.33.165). Repentance was verbalized in the renunciation of Satan, even as faith was verbalized in confession: "When we come to the grace of baptism," we renounce "all other gods and lords, we confess the only God, Father, Son, and Holy Spirit."[66]

Like Gregory (see below), Origen saw the words connected with baptism as "covenants" (*Mart.* 12, 17). Origen compared the soldiers' oath (*sacramentum*) to the baptismal vows (*Hom. Jos.* 5.1–2). For Clement of Alexandria too, instruction, faith, and repentance were essential to baptism. "Instruction leads to faith, and faith together with baptism is trained by the Holy Spirit, since faith is the one universal salvation of humanity" (*Paed.* 1.6.30.2). Clement proceeds to include repentance:

---

61. B. Darrell Jackson, "Sources of Origen's Doctrine of Freedom," *Church History* 35 (1966): 13–23; repr. in *Doctrines of Human Nature, Sin, and Salvation in the Early Church,* edited by Everett Ferguson, 1–11 (New York: Garland, 1993).

62. Hans Jörg auf der Maur and Joop Waldram, "*Illuminatio Verbi Divini—Confessio Fidei—Gratia Baptismi:* Wort, Glaube und Sakrament in Katechumenat und Taufliturgie bei Origenes," in *Fides Sacramenti Sacramentum Fidei,* edited by Hans Jörg auf der Maur, et al., 41–95 (Assen: Van Gorcum, 1981).

63. Origen, *Hom. Lev.* 6.2.5; trans. Barkley; cf. "the word of God in the heart" and "the word of faith" in *Hom. Ex.* 10.4. The catechumen was devoted to hearing the law of God daily (*Hom. Jos.* 4.1)

64. Cf. *Comm. Rom.* 5.10.2.

65. *Hom. Lc.* 21.4; trans. Joseph T. Lienhard, FC 94. On quitting a life of sin prepared one to receive the Holy Spirit, see *Hom. Lev.* 6.2.5.

66. *Hom. Ex.* 8.4; trans. Heine; cf. the verbal "confession of the voice," *Comm. Rom.* 5.10.4.

There follows of necessity to the one who has been reminded of better things repentance for the worse things.... In the same manner we ourselves, having repented of our sins, having renounced our faults, and being purified in baptism run back to the eternal light, children to their Father. (*Paed.* 1.6.32.1)

"The sins committed before coming to faith are forgiven before the Lord in order that they may be as if they had not been done" (*Str.* 4.24.153.3). "An adequate cleansing for a person is genuine and sure repentance" (*Str.* 4.22.143.1).[67]

The necessity of instruction, faith, and repentance made baptism in extremis and of infants problematic for Gregory of Nazianzus. He did not reject either practice, but both were anomalous to his basic understanding of baptism. Concerning deathbed baptism, he regarded it as undesirable that the decision might be made by someone else (*Or.* 40.11).

Concerning infants he gave a fuller discussion. He responded to the question, "What have you to say about those who are still children and conscious neither of the loss nor of the grace? Are we to baptize them too?" His answer was, "Certainly, if any danger threatens. For it is better that they should be unconsciously sanctified than that they should depart unsealed and uninitiated" (*Or.* 40.28). Under "Old Testament Connections," above, we cited his justifications for his response. In regard to those children not in danger, "I give my opinion to wait till the end of the third year, or a little more or less, when they may be able to listen and answer something about the sacrament" (*Or.* 40.28). For Gregory children were not guilty of sin, so the age of receiving the seal of belonging to Christ could be postponed. He said that infants who died unbaptized would be neither glorified nor punished in the afterlife. Nevertheless, as part of his encouragement to all to come to baptism, he specifically included the "infant child," telling the parents to give their child the Trinity instead of amulets and incantations (*Or.* 40.16).[68] Gregory's recommendation of waiting until the end of the third year of life and his exhortation to parents to bring their child to baptism make more sense as responses to a recent development of infant baptism in nonemergency situations than as an innovation in a regular practice. His encouragement for all to be baptized carried the day, for there is no indication that his recommendation of three years of age had a following.

---

67. See also *Str.* 2.3.11.2.
68. A "seal for infants" that "wards off evil" in *Poemata arcana* 8.87–95 probably refers to infant baptism.

Origen too dealt with questions about the propriety of baptizing infants, but his approach was different. He defended the practice as "a tradition from the apostles" (*Comm. Rom.* 5.9.11) and justified it as forgiving the impurity attached to birth. The question he addressed was "Why, since the baptism of the church is given for remission of sins, is baptism given even to infants?" "If there is in infants nothing which ought to pertain to forgiveness and mercy, the grace of baptism would be superfluous."[69] In all three passages where Origen justifies infant baptism, he appeals to Job 14:4–5, and twice he adds Psalms 51:5.[70] He understands these texts as referring to "stains of birth" requiring purification (Lev. 12:6–8; Luke 2:22). Although Origen recognized the distinction between "stains" and "sins," he used the "forgiveness of sins" to explain the baptism of small children, who have no sin of their own, since they need purification. To that extent he qualified earlier (and later Greek) affirmations of the innocence of children. Nevertheless, this ceremonial, bodily impurity differed from Augustine's view of guilt inherited from Adam's sins, for the stain attached to the birth of Jesus, as well (*Hom. Lc.* 14.3–4). Origen may have had primarily emergency baptisms in view, for no surviving passage reconciles infant baptism with the importance he attaches to hearing and personal faith.

All three of these authors stress the moral consequences of one's baptism. The laver (or bath) is "not merely a washing away of sins in you, but also a correction of your manner of life" (*Or.* 40.32). The baptismal ceremony constituted "covenants before God for a second life and a purer manner of life" (*Or.* 40.8). Baptism was only one step on the road to salvation, a beginning that one must continue to pursue (*Or.* 40.7, 22). "The work of your salvation is one upon which you should be engaged at all times" (*Or.* 40.14). Origen connected the confession of faith to the subsequent life of good works:

Surely in that passage [1 John 4:2] it is not the one who shall have declared these syllables and pronounced them in this common confession that shall seem to be led by the spirit of God [Rom. 8:14], but the one who has fashioned his life in such a way and has produced the fruit of works.[71]

69. *Hom. Lev.* 8.3.5, trans. adapt. Barkley.
70. *Hom. Lc.* 14.3, 5; both texts in *Hom. Lev.* 8.3.5; *Comm. Rom.* 5.9.11
71. *Comm. Rom.* 5.8.10; trans. Scheck.

In refuting Celsus' charges against Christians, Origen referred to the testing of the behavior of candidates for baptism and emphasized Christianity's moral purpose of improvement of conduct (*Cels.* 3.51, 59–60, 69). With reference to Romans 6:4, "walk in newness of life," he insisted: "For you must not imagine that the renewing of the life, which is said to have been done once, suffices. On the contrary at all times and daily, this newness must, if it can be said, be renewed."[72]

Clement of Alexandria makes a direct connection between the doctrine of baptism and the subsequent moral life.

We who have put off the old person, removed the old garment of evil, and put on the incorruption of Christ in order that we may become a new, holy people, having been regenerated, we keep the new person undefiled and are innocent as a baby of God, having been cleansed from fornication and wickedness. (*Paed.* 1.6.32.4)

The work *Exhortation to Endurance, To the Newly Baptized* implies post-baptismal moral instruction. It is preserved as a work of Clement of Alexandria, but it has been attributed to Gregory of Nazianzus,[73] a recognition of the similarities in the two authors.

Conclusion

Gregory of Nazianzus's baptismal theology provides one tributary to the common sea of early Christian experience. The Alexandrian tradition was one of the streams flowing into his contribution to this sea.

72. *Comm. Rom.* 5.8.13; trans. Scheck.
73. Augusto Guida, "Un nuovo testo di Gregorio Nazianzeno," *Prometheus* 2 (1976): 193–226.

William Tabbernee

6. Gregory of Nazianzus, Montanism, and the Holy Spirit

As is well known, Gregory of Nazianzus (ca. 329–390) arrived in Constantinople in September 379 to commence a theological preaching and teaching mission. His mission had as its aim the advancement of Nicene orthodoxy in the city and the establishment of a viable unity among the members of the then current theological factions, who strongly disagreed about various aspects of the way in which the Trinity should be defined and understood. What is not so well known is that Gregory, as part of his rhetorical strategy, made use of polemical references to Montanus (d. ca. 175) and Montanists.[1] Gregory portrays Montanus as a prime example of one whose own *evil* spirit was *against* the *Holy* Spirit, just as he portrays those who deny the (full) divinity of the Holy Spirit as "Pneumatomachians" ("Fighters against the Spirit").

---

1. On Montanism, see Christine Trevett, *Montanism: Gender, Authority and the New Prophecy* (Cambridge: Cambridge University Press, 1996); William Tabbernee, *Fake Prophecy and Polluted Sacraments: Ecclesiastical and Imperial Reactions to Montanism,* Supplements to Vigiliae Christianae 84 (Leiden: Brill, 2007); and Tabbernee, *Prophets and Gravestones: An Imaginative History of Montanists and Other Early Christians* (Peabody, Mass.: Hendrickson, 2009); literary sources include Ronald E. Heine, *The Montanist Oracles and Testimonia* (Macon, Ga.: Mercer University Press, 1989); epigraphic sources include Tabbernee, *Montanist Inscriptions and Testimonia: Epigraphic Sources Illustrating the History of Montanism,* Patristic Monograph Series 16 (Macon, Ga.: Mercer University Press, 1997) [abbreviation *IMont* with inscription number]. This corpus was produced while Frederick W. Norris was editor of the North American Patristic[s] Society's Patristic Monograph Series in which it was published, and benefited greatly from his insightful comments and editorial expertise. It is a joy for me to contribute this chapter on Gregory of Nazianzus and Montanism to the Festschrift honoring Professor Norris.

Gregory of Nazianzus' Sources for His Knowledge of Montanism

None of Gregory's extant works written prior to 379 mentions Montanus or Montanism. This is not surprising. Montanism was not (or certainly was no longer) a pressing concern in Cappadocia. In the early 230s, Firmilian of Caesarea (bp. ca. 230–268) had attended a council at Iconium in neighboring Phrygia that decided that Montanists wishing to join the "catholic" church needed to be (re-)baptized.[2] Whether Firmilian himself, *in Cappadocia*, ever had occasion to implement pastorally the policy established at Iconium is not known. Even if so, that was almost 150 years earlier, and Gregory's one-time close friend Basil, the current bishop of Caesarea (bp. 370–379) gives no indication that there were any contemporary Montanists in his jurisdiction. This jurisdiction included Sasima, the see to which Basil, in 372, appointed Gregory against his will as part of Basil's strategy to counter the ambitions of the neo-Arian Anthimus of Tyana (bp. 370s). However, as Gregory never took up his position, if there were Montanists at Sasima (which is unlikely), Gregory had no personal contact with them. Nor does he mention the presence of any Montanists at Nazianzus.

Gregory's lack of personal contact with Montanists before he went to Constantinople does not mean, of course, that he was unfamiliar with anti-Montanist traditions. The absence of earlier comments can be explained simply on the basis of the lack of pastoral or theological necessity to mention Montanus and/or Montanists at an earlier time. When the need arose, however, Gregory of Nazianzus, Basil, and Basil's brother, Gregory of Nyssa (bp. 372–ca. 395), were ready and willing to demonstrate their knowledge of the Montanist "heresy" as part of their defense of orthodoxy.

Amphilochius the Elder and Amphilochius the Younger

After studying for a time with the local grammaticus in Nazianzus (*Or.* 7.6), Gregory and his younger brother Caesarius (ca. 331/332–368) moved, in ca. 343, to Iconium to further their education at the estate of their maternal uncle, Amphilochius the Elder (d. post-374). Amphilochius, a renowned

2. Firmilian, *Ep., ap.* Cyprian *Ep.* 75.7.4; 75.19.4.

lawyer and rhetorician, took personal responsibility for and an active role in Gregory's education. It is almost certain, therefore, that while Gregory was being instructed in the history of Christianity of the region, Amphilochius told him about the council that had been convened at Iconium to deal with the pastoral problems presented by Montanism in that part of Asia Minor in the previous century.

Although Montanism no longer existed in Cappadocia, there were still contemporary Montanists in Phrygia, including Iconium in the 340s. Thirty years later, Basil responded to a series of questions put to him by Amphilochius the Younger (ca. 340/345–ca. 398/404) after Basil had appointed him bishop of Iconium in 373.[3] The first of these questions related to the validity of baptisms performed by Novatianists and Montanists.[4] Like his cousin Gregory, Amphilochius had, presumably, first learned from his father all about the decisions made at the Council of Iconium, but Amphilochius wanted up-to-date canonical advice from Basil, especially since there had been a new development since the council had been held.

At the time of the Council of Iconium, Novatianists did not yet exist— having arisen only in the aftermath of the Decian persecution (250–251). When Constantine I (r. 307–337) decided to champion "catholic" Christianity and support it by anti-heretical legislation, he initially treated Novatianists and Montanists alike. In ca. 325/326, he forbade members of both groups to assemble and threatened to confiscate any property where Novatianists or Montanists were caught gathering for worship or other activities. Constantine also enacted the burning of their books.[5] However, Constantine soon changed his mind about the Novatianists and, on September 25, 326, allowed them once more to have their own places of worship and cemeteries.[6] The case had, presumably, been made that Novatianists, *unlike* Montanists and others specified in the earlier legislation, were *schismatics* rather than *heretics*. Constantine's more tolerant attitude to Novatianists than to the Montanists resulted in the merging of the two groups in some locations. Perhaps it is more than coincidental that, in two of the three instances where Gregory of Nazianzus refers to the Montanists, he also mentions Novatianists.[7]

3. Basil, *Ep.* 188, 199, 217.   4. Basil, *Ep.* 188.1.
5. Eusebius, *V. Const.* 3.64–66.   6. *Cod. Theod.* 16.5.2.
7. *Or.* 22.12; DVS 1174–75.

Laodicea Combusta, less than 40 km from of Iconium, had a "merged" Novatianist/Montanist community at least from the 340s.[8] Amphilochius' question to Basil about the validity of Novatianist and Montanist baptisms, therefore, may have been prompted by the existence of Novatianists/Montanists in and around Iconium, if not by the continued presence of members of separate Montanist groups in the region. As we shall see, Gregory appears to have received copies of the correspondence on the Montanists and Novatianists between his cousin and Basil.

Eusebius and Origen

After they left Iconium, Gregory and Caesarius studied briefly at Caesarea in Cappadocia.[9] There they probably met Basil for the first time. The next occasion for Gregory to learn more about Montanism, however, was in 347/348—the year the young men lived in Caesarea Maritima in Syria Palaestina.[10] Issues relating to Nicene Christianity and Arianism were central during their studies there, but the writings of Origen (ca. 185–ca. 253), who had taught in Caesarea from ca. 232, and of Eusebius (ca. 264/265–ca. 339/340), the church historian and bishop of Caesarea from ca. 313, were also influential and formative.

The great library at Caesarea,[11] founded by Origen's disciple Pamphilus, gave Gregory access to the writings of Eusebius and Origen containing information about Montanism. His access to the library does not, of course, guarantee that Gregory definitely read the anti-Montanist material there, but there are sufficient linguistic hints in his later comments about Montanism to suggest that he did. For example, the adherents of the movement founded by Montanus referred to the movement as the "New Prophecy." Eusebius and his own sources about Montanism, however, refer to "the New Prophecy" as "the sect/heresy of those named after the Phrygians."[12] Gregory, similarly, in *Or.* 22.12, employs the word "Phrygians" to refer to those we now call "Montanists."[13]

---

8. *IMont* 69–70; see Tabbernee, *Montanist Inscriptions*, 425–44.

9. *Or.* 43.13.

10. *Or.* 7.6; Jerome, *Vir. ill.* 113.

11. On which, see Andrew J. Carriker, *The Library of Eusebius at Caesarea* (Leiden: Brill, 2003).

12. E.g., *Hist. eccl.* 5.16.1: τὴν λεγομένην κατὰ Φρύγας αἵρεσιν, or "the sect/heresy of the Phrygians" (e.g., 4.27; cf. Anonymous, *Fr., ap.* Eusebius, *Hist. eccl.* 5.16.22).

13. The term "Montanists" appears first in the published version of Cyril of Jerusalem's *Catechetical*

The anonymous Phrygian bishop who was Eusebius' primary source for what he wrote about "the Phrygian heresy" in his *Ecclesiastical History* condemned Montanus and Montanus' prophetic companions Maximilla and Priscilla for their frenzied manner of prophesying.[14] He argued that a true prophet/ess has no need to speak "in ecstasy,"[15] and that prophesying ecstatically is a sign of false prophecy:

A false prophet, indeed, is the one in extraordinary ecstasy (ἐν παρέκστασει) in which state the prophet speaks without restraint and without fear, beginning with voluntary ignorance but ending up in involuntary madness of soul (μανίαν ψυχῆς).[16]

An echo of the Anonymous' words can be heard in Gregory of Nazianzus' statement that the madness (μανία) of the Phrygians was still alive in his day (*Or.* 22.12). Even if Gregory had not first read these comments in the library at Caesarea, he had apparently at least come across Eusebius' *Historia ecclesiastica* at some stage.

There can be no doubt that Gregory spent time reading the works of Origen in Caesarea and that what he learned from Origen influenced greatly his theological and intellectual development and strengthened his commitment to an ascetical lifestyle.[17] Either already in Caesarea, or at least in ca. 358/359– ca. 362, when he and Basil composed the *Philocalia,* an anthology of extracts from Origen's works,[18] Gregory must have come across statements by Origen about Montanism.

Two of Origen's statements refer specifically to the Montanists' erroneous understanding of the Holy Spirit. In his *Commentary on Matthew,* Ori-

---

Lectures (16.8: τοὺς Μοντανούς), delivered ca. 348. It was also common, especially in the post-Constantinian era, to refer to Montanists as "Cataphrygians" (οἱ Κατάφρυγας), a new term created by erroneously joining the two originally separate words κατά ("after") and Φρύγας ("Phrygians").

14. *Fr., ap.;* Eusebius, *Hist. eccl.* 5.16.9.

15. *Fr., ap.;* Eusebius, *Hist. eccl.* 5.17.1.

16. *Fr., ap.;* Eusebius, *Hist. eccl.* 5.17.2. On the early charges that Montanist prophecy, and therefore Montanism itself, was an expression of madness (μανία), see Tabbernee, *Fake Prophecy,* 92–100; cf. Laura S. Nasrallah, *"An Ecstasy of Folly": Prophecy and Authority in Early Christianity* (Cambridge, Mass.: Harvard University Press, 2003). Unless indicated otherwise, all translations from ancient sources in this essay are my own.

17. On Origen's influence on Gregory of Nyssa, see Joseph W. Trigg, "Knowing God in the *Theological Orations* of Gregory of Nazianzus," in *God in Early Christian Thought: Essays in Memory of Lloyd G. Patterson,* edited by Andrew B. McGowan, Brian E. Daley, and Timothy D. Gaden, 84–101, Supplements to Vigiliae Christianae 94 (Leiden: Brill, 2009); Beeley, *Gregory of Nazianzus on the Trinity,* 272–74.

18. Gregory of Nazianzus, *Ep.* 6.4, 115; *Philocalia,* preface.

gen points out that while the Gospel attributed to John is well known, not all Christians have paid attention to what it says about the Holy Spirit. According to Origen, heeding the spirit of error and the teaching of demons has allowed these false spirits to make pronouncements in the great name of the Paraclete.[19]

Similarly, in the *De principiis,* a primary source for the *Philocalia,* Origen states:

Some, who hear the Spirit called "Paraclete" in the Gospel, since they do not observe these distinctions and differences, nor do they consider for what work or activity the Spirit is named "Paraclete," ... *by holding views that are less than worthy of the Paraclete's deity,* have ... delivered themselves to errors and deceptions, seduced by some erring spirit more than informed by the instructions of the Holy Spirit.[20]

Significantly, Origen's portrayal of Montanists as persons whose view of the Holy Spirit opposes and undermines the Paraclete's deity—and Gregory's adoption of Origen's portrayal—may explain why Gregory, in his later defense of the full deity of the Holy Spirit, cites the Montanists as historic and contemporary examples of those who erroneously fight against the Spirit.

Cyril of Jerusalem and Epiphanius of Salamis

At the very time Gregory was in Caesarea Maritima, Cyril of Jerusalem was delivering, for the first time, his *Catechetical Lectures* in Jerusalem. Gregory may have heard about Cyril while in Caesarea[21] but it is unlikely that Gregory saw a copy of the published version of those lectures as early as ca. 347/348.[22] It is clear, nevertheless, from Gregory's own *Theological Orations,* delivered in Constantinople in 380, that, if he did not see them in 347/348, he had read Cyril's lectures in the meantime and incorporated their content into his own theological framework.[23]

Cyril's animosity toward the Montanists, fueled by the threat that Montanist teaching about the descent of the *New* Jerusalem (Rev 21) *at or near Pepouza,* the administrative and spiritual center of Montanism in Phrygia,[24]

19. Origen, *Comm. Mt.* 15.30.
20. *Princ.* 2.7.3, adapt. Heine, trans., *Montanist Oracles,* 95–96, emphasis added.
21. See Norris, *Faith Gives Fullness to Reasoning,* 119–20; McGuckin, *Saint Gregory of Nazianzus,* 39.
22. See, however, Norris, *Faith Gives Fullness to Reasoning,* 3.
23. E.g., cf. *Or.* 28.3, 15–16 with *Catech.* 6, and *Or.* 28.22–30 with *Catech.* 9; see Norris, *Faith Gives Fullness to Reasoning,* 109, 119, 123, 126.

rather than at or near Jerusalem itself, presented his own city as a center of pilgrimage and eschatological expectation.[25] Cyril accused Montanus *personally* of slaughtering and cutting into pieces women's wretched little children for unlawful food on the pretext of their so-called sacred rites (*Catech.* 16.8).

Cyril's charges of infanticide and cannibalism against the Montanists are taken by later Fathers to refer to a Montanist practice whereby infants were pricked by copper needles and blood extracted.[26] According to Augustine of Hippo (b. 395–430), the purpose of extracting the blood was to mix it with flour in order to bake polluted eucharistic bread (*Haer.* 26). Epiphanius of Salamis (b. 367–403/405), on the other hand, sees the function of the alleged Montanist blood extraction as primarily initiatory, rather than eucharistic, declaring that the piercing of an infant with copper needles was performed at Easter (*Pan.* 48.14.6), the traditional time for conducting baptisms.[27] It is very probable that, underlying the distorted reports of infanticide, cannibalism, and polluted eucharistic meals among the Montanists, was an actual practice of baptismal tattooing—permanently marking the initiate with a Christian sign.[28]

Gregory of Nazianzus, of course, never read Augustine's *De haeresibus*—which was not written until 428/429. It is possible, however, that Gregory had come across a copy of Epiphanius' *Panarion* (composed before 377) while a resident at St. Thecla's Monastery in Seleucia ad Calicadnum, in Cilicia, from ca. 375 until the fall of 379.

Athanasius and Didymus the Blind

Christopher Beeley is undoubtedly correct in concluding, even though Gregory had spent a year (348) in Alexandria before continuing his studies in Athens, that Gregory's view of the Holy Spirit was not influenced by Athanasius of Alexandria (b. 328–373) or Didymus the Blind (ca. 310/313–ca. 431).[29]

24. Tabbernee, "Portals of the New Jerusalem: The Discovery of Pepouza and Tymion," *JECS* 11 (2003): 87–94; Tabbernee and Peter Lampe, *Pepouza and Tymion: The Discovery and Archaeological Exploration of a Lost Ancient City and an Imperial Estate* (Berlin: Walter de Gruyter, 2008).

25. Jan W. Drijvers, *Cyril of Jerusalem: Bishop and City,* Supplements to Vigiliae Christianae 72 (Leiden: Brill, 2004), 6n26.

26. E.g., Epiphanius, *Pan.* 48.14.6; 48.15.7.

27. See Tabbernee, *Fake Prophecy,* 353–55.

28. For a full discussion of the likelihood of Montanist baptismal tattooing, including contemporary Carpocratian and later Christian parallels, see Tabbernee, *Fake Prophecy,* 356–58.

29. Beeley, *Gregory of Nazianzus on the Trinity,* 8, 277–84.

Nor does it appear that Gregory's knowledge of Montanism was derived from Athanasius or Didymus.

Athanasius refers to "Phrygians" (or "Cataphrygians") five times as heretics who commit errors similar to those committed by Arians.[30] As we shall see, Gregory and Basil utilize the same strategy, but Athanasius' references contain no information about Montanists that Gregory could not have obtained from other sources. Interestingly, in *Oration* 21, a panegyric commemorating Athanasius delivered in Constantinople on May 2, 380, Gregory does not refer to the above-mentioned works by Athanasius, which probably means that he was unaware of their existence (and of the anti-Montanist comments contained in them).

Similarly, if Gregory read any of Didymus the Blind's commentaries written before 379–381—when Gregory's own comments on Montanism were penned—there is no hint in Gregory's writings that he did so. He definitely could not have read these commentaries in Alexandria, as Didymus' published commentaries were written no earlier than 350. Consequently, the references by Didymus in *Fr. Ac.* 10.10 and *Fr. 2 Cor.* 5.12 to Montanist ecstatic prophesying may not have been seen by Gregory. Certainly Gregory did not see Didymus' *De Trinitate,* with its explicit references to Montanism, before 381, as it was written well after that date.[31]

The *Dialogus Montanistae et Orthodoxi* and Jerome

While it seems clear that Gregory of Nazianzus did not gain any of his knowledge about Montanism from Athanasius or from Didymus, it is possible that he came to know of one specific late anti-Montanist charge from a work traditionally (but wrongly) *attributed* to Didymus. This work, the *Dialogue between a Montanist and an Orthodox,* used as a source by Didymus, contains material that is almost identical to some data about Montanism in the *De Trinitate.*

In addition to accusing the Montanists of a modalist-like view of the Godhead by not distinguishing properly between Father, Son, and Holy Spirit,[32]

---

30. *C. Ar.* 1.3; 2.43; 3.47; *Syn.* 4; 13.

31. Didymus, *Trin.* 2.15; 3.18–19; 3.23; 3.38; 3.41. On the possibility that Didymus' later works may have been influenced by Gregory of Nazianzus, see Beeley, *Gregory of Nazianzus on the Trinity,* 284.

32. *Dial.* 2.5–3.4; cf. Didymus, *Trin.* 2.15; 3.18–19; 3.23; 3.38; 3.41.

the "Orthodox" in the *Dialogus* claims that Montanus had been a pagan priest, "the priest of an idol."[33] Jerome similarly describes the founder of Montanism as "the mutilated and emasculated half-man Montanus" (*Ep.* 41.4). Jerome's wording may well be a not-so-subtle allusion to the view that Montanus had been a castrated priest of the cult of the Phrygian Mother goddess Cybele. The *Dialogus,* on the other hand, calls Montanus "the priest of Apollo" (4.5). Hirschmann, however, has shown recently that, in the particular region of Phrygia where Montanism started, the cults of Apollo and Cybele were closely interrelated.[34]

Gregory of Nazianzus characterizes the "Phrygians" as both "initiators" and "initiates" (*Or.* 22.12: τελούντων τε καὶ τελουμένων). No doubt he is referring here primarily to Montanist baptism (presumably the strange baptism involving pricking infants with copper needles) but, in his typical rhetorical style, cannot help adding that these "Phrygian" initiations call to mind somewhat related practices of earlier times (*Or.* 22.12b: μικροῦ τοῖς παλαιοῖς παραπλήσια). None of his hearers (or readers) would miss the allusion to the *taurobolium*—the ancient Phrygian ritual by which men would castrate themselves and slash their bodies while being spattered by the blood of a sacrificed bull as part of their initiation into the priesthood of Cybele.

Oration 22 was probably delivered in late September 379, soon after Gregory arrived in Constantinople. Jerome did not write his letter containing the comment about Montanus being a "mutilated and emasculated half-man" (*Ep.* 41.4) until the mid-380s. Therefore, while it is certain that Jerome and Gregory had close personal contact from June 380 onward[35] and that Jerome considered Gregory his teacher and mentor,[36] Jerome could not have been Gregory's source for the charge that Montanus had been a priest of Cybele and/or Apollo. Gregory most probably gained that (alleged) detail about Montanus from the *Dialogus*. Basil, as we shall see, appears to have read the *Dialogus* sometime before 363/364. If Basil had a copy of the *Dialogus* in his possession, Gregory may have seen and read it himself as early as the 360s.

---

33. *Dial.* 4.6; cf. Didymus *Trin.* 3.41.3.

34. Vera-Elisabeth Hirschmann, *Horrenda Secta: Untersuchungen zum frühchristlichen Montanismus und seinen Verbindungen zur paganen Religion Phrygiens,* Historia, Einzelschriften 179 (Stuttgart: Steiner, 2005), esp. 15–19, 39, 54, 70–79, 86–92, 139–45.

35. See McGuckin, *Saint Gregory of Nazianzus,* 277–78.

36. *Ep.* 50.1; 52.8; *Vir. ill.* 117.

Basil the Great

It can no longer be assumed that Basil of Caesarea was the leading theologian among the three so-called Cappadocian Fathers, from whom Gregory of Nazianzus and Gregory of Nyssa took their lead.[37] Nor, after the Sasima debacle, was the relationship between Basil and Gregory ever the same as it had been during their time as fellow students in Athens (348–355) or during their early years back in Cappadocia after 358. Nevertheless, the two men kept in relatively close contact, worked together on a number of occasions, and kept up an active correspondence—which Gregory published toward the end of his life, with the assistance of his grandnephew Nicobulus (*Ep.* 52–53). There can be little doubt that Gregory received and/or collected copies, not only of important letters that Basil wrote to others, such as Gregory's own cousin Amphilochius of Iconium, but that he received and read many, if not most, of Basil's important treatises—some of which included information about Montanism.

Basil's first reference to Montanus and Montanism is contained in his treatise against Eunomius of Cyzicus (bp. 360–394). Eunomius, a close associate of Aetius of Antioch (ca. 313–ca. 365/367), was Aetius' successor as leader of a group best described as "Heterousians" rather than (as traditionally) "Anomoians."[38] The "Heterousians," in opposition to the strictly Nicene "Homoousians," argued that the Son, instead of being of the *same* essence as the Father, was in some (although not all) aspects *unlike* (ἀνόμοιος) the Father. Ontologically, therefore, according to this position, the Son did not (quite) share the same essence (οὐσία) as the Father.[39] Basil wrote his *Contra Eunomium* ca. 363/364 at a time when the relationship between him and Gregory of Nazianzus was still cordial. Gregory undoubtedly received a copy of the treatise, perhaps as early as 364, when he visited Basil that year.

In *Eun.* 2.34 Basil, using a standard ploy, accuses Eunomius of being like (the heretic) Montanus, who, in Basil's view, was (like Eunomius) furious against the Spirit. According to Basil, Montanus, out of arrogance, insulted

---

37. See Beeley, *Gregory of Nazianzus on the Trinity,* 10, 10n28, 292–303.

38. See Beeley, *Gregory of Nazianzus on the Trinity,* 21 and 21n58.

39. Aetius and Eunomius, as well as other Heterousians, were exiled for their views. Coincidentally, but interestingly, given the topic of this essay, Aetius was exiled by Constantius II (r. 337–361) to Pepouza (Philostorgius, *Hist. eccl.* 4.8).

the Spirit through humiliating names and devalued the Spirit's nature by declaring that it would be a dishonor for the Spirit to proceed from the Creator.
The accusation appears to be Basil's first, but here somewhat veiled, reference
to the charge that he expresses more clearly later that the Montanists "blas-
phemed against the Holy Spirit by unlawfully and shamelessly attributing the
name Paraclete to Montanus and Priscilla."[40] Presumably, Gregory of Nazianzus has the same accusation (and, particularly, about Priscilla) in mind when
he refers to "Montanus' evil and feminine spirit" (*Or.* 33.16).[41]

The charge that Montanus equated himself with the Holy Spirit was not
made explicitly until the fourth century,[42] and gradually extended to include
Priscilla and Maximilla.[43] The charge is patently false. It arose out of the practice by the founders to speak in the first person as the mouthpiece(s) of the
Father, Son, and Holy Spirit—not just the Paraclete.[44] This approach, in fact,
differed little, if at all, from Gregory of Nazianzus' own practice of claiming to
be a musical instrument played by the Spirit to convey what God, through the
Spirit, wants the church to know (*Or.* 12.1).[45]

The second part of Basil's accusation against Montanus (and/or the Montanists) is reducing the status of the nature of the Spirit by arguing that it
would be a dishonor for the Spirit to have proceeded from the Creator. No
extant oracle by Montanus (or for that matter by Maximilla or Priscilla) uses
the language of "procession." Nor would we expect any founding Montanist
oracle to have included such terminology, which is an integral part of *fourth*-
century, rather than *second*-century, Trinitarian theology. The source of Basil's
comments about Montanus' denial of the Holy Spirit "proceeding" from the
Creator appears to have been the *Dialogue between a Montanist and an Orthodox* referred to above.

In the *Dialogus,* the "Orthodox," obviously well-versed in the Trinitarian
debates of the mid-to-late fourth century, declares: "God is one by reason of
nature (φύσεως), however in terms of hypostasis (ὑποστάσει), the Father and the
Son and the Holy Spirit differ from one another" (3.6; cf. 3.14a). The "Orthodox" chides the "Montanist" for not acknowledging the "clear distinction of

40. *Ep.* 188.1; Heine, *Montanist Oracles,* 129–30.
41. Trans. Browne and Swallow, NPNF 2.7:333.
42. E.g., Cyril of Jerusalem, *Catech.* 16.8.   43. Theophylact, *Ennarrat. Lk.* 24.
44. Tabbernee, *Fake Prophecy,* 381.
45. Cf. Montanus, *Fr., ap.,* Anti-Phrygian, *Fr., ap.* Epiphanius, *Pan.* 48.4.1.

the three hypostases" (3.11), accusing the "Montanist" of a kind of modalism. In an attempt to not fall into the trap of the opposite heresy ("Tri-theism") the "Orthodox" emphasizes that in his view:

the Father is everywhere, and the Son is everywhere, and the Holy Spirit is everywhere; and just as there is nothing between mind and speech and breath, so there is nothing between the Father, Son, and Holy Spirit. (3.12)[46]

The "Orthodox" concludes: "you must understand that the Father is complete, and the Holy Spirit, *who proceeds from the Father,* is complete, with a complete hypostasis" (3.13a). To this, the "Montanist" replies: "How can this be?" (3.13b).

The purpose of the *Dialogus* is to portray Montanists as modalists unable or unwilling to accept "orthodox" Trinitarian theology expressed through the confession of one God in three independent but co-equal hypostases. Assuming that Basil read the *Dialogus,* it seems that he took the alleged denial (or at least questioning) by the "Montanist" of the statement by the "Orthodox" that the Holy Spirit proceeded from the Father to have meant that Montanus himself (sic), as a "modalist," demeaned the nature of the Spirit by not acknowledging a separate hypostasis achieved through "procession." The extent to which Montanists were modalists is debatable. There was a split among the Montanists over modalism in Rome during the latter part of the second century,[47] but, apart from that, there is no evidence for Montanist modalists other than the author of the *Dialogus'* portrayal of the "Montanist" (and Montanus!) as modalists. Whether (some?) fourth-century Montanists were indeed modalists is, however, somewhat irrelevant. The mere fact that Montanists were *perceived* to be modalists was sufficient for them to be cited negatively by Catholic/orthodox authors as examples of anti-Trinitarian heretics.

Basil's strongest denunciation of Montanism appears in *Ep.* 188, a canonical letter written, as already noted, to Amphilochius ca. 175. In this letter Basil not only accuses Montanists of blasphemy against the Holy Spirit by equating the Paraclete with human beings (Montanus and Priscilla)—thereby committing the unpardonable sin (Mt 12:31)—but charges them with heretical baptisms. Applying the logic underlying the decisions made at the Council of Iconium a century and a half earlier, he argues:

46. Heine, *Montanist Oracles,* 121.   47. Pseudo-Tertullian, *Haer.* 7.2.

What basis to be regarded as authentic then has the baptism of these who baptize into Father, Son, and Montanus or Priscilla? For they have not been baptized who have been baptized into something not handed down to us. (*Ep.* 188.1)

Basil's statement is often taken to mean that he believed Montanists used a baptismal formula that employed the formula "in the name of the Father, the Son, and Montanus (or Priscilla)."[48] A fascinating inscription from Mascula in Numidia (modern Kenchela, Algeria) appears, at first glance, to confirm that Montanists did this: "Flavius Avus, *domesticus,* has fulfilled what he promised in the name of the Father, and of the Son (and) of *dominus* Montanus" (*IMont* 71).

This inscription, however, rather than recording a Montanist baptismal formula, reports the fulfillment of a *vow* made in the name of the Trinity[49] *and* the orthodox Carthaginian martyr Montanus, who was put to death on May 23, 259—not Montanus, the founder of Montanism.[50] Nor does Basil actually say that Montanists baptized with an altered formula that substituted "Montanus" or "Priscilla" for "Holy Spirit." His point is more subtle: even using the correct baptismal formula, but believing that Montanus or Priscilla are to be equated with the Paraclete, alters the meaning of the correctly worded formula. Montanists are baptizing heretically when they have a heretical understanding of the meaning of one of the terms of the Trinitarian formula they employ.

Gregory of Nyssa

Basil's brother Gregory of Nyssa wrote a significant polemic against Montanism. Extensive excerpts from this now-lost work were included alongside those of Hippolytus (ca. 170–ca. 236/237) in the anti-Montanist section of an (unfortunately also lost) *florilegium* compiled by Stephen Gobarus in the sixth century (Photius, *Cod.* 232). This treatise may have been one of Gregory of Nazianzus' sources for his knowledge of the "Phrygian heresy." Unfortunately, as the treatise is no longer extant and it is unclear when exactly it was written, it is difficult to know whether Gregory of Nyssa's work influenced in any way the three passages referring to Montanism in Gregory of Nazianzus' extant works.

---

48. See Trevett, *Montanism,* 219.

49. The current absence of the words "and of the Holy Spirit" may simply be the result of bad weathering of the stone in the place where the words *et spiritus sancti* may have been inscribed originally.

50. See Tabbernee, *Montanist Inscriptions,* 445–52.

Gregory of Nazianzus' References to Montanism in the Context of His Defense of the Full Divinity of the Holy Spirit

From the time Montanus, Maximilla, and Priscilla began the New Prophecy movement in ca. 165 CE, they had numerous charges leveled at them by their "catholic/orthodox" opponents. These charges may be classified into three broad categories: false prophecy, novel practices, and heresy.[51] Although Gregory of Nazianzus, presumably, was aware of a number of these accusations, he ignores most of them—concentrating only on those that related directly to the Montanists' actual (or alleged) understanding of the Holy Spirit.

Oration 22

Gregory's first reference to Montanus, whom, like Cyril of Jerusalem, he treats as the personification of the whole movement, is contained in *Oration* 22. The oration clearly reveals Gregory's emphasis on the full divinity of the Holy Spirit. His careful wording of the Trinitarian formula that he presents, however, also indicates his continued efforts at achieving a peaceful way by which the rival parties can reach common ground. Focusing on their worship of the one Trinitarian God, Gregory challenges his audience to accept a definition that is centered on worshipping the single divinity and power in the three: Father, Son, and Holy Spirit (*Or.* 22.12a). He calls upon his listeners to avoid the extremes of worshipping the one Godhead "too much" or "too little" (*Or.* 22.12b).

By those who worshipped the one Godhead "too little," Gregory had in mind not only "Arians," but some to whom he refers to elsewhere as Pneumatomachians. These "Spirit-Fighters," apparently followers of, or at least influenced by, Eustathius of Sebaste (bp. ca. 356–pre-381),[52] denied the full divinity of the Holy Spirit, even though most of them affirmed the full divinity of the Son. As in the case of all derogatory labeling, those called "Pneumatomachians" by their opponents never used this designation of themselves. Gregory

---

51. For a detailed discussion of all the charges, see Tabbernee, *Fake Prophecy*.

52. The same group may also have had a connection with Macedonius of Constantinople (bp. ca. 342–360), after whom they are sometimes called (e.g., Gregory of Nazianzus, *Ep.* 202.5; Gregory of Nyssa, *Spir.* 3.1.89t3; Socrates, *Hist. eccl.* 1.8.24).

of Nazianzus appears to have been the first in Asia Minor to utilize the term. Whether Gregory simply made up the term Pneumatomachians or borrowed it from a written or oral source is undocumented. As early as 357–378, Athanasius had used the expression πνευματομαχεῖν ("to fight against the Spirit") in describing the beliefs of a group of Christians in Egypt reported to him by Serapion of Thmuis (bp. ca. 330–post-362),[53] but, as noted, Gregory of Nazianzus does not seem to have been very familiar with Athanasius' writings. In any case, there does not seem to have been any direct physical link between the Egyptian "Pneumatomachians" and the ones who listened to Gregory's orations. Theologically speaking, however, they did share the view that the Holy Spirit, in some ways, was a created entity and, therefore, was not divine in the full sense in which the Father and the Son were divine.

It was in the context of his attempts to persuade contemporary Pneumatomachians that Gregory lists Montanus and Novatian (ca. 200–258) as the first among (relatively) recent examples of persons who split the church:

I ask you ... was not Montanus' evil spirit directed against the Holy Spirit enough; and Novatian's arrogance, or rather, impure purity trying to lure the multitude with fair-seeming words? (*Or.* 22.12b)[54]

Then, bringing his list of heretics, heresies, schismatics, and schisms up to date and closer to home, Gregory refers to the ongoing "mania of the Phrygians" (*Or.* 22.12b).

As noted already, the term "Phrygians" here primarily refers to the Montanists ("Phrygian heretics") but contains a secondary allusion to the adherents of the Phrygian cult of Cybele. Gregory describes the *mania* of the Phrygians as still continuing today—a reference to the presence of Montanists at that time, not only in Phrygia, but even in Constantinople.[55] Gregory may have presumed that Montanists in Constantinople, as well as those in Phrygia, practiced horrific bloodletting baptisms as part of their initiatory practices. In any case, if, as taken for granted above, Gregory had read Basil's letter to Amphilochius (*Ep.* 188.1), he would have deemed any kind of Montanist baptism to have been heretical because of the Montanists' (alleged) heretical view

53. *Ep. Serap.* 1.32; 4.1.
54. Gregory of Nazianzus, *Select Orations,* trans. Vinson, 126, altered.
55. As late as 530–531, Justinian I (r. 527–565) was still trying to eradicate Montanists from the capital (*Cod. Justin.* 1.5.20.3–4; 1.5.21.1–2).

of the Holy Spirit—even if they used a correct baptismal formula. The pneumatological irregularity of Montanist baptism would have been particularly troublesome to Gregory, as he had an extremely high view of the importance of baptism as the means of a Christian's own "divinization" (θέωσις) and the Holy Spirit's role in that baptismal (and life-long) process of becoming "godlike" (*Or.* 31.29; 40.7–8).[56] The Montanists' erroneous view of the Holy Spirit would have invalidated that process and nullified its effects.

Oration 33

In a lifetime of traumatic events, Easter 380 must rank as one of the most traumatic in the life of Gregory of Nazianzus. During the Easter Vigil, Gregory and the others present, including baptismal candidates, were attacked by a stone-throwing mob.[57] Soon afterward a young man broke into Gregory's residence and tried to murder him.[58] Both incidents appear to have been prompted by loyalty to the city's "Arian" (homoian) bishop Demophilus (bp. 370–380), whose status and activities were threatened by Gregory's presence.

Oration 33 was delivered in the aftermath of these events. In the first part of the oration, Gregory counters the charges that his "Arian" opponents, Demophilus' supporters, made concerning his right and qualifications to exercise an episcopal ministry in Constantinople (*Or.* 33.1; 31.6–13). He also contrasts his own nonreactive behavior and forgiving attitude in the midst of the recent events with the violent actions of the "Arians" against him in Constantinople and against other "pro-Nicene" bishops elsewhere (*Or.* 33.3–14). Gregory, still trying to win over his opponents, declares that he is already counting among his sheep and shepherds persons who are currently wolves (*Or.* 33.15)—opening the door of his fold, and even potential leadership positions in that fold, to Homoians, Heterousians, and Pneumatomachians as well as to Homoousians.

Basing his next rhetorical move on the words of the Good Shepherd (Jn 10:11–18), Gregory portrays himself as a shepherd who teaches the truth as contained in Scripture and handed down by the Fathers (*Or.* 33.15). His sheep know him; they know his voice; and they follow him (*Or.* 33.15–33.16). Conversely, sheep such as his will not follow strange shepherds, because they

---

56. See Beeley, *Gregory of Nazianzus on the Trinity,* 116–22; 174–78, 181.

57. *DVS,* 655–57; *Ep.* 77; *Or.* 41.5.

58. *DVS,* 1440–70.

have learned to distinguish the voice of their own true shepherd from that of strangers. Instead they will flee from such false shepherds:

They will flee from Valentinus with his division of one into two, refusing to believe that the Creator is other than Good.... They will flee from Marcion's god, compounded of elements and numbers; from Montanus' evil and feminine spirit;... from Novatian's boasting and wordy assumption of purity;... from the difference of nature taught by Arius and his followers. (33.16)[59]

As in *Oration* 22, the reference to Montanus as a personification of heresies in this list is to supply Gregory's audience with a negative benchmark against which true doctrine may be judged. The true Holy Spirit is not the evil spirit whom Montanists equate with Montanus and (the *female*) Priscilla (and Maximilla). Nor is the true Holy Spirit the less-than-fully-divine deity worshipped by the "Arians."

De vita sua

After Theodosius I (r. 379–395) became emperor and declared his intention to enforce pro-Nicene orthodoxy in the capital and elsewhere, it was virtually inevitable that Gregory would ultimately gain the ascendency over Demophilus and others, such as a man named Maximus, who in 380 was supported by the Alexandrians in his claim to the see of Constantinople (*DVS* 736–1043). Demophilus, who had refused to assent to the Nicene Creed, was exiled, and Gregory was installed by Theodosius as archbishop on November 27, 380. Gregory's appointment was confirmed ecclesiastically in May of the following year, at the beginning of the Council of Constantinople.

As everyone familiar with the story knows, the council did not go well for Gregory, even after he, in June 381, became the presiding bishop. For political as much as theological reasons, the majority of the bishops refused to go all the way with Gregory in his attempt to have the council adopt a Trinitarian position that affirmed unambiguously the full divinity of the Holy Spirit. Later that same month, Gregory resigned both the presidency of the council and his episcopate of Constantinople, preached a farewell sermon (*Or.* 42), and returned to Cappadocia—where, the next year, he wrote (among other works) his autobiographical poem, the *De vita sua* ("Concerning his Own Life").

59. Trans. adapt. Browne and Swallow, NPNF 2. 7:333–34.

Gregory's third and last known reference to Montanus and Montanism is contained in the *De vita sua* (l.1174). The reference appears in the context of a section where Gregory is describing his congregation in Constantinople (1140–45), some members of which, in particular, were drawn to Gregory by his preaching on the Trinity (1120), not just his eloquence (1125–29; 1187–272). While praising their steadfastness in orthodoxy, which resulted from his preaching (1137–39), Gregory cannot help mentioning that some of these same people, in the absence of an orthodox teacher, went to any teacher available, delighting in doctrine rather than truth (1140–45).

Almost as an aside, Gregory then provides a long list of persons and groups who follow aberrant doctrines (1146–86). This list reads in part:

[there] are those who concoct deity out of scripture, who allot the Old and New Testaments to two separate gods, an austere and a beneficent; ... There are those who delight in the primal darkness of Mani, *and those who vehemently reverence the spirit of Montanus* or the hollow pride of Novatian. And there are the destroyers, too, of the incorruptible Trinity, the dividers of the indivisible nature. Again from these latter, as from a single hydra, spring many heads of impiety: the teaching that puts among created things the Holy Spirit only. (1167–80)[60]

As with the list of heretics and heretics enumerated in *Oration* 22, Gregory mentions the Montanists and Montanus' spirit as a graphic contrast between a *false* spirit and the Holy Spirit—which allows him to segue into a denunciation of those who, unlike himself, do not believe in the full divinity of the Holy Spirit.

Conclusion

Gregory of Nazianzus was fighting an uphill battle in defending the full divinity of the Holy Spirit and needed all the weapons at his disposal to do so. One of these weapons was his rhetorical use of references to Montanus and the Montanists. He could presume that his audience at least knew a little about these aberrant Christians—either historically or perhaps even as contemporaries in Constantinople. Referring to these Phrygians conjured up not only blasphemous views of the Holy Spirit, but also pagan practices, heretical baptisms, polluted sacraments, orgiastic initiations, bloodletting, and even

60. Trans. adapt. Meehan, emphasis added.

infanticide. Whether or not these conjured-up images were based in historical reality was, to a large extent, irrelevant for Gregory's purposes. All that was important was that Gregory's listeners and readers got the point that they should not fall into past or present pneumatological errors, but flee from any person (or group of persons) who in any way denigrated the Holy Spirit—especially those who denigrated the Spirit by not acknowledging the Spirit's right and proper place in the Godhead.

Claudio Moreschini

7. Gregory Nazianzen and Philosophy, with Remarks on Gregory's Cynicism

TRANSLATED BY CAROL CHIODO

Philosphia

It is well known that for the Cappadocian fathers—and especially for Gregory of Nazianzen—the term "philosophy" signifies "the Christian life" or "the contemplation of Christian truth."[1] When referring to the contemplation of Christian truth, *philosophein* and *theologein* are almost equivalent in Gregory's works, though *philosophein* occurs with greater frequency. Yet, in addition to these basic senses, *philosophein* carries a controversial meaning, as well. This polemical sense reflects Gregory's sophistic art and his refined use of *logoi*: "[the doctor] discoursing learnedly on your disease after you are dead," as he puts it in one of his orations.[2]

Gregory also uses the terms *philosophos* and *philosophein* ironically in order to describe himself and his lifestyle in a way that differs from that of the powerful and the cultured, "intelligent" inhabitants of Constantinople. "But

---

1. As evidenced by the classic study (though now in need of updating and further analysis) by Anne Marie Malingrey, *Philosophia: Étude d'un group de mots dans la littérature grecque des Présocratiques au IVème siècle après J.-C.* Études et Commentaires 40 (Paris: C. Klincksieck, 1961).

2. *Or.* 40.11, trans. Browne and Swallow; see also *Or.* 41.2: "however, if there be any more lofty reason than this [the number seven], let others discuss it (*philosopheitosan*)." Other examples may be found in *Or.* 36.6; 38.8, 10; 39.8,11; 39.17; 40.3; 41.1.

I am so old fashioned and such a philosopher as to believe that one heaven is common to all; and that so is the revolution of the sun and the moon!"³ In other passages Gregory speaks of philosophy to distinguish his own views from those of his opponents: "Since I have argued with you in a petty way about these matters, I will now proceed to take a larger and more philosophic view of them."⁴ In *Oration* 33.6, in reply to some offensive comments made by his enemies regarding his provincial origins ("your city, you say to me, is a little one, or rather is no city at all, but only a village, arid, without beauty, and with few inhabitants),"⁵ Gregory writes,

If like the just man I do not become my own accuser right away, at any rate I gladly receive healing from another.... But, my good friend, this is my misfortune, rather than my fault, if indeed it be a misfortune. If it is against my will, I am to be pitied for my bad luck, if I may put it so; but if willingly, then I am a philosopher.⁶

The Secular Disciplines

For Gregory Nazianzen it is necessary to distance oneself from the secular disciplines, or at least not hold them in too high esteem, and to dedicate oneself above all to the true philosophy. Gregory makes such statements in his funeral oration for his brother Caesarius and his memorial oration for his friend Basil; yet, however accurate these passages may be about their ostensive subjects, Gregory is clearly expressing his own ideal of the Christian life. Regarding the secular disciplines cultivated by Caesarius, Gregory observes that he

gathered all that was helpful—I mean that he was led by the harmony and order of the heavenly bodies to reverence their Maker—and avoided what is injurious; not attributing all things that are or happen to the influence of the stars, like those who raise their own fellow-servant, the creation, in rebellion against the Creator, but referring, as is reasonable, the motion of these bodies, and all other things besides, to God. In arithmetic and mathematics, and in the wonderful art of medicine, in so far as it treats of physiology and temperament, and the causes of disease, in order to remove the roots and so destroy their offspring with them, who

---

3. *Or.* 33.9, trans. Browne and Swallow; see also *Or.* 33.15: "this too I reckoned and still reckon with myself, and you decide if it is not correct. I have often discussed it (*ephilosophesa*) with you before"; *Or.* 36.4, "why indeed did we adopt a strange and outlandish creed ... why did we discuss (*ephilosophoumen*) strange and abnormal things"; trans., adapt. Vinson.
4. *Or.* 33.11, trans. Browne and Swallow.   5. *Or.* 33.6, trans. Browne and Swallow.
6. *Or.* 33.6, trans. Browne and Swallow.

is so ignorant or contentious as to think him inferior to himself, and not to be glad to be reckoned next to him, and carry off the second prize?[7]

Basil in his youth was

an orator among orators, even before the chair of the rhetoricians, a philosopher among philosophers, even before the doctrines of philosophers [...] Eloquence was his by-work, from which he culled enough to make it an assistance to him in Christian philosophy, since power of this kind is needed to set forth the objects of our contemplation. For a mind that cannot express itself is like the motion of a man in a lethargy. His pursuit was philosophy, and breaking from the world, and fellowship with God, by concerning himself, amid things below, with things above, and, where all is unstable and fluctuating, winning the things that are stable and remain.[8]

Speaking of Basil's student days in Athens:

Who had such power in Rhetoric, which breathes with the might of fire, different as his disposition was from that of rhetoricians? Who in Grammar, which perfects our tongues in Greek and compiles history, and presides over meters and legislates for poems? Who in Philosophy, that really lofty and high reaching science, whether practical and speculative, or in that part of it whose oppositions and struggles are concerned with logical demonstrations; which is called Dialectic, and in which it was more difficult to elude his verbal toils, if need required, than to escape from the Labyrinths? Of Astronomy, Geometry, and numerical proportion he had such a grasp, that he could not be baffled by those who are clever in such sciences: excessive application to them he despised, as useless to those whose desire is godliness.... Medicine, the result of philosophy and laboriousness, was rendered necessary for him by his physical delicacy, and his care of the sick. From these beginnings he attained to a mastery of the art, not only in its empirical and practical branches, but also in its theory and principles.[9]

For his part, Cyprian, while still a pagan, was "the flower of youthfulness, the monument of nature, a bastion of learning not only in philosophical studies but in the other disciplines and any of their divisions."[10] In another passage, Gregory divides oratory into three groups: those destined to morally edify all, those whose subject matter is the teaching of Christian dogma, and those which celebrate the lives of illustrious men (*Or.* 24.13). According to George Kennedy, these three categories correspond to the deliberative genre (in which Cyprian advises his listeners on a course of action), the judiciary genre (because

---

7. *Or.* 7.7, trans. adapt. Browne and Swallow.   8. *Or.* 43.13, trans. adapt. Browne and Swallow.
9. *Or.* 43.23, trans. Browne and Swallow.
10. *Or.* 24.6, trans. Vinson.

both present and past human activities are judged according to the teachings of Scripture), and the epideictic.[11] The first two categories may take the form of homilies or sermons on a theme.

Against Philosophy

Gregory expresses his condemnation of philosophy by traditional means, which in themselves merit little interest. Naturally, there are plentiful examples in his two *Invectives against Julian,* where he derides Plato, Chrysippus, the Peripatetics, and the austere Stoa, as well as the artifice of philosophical language, geometry, discussions of justice, and even the principle that it is better to suffer an offense than to commit one. He learned these things from his noble instructors (in other words, theurgists such as Maximus of Ephesus) and the defenders and legislators of the realm, those whom he found at the crossroads and in the slums (the Cynics), masters in impiety and not eloquence (*Or.* 4.43). The philosophers imagine inexistent and ideal cities, yet adore the splendor of tyrannies (an allusion to Plato and his submission to Dionysius, the tyrant of Syracuse). There are many erroneous philosophical doctrines: the nonexistence of God and of his Providence, the assertion that everything moves by chance, by necessity or by astral movement; and the stars then are moved by unknown movers in unknown locations. Other philosophers support hedonism. All of them, immersed in the mud and the shadows of error, are as incapable of teaching as demons, and they are unable to raise themselves to a level worthy of their Creator. Or, even if they did glimpse some truth, because they did not have the *Logos* and God guiding them, they were swayed by things that were easier to believe because of their proximity to the thought of common people and the ignorant.[12]

Famous philosophers are the object of Gregory's scorn: Crates, Antisthenes, Diogenes, Epicurus, Socrates, Aristotle, Cleanthes, Anaxagoras, and Heraclitus.[13] Gregory speaks ironically of Julian's ideal to unite the reign under philosophy.[14] He condemns Pythagoras, the Orphics, Plato for his doctrine of ideas, metensomatosis, anamnesis, and ephebic love. He condemns

---

11. See George A. Kennedy, *A History of Rhetoric,* vol. 3, *Greek Rhetoric under Christian Emperors* (Princeton: Princeton University Press, 1983), 217.

12. *Or.* 4.44.						13. *Or.* 4.72.

14. *Or.* 4.45.

Epicurus, as well as Aristotle for his restricted view of providence, his subtlety, his ideas concerning the mortality of the soul, and the meanness of his doctrines. He condemns the arrogance of the Stoa and the gluttony and vagrancy of the Cynics; he also condemns the Atomists for their doctrines of fullness and void.[15] There are polemical allusions to Sextus Empiricus, Pyrrho, and the Skeptics' stance of "contesting everything":[16] "and babbling is reputed culture, and, as the book of the Acts says of the Athenians, we spend our time in nothing else but either to tell or to hear some new thing."[17] He condemns the futility of the arts of *paideia,* syllogisms, letters, and geometry, and marveling at the movement of the stars.[18]

After his death, Caesarius will therefore not devote his time to the medicine of Hippocrates and Galen or their adversaries, or to the geometry of Euclid, Ptolemy, and Heron, or to the boasts of Plato, Aristotle, Pyrrho, or other characters like Democritus and Heraclitus, Anaxagoras, Cleanthes, and certain other philosophers from the solemn Stoa or the Academy.[19]

Polemic Against Contemporary Philosophy

Gregory's hostile stance toward philosophy is considerably more lively and interesting when he turns his attention to contemporary philosophical movements and to the mystery cults. He refers to "all the details about the gods and the sacrifices and the idols and demons, whether beneficent or malignant, and all the tricks that people play with divination, evoking gods, or souls, and the power of the stars."[20] There is "our much touted sophistic, or grammatic (not to say philosophy), a pursuit that is all the rage among our young people."[21]

Gregory's polemic with Julian encapsulates his indictment of philosophy and paganism. Julian was misled by the impiety of the Asian philosophers (most likely local neo-Platonists, descendents of Iamblichus's teachings) and was pressed by them into dedicating himself to astrology, horoscopes, divination, and the magical arts.[22] To this false philosophy Julian joined the mystery cults that encouraged self-mutilation, Phrygian orgies, and Mithraism,[23] secret

15. *Or.* 27.10.
16. *Or.* 21.12.
17. *Or.* 21.12, trans. Browne and Swallow.
18. *Or.* 25.7.
19. *Or.* 7.20.
20. *Or.* 27.9, trans. Browne and Swallow.
21. *Or.* 22.3, trans. Vinson.
22. *Or.* 4.31; 5.20.
23. *Or.* 4.70.

ceremonies,[24] Orphism, nocturnal rites,[25] and astrology, whose only redeemable aspect was the star that guided the three Magi to Bethlehem.[26] These are all details that derive from a direct acquaintance with Julian.

In addition, Gregory criticizes the neo-Platonic interpretation of ancient myths to which Julian was devoted. The immortality of the myths had been challenged by the pagans themselves,[27] yet the allegorical interpretation put forward was not convincing (*Or.* 4.114). Even though allegory was practiced by Christians, as Gregory knew well, in the sense proposed by Julian and his friends pagan allegorical exegesis was arbitrary. Gregory admits that the sacred text possesses an external meaning, but the most important meaning is the deeper one with which one educates the faithful. In any case, how would Julian behave if invited to educate the pagans with his authoritative texts such as Homer, Hesiod, and the Orphics, which constitute a series of immoral stories?

And yet these stories, if true, you should not be ashamed of; but you ought to glory in them, or at any rate to prove that they are not shameful. And what good is there in taking refuge in the word "fable" as a veil for shame; for a fable is the resource not of those who are confident in their cause, but of those giving it up. But if these tales are fictions, in the first place let them show us their undisguised theologians, so that we can deal with them; and next let them explain how it is not silly to boast of the very things of which they feel ashamed: and the things that it was possible to conceal from the vulgar (for education does not belong to all), to make these public to everybody's eyes, by means of statues and figures.[28]

---

24. *Or.* 5.30.   25. *Or.* 5.31.

26. *Or.* 5.5. This detail, that the only star that had truly predicted the future was that of the three Magi, also appears in the *Carmina arcana* (*Carm.* 1.1.5.53–69). The comet, which appeared at the Christ's birth, signified the submission of pagan astrology to Christian religion; see Donald A. Sykes' comments in Moreschini, ed., *Poemata Arcana,* ad locum.

27. That the pagans allegorically interpreted their myths was a well-known fact for several centuries. Macrobius (*Commentariorum in somnium Scipionis* 1.2.7–21) refers to a statement by Porphyry in which he asks which parts of philosophy might use myths. Julian poses the same question in a lengthy section in his *Against the Cynic Heraclius*. Like Macrobius (*Comm. in somn. Scip.* 1.2.17), he evokes Porphyry's statement that "nature loves to hide itself" (*Heracl.* 11.216C); on this topic, see Jean Bouffartigue, *L'empereur Julien et la culture de son temps,* Collection des Études Augustiniennes, Série Antiquité 133 (Paris: Études Augustiniennes, 1992), 629ff. Julian's thinking is that scandalous myths are helpful to certain philosophical procedures. The more absurd and unseemly the myth, the more necessary is allegorical interpretation, and people of lively intellect are stimulated to discover the true meaning. We find a similar statement in another one of Julian's orations (*Mater deorum* 10.170a), another recycled idea, which had already been expressed by Maximus of Tyrus (*Diss.* 4.6a) and by Plutarch (*Vita et poesi Homeri* 6); see also Proclus *Commentarius in Platonis libros de Republica* 1.44.14–15, which derives in all probability from Iamblichus. Gregory notes even fifteen years later, in 380, that the pagans themselves criticized the immorality of their myths (*Or.* 31.16).

28. *Or.* 4.116, in *Julian the Emperor, Containing Gregory Nazianzen's Two Invectives and Libanius'*

Gregory admits that there are Christian stories that contain a hidden meaning, such as those from the Old Testament that must be interpreted allegorically, but in any case their first meaning is not an immoral one. It is inadmissible that God's doctrine could be unseemly and unworthy of its hidden meaning (*Or.* 4.118). With the pagans, however, the hidden meaning of myths is unbelievable, and the immediate meaning is dangerous.

These polemical remarks are certainly based on a solid foundation, and they are not trite repetitions of tradition motifs. Gregory could have read some of Julian's works or, perhaps, Salustius' *Gods and Men*. In any case, he was informed of what was said by the men of pagan letters, in the court and outside of it, in order to defend the deeper meaning of myth through allegorical interpretation.

True Philosophy

Platonism and Rhetoric

The problem that interests us here is one common to the majority of Christian writers: does a true philosophy exist outside of Christianity? Certainly not. Only Christianity possesses the truth, and pagan philosophy is nothing other than a lower form of knowledge; it may provide, at best, some conceptual instruments that clarify and deepen what Christianity possesses from revelation and tradition. For the Cappadocian Fathers and a number of other Christian writers, many of these conceptual instruments stem from Platonism. We, too, have followed this line of study, and it is therefore not necessary to retrace the results of research on the philosophy of Gregory of Nazianzus; although this research is still valid, some of its conclusions might be corrected or modified.

It is important to note at this point Frederick W. Norris' interpretation, which is innovative in many aspects.[29] This scholar has traveled a path that differs from those of us who have simply considered the presence of Platonism in Gregory's thought. Instead, Norris views philosophical rhetoric as essential in the cultural formation of Gregory, who, unlike other Christian writers, was

Monody with Julian's Extant Theosophical Works, trans., adapt. C. W. King (London: George Bell and Sons, 1888), 1–121.

29. See Norris, *Faith Gives Fullness to Reasoning,* 17–39.

educated in Athens. The rhetoric that Gregory studied was that of the Second Sophistic, in which philosophy played a significant role. Furthermore, various neo-Platonic commentators of Aristotle considered the *Rhetoric* and the *Poetics* of the Stagirite part and parcel of his logic.[30] Accordingly, Norris has detected the presence of logical methods derived from philosophical rhetoric, such as the enthymeme, in various passages of Gregory's *Theological Orations*. This could be the way that "faith gives fullness to reasoning," as Norris has titled his commentary.

Cynicism

It is curious that, in spite of his Platonism, Gregory attempts to define Christian philosophy drawing from Cynic doctrines. In this way, the function of Christian philosophy is limited to morals, for Cynicism was a strictly moral philosophy. True wisdom, therefore, sets itself against sophistry: "You savants and philosophers with your majestic cloaks and beards, you professors and teachers [*grammatistai*], avid for public acclaim, I do not see how you can be called wise."[31]

Gregory expressed this view following his encounter with Maximus the Cynic in the summer of 380. He delivered two orations on the subject (*Or.* 25 and 26) and in praise of Maximus; he also probably composed his Cynic poems sometime between 379 and his fallout with Maximus in August 380. Later on, however, Gregory no longer identifies Christian morals, the true philosophy, with Cynicism.

The problem concerning Gregory's use of Cynic doctrines was posed at the end of the nineteenth century by a brief, but still valuable, contribution by Rudolf Asmus. It was then picked up briefly by Julius Geffcken and, more extensively, in a monograph by Joseph Dziech.[32] Since then, for an extensive period of time, the problem has been neglected, and even recent studies on Cynicism have ignored Gregory.[33] Those studies are now outdated: they do not

---

30. With this interpretation, Norris develops Kennedy's hypothesis in *Greek Rhetoric,* 215–39; Kennedy had limited himself to pointing out the most openly rhetorical elements of Gregory's rhetoric.

31. *Or.* 36.12, trans. Vinson.

32. See Rudolf Asmus, *Gregorius von Nazianz und sein Verhältnis zum Kynismus,* Theologische Studien und Kritiken 67 (Leipzig: Teubner, 1894), 314–39; Julius Geffcken, *Kynika und Verwandtes* (Heidelberg: Winter, 1909), 18–19; and Joseph Dziech, *De Gregorio Nazianzeno diatribae quae dicitur alumno,* Poznańskie Towarzystwo Przyjacioø Nauk, Prace Komisji Filologicznej 3 (Poznań: 1925).

33. See Marie-Odile Goulet-Cazet and Richard Goulet, *Le cynisme ancien et ses prolongements:*

deal with the sociopolitical structure that induced Gregory to be attracted by Cynicism, and in the interest of comprehension they gathered under the common name of Cynicism even the most generic moral considerations, proper to both Christianity and paganism, without sufficient regard for their differences. As it has been rightly observed,

> Mere stress on the difficulty of the moral life, if it is not associated with a particular Cynic figure as its exemplar, should not be allowed to count. [...] Perhaps a distortion is practiced if these points of contact are made the grounds for assigning them formally to one or another school, and above all if—as has sometime been the tendency—any popularizing text that cannot be attributed securely to one of the great institutionalized schools is for that reason categorized without further ado as "Cynic."[34]

Today, Cynic ethics appear far more problematic than these earlier studies suggest.

Gregory's Theoretical Definition of Cynicism

Oration 25 is an extraordinarily innovative document, because it clearly presents a conciliatory project between Christian morals (which remain in any case above pagan ones) and Cynicism. Gregory contests the false wisdom of other philosophies and sets them against the courage and the sincerity of the Cynic philosopher (*Or.* 25.2). Maximus is the most perfect of all philosophers and martyrs of truth; his commitment to Christian ethics is immense. He is a Dog, thanks to his frank speech (*parrhesia*) in defense of the upright faith, which was being threatened by the Homoians still in power in Constantinople (*Or.* 25.3). In this way, Maximus has earned true nobility, which is not that of bloodline, but of true Christian existence. For this reason, Maximus is a citizen of the entire earth (Cynic philosophers do not suffer being bounded by restricted borders), even if, as far as his body is concerned, he is a citizen of the city of Alexandria. To better preach his ideas, Maximus prefers the active life to the hermitic one; he would like to exhibit the social relations and the

---

Actes du Colloque international du CNRS, edited by Marie-Odile Goulet-Cazet and Richard Goulet (Paris: Presses universitaires de France, 1993), and its English translation, R. Bracht Branham and Marie-Odile Goulet-Cazé, *The Cynics: The Cynic Movement in Antiquity and Its Legacy,* Hellenistic Culture and Society 23 (Berkeley: University of California Press, 1997); as well as Dieter Krueger, "Diogenes the Cynic among the Fourth Century Fathers," *Vigiliae Christianae* 47 (1993): 29–49, here 39–42.

34. Cf. Michael B. Trapp, "On the Tablet of Cebes," in *Aristotle and After,* edited by Richard Sorabji, 159–80, Bulletin Supplement 68 (London: Institute of Classical Studies, School of Advanced Study, University of London, 1997), esp. 171.

philanthropy of charity. His Christian Cynicism is therefore a polemic against the pride of the Greeks (*Or.* 25.5).

Oration 25 also contains a *comparatio vitarum*, in the same manner of that found in *Poem* 1.2.8:

[Maximus] rejects and banishes as far away as possible the Peripatetics and the Academics and the austere Stoa and Epicurus with his mindless world and atoms and hedonism, after crowning them with fillets of wool, just as one of them had done with the poet. As for the Cynics, finding their godlessness utterly repugnant but their unpretentiousness appealing, he is what you now see, a Dog opposed to actual dogs, a lover of wisdom against those who lack it, and a Christian working for everyone's well-being. Through his outward resemblance he quashes their arrogant self-righteousness, and by his novel dress, the studied simplicity of some in our own camp. In this way he provides living proof that piety does not reside in superficial details or a philosophical temperament in a gloomy countenance, but rather in steadfastness of soul and purity of mind and an inclination toward virtue that is genuine, regardless of the clothes we wear and the company we keep. This holds true whether that company is ourselves alone and we insulate our minds from the senses, or whether it is a crowd of our fellow-creatures amid whom we maintain an inner solitude, practicing our philosophy among non-philosophers (just like Noah's ark, which, though in the flood, was unscathed by it, and Moses' great sight, the bush on the mountain, which the fire burned but did not consume), neither adversely affected ourselves in any way by contact with the mass any more than adamant is by those who strike it, but by our personal example making others better to the utmost of our ability. Of this philosophy the fruit does not lie in ideal states conjured up with words (*scindapses,* as it were, to use their own expression, and *tragelaphs,* that is, just so many meaningless sounds), or in what they call categories and logical reductions and syntheses, or complete and incomplete predicates and rhetorical niceties, or mathematical lines of some sort that exist nowhere, or astronomical conjunctions and configurations dreamed up in defiance of God's providence. These things he regarded as trifling and secondary, and he played with them merely to avoid being played with by those who sport a knowledge of them.

[What, then, was his primary goal?] To plead the cause of justice before magistrates, to speak his mind freely and unselfconsciously in the presence of kings ... to contain the turmoil of a disgruntled populace, the peremptoriness of potentates, the pain of houses divided against themselves, the narrow-mindedness of the ignorant, the self importance of the educated, the wealth that is full of pride, the excess that breeds arrogance, the poverty that invites crime, the anger that goes too far and takes judgment with it, ... immoderate pleasure, uncontrollable laughter; to put an end to the anguish of grief, the waywardness of youth, the peevishness of old age, the widow's loneliness, the orphan's despair.... Will not anyone of sense much prefer these pursuits to syllogisms and linear measurements and star-gaping, once he realizes that if we all spent our time studying logic or geometry or astronomy the quality of our life would not for all that be improved one iota (indeed our society would completely fall apart); while if, on the other hand, the concerns I have listed are passed over, the result is utter

confusion and chaos? Need we add how much better and superior these endeavors are to Antisthenes' sophisticated nonsense, Diogenes' dainty diet, and Crates' free love?[35]

In sum, the ethical ideal that Gregory intends to propose is that of Cynic
philosophy, which devotes its attention exclusively to the education of man.
Cynicism is modified to the historical and social context of Christianity in the
fourth century, a time in which the choice of a perfect Christian life was discussed, whether it be the monastic or contemplative life or the practical life
in the midst of society. Gregory proposes a compromise between the two demands: he picks up the moral principles of Cynic philosophy, such as disdain
for worldly goods, candor of speech, freedom of the soul in the presence of the
powerful, and the conviction that one is a "citizen of the world,"[36] and he interprets them in a Christian key.

Cynicism in Gregory's Poetry

The moral themes expressed in *Oration* 25 return in various poems.
Among these, the poem "On Virtue" (*Carm.* 1.2.10) is significant. Gregory
praises the Cynic's cloak (*tribon*) and his cane (*Carm.* 1.2.10.242–72; 286–90),
yet Gregory's ideal of the virtuous life is emphatically drawn from Christian
asceticism. In order to attain virtue, useful examples can be found in pagan
writings:[37] poverty (vv. 214–579), asceticism (*enkrateia*, vv. 580–616), strength
(vv. 676–766), temperance (vv. 773–897).[38] Gregory uses paradigmatic *topoi*
and *chreiai* drawn from a common legacy of *Popularphilosophie,* employing
as well stylistic details from the diatribe such as the apostrophe and rhetorical questions.[39] He recalls the most significant Cynics, such as Diogenes and
Crates, and presents a series of examples of willed poverty, which was the result of an autonomous decision (vv. 244–58). But he is careful to note the
Christian perspective that gives them their real significance: "These examples,

35. *Or.* 25.6–7, trans., adapt. Vinson. We will discuss these figures later; for the time being, let us note
that, in Gregory's view, Maximus is indeed a Cynic, but as a Christian he is markedly superior to the famous Cynic philosophers of the past.
36. These are Cynic statements that, as noted above, have occupied many scholars. Among the latest, see Gilles Dorival, "L'image des cyniques chez les pères grecs," in *Le cynisme ancien et ses prolongements,* edited by Goulet-Cazet and Goulet, 419–43, especially 441.
37. See Gregory of Nazianzus, *Sulla virtù: Carme giambico [1.2.10]*, introduction, critical text, and
translation by Carmelo Crimi, commentary by Manfred Kertsch, Poeti cristiani 1 (Pisa: ETS, 1995), 34–35.
38. Gregory of Nazianzus, *Sulla virtù: Carme giambico,* 30, 38–39.
39. Gregory of Nazianzus, *Sulla virtù: Carme giambico,* 41.

therefore, are practically the same as my laws, which allow me fly to life as a bird, with daily unsown food, to the beauty of lilies, splendidly dressed. They provide a shelter of simple dress, on the condition that we adore the one great God" (vv. 259–64).[40]

But Cynicism can be understood in a Christian sense inasmuch as it condemns human defects. Human insatiability, according to Gregory, derives from the imperfection of nature, caused by the fall of our progenitors (vv. 468–80). Besides, it is futile to seek this knowledge in the doctrines and the fictions of the pagans, since Christian doctrine provides numerous exhortations to virtue. For this reason Gregory contrasts worldly goods with those of the afterlife: wealth and fortune's largesse are countered by God and celestial things (vv. 449–51); worldly power is countered with Christ's cross. In a *sententia* typical of Gregory's rhetoric, he writes in verse 467 that one should toss away "everything that is destined to be eaten by moths and depends on a roll of the dice,"[41] namely sumptuous clothing and all that is in the hands of chance. From verse 265 on, Gregory states that the examples of pagan virtue, though admirable, were corrupted by a series of flaws that diminished their virtue, particularly ostentation and gluttony, which presented itself in subtle forms, "as if some made poverty a subject of pleasure." He notes as well that even some wise pagans were afflicted with the most reprehensible vices, such as pederasty in the case of Socrates, adulation in the case of Plato, or luxury in the case of Aristippus. For them, appearances were more important than a true quest for virtue (v. 270); and their virtuous behavior was vain (v. 215). To sum up: Considering the truth of the moral teachings of Christianity, then, even Cynicism may be criticized, for its impudence, arrogance and ungodliness are unacceptable.

Cynic Philosophers as Examples of Virtue

Diogenes, the archetype of the Cynics,[42] was admirable for his poverty (*euteleia*) and for his simple diet (*Carm.* 1.2.10.218–25). He was an example for Christians even in his provocative antisocial behavior, which violated the rules of courtesy: "The man from Sinope approached the women leaving the broth-

40. An elaboration of Mt 6:25–28, as is evident.
41. It is a Heraclitean metaphor, like those indicated in note 64.
42. On Diogenes, see also Gregory's *Or.* 4.72.

els and insulted them, it is said. What did he expect in doing this? He wanted to bear offense more easily by reciprocating offense. Consider this and scorn offense."[43] Crates of Thebes was also famous; he claimed to have obtained freedom by his own hand through the destruction of his wealth (*Carm.* 1.2.10.228–35). Gregory recalls Crates' behavior in his *De vita sua* (*Carm.* 2.1.11.270ff.), and he attempted to imitate him in this regard:[44] "The first step in my concept of the philosophic life had long been this: to sacrifice to God as well as everything else the labor of letters too, like people who abandon their property to be grazed by sheep, or cast the treasure they have amassed to the bottom of the sea" (vv.270–73).[45]

In *Poem* 1.2.10.598–600, Gregory recalls "the excellent Cercidas, who ate salt and spat salt at those who lived sumptuously in the very same luxury."[46] The salt in question is the *sal niger* for which Bion of Borysthenes' corrosive and caustic eloquence was famous. According to Horace, "After all, men have not all the same tastes and likes. Lyric song is your delight, our neighbor here takes pleasure in iambics, the one yonder in Bion's satires with their caustic wit."[47]

Gregory calls Maximus a "dog of the heavens" in *Poem* 2.1.11.938, an expression derived from Cercidas.[48] This shows that Gregory wanted Cynicism to be Christian: Maximus, instead, was simply a dog—that is, a contemptible Cynic (vv. 924–26). Following Cynic preaching, Gregory also cites negative examples: Midas as an example of avarice (*Carm.* 1.2.10.408–11);[49] Aristippus as an example of luxury (*Carm.* 1.2.10.319ff); Sardanapalus as an example of

43. *Carm.* 1.2.25.494–96.

44. Learned references to this episode with Crates can be found in Jungck's commentary in Gregory of Nazianzus, *De vita sua: Einleitung, Text, Übersetzung, Kommentar;* Wissenschaftliche Kommentare zu griechischen und lateinischen Schrifstellern (Heidelberg: Winter, 1974).

45. Trans. Meehan; see also *Or.* 4.72; 36.12 (though Crates is not named); 7.10. The episode is also recalled by Julian, *Or.* 6.

46. See Kertsch's note at Gregory of Nazianzus, *Sulla virtù: Carme giambico*, 598–600.

47. "Denique non omnes eadem mirantur amantque:/ carmine tu gaudes, hic delectatur iambis, / ille Bioneis sermonibus et sale nigro"; *Ep.* 2.2.58–60, Horace, *Satires, Epistles and Ars poetica*, trans. H. Rushton Fairclough (Cambridge, Mass.: Harvard University Press, 1926).

48. See Geffcken, *Kynika und Verwandtes*, 18–19, and Kertsch's note at Gregory of Nazianzus, *Sulla virtù: Carme giambico*, 938.

49. The example is certainly a commonplace, and it surfaces again in another diatribic context: see *Carm.* 1.2.28.148–50; 2.1.88.13ff. The example of Sardanapalus is similar: a few lines following (1.2.10.613), Sardanapalus, corrupted by weakness and luxury, "desired a throat longer than that of a crane, to prolong his pleasure."

weakness (*Carm.* 1.2.10.612–616); and Giges as an example of greed for money (*Carm.* 1.2.10.31–33; 2.1.88.7ff).

In *De vita sua* (2.1. 11.1030ff), written after Maximus' betrayal, Gregory contrasts the Cynicism of his time, which was so depraved as to be represented by Maximus, with the Cynicism of the ancients like Diogenes, Antisthenes, and Crates. Yet earlier in the poem Gregory had already mentioned Maximus in connection with the difficulties his community experienced when they were forced to include untrustworthy members.[50] Then Maximus played a role that can still serve as an edifying example to Christians: "a Dog tread on my episcopal seat, and worshipped Christ instead of Heracles" (vv. 974–75).

Other Cynic Themes in Gregory

The Praise of Poverty (Uteleia) *and the Condemnation of Luxury* (Tryphé) There are additional Cynic themes that appear numerous times in Gregory's work. The spare diet, for example, merits special praise:[51]

Others can have their gold and silver: their passion to be surrounded by innumerable possessions brings them sparse satisfaction and much trouble. Plain fare is my delight, coarse food I find sweet, and salt and a meager board, and with it all a fasting draught of water. Such, with Christ, who ever elevates my mind, is my best wealth.[52]

Speak to me of your ornaments: your home, the lustful woman, children, possessions, superintendents, tax collectors, edicts and disputes, all filled with worries and affairs, and the table filled with renowned dishes.[53]

The soft weave of silk did not ensnare me. I took no pleasures in the luxuries of the table, in catering to an insatiable belly, which is the wanton mother of lust. Living in great and brilliant houses did not please me.[54]

Gregory's critics, who were both the powerful and the admirers of the powerful, insulted him because he ate salt (or humble foods), yet at the same time "refused with 'salted disdain' refined and magnificent banquets" (*Carm.* 2.1.11.705–7). The enigmatic expression "you refuse with salted disdain (*halmyròn kataptyeis*)" must signify the severity with which Gregory scorns luxury: "Bread is my condiment, I have drink. Every pleasure of mine comes from salt:

---

50. This is the meaning of the image in v. 971: "to gather something even from straw."
51. See Ludwig Deubner, "Kerkidas bei Gregor von Nazianz," *Hermes* 54 (1919): 438–39.
52. *Carm.* 2.1.1.71–76.   53. *Carm.* 2.1.12.610–16, *De seipso et de episcopis.*
54. *Carm.* 2.1.1.65–67.

through it I spit salt at those who enjoy luxury."[55] Similar to his condemnation of luxury is that of the pleasures of the belly (*Carm.* 1.2.1.44; 2.1.1.283; 65–67) or his condemnation of gluttony (*Carm.* 1.2.10.313–18). The contrast between *tryphé* and *euteleia* is also found in *Carm.* 1.2.10.259 and in *De se ipso et de epis-copis* (*Carm.* 1.1.12.297ff).

Wealth   Gregory describes wealth as a "game of the moment," like all earthly things (*Ep.* 204; *Carm.* 1.2.16.9; 1.2.3.92; 1.2.10.443–48). It is "transient pride" (*Carm.* 2.1.88.28). The Christian, therefore, must scorn wealth and the gifts of fortune (*Carm.* 1.2.10.25–26); indeed, wealth is a wicked counselor (*Carm.* 1.2.8.102–3, 159). In opposition to the vanity of this life, there is true wealth in Christ (*Carm.* 2.1.82.1ff). The sentence is structured in the traditional form: "to some gold, to others silver, to others the sumptuous table; but for me, Christ is the great wealth."[56]

On this point Theognides was a poor teacher because he taught the opposite: better to throw oneself to the sea or from a cliff rather than endure poverty (*Carm.* 1.2.10.393). Instead, poverty is preferable to unjust wealth (*Carm.* 1.2.33.129; 1.2.28.145; 2.2.5.260ff).[57] Gregory reaffirms the idea in various poems written against the wealthy (Carm. 1.2.26–28).

Human Glory   In *Poem* 1.2.26.1–6, "For a Noble of Ignoble Morals," Gregory tells the following tale:

A man of noble origins, but evil to the bone, threw his ancestors in the face of a man of excellent status, but without noble origins. And the latter, smiling mildly, responded with a motto worthy of remembrance: "My family is to my dishonor, as you are to yours." Hold close this saying so you place nothing before virtue.

Even the pagan philosophers' scorn for glory is nothing other than vainglory: "Know that the desire for vain things is vain opinion, and that glory is the appearance to us in this way or in that" (*Carm.* 1.2.10.270–71).[58] And again: "Follow glory, but not all of it, and not too much. It is better to be than to

55. See also *Carm.* 1.2.8.96–98.
56. See also *Carm.* 1.2.10.456ff.
57. A very common *sententia:* see Ulrich Beuckmann, *Gregory of Nazianzus, Gegen die Habsucht (Carmen 1,2,28): Einleitung und Kommentar,* Studien zur Geschichte und Kultur des Altertums, Neue Folge. 2, Reihe, Forschungen zu Gregor von Nazianz 6 (Paderborn: F. Schöningh, 1988), line 260.
58. See also *Carm.* 1.2.34.97–99.

seem. If you are instead excessive, do not go seeking vain or youthful glory. What does a monkey gain by appearing like a lion?" (*Carm.* 1.2.33.93–96)[59]

Gregory frequently criticizes the conviction that a noble birth in itself constitutes a merit. In *Poem* 1.2.25.447–48 he writes that "a small glory[60] and the ease and nobility of the race are child's play."[61] In another poem he asks:

And you who are so wicked, do you call yourself noble? Idle chatter. Let the plumb-line show your rectitude, and then I will be persuaded. You say that even if I am a free man, I am of obscure origins. And I laugh at your wickedness if you think that in your evil you might obscure your ignoble soul with noble origins. It was wealth, not honesty, that distinguished the nobility, perhaps even your ancestors, but let us suppose that it was honesty: what does nobility have to do with you, if it is evil? Those who are noble by birth but ignoble in soul I deem a corpse that makes even perfumed ointments stench. The only nobility is to have honesty of the soul.[62]

All things connected with social status are therefore to be considered vain. Even thrones and empires are "the transient pride of the times."[63] Gregory thus praises Vitalian for having avoided such snares:

In exchange for all of your wealth you received one precious pearl for the last day, uniting Christ and your sainted intellect, and you wore a cloud that descended from above. Distanced from the earthly world and rising in the middle of a wall, you halted the violence of the unfillable void. You disdained the prideful thrones, throwing to the ground the empty arrogance of vainglory.[64]

Even homeland belongs to the category of indifferent things: "one's native country is a chasm, the foreign land a disgrace" (*Carm.* 1.2.16.21).[65] For, ac-

59. Another use of an Aesopic fable to emphasize the scorn of glory: see *Carm.* 1.2.10.439–42.

60. In Greek *doxarion*. Diminutives are frequent in the diatribe to express commiseration: see Epictetus, *Diss.* 2.22.11, and Gregory of Nazianzus, *Ep.* 178.10, similarly a catalogue of worldly goods; *Or.* 19.4 and 32.17, among many examples. See the comments in Gregory of Nazianzus, *Synkrisis bion,* ed. Henricus Werhahn (Wiesbaden: H. M. Werhahn, 1953), 88, and Michael Oberhaus, *Gregory of Nazianzus, Gegen den Zorn (Carmen 1,2,25): Einleitung und Kommentar,* Studien zur Geschichte und Kultur des Altertums, Neue Folge. 2, Reihe, Forschungen zu Gregor von Nazianz 8 (Paderborn: F. Schöningh, 1991), lines 447–48.

61. The expression is Heraclites' (VS 22 B 70), who designates with this term the opinions of men; see Bernhard Wyss, "Zu Gregor von Nazianz," in *Phyllobolia für Peter von der Mühll zum 60. Geburtstag am. 1 August 1945,* edited by Olof Gigon, Karl Meuli, Willy Theiler, Fritz Wehrli, and, Bernhard Wyss, 153–83, 179n1 (Basel: Schwabe, 1946), which refers to *Or.* 14.20; Gregory of Nazianzus, *Synkrisis Bion,* ed. Henricus Werhahn, 94–101; see also Gregory's *Carm.* 1.2.10.417–20, and the two poems 1.2.26–27.

62. *Carm.* 1.2.27.23–33.   63. *Carm.* 2.1.88.27–28.

64. *Carm.* 2.2.3.273–79, "To Vitalian"; see also *Carm.* 2.1.85.10–12: "All things shake down time here, like dice: beauty, fame, wealth, power and treacherous happiness"; *Carm.* 2.1.32.52–54; and the gnomic *Carm.* 1.2.34.82–85, 96–97.

65. See also *Carm.* 1.2.26.23–24; 1.2.10.421–26.

cording to a well-known saying that Gregory takes up, the true Cynic is a citizen of the world.

Similarly, the value of fortune's gifts is small (*Carm.* 1.2.16.9ff), particularly that of beauty: "consider beauty to be the order of your thoughts, not that drawn by the hand or that time dissolves" (*Carm.* 1.2.33.81–82).[66] Yet the same holds true for all worldly experiences in themselves: "The pains have arrived, pleasures, arrogance, fear, wealth, glory, infamy, realms. May they go as they please. No unstable thing touches the man who proceeds well."[67]

The Debasement of Marriage   This ascetic theme is found in *Poem* 1.2.10.53–56, but it is necessary to distinguish here (more so than elsewhere) between pagan Cynicism and Christian Cynicism. Because the debasement of marriage and sexuality was such a widespread theme in ancient Christianity (both orthodox and heretical), it would be arbitrary to trace such a condemnation back to popular pagan philosophy. There is no need to recall the theme of the *incommoda nuptiarum* developed by Jerome, who studied for a time under Gregory of Nazianzus. In *Poem* 1.2.1.623ff, Gregory expresses this theme programmatically: "Since you have considered and reflected upon this, consider also the distresses of marriage, which exists for the slaves of the flesh."[68] Again:

They walk the righteous path those whose life is not on this earth; three times blessed, they live on the earth above the flesh, without the marital yoke, scornful of the world, inhabitants of the heavens, without wealth, sorrowful, they sleep on the ground and own only one chiton, possess only one treasure, poverty and the gaze directed at God.[69]

Which Is the Better Life?   As in *Oration* 25, in *Poem* 1.2.8, "The Comparison of Lives," there is a synthesis of Cynicism and Christian ethics by means of a debate between the active and the contemplative lives. It is analogous to a debate found in pagan Cynicism: whether the life of the philosopher, the king, the rich man, or the wise man is better.[70] Each of the two contenders exhibits his individual merits and claims to excellence with respect to

---

66. See also *Carm.* 1.2.3.59–60; 2.2.6.3ff; 2.1.45.234–42. Christian reflection on this theme can already be found in Clemement of Alexandria, e.g., *Paed.* 3.11.64.1: "the best beauty is above all, that of the soul."

67. *Carm.* 1.2.33.85–88, "*Tetrastichae sententiae.*"   68. See also *Carm.* 1.2.6.23–25.

69. *Carm.* 2.2.5.147–50.

70. The debate between the active life and the contemplative life is analogous in form to that which takes place in the first of a series of poems that Gregory composed to celebrate virginal life; *Carm.* 1.2.1.

mankind (vv. 6–18). The active life presents among its titles that of inherited nobility (v. 41), to which the contemplative life replies: "Of what descent? Which creator? Don't you know that mud is the same for everyone? There is only one nobility: the imitation of God. You are strong by means of sepulchers and new laws" (vv. 42–45). The active life counters with wealth (vv. 46–48), but the contemplative life objects:

Poverty does not allow enemies, and compassion is more certain than envy. Elevated thrones are subject to transience, and friends are more friends of circumstance. If they remain, it is better to obey God than to possess distinguished things among visible things or to be superior to all things visible (vv. 49–55).

The *topos* of the advantages that come with wealth follows, as well as those that come with *tryphé* (satiety, the pleasures of the table and of life), which are then countered by the damage they procure (vv. 74ff). The poem's conclusion seems obvious: "if one is not mad" the winner is the contemplative life; but the author also adds:

Now go. It is preferable that you are at peace with each other and with the great God, you awarding the first honors to the first type of life and you taking the second type as a brother. If it does not possess the first honors, what prevents it from having the second ones? This is not dishonor. In this way life could be secure (vv. 249–55).

The conciliatory proposal between the two types of life was probably prompted by the practical necessities of Gregory's ministry. This suggestion is found also in Gregory's panegyric of Athanasius, where he distinguishes between hermitic life and a life dedicated to helping the poor before concluding that there isn't a conflict between the two, and that both should be sought (*Or.* 21.19–20 and 6).

Conclusion

After having outlined some fundamental aspects of Gregory's Cynicism, Asmus asked what prompted Gregory to attempt what he considered a real synthesis between Cynicism and Christianity.[71] In Asmus' view, there is a common aim to both systems: the salvation of the human being within society and within his own conscience. It was a very nineteenth-century assessment

71. Asmus, *Gregorius von Nazianz,* 330–31.

(Asmus even uses the term *Kulturkampf*). The Cynic ideal received renewed attention under Julian's dominion, Asmus reasoned. As Cynicism developed and grew from the fragments of the ancient philosophical, theological, and political systems, so too did Christianity under Julian and after him: and the affinity between the two ideologies consists in this. On this basis, Asmus develops an improbable parallelism between Christianity and Cynicism.[72]

I propose a different route, which begins with the fact that Julian the Apostate considered the Cynics analogous to the detested "Galileans." Demonstrating his revulsion toward the Cynic Heraclius (*Heracl.* 18.224a), the emperor confirms his desire to assign the Cynics the name of *apotaktitai,* a term used for a sect of Christian encratites (and Julian adds that the name was assigned to them by the impious "Galileans"). In his oration *Against the Ignorant Cynics* (*Or.* 12.192d), Julian declares, "You recognize, I believe, the words of the Galileans," referring to Genesis 9.3 (*lachana chortou*), on the basis of which Christians felt they were not required to observe restrictions in their diet. Julian scornfully dubs them "the omnivores."[73] We also find scorn for such contemptible freedom of the Christians in Julian's *Against the Galileans* (Fr. 58.23 and 74.3 Masaracchia). Even Heraclius was Egyptian like Maximus, and, like Maximus, lived a life that was not that of a Cynic, but was quite different from that of the Cynics of earlier times, particularly Diogenes, whom Heraclius accuses of vainglory. Julian too, like Gregory, contrasts the arrogant and impoverished Cynics of his time with the Cynics of the past, who were truly free men. The Cynic whom Julian targets in *Against the Ignorant Cynics* possesses, among the many characteristics of his sordid conduct, the vice of admiring the "macabre life of wretched women" (*Or.* 20.203c), referring to encratite women who lived in the manner of the dead, refusing all good that life offered. According to Margarethe Billerbeck, the fact that Julian reprimands the Cynics of his time for accusing Diogenes of vanity, degenerating Cynicism in this way

---

72. Asmus, *Gregorius von Nazianz,* 331: "Virtue must be the field of the Christian as *philanthropia* is the field of the Cynic. The master of one is the Son of God, Jesus Christ, for the others Heracles, son of Zeus. As the apostles follow one, so the Cynics follow the other. Neither knows a home country; both roam from one place to another, teaching and fearing no one. They do not speak to the world's powerful, but to the poor and the oppressed. They speak in the manner of the people. They point to true and eternal goods, beyond the fleeting. They reinforce self-conviction and the patience of the meek with the warning that they must think of true freedom."

73. Julian, *Giuliano Imperatore contro i cinici ignoranti,* ed., trans., and commentary Carlo Prato and Dina Micalella (Lecce: Università degli Studi, 1988), which contains further details on Julian's critical, yet favorable stance toward Cynicism.

from its original form, expresses an opinion that is similar to Gregory's, who accused the great Cynics of the past of ostentation.[74] It is possible, then, that the Cynics targeted by Julian are, like Gregory, Christians.

In reality, such a close resemblance between Cynicism and Christianity was not obvious; rather, it is suggested by the different interpretations (some equivalent and some contrary) given by Gregory of Nazianzus and Julian, whose personalities were, in some aspects, very similar. As Gilles Dorival has rightly observed, two types of Cynicism in the fourth century have emerged: one that was defined by a specific *telos* and was completely incompatible with Christianity, and one that did not have its own proper *telos*, but was reduced to a form of life, and therefore was compatible with other philosophical *tele*, even a Christian one.[75]

The search for a morality modeled on Cynicism, or perhaps a "popular philosophy," was much stronger in Gregory of Nazianzus than in Gregory of Nyssa, and even in Basil. Gregory Nazianzen viewed ancient Cynicism, more so than its contemporary forms, as an authoritative source for a life detached from the world, and it was for this reason that he assumed a moderately approving stance toward it (as he did for Platonism). But he did not accept it without reservation, and this is, after all, the customary attitude of Christian culture with respect to that of the Greeks.

74. See Margarethe Billerbeck, "Le cynisme idéalisé d'Epictète à Julien," in *Le cynisme ancient,* ed. Goulet-Cazet and Goulet, 319–38, here 335–36; see also a brief note by Krueger, "Diogenes the Cynic," 42.

75. See Dorival, "L'image des cyniques," 443.

PART 2 ❧ HISTORY AND
AUTOBIOGRAPHY

Suzanne Abrams Rebillard

8. Historiography as Devotion

Poemata de seipso

It is difficult to distill Gregory of Nazianzus' poetic project from his *Poemata de seipso:* the pieces are too disparate in form, style, and focus to allow generalization, and the grouping as a collection is a modern one, not Gregory's own.[1] Monks of St. Maur first collected the ninety-nine poems together in the eighteenth century, a grouping that Migne retained in his volume devoted to Gregory's poetic corpus as book 2, section 1, the *Poemata historica: poemata de seipso.*[2] The widely held perception of these poems as a trustworthy histori-

1. On the difficulty of categorizing, see Gregory of Nazianzus, *Oeuvres poétiques, Vol. 1.1, Poèmes personnels,* edited by André Tuilier and Guillaume Bady, trans. and notes by Jean Bernardi (Paris: Les Belles Lettres, 2004), lxviii–l (the authors argue for Gregory's having collected these poems himself); and regarding *Carm.* 2.1.11, but with applicability to much of the collection, see Gregory of Nazianzus, *De vita sua,* ed. Jungck, 13–16. The organizational structure for my study of the collection in my dissertation is thematic: Suzanne Abrams Rebillard, "Speaking for Salvation: Gregory of Nazianzus as Poet and Priest in his Autobiographical Poems" (Ph.D. diss., Brown University, 2003). Other approaches include McGuckin, "Gregory: The Rhetorician as Poet," in *Gregory of Nazianzus, Images and Reflections,* edited by Jostein Børtnes and Tomas Hägg, 193–212 (Copenhagen: Museum Tusculanum Press, 2006); and Kristoffel Demoen, *Pagan and Biblical Exempla in Gregory Nazianzen,* Corpus Christianorum Lingua Patrum 2 (Turnhout: Brepols, 1966), 61–63.

2. The *PG* was the standard edition for ninety three of the ninety-nine poems until the 2004 Budé edition of poems 1–11. The first three exceptions are: 2.1.1: Rolande-Michelle Bénin, "Une autobiographie romantqiue au IVe siècle: Le poème 2.1.1 de Grégoire de Nazianze, Introduction, texte critique, traduction et commentaire" (Ph.D. diss., Université Paul Valery-Montpellier III, 1988); 2.1.11: Gregory of Nazianzus, *De vita sua,* ed. Jungck, and John Thomas Cummings, "A Critical Edition of the Carmen *De vita sua* of St. Gregory Nazianzen" (Ph.D. Diss., Princeton University, 1966); and 2.1.12: Gregory of Nazianzus, *Über die Bischöfe (Carmen 2.1.12),* edited and translated with an introduction and commentary by Beno Meier, Studien zur Geschichte und Kultur des Altertums, n.F. 2 Reihe: Forschungen zu

cal source likely stems in part from this grouping and its titles in the *Patrologia Graeca;* and the titles of recent translations, continue this tradition: the "autobiographical poems" in White's volume, and the "poêmes personnels" of the 2004 Budé edition. The poems' seductive exhibition of emotions has led to the assumption that they reveal clearly the man and his times, with inadequate attention paid to the separation between the author as a "real" man and his textual identity.[3]

Such straightforward reading of the poems, however, has come under recent and increasing fire as scholars have begun to deconstruct Gregory the man as constructed in his texts. Marie-Ange Calvet-Sébasti, for example, wrote in 2001: "Grégoire n'est évidemment pas un historien."[4] Her generic definition raises the question: by whose definition is Gregory not a historian? The author himself expresses a wish, albeit rhetorical, to write like the premier classical historians: "Who might grant me the erudition and tongue of Herodotus and Thucydides, in order that I pass on to future times the malignance of this man [Julian] and inscribe on a stele for posterity these current events?" (*Or.* 4.92) The wish calls to mind the statements of purpose of both these models, echoing their concern for the future and the conception of their works as monuments; it suggests to a reader knowledgeable about the Greek historiographical tradition that Gregory is well-versed in classical historiography. It is not in the orations, however, or even the letters where one finds his most aggressive self-promotion as an authoritative recorder of events, but in some of the *Poemata de seipso* (specifically, *Carm.* 2.1.10–14, 19, 34, 39, and 68),[5] where he intrudes upon accounts of his personal experiences with commentary about his authorial function, giving an historical meta-narrative. The similarities of this meta-narrative to those found in classical models suggest that at least this group of the *Poemata de seipso* should be approached as historiography. There

Gregor von Nazianz (Paderborn: F. Schöning, 1989). To these can now be added *Carm.* 2.1.10, 19, and 32 in Christos Simelidis, *Selected Poems of Gregory of Nazianzus: 1.2.17; 2.1.10, 19, 32: A Critical Edition with Introduction and Commentary,* Hypomnemata 117 (Göttingen: Vandenhoeck and Ruprecht 2009).

3. On the distinction, see Susanna Egan, "Faith, Doubt, and Textual Identity," *Auto/Biography Studies* 23, no. 1 (2008), 52–64.

4. Marie-Ange Calvet-Sébasti, "L'évocation de l'affaire de Sasimes par Grégoire de Nazianze," in *L'historiographie de l'église des premiers siècles,* edited by Bernard Pouderon and Yves-Marie Duval, 481–97, Théologie historique 114 (Paris: Beauchesne, 2001), quotation on 496.

5. Henceforth all poems from the *Poemata de seipso* will be cited by poem and line number only, omitting the book and section numbers from Migne.

emerges from these pieces a portrait of Gregory as a *histor,* an accurate recorder of events on the basis of not only his own experience and interpretative skill, but more importantly, his relationship with the divine. The meta-narrative of the *Poemata de seipso* can be interpreted as a depiction of the historian at work, a portrait that is meant to be emulated with a view toward proper devotional practice.

Any reconstruction of authorial intent based on internal evidence of these poems, which are universally recognized as pedagogical, is speculative, and quests for the "real" Gregory are thwarted by the construction of Gregory the Christian paradigm. What we can do is to discover how a group of poems universally recognized as pedagogical creates such a paradigm. The following argument is not an account of specific allusions to classical historical meta-narrative in the *Poemata de seipso,* nor does it define a genre of historiography and its practitioners in late antiquity; rather, it aims to discover some characteristic elements that might provide an interpretive context for this particular group of texts.[6]

Some scholars have regarded the poems' façade of personal introspection as modern, both in its tone and in its assumed conception of personal interiority,[7] and the poetry's anticipation of modern autobiography is held to be without precedent in Gregory's contemporary literature.[8] Still others have argued that the poems are dependent upon classical and second sophistic models, and as hybrids of, among other things, epic, elegy, lyric, and rhetoric normally at home in prose, though their similarity to classical historiography has not been

6. I avoid making a generic argument primarily because of the diverse nature of the poems and follow the arguments regarding the variegation of historiography in John Marincola, "Genre, Convention, and Innovation in Greco-Roman Historiography," in *The Limits of Historiography: Genre and Narrative in Ancient Historical Texts,* edited by Christina Shuttleworth Kraus, 281–324, Mnemosyne Supplement 191 (Leiden: Brill, 1999).

7. See Georg Misch, *A History of Autobiography in Antiquity,* trans. E. W. Dickes, (London: Routledge and Kegan Paul, 1950), 2: 600–24; and more recently Gregory of Nazianzus, *Autobiografia: Carmen de vita sua,* edited by Francesco Trisoglio, Collana Letteratura cristiana antica, n.s. 7 (Brescia: Morcelliana, 2005), 9; Gilbert, ed., *On God and Man,* 3, and Gregory of Nazianzus, *Selected Poems,* trans., with an introduction by John A. McGuckin (Oxford: SLG Press, 1986), xx.

8. For a critique of a modern/romantic approach, see Maria G. Bianco, "Poesia, teologia e vita in Gregorio Nazianzeno, *Carm.* 2.1.1," in *La poesia tardoantica e medievale, Atti del I Convegno Internazionale di studi, Macerata, 4–5 maggio 1998,* edited by Marcello Salvadore, Quaderni 1 (Alexandria: Edizioni dell'Orso, 2001), 217–30; and despite his comment in the preceding note, McGuckin, "Autobiography as Apologia," *Studia Patristica* 37, no. 4 (2001): 160–77, esp. 161.

expanded upon.[9] Yet the personal nature and the classical elements of the poems are rarely viewed as interdependent. My reading of the *Poemata de seipso*
as historiography addresses this separation by exploring with a narratological
approach the nature of intrusions by the author as *histor,* the composer of the
narrative.[10] Gregory's meta-narrative brings his compositional decisions to the
forefront, like Herodotus' and Thucydides', constantly shifting the audience's
attention from the narrative to the *histor* and back again. However, because
this is autobiography, the narrator is also the central actor in the events described—the object of the narrative. When the interplay of these roles of *histor,* character narrator, and narrative object is examined from a narratological
perspective, it appears to be precisely Gregory's likeness to the classical historiographers in this multiplication of roles relative to the narrative that produces
the "personal" character so often viewed as modern.

We will first locate the *Poemata de seipso* in the historiographical tradition
by comparing their historical meta-narrative to Herodotus' and Thucydides'.
Having established the historiographical context as a legitimate framework
for interpretation, we then embark on a case study of *Poem 34, On Silence
During Lent,* closely analyzing the poem in light of recent narratological work
on Herodotus' project. Like the Herodotean text, Gregory's piece reveals a
variety of hermeneutical possibilities while simultaneously making the audience aware of the *histor*'s compositional processes. The *histor* who emerges is
a salvific and cosmological presence that focalizes the divine, thereby serving
as an example of proper human/divine relations. The poem would transform
its audiences into focalizers of the divine in their lives by similar analytical and
compositional processes as those of the *histor* who focalizes the divine in his
text. This pedagogy is for Gregory the devotional responsibility of a priest.

9. Libanius, Ovid, a poetic epistle, a political autobiography and "eine politische Verteidigungs-
schrift in Briefform," Gregory of Nazianzus, *De vita sua,* ed. Jungck, 13–15. Demoen *(Pagan and Biblical
Exempla)* and Wyss ("Gregor von Nazianz," *RAC* 12, cols. 793–863) both note Gregory's use of Herodotus and Thucydides, but not in the context of writing historiography.

10. For classical conceptions of the *histor,* see W. Robert Connor, "The *Histor* in History," in *No-
modeiktes: Greek Studies in Honor of Martin Ostwald,* edited by Ralph M. Rosen and Joseph Farrell (Ann
Arbor: University of Michigan Press, 1993), 3–15, and Carolyn Dewald, "'I Didn't Give My Own Ge-
neaology': Herodotus and the Authorial Persona," in *Brill's Companion to Herodotus,* edited by Egbert J.
Bakker, Irene J. F. de Jong, and Hans van Wees, 267–90, Brill's Companions in Classical Studies (Leiden:
Brill, 2002).

Poetry As Historiography

On a most basic level, the explicit purpose of both Herodotus and Thucydides, which Gregory echoes, is to make a record and monument for the future.[11] The Herodotean text opens:[12]

I, Herodotus of Halicarnassus, am here setting forth my history, that time may not draw the color from what man has brought into being, nor those great and wonderful deeds, manifested by both Greeks and barbarians, fail of their report, and, together with all this, the reason why they fought one another. (1.1)

The oft-commented statement of purpose from the opening book of the Thucydidean text reads:[13]

It will be enough for me, however, if these words of mine are judged useful by those who want to understand clearly the events that happened in the past and that (human nature being what it is) will, at some time or other and in much the same ways, be repeated in the future. My work is not a piece of writing designed to meet the taste of an immediate public, but a possession to last for ever. (1.22.4)

Gregory's statements of purpose follow in this tradition—for example, *Poem* 19.49–50: "Truly, let it be heard and be written for those to come, both people and leaders, hostile and benevolent"; and 11.402–45:

> This is why I have undertaken to pass on these events to the ages—
> for it is not dear to me to rhapsodize extensively in vain—
> listen everyone, you who are contemporaries and those to come.

11. John Marincola, *Authority and Tradition in Ancient Historiography* (Cambridge: Cambridge University Press, 1997) recognizes all of the historiographical aspects of the *poemata de seipso* discussed below as part of the classical tradition.

12. Herodotus, *The History*, trans. David Grene (Chicago: University of Chicago Press, 1987), 33. On Herodotus' work as a monument, see Charles Hedrick, "The Meaning of Material Culture: Herodotus, Thucydides, and Their Sources," in *Nomodeiktes: Greek Studies in Honor of Martin Oswald*, edited by Ralph Rosen and Joseph Farrell (Ann Arbor: University of Michigan Press, 1993), 25, esp. note 26 for bibliography.

13. Thucydides, *History of the Peloponnesian War*, trans. Rex Warner, with an introduction and notes by M. I. Finley (New York: Penguin 1972), 48. The bibliography on Thucydides' purpose is extensive, but see, e.g., Dewald, "The Figured Stage: Focalizing the Initial Narratives of Herodotus and Thucydides," in *Thucydides*, edited by Jeffrey S. Rusten, 128–40, Oxford Readings in Classical Studies (Oxford: Oxford University Press, 2009); Tim Rood, "Objectivity and Authority: Thucydides' Historical Method," in *Brill's Companion to Thucydides*, edited by Antonios Rengakos and Antonis Tsakmakis, 225–50, Brill's Companions in Classical Studies (Leiden: Brill 2006).

> I am compelled to tell of my experiences
> from earlier on, even if it should be necessary to go on at length,
> lest a false account overpower mine.[14]

Gregory's concern with monumentalizing his work (in the literal sense of making it a stele) is evident in 11.748–49: "May my account become an everlasting stele to my ills"; and 34.209–10: "Receive these offerings, spoken by my hand so that you might have / a speaking memorial of my silence."

The second similarity is what one might call the authorial signature or authorial self-consciousness. In both classical texts, the author's name begins the first sentence. Gregory's self-naming can be seen to mimic this practice.[15] For example, consider 10.35–36: "This is the *logos* of Gregory, whom the land of the Cappadocians nurtured, who stripped himself of all for Christ."[16] In these lines, the author names and identifies himself within physical (Cappadocia) and socioreligious (Christian) spheres that the audience can recognize beyond the limits of the text—i.e., as a "real" person, or an "extra-textual" individual.[17]

A third major point suggesting Gregory's reliance on classical historiography as a compositional model is his concern with creating the definitive account of events in the face of others that are in circulation, a process that, since Herodotus and Thucydides, demands presentation of research methods.[18] Herodotus consistently presents numerous accounts.[19] At 2.99 he describes his collection of material:

14. Emended text of Gregory of Nazianzus, in *Poèmes personnels*, ed. Tuilier and Bady, 59. All translations of the poems are my own; cf. 11.1351–52 and 12.45–47.

15. See Marincola, *Authority and Tradition*, 271–75, on the tradition of self-naming; also, Irene J. F. de Jong, "Herodotus," in *Narrators, Narratees, and Narratives in Ancient Greek Literature, Studies in Ancient Greek Narrative*, edited by Irene de Jong, René Nünlist, and Angus Bowie, 1: 102–3, Mnemosyne Supplements 257 (Leiden: Brill 2004), and Rood, "Thucydides," 115–21.

16. See Simelidis, *Selected Poems*, 149–52, for similarity to a Hesiodic and Theognidian *sphragis*. Egbert Bakker identifies as historiographical a Theognidian *sphragis* that ultimately derives from inscriptional language in "The Making of History: Herodotus' *Historiēs Apodexis*," in *Brill's Companion to Herodotus*, edited by Bakker, de Jong, and van Wees, 30–31.

17. Marincola, *Authority and Tradition*, 271–75. On Thucydides' affirming his authority by self-identification within a socio-political context, see Rood, "Objectivity and Authority," 228–33.

18. Their "objectivity" and "reliability" have been debated in light of new interpretive trends; see Emily Baragwanath, *Motivation and Narrative in Herodotus*, Oxford Classical Monographs (Oxford: Oxford University Press 2008), 55–59, tracing the debate back to Plutarch's criticism of Herodotus; and Simon Hornblower, "Narratology and Narrative Techniques in Thucydides," in *Greek Historiography*, edited by Simon Hornblower, 54–72, 131–66 (Clarendon Press: Oxford 1994).

19. Herodotus, *The History*, 1.4–6, trans. Grene. On varying accounts, see Robin Waterfield, "On 'Fussy Authorial Nudges' in Herodotus," *Classical World* 102, no. 4 (2009), 490–91.

So far it is my eyes, my judgment and my searching that speak these words to you; from this on, it is the accounts of the Egyptians that I will tell to you as I heard them, though there will be, as a supplement to them, what I have seen myself.[20]

Thucydides defends his research methods in 1.22.4:

And with regard to my factual reporting of the events of the war I have made it a principle not to write down the first story that came my way, and not even to be guided by my own general impressions; either I was present myself at the events that I have described or else I heard of them from eye-witnesses whose reports I have checked with as much thoroughness as possible.[21]

Like Herodotus and Thucydides, Gregory recognizes a proliferation of accounts to be sifted and interpreted, as in the passage quoted above from *De vita sua* (11.40–45).[22] His repeated references to contemporaries' support for his claims suggest that a multiplicity of stories is in circulation—for example, 13.57–58: "For those who know it, this is the story of my trouble."[23] Two poems open with a recitation of what his enemies say about him, to which he responds at length (12.1–10 and 68.1–32). He again acknowledges the possibility of different interpretations of events and offers his solution to countering these conflicting accounts: the presentation of evidence selected in accordance with sound judgment, the clear objective stated in 11.1–5:

> The purpose of this work is to explore
> the course of my misfortunes, or even my successes:
> for some see them as the former, others as the latter,
> each depending, I think, upon his penchant.
> But inclination is not a solid ground for judgment.[24]

20. Herodotus, *The History,* trans. Grene. On the passage: Caroline Dewald, "Narrative Surface and Authorial Voice in the *Histories,*" *Arethusa* 20 (1987): 147–70, and Nino Luraghi, "Meta-*historiē*: Method and Genre in the Histories," in *The Cambridge Companion to Herodotus,* edited by Dewald and John Marincola, 83 (Cambridge: Cambridge University Press, 2006).

21. Thucydides, *History of the Peloponnesian War,* trans. Warner.

22. On Gregory's concern with circulating his version, see Neil McLynn, "The Voice of Conscience: Gregory Nazianzen in Retirement," in *Vescovi e pastori in epoca Teodosiana: In occasione del XVI centenario della consecrazione episcopale di S. Agostino, 396–1996: XXV Incontro di studiosi dell' antichità cristiana, Roma, 8–11 Maggio 1996,* 2:299–308, Studia ephemeridis Augustinianum 58 (Rome: Institutum Patristicum Augustinianum, 1997).

23. Also see *Carm.* 30.5–11.

24. Cf. *Carm.* 12.65–70. On Gregory's self-quotation, see Abrams Rebillard, "The Autobiographical Prosopopoeia of Gregory of Nazianzus," *Studia Patristica* 47 (2010): 123–28.

Carolyn Dewald has pointed out regarding the classical historiographers: "Herodotus and Thucydides as people with lives of their own are conspicuously absent from their narratives of events. In one sense, it is this absence of personal biographical detail that makes the emergence of the authoritative narrator's persona within the historical narrative possible."[25] In the meta-narrative of the *Poemata de seipso,* however, precisely the opposite occurs: the personal experience of the author—the very object of the narrative—is claimed to be recognized by contemporaries, which supports the "truth" of the narrative and the reliability of its author as *histor* and character narrator.

Gregory's greatest support for reliability as *histor* is his proximity to the divine, which often combines with an assertion of compulsion to speak and a comparison of himself to prophets or other biblical figures with divine favor. Compulsion arises in an interjection of the narrator's voice at 11.1273: "I was going to stop my account here, but later events compel me to continue"; and at 11.1527: "It is not right to conceal the truth." In poem 13.18ff, he compares his speech born of suffering to a wave under rocks that cannot be contained, an image of compulsion that in the following lines is related to his relationship with the Trinity. "Such things I have suffered, I am unable to contain my anger within," he writes in lines 23–24, before commenting on the sufferings of Christ as a mortal and on himself as a victim of "the mad one" who threw Adam from Paradise. His closing lines in poem 10, identifying him as an author who has stripped himself of all for Christ, suggests that the suffering that provides the knowledge requisite for writing comes from his devotion to the divine, and hence has divine sanction.

Force is added to the compulsion to speak through its links to a prophetic role. In poem 14, having stated that no one will prohibit him from speaking about the Trinity even though he has left the bishop's throne ("I have a voice, you have the cities and the illustrious thrones" [14.47]), he ends the poem with a comparison of himself to Isaiah, the three young men in the fire, Daniel, Paul, Peter, and the Prodromos. Consider also 19.38–39: "I will speak what my mind compels"; here "mind" is a translation of νοῦς, that part of a human being that is naturally most akin to the divine in Gregory's anthropol-

---

25. Dewald, "Paying Attention: History as the Development of a Secular Narrative," in *Rethinking Revolutions through Ancient Greece,* edited by Simon Goldhill and Robin Osborne, 164–82 (Cambridge: Cambridge University Press, 2006), quotation at 173.

ogy—hence it is in a sense God who compels him to speak. Gregory offers a prayer to God to accept his speech earlier in this poem (lines 6–9), which dedication to God functions as a support of its truthfulness; and finally, after claiming the work is for generations to come, he compares himself as poet to Job in the latter's prophetic capacity. In poem 68, truth versus what the envious speak is combined with the messenger's role: lines 1–32 contain the calumnies of his enemies; lines 33–34 state gnomically that those who speak without envy speak accurately, and then in 35–38 Gregory says he will speak; twenty-odd lines later (63ff) he compares himself with Jonah the messenger (κῆρυξ). The *histor*, by linking himself with the prophets, indicates that the narrative is a nexus of truth and prophesy compelled by God.

Dewald writes that Herodotus' and Thucydides' "achievement was revolutionary in that both authors attempted as narrators not to invent a world (even one 'realistically' constructed), but rather to encode into their texts their own efforts as authors to understand and represent the ordinary world of social experience that had been lived through by other real human beings."[26] Following in their footsteps, Gregory's historiographical project is an effort to set the record straight on certain events with commentary—explicit and implicit—on how one does so effectively, all with a view to Christian devotion. The following section on the similarity in relating to an audience between his project in 2.1.34 and the Herodotean project explores how both these aspects are necessary for the successful performance of his pedagogical act of devotion.

Herodotus and Gregory's *Poem* 34

If we assume that the project in Gregory's more narrative poems is to fulfill the wish in *Oration* 4.92, or, as he writes in the prologue to *De vita sua*, to investigate (ἐξιστορεῖν) events of his life, what conceptions of the *histor* can be extracted from the text?[27] Close analysis of poem 34, *On silence during Lent*,

26. Dewald, "Paying Attention," 169.

27. Post-Herodotus, terms from the *histor-* root do not appear in historiography for self-reference (Connor, "The *Histor* in History"), yet they appear frequently in Gregory's corpus in relation to telling stories, particularly in the discourses against the emperor Julian (*Or.* 4.20, 77; *Or.* 5.5, 23, 33), from which one might argue that Gregory conceived of the term as "pagan," requiring Christian appropriation. Cf. *Poem* 12.675. The root appears five times in the *Poemata qui spectant ad alios* (PG 37:1474.5, 1510.6 (twice), 1522.3, 1522.4).

in relation to Herodotus reveals a similarity between the *histor* of the *Poemata de seipso* and that of the Herodotean text as he has been painted by recent scholarship.

The 105 elegiac couplets of poem 34 expound upon Gregory's ascetic achievement of keeping silent for Lent in 382, just after his retreat from Constantinople; the poem demonstrates how the author controls his potentially dangerous tongue, turning its power from strife to orthodox theological instruction. The piece is a sophisticated literary reflection of devotion to God and a proof of ascetic prowess, theological orthodoxy, and mastery of language. Though it does not seem overtly historiographical on first reading, it is a record of an "event," and there is a meta-narrative that can be read as reflecting Herodotean influence. Moreover, the succinct retelling of Polykrates' tale at the end of the piece is demonstrably a reference to Herodotus' *Histories*.

Dewald has taken a narratological approach to the Herodotean text and discovered there two overlapping "authorial registers": the "I" of the *histor*, who composed the text, and the "I" of the narrator, who tells the story.[28] She argues that the text demands its readers consider both simultaneously, with the result that "the doubleness of his overt authorial persona reflects his own efforts in the service of knowledge" and can function as a model for understanding human experience.[29] A similar approach can be taken to the voices in Gregory's *Poem 34*. Transitional commentary in the *histor*'s voice, distinct from the character narrator who relates the details of ascetic achievement, intrudes between large subsections of the poem. This meta-narrative prepares the reader for what follows and offers interpretive comment on what precedes, thereby establishing relationships between the *histor* and his audiences (both internal and external) and characterizing the *histor* as distinct from the character narrator. In other words, the meta-narrative allows the author at least two voices and recognizes an interpretive role for the audience(s). But whereas in the Herodotean text a "real" figure of Herodotus as actor is absent from the narrative, which lends credence to the *histor* as an objective observer, it is, as we shall see, precisely the addition of the third role for Gregory as the object of the narrative that underscores the reliability of his persona of *histor* as a pedagogical and devotional model.

28. Dewald, "Herodotus and the Authorial Persona," esp. 272–73, but *passim;* and Dewald, "Paying Attention," 170–77.
29. Dewald, "Herodotus and the Authorial Persona," 288–89.

The poem's opening voice is that of the *histor,* seeming to speak at the time of the poem's composition and/or to recur with each rereading of the poem, which enhances the trustworthiness of his voice.[30] There is a shift to a character narrator in the following ten lines (3–12), where the opening mono-logue ceases and the narrator turns to an audience external to the poem. A straightforward account of past events begins in line three: "When [ἡνίκα] ... forty days ago in the manner of Christ the king"; and continues with tem-poral adjectives: "first [πρῶτα μὲν] ... and then [αὐτάρ ἔπειτα]," the events tak-ing place in a human timeframe (3, 5, 7, 9). The *histor* then breaks the flow of that narrative to indicate that the next section is explanatory: "The reason [τὸ αἴτιον]?[31] In order that I learn / to measure my words, controlling all" (11–12).

The partitioning of the narrator's self in the opening couplet of poem 34 is instrumental in characterizing the author on various levels: "Check yourself, dear Tongue. And you, Pen, inscribe for me words / of silence, and sound the matter of my heart for the eyes" (1–2). The *histor* reveals himself to be separa-ble into elements: a tongue, an implied hand, a heart. This fracturing continues later in the poem with the addition of νοῦς: "I speak from my hand, which has received in succession from my mind" (158); and in the closing couplet of the poem: "Receive these offerings spoken by my hand" (209). In the first two lines of the poem, the narrator's voice is distinguished from his tongue's voice; but as the two have their source in a single body, the couplet can be read as a mono-logue. Moreover, the initial characterization of the *histor* from the first dozen lines of the poem is of a man with keen self-awareness: he addresses part of him-self, indicating a capacity to distinguish between the various functions within himself and careful consideration of how best to communicate. As the follow-ing phrases reveal, he acts and writes methodically: "when ... first ... then ... for the following reason." The *histor's* methodical nature as inquirer is later under-scored by the introduction to the Polykrates episode: "I hear [πυνθάνομαι] that a lord of Samos...." (193)[32]

---

30. On changes from narrating to narrative time illustrating the predictive function of the historian, see Roland Barthes, "The Discourse of History," trans. Stephen Bann, *Comparative Criticism* 3 (1981): 9–10.

31. On *aitiai* in the opening of Herodotus and its relevance to the genre, see Bakker, "The Making of History"; Donald Lateiner, *The Historical Method of Herodotus,* Phoenix Supplement 23 (Toronto: University of Toronto Press, 1989), chap. 9.

32. Demoen ("The Attitude towards Greek Poetry in the Verse of Gregory Nazianzen," in *Early Christian Poetry,* edited by Jan den Boeft and Anton Hilhorst, 245, Supplements to Vigiliae Christianae 22 [Leiden: Brill, 1993]) sees this verb as introducing indirect quotation of earlier Greek poetry.

The opening narrative situation provides intimacy between narrator and audience. The multiplication of narrative voices, mirrored in the variety of communicative body parts, entails a multiplication of audiences that will intrude upon the initial intimacy between the narrator and reader.[33] This shifting continues throughout the poem. The *histor* addresses an unnamed individual three quarters of the way through the poem: "dear friend" (147). Thus in addition to an implied general audience of the poem, someone specific is the intended recipient—someone "dear" to the *histor,* who to the wider audience is a potential witness outside the text to the veracity of that text.[34] Just after this, the *histor* explicitly invites an implied general audience to attend his account of ascetic acts and his justification of his behavior as a priest/bishop: "Come, if you will, and listen to another story of my silence, whoever is hostile and whoever is kindly disposed."(151–52) Finally, in the closing lines of the poem, the Trinity is presented as an offering, transforming the act of composition into an act of devotion:

> But indeed, restrain Envy, you remedy for mortals; having snatched me
> from sharp tongues, may you lead me to your light.
> There, honoring you with the radiant eternal beings,
> I will celebrate in song with a harmonious sound from my mouth.
> Receive these offerings, spoken by my hand, so that you
> might have a speaking memorial of my silence. (205–10)

There are numerous dialogues among the *histor,* the character narrator, and their human and divine audiences; the shifts in speaker and consequent overlaps of dialogue recreate the cosmos and implicate the audience's role in it.[35] The common thread between historian and audience that allows for such a dialogism in Herodotus is, according to Dewald, "'secular' common sense," but in the *Poemata de seipso* it is faith.[36]

The intruding *histor* enables a dialogue between the audiences and the divine. Gregory asserts in all but narratological terms that as *histor* he is focaliz-

33. De Jong, "Herodotus," 110–11, lists multiple narrates; more thorough is Baragwanath, *Motivation and Narrative.*

34. A recipient of *Ep.* 107–19, also concerning this Lenten silence, may have also received the poem.

35. On participation in the Trinity in Gregory's writings, see Stratis Papaioannou, "Gregory and the Constraint of Sameness," in *Gregory of Nazianzus,* ed. Børtnes and Hägg, 59–81; and Christopher A. Beeley, *Gregory of Nazianzus on the Trinity and the Knowledge of God: In Your Light We Shall See Light,* Oxford Studies in Historical Theology (Oxford: Oxford University Press, 2008), esp. 228–33.

36. Dewald uses Bakhtin; Dewald, "Paying Attention," 180–82.

ing the divine when he identifies himself as "an instrument of God" (69–70). This serves as introduction to a *recusatio* of classical literature and an assertion, by the character narrator, of his own appropriate and controlled communication, thereby linking learned poetry with divine inspiration. Such behavior, the *histor* notes in closing before shifting back to the character narrator's account of his ascetic acts, "is the command of Christ the Great Lord, / thereupon the rudder of our minds" (139–40). This divine rudder controls the message spoken by his hand (145–48):

> But the all-shining Word orders you, O most noble one,
>> to contain the flow of all the evils where it begins.
> These are the goals, dear friend, of our silence.
>> I speak from my hand, which has received in succession from my mind.

From God via Gregory's mind, then hand, to the recipient of the poem and the more general audience, comes an invitation to participate in the divine economy, but a participation that is active rather than passive.

A demanding relationship with the audience through the presentation of various hermeneutical possibilities is a well-recognized characteristic of the Herodotean text.[37] Like Herodotus, Gregory includes sections that require analysis to make sense of their function in the wider narrative. One example of this is the Polykrates episode at the end of poem 34. The passage is marked by a sudden shift in narrative style, and on first reading it is surprising, given the earlier *recusatio* of classical literature, but the sudden shift itself is a clue to readers to look for Herodotus.[38]

Our primary source for the tale of Polykrates and his ring is book 3 of Herodotus' *Histories*. Bernhard Wyss and Kristoffel Demoen both assume that this instance of the story in Gregory is one of his numerous allusions to Herodotus.[39] However, as Charles Fornara has indicated regarding Ammianus, much Classical material that appears in fourth-century CE texts was common intellectual property and cannot necessarily be identified as a specific al-

---

37. See the contributions in *Arethusa* 20 (1987); Lateiner, *Historical Method of Herodotus;* Baragwanath, *Motivation and Narrative;* and Elizabeth Irwin and Emily Greenwood, eds., *Reading Herodotus: A Study of the* Logoi *in Book 5 of Herodotus' Histories* (Cambridge: Cambridge University Press, 2007).

38. Baragwanath, *Motivation and Narrative,* 28, on awkward juxtaposition of episodes requiring analysis.

39. The story appears in Herodotus at 3.39–46, 54–56, and the murder in 120–25; see Wyss, "Gregor von Nazianz"; Demoen, *Pagan and Biblical Exempla,* 350.

lusion on the basis of content.⁴⁰ Gregory's Polykrates is an excellent example of this problem: many of the key terms in poem 34 are not the same as those in the Herodotean text. The ring in the former is πόρκη, but in Herodotus σφραγίς. Good fortune in poem 34 is εὐδρομίη, but in Herodotus εὐτυχία. Fisherman is ἰχθυβόλος, but in Herodotus ἁλιεύς. In the poetic version, the king's servants find the ring ἐν λαγόσιν, but in Herodotus ἐν τῇ νηδύϊ.

This lack of repetition of key vocabulary might argue against reading a reference to the Herodotean version, but the historical meta-narrative opening and closing the Polykrates episode indicates that it is precisely Herodotus' Polykrates, not simply the figure from a well-known story, who appears in *Poem* 34.

> I hear that a lord of Samos in order to satisfy Envy,
>> Fearing good fortune contrived this protection:
> A ring from his father, which he loved, he threw into the sea,
>> And a net caught the fish that swallowed the ring,
> A fisherman gave the fish to the lord, who gave it to his servant,
>> And the ring was in the belly of the fish;
> The lord's stomach received the fish, and his hand, the ring.
>> A great wonder—not even willingly did that man find misfortune!
> So it is also for me, for Envy always keeps a sharp eye out
>> For my speech; I welcomed the depth of silence.
> So much of the Samian for me. I do not know tomorrow clearly,
>> Whether a bad or good end might meet me. (193–204)

The story is launched with a typically Herodotean comment on inquiry: "I hear that a lord of Samos...." (193)⁴¹ The closing formula for the account, "So much of the Samian for me" (203), which cuts two significant elements of the Polykrates story that we know from Herodotus: Amassis of Egypt and the Samian's gruesome death, dams the flow of the story. This narrative technique in Herodotus, whose formulae are categorized by Donald Lateiner, indicates that the author thinks he has strayed too far from his main point or has told enough of the story to make that point.⁴²

40. Charles Fornara, "Studies in Ammianus Marcellinus: II: Ammianus' Knowledge and Use of Greek and Latin Literature," *Historia* 41 (1992): 420–38.
41. On Herodotus' emphasis on inquiry, see Dewald, "Narrative Surface"; Matthew Christ, "Herodotean Kings and Historical Inquiry," *Classical Antiquity* 13 (1994): 167–202; and Christopher Pelling, "Epilogue," in *The Limits of Historiography*, esp. 335–43.
42. Lateiner, *Historical Method of Herodotus*, 44–50.

In *Poem* 34 where the story breaks off, Gregory's Polykrates does not know the misfortune in store for him and Gregory himself, as he says just after leaving off the tale, does not "know tomorrow clearly." Hence if, on the one hand, the preceding comment, "so much of the Samian for me," is read as likening the author to Polykrates, just as the Samian perceives himself to have staved off divine envy upon the return of his ring, so too Gregory might like to consider himself in his silent retirement beyond the reach of the envy of his episcopal colleagues. On a cosmological level, moreover, this life will be followed by another; the divine cosmological story does not finish within the human time frame, and human retelling is limited by its mortality. Though if, on the other hand, the "so much of the Samain" comment suggests the likeness between them has ended, Gregory could be saying that, rather than attempting to trick Envy by tossing out a ring, he converts the cause of his suffering to the devotional acts of silence and poetic composition. The reader is left "operating on a level of conjecture."[43]

The first installment of the Herodotean version of Polykrates' story is, like Gregory's, limited, omitting the king's murder.[44] In the second installment of the Polykrates story in Herodotus, the *histor's* voice intrudes to introduce the reported reasons for the murder of the king, explicitly calling on his audience for interpretive participation: "These are the two reasons (αἰτίαι) given for Polycrates' death; you may believe which you prefer."[45] We know that Gregory was familiar with the whole Herodotean version because he includes Polykrates' death in another poem.[46] His omission of the murder echoes the Herodotean narrative structure in delaying completion of the story—indicating not only Gregory's compositional choice as *histor,* but his cosmological limitations as a mortal object of the narrative.

J. E. van der Veen has argued that the ring episode in Herodotus subtly suggests it is not divine interference that causes Polykrates' downfall, but his failure to follow Amassis' advice to the letter.[47] He divests himself of something whose loss only irritates him, not what is most dear to him—namely his

---

43. Baragwanath, *Motivation and Narrative,* 2–3.

44. See Waterfield, "'Fussy Authorial Nudges,'" 491, on Herodotus' presentation of variant versions of Polykrates' murder.

45. Herodotus, *The History,* 3.122, trans. Grene.

46. *Carm.* 2.2.3.421–25; Demoen, *Pagan and Biblical Exempla,* 98.

47. J. E. van der Veen, "The Lord of the Ring: Narrative Technique in Herodotus' Story on Polycrates' Ring," *Mnemosyne* 46, no. 4 (1993): 433–57.

power, so divine envy is not placated. Gregory's reading of his own behavior and of Herodotus could have been similar to van der Veen's: like Polykrates, he failed to recognize the import of his colleagues' envy while in Constantinople, and as a result, had to retreat (187–89). Through the meta-narrative, the audience can perceive Gregory the narrative object as a negative exemplar and Gregory the *histor* as the wise advisor and reach the conclusion that Gregory, unlike Polykrates, has learned to interpret his own errors within a cosmological framework. The productive use of the lapse in time between his actions as narrative object and his composition as *histor* grants Gregory credibility in the latter role as an interpreter of events while allowing him to serve as an exemplar of self-evaluation. Moreover, Roland Barthes' concept of meta-narrative dechronologizing the historical text becomes applicable, allowing an audience to locate Gregory as *histor* in a cosmological interpretive framework. Clearly, like Herodotus, Gregory offers his readers an invitation to interpretation, and even an explicit one in lines 201–2. This invitation is accepted and pursued below in terms of the overlapping of his three roles relative to the narrative—*histor,* narrator, and character—demonstrating the multiplicity of possibilities and consequent responsibilities for the audience to participate in the text, and by implication, in the divine economy.

First, if the narrative object is meant to resemble Polykrates, we might read the forfeited ring as the see of Constantinople: Gregory sacrificed his position for the sake of ecclesial harmony. Alternatively, the ring could represent the see of Nazianzus, which he forfeited on going to the capital, but then has the "good fortune" to win back. Like Polykrates' ring, the church at Nazianzus is for Gregory something of a paternal heirloom. The reference may be conciliatory, when the audience of the poem is local: claims of prizing his home church ameliorate the insult of his earlier temporary desertion to Seleucia and then to the capital. In a second interpretation, Gregory as narrator could be the ring and Constantinople the Polykrates who might still win him back—or in fact has won him through his poetry. Gregory writes as character narrator in line 201 following the end of the story that he "welcomed the depth of silence," a marine metaphor that connects him in his silent depths to Polykrates' ring in the sea. The comparison implies, moreover, that like the ring, Gregory will return from his silence to preach again; hence his comment at line 191: "check yourself only a little while, Tongue; you will not be fettered to the end." A third possibility is that as *histor*, he is an architect of his own destiny. Polykrates makes choices that affect his fate; Gregory's interpretive and compositional decisions affect his own and his audience's participation in the divine story of salvation.

Envy also links the stories of Polykrates and Gregory. It frames Gregory's retelling, appearing in lines 193, 201, and 205. In scores of places in the *Poemata de seipso*, Gregory attributes his treatment by clerics in Constantinople to their envy of him, particularly of his rhetorical talents. In poem 34 he blames his suffering specifically on his failure to recognize this envy: "But a foolish speech crushed me. I certainly did not think / so earlier, but it crushed me nevertheless; / it made me an object of envy to all my friends. O Envy, even / you took from me! Check yourself, dear Tongue" (187–90). One might argue that the ascetic act of keeping silent is Gregory's prophylactic against envy, and thus his speech is the equivalent of Polykrates' ring. Herodotus, too, points to Amassis' fear of divine envy as the cause of Polykrates' decision to divest himself of the ring.

If the reader is familiar with Herodotus' version, he looks in Gregory for an advisory figure, a recurring Herodotean type, to make sense of the tale.[48] What he discovers is that given the pedagogical tone throughout the poem and directly following the Polykrates passage, the moral advisor is Gregory himself: as *histor*, constructing a beneficial narrative; as character narrator, with a preaching tone about the ills of the tongue for all men; and as object of the narrative as behavioral exemplar. Yet as Deborah Boedeker has pointed out regarding the Demaratus episode in Herodotus, the moral is found in an even wider context than the text.[49] The moral in poem 34, if the recommendation to silence is labeled as such, is more forcefully conveyed in consideration of Gregory's other accounts of recent experiences and of his relationship with the divine.

Conclusion

It is clear that Gregory did not spit out the salt of the earlier pagan books. Like Herodotus, who claims in his prologue to write of wondrous deeds, Gregory as *histor* claims to be retelling a "great wonder" in his Polykrates episode.

48. See Christ, "Herodotean Kings."
49. Deborah Boedecker, "The Two Faces of Demaratus," *Arethusa* 20 (1987): 185–201, esp. 185.

Through Polykrates and Herodotus, he provides a speaking memorial of his silence, as promised, but also of himself as narrative object and *histor*. When Gregory wrote about isolating and silencing himself he transformed himself into a narrative object, even objectifying himself to the point of presenting himself as his own body parts; he created a paradigm for inaction, and his experience became a great non-event to be replaced by the event of the poem and its interpretation. The *histor* that comes to life from the meta-narrative in the text becomes the "great wonder" and the "speaking monument." With his meta-narrative, he exposes the process of focalizing a divine narrative—the rudder of his mind moves his hand—to provide his audiences with a model for proper consideration of one's relationship to God. What in Herodotus has been identified as a triangular model of author/performance-text/audience has become in Gregory's *Poem* 34 and other poems in the group a four-pointed model: God/*histor*/text/audience.

Gregory's likening of himself as author to classical historiographers through historical meta-narrative and narratological techniques and his further connection of himself to the divine strengthen his authority as historiographer. He is, by his own admission in numerous places, Marincola's lonely historian, who "seeks to mark out for himself a place in the historiographical tradition," following his predecessors, yet innovating.[50] The *histor* of the *Poemata de seipso* forges a link between his historical meta-narrative, the narrative, its object, and the divine, transforming an authoritative account by classical historiographical standards—an impartial, true portrayal of events—into a narrative related to prophesy in which the "event" (or even the "man") is subsumed beneath the pedagogy. By judiciously organizing his narrative and consistently connecting it to the divine, Gregory, in the words of Greenwood and Irwin, molds "events into a chain of causation"[51] whose end lies with the Trinity. These selections from the *Poemata de seipso* are a performance not only of the author's judgment, but of the proper relationship between human and divine, and in providing their audience with a model, they fulfill the poet/priest's pedagogical responsibility and divine vocation, transforming historiography into devotion.

50. Marincola, *Authority and Tradition*, 218.
51. Irwin and Greenwood, eds., *Reading Herotodus*, 36.

Andrew Hofer, OP

9. The Stoning of Christ and Gregory of Nazianzus

"Children, for my sake, 'guard what has been entrusted to you'; remember my stoning! The grace of our Lord Jesus Christ be with you all! Amen!"[1] With these words, Gregory of Nazianzus ends his Farewell to the Bishops, dramatically set in his departure from Constantinople in 381.[2] Gregory ensures that people would remember his stoning from the Easter Vigil of 380 by referring or alluding to it throughout his writings.[3] For example, it is here evoked in Pauline fashion.[4] What is the significance of this oft-recalled episode of Gregory's life for his Christology?[5]

1. *Or.* 42.27, trans. Daley. An earlier version of this chapter was presented at a session chaired by Frederick Norris and devoted to Gregory of Nazianzus on May 21, 2009 at the North American Patristics Society annual meeting.

2. For a study of this oration as a certificate of discharge, see Susanna Elm, "Inventing the 'Father of the Church': Gregory of Nazianzus' 'Farewell to the Bishops' (*Or.* 42) in Its Historical Context," in *Vita Religiosa im Mittelalter: Festschrift für Kaspar Elm zum 70. Geburtstag,* edited by Franz J. Felten and Nikolas Jaspert, 3–20 (Berlin: Duncker and Humblot, 1999).

3. The year 380 is ascertained by McGuckin, who dates Gregory's entrance to Constantinople after the synod in 379 called by Meletius of 150 bishops in Antioch. Gregory's stoning could then not have occurred on Easter 379 as Gallay held; see John A. McGuckin, *Saint Gregory of Nazianzus: An Intellectual Biography* (Crestwood: N.Y.: St. Vladimir's Seminary Press, 2001), 240; cf. Paul Gallay, *La Vie de Saint Grégoire de Nazianze* (Lyons: Emmanuel Vitte, 1943), 136–39.

4. See 1 Tim 6:20; Gal 6:17–18; and Col 4:18.

5. Some of the most substantial treatments of Gregory's Christology are Frederick W. Norris, "Gregory Nazianzen's Doctrine of Jesus Christ" (PhD diss., Yale University, 1970); Donald F. Winslow, *The Dynamics of Salvation: A Study in Gregory of Nazianzus,* Patristic Monograph Series 7 (Cambridge, Mass.: Philadelphia Patristic Foundation, 1979); and Christopher A. Beeley, *Gregory of Nazianzus on the*

To answer this question, the present chapter falls into three parts. The first exposes the Christocentric quality of Gregory's autobiography, highlighting what may be a surprising comparison between Gregory and a non-Christian contemporary. The second shows the autobiographical context of Gregory's Christology, featuring some ways that Gregory finds himself when considering Jesus Christ's incarnation and mysteries within salvation history. These two settings prepare us for the paper's third part, where we encounter the parallel that Gregory invites his readers to see in the stonings of Christ and himself. The chapter concludes by noting some significance of the stonings for deification, both in Gregory's imitation of Christ and his pastoral ministry. In drawing connections between Gregory's writing of the life of Christ and the literary fashioning of his own life, the chapter is offered in tribute to Frederick Norris, whose many penetrating studies on the Theologian includes one provocatively named "Gregory Nazianzen: Constructing and Constructed by Scripture."[6] I argue that Gregory's recurrent treatment of Christ's threatened stonings, as recorded in John 8.58–59 and 10.30–39, and his own, from the Easter Vigil of 380, provides a valuable case demonstrating what can be called a Christomorphic autobiography and an autobiographical Christology. Gregory uses his rhetoric in reflexive fashion so that he speaks of Christ's life as blended with his own. Gregory's teaching on Christ points to salvation for his own life, and the account of his own life bears the marks of his Savior.

Christomorphic Autobiography

Gregory once comments that he is "the kind of person who relates everything to myself."[7] Arguably more than any other Father of the Church, Gregory draws attention to the way he thinks, the prayers he makes, the sufferings he

---

Trinity and the Knowledge of God: In Your Light We Shall See Light, Oxford Studies in Historical Theology (Oxford and New York: Oxford University Press, 2008), 115–51. For a brief consideration of the importance of Gregory's stoning to his life and writings, see John A. McGuckin, *Saint Gregory of Nazianzus: An Intellectual Biography* (Crestwood, N.Y.: St. Vladimir's Seminary Press, 2001), 257–58.

6. Frederick W. Norris, "Gregory Nazianzen: Constructing and Constructed by Scripture," in *The Bible through the Ages,* vol. 1, *The Bible in Greek Christian Antiquity,* edited by Paul M. Blowers, 149–62 (Notre Dame, Ind.: University of Notre Dame Press, 1997).

7. *Or.* 26.9; trans. Daley; cf. Kristoffel Demoen, *Pagan and Biblical Exempla in Gregory Nazianzen: A Study in Rhetoric and Hermeneutics,* Corpus Christianorum Lingua Patrum 2 (Turnhout: Brepols, 1996), 289.

endures, the illnesses he bears, the enemies he fights, and the causes he champions.[8] With little exaggeration, one could say that all Gregory's writing is autobiographical—as he almost never gives an account of anything disconnected from his own life.[9]

This autobiographical turn can be compared profitably to other prominent thinkers—both Christian and non-Christian—of the third and fourth centuries. Like Raymond Van Dam, we could contrast Gregory's attitude to the "blank sheet" of Basil, who does not invite his readers to share his personal life.[10] Moreover, Gregory's approach differs considerably from Plotinus, of whom Porphyry tells us that he "could never be induced to tell of his ancestry, his parentage, or his birthplace."[11] On the other hand, comparisons can be fruitfully made between Gregory and Julian, especially in their similar descriptions of a philosophical life.[12] Reviewing three opinions current in his day, Julian considers whether philosophy is "the art of arts and the science of sciences or as an effort to become like God, as far as one may, or whether, as the Pythian oracle said, it means 'Know thyself.'"[13] Gregory's autobiographical writing embodies all three descriptions of philosophy—and all three bear the form of Christ for Gregory. It is the Word who enables Gregory to know himself as created to be like the Word; it is the Word who became human so that Gregory could become divine; it is the Word who gives Gregory the gift of words to practice the art of arts in the priestly ministry of preaching and writing. This threefold exploration would give further support to Anne Marie Ma-

8. Musurillo writes: "With the exception of Augustine, no other Father of the Church reveals so much of his own interior longings, his doubts, and his anxieties. Thus the greatest value of Gregory's poetry is the personal insight into the heart of one of the most brilliant of early Greek theologians"; see Herbert Musurillo, "The Poetry of Gregory of Nazianzus," *Thought* 45 (1970): 45–55, at 46.

9. Cf. Raymond Van Dam, *Kingdom of Snow: Roman Rule and Greek Culture in Cappadocia* (Philadelphia: University of Pennsylvania Press, 2002), 204.

10. Raymond Van Dam, *Becoming Christian: The Conversion of Roman Cappadocia* (Philadelphia: University of Pennsylvania Press, 2003), 163–70.

11. Porphyry, *On the Life of Plotinus and the Arrangement of his Work* 1, in *Plotinus: The Enneads*, trans. Stephen MacKenna, Classic Reprint Series (Burdett, N.Y.: Larson Publications, 1992), 1.

12. For connections between Julian and Gregory, see Susanna Elm, "Orthodoxy and the Philosophical Life: Julian and Gregory of Nazianzus," *Studia Patristica* 37 (2001): 69–85; Elm, "Historiographic Identities: Julian, Gregory of Nazianzus, and the Forging of Orthodoxy," *Journal of Ancient Christianity* 7 (2003): 249–66; and Elm, "Hellenism and Historiography: Gregory of Nazianzus and Julian in Dialogue," *Journal of Medieval and Early Modern Studies* 33 (2003): 493–515.

13. Julian, *Or.* 6.3, in Julian, *The Works of the Emperor Julian*, vol. 2, trans. Wilmer Cave Wright (New York: Macmillan, 1913), 11.

lingrey's conclusion that philosophy for Gregory can be summed up as "life of intimacy with Christ."[14] Yet it is to another of Gregory's non-Christian contemporaries that we turn for an autobiographical comparison precisely with Gregory's Christology.

The famed rhetor Libanius shares much in common with Gregory and provides a contemporary parallel. Next to Libanius, Gregory does not seem as oddly self-obsessed as he might. Libanius wrote much of his *Autobiography* (1–155) in 374 and circulated it among friends; the rest (156–285) was added from private diary entries after his death. Raffaella Cribore notes, quoting Malcolm Heath's assessment of the scholarship, that Libanius has the reputation of being "a disturbed old man and an 'embittered egocentric' whiner."[15] This is not far from some modern caricatures of Gregory![16] Libanius tells his story with details and themes that are also emphasized in Gregory's own account: family struggles and an extraordinary devotion to his mother; a teenage love for letters; the offering of himself as a model for philosophy and rhetoric; recurrent treatments of those he admires and those he rivals; the calling of himself old at a fairly young age; an incident threatening his eyesight; complaints of illnesses; the recounting of a global fame; dedications and supplications to the divine; and the extolling of a certain religious outlook from a minority position.

Significantly, both Gregory and Libanius tell their stories to a heavenly person. The *Autobiography* of Libanius features Fortune (*tychē*)—the goddess overseeing his life. At the beginning of the work, he says that he is neither the happiest of mortals based upon the applause of his oratory nor the most wretched based upon the perils and pains he suffers—although that is how his life is perceived by others.[17] Libanius finds that the gods have mixed the things

14. Anne Marie Malingrey, *"Philosophia" Étude d'un groupe de mots dans la literature grecque, des Présocratiques au IVe siècle après J.-C.*, Études et Commentaires 40 (Paris: Librairie C. Klincksieck, 1961), 298.

15. Raffaella Cribore credits Malcolm Heath's assessment of this general impression in modern accounts of Libanius; see Raffaella Cribore, *The School of Libanius in Late Antique Antioch* (Princeton: Princeton University Press, 2007), 13; cf. Malcolm Heath, *Menander: A Rhetor in Context* (Oxford: Oxford University Press, 2004), 186.

16. For example, Raymond Van Dam spends several pages on "Self-Pity" in chap. 10, "'The Trail of Sorrows': The Autobiographies of Gregory of Nazianzus," in Van Dam, *Becoming Christian*, 171–85, esp. 171–75. For a more positive reading of Gregory's autobiographical writing and character, see Čelica Milovanović-Barham, "Gregory of Nazianzus's *De rebus suis* and the Tradition of Epic Didactic Poetry," *Zbornik radova Vizantoloskog instituta* 45 (2008): 43–69.

17. Text and translation in Libanius, *Libanius: Autobiography and Selected Letters*, vol. 1, ed., trans. Albert F. Norman (Cambridge, Mass.: Harvard University Press, 1992).

of Fortune for him.[18] At the end of the first half of the *Autobiography,* Fortune herself speaks to console Libanius in the midst of his troubles by reminding him that he has been granted a reputation for excellence in rhetoric.[19]

Gregory's life is likewise thought to hold the greatest blessings or the worst sufferings, as he expresses at the beginning of his *De vita sua,*[20] but his story is told frequently in the presence of Christ, not Fortune. Thanks to Suzanne Abrams Rebillard's study and translations of many poems previously overlooked, we are in a better position to see how pervasively Gregory turns to Christ when writing poetry on his own life.[21] At times, Fortune and Christ in the respective works of Libanius and Gregory have similar roles, such as steering the cosmos and the individual life. But even though Fortune has a presence in life that Libanius can even hear, he does not believe in an incarnation of Fortune. For Gregory, Christ is not some lesser deity guiding the course of human life. Rather, Christ is the eternal Word who became flesh, whose blood has redeemed Gregory, and who continues to dwell in Gregory's soul and accompanies him to the light of heaven's glory. In this way Gregory experiences the mixture of being blended with divinity, thanks to Christ's presence.

Indeed, obvious differences separate the two fourth-century rhetors, but some striking similarities remain. For example, both Gregory and Libanius speak of being stoned in the midst of activities that define their lives. Libanius says that a man frequently tried to stone him, but gives in detail only one incident when he was alone on a summer day at noon engrossed in Demosthenes.[22] Demosthenes, of course, was hailed as the premier orator of ancient Athens and felt his life so threatened that he committed suicide. Libanius consciously imitated Demosthenes and felt his own life threatened.[23] In his autobiography, Libanius credits divine help that he was not stoned to death. Gregory's stoning, on the other hand, is at the hands of heretical monks while he led the Easter Vigil's initiation of new Christians. This similarity of life-defining activities exposes yet another difference between the two rhetors.

18. Libanius, *Autobiography,* 1.   19. Libanius, *Autobiography,* 155.
20. See *De vita sua* 1–5, ed. Jungck.
21. Suzanne Abrams Rebillard, "Speaking for Salvation: Gregory of Nazianzus as Poet and Priest in His Autobiographical Poems" (Ph.D. diss., Brown University, 2003).
22. Libanius, *Autobiography,* 235–38. Libanius authored hypotheses on Demosthenes' orations and, like many others, considered him the ideal classical orator.
23. Cf. Raffaella Cribiore, *The School of Libanius in Late Antique Antioch* (Princeton: Princeton University Press, 2007), 150–51.

Whereas Libanius strove to be a new Demosthenes, Gregory sought to live the life of Christ. That he was stoned during the Easter Vigil makes the stoning take on a tremendously Christological significance: Gregory suffers like Christ while initiating others into Christ's mysteries.

This single incident of Gregory's identification with Christ in the Easter Vigil's liturgy, referenced many times in his writing, represents his life-long commitment. Gregory (whose rhetoric rivals that of Libanius) devotes his words to the Word, patterning his whole life on the life of Christ. He says:

> I cling to the Word alone, as servant of the Word, and would never willingly neglect this possession, but on the contrary honor him and embrace him and take more pleasure in him than in all other things combined that delight the multitude; and I make him the partner of my whole life.[24]

As the Word's minister, Gregory expresses his philosophy of life—through the power of his rhetoric—in a life of intimacy with Christ.[25]

Autobiographical Christology

Such Christocentric devotion occurs because of the double blending that Gregory expounds in many places. In the incarnation the Word mixes with the human life that Gregory knows as his own, and in divinization Gregory is mixed with the Word's divinity. For example, Gregory in the fourth *Theological Oration* says:

> As the "form of a slave" [the Word] comes down to the same level as his fellow-slaves; receiving an alien "form" he bears the whole of me, along with all that is mine, in himself, so that he may consume within himself the meaner element, as fire consumes wax or the sun ground-mist, so that I may share in what is his on account of the intermingling.[26]

Incarnation and divinization are two sides of the same coin for Gregory. As we will see, Gregory in a particular way experiences suffering as the intermingling between Christ's life and his own.

---

24. *Or.* 6.5, trans. adapt. Vinson.

25. For other key examples of philosophy as sharing the life of Christ, see *Ep.* 178, *Or.* 4.73; 26.6, 12; and 43.63.

26. κἀγὼ μεταλάβω τῶν ἐκείνου διὰ τὴν σύγκρασιν, *Or.* 30.6, trans. adapt. Wickham. The images of wax melting before fire and the sun drying up the mist from the ground are biblical; cf. Psalm 67:3 (LXX) and Sirach 43:4 (LXX).

Gregory evokes the blend between Christ and himself not only in Christ's incarnation, but also in the mysteries of Christ's life. The festal orations give eloquent testimony to Gregory's fascination for the events in Christ's life. For example, he begins *Oration 39, On the Holy Lights,* with this acclamation: "Once again my Jesus, and once again a Mystery!"[27] In fact, the first oration from Gregory's corpus stresses the Pauline theme of baptismal union with the mysteries of Christ that echoes throughout Gregory's writings. With theological accents proper to his autobiographical Christology, Gregory exclaims:

Yesterday I was crucified with Christ, today I am glorified with him; yesterday I died with him, today I am made alive with him; yesterday I was buried with him, today I rise with him. But let us make an offering to the one who died and rose again for us.... Let us offer our own selves, the possession most precious to God and closest to him. Let us give back to the Image that which is according to the image.[28]

Gregory urges his listeners to become "like Christ, since Christ also became like us."[29] In this deification where Gregory exhorts the faithful to become gods, he continues that again it is a matter of complete conformity in life to Christ: "But one can give nothing comparable to oneself, understanding the mystery and becoming because of him everything that he became because of us."[30]

All history culminates for Gregory in Christ's coming so that Gregory and those with him can experience Christ's life in baptismal grace. This is vividly expressed in the last of the *Poemata arcana, On the Testaments and the Coming of Christ.*[31] Gregory begins by asking his reader to consider the reason for the twofold law. The duality of covenants is not due to God leading humans by fractious or vacillating teachings, for the Word is skilled in all things.

27. *Or.* 39.1, trans. Daley.   28. *Or.* 1.4; trans. Harrison.
29. *Or.* 1.5; trans. Harrison.   30. *Or.* 1.5; trans. Harrison.

31. I am assisted by Peter Gilbert's translation and commentary found in "Person and Nature in the Theological Poems of St. Gregory of Nazianzus" (Ph.D. diss. The Catholic University of America, 1994), 487–517; and by the work of Donald A. Sykes and Claudio Moreschini in St. Gregory of Nazianzus, *Poemata Arcana,* ed. with a textual introduction by Claudio Moreschini; introduction, translation, and commentary by D. A. Sykes; English translation of textual introduction by Leofranc Holford-Strevens, Oxford Theological Monographs (Oxford: Clarendon Press, 1997), 41–47 and 251–64. In this work, Sykes changes his mind about what he expressed earlier and says that the addendum of 60 lines following line 18 do not belong there. For his earlier position, see Sykes, "The *Poemata Arcana* of St. Gregory Nazianzen," *Journal of Theological Studies* 21 (1970): 32–42 and Sykes, "The *Poemata Arcana* of St. Gregory Nazianzen: Some Literary Questions," *Byzantinische Zeitschrift* 72 (1979): 6–15. However, Sykes still considers these lines to be genuine lines of Gregory's authorship. Gilbert takes note that the 60 lines are an addendum, but treats them as he does the rest of the poem.

Rather, God's loving assistance considers the need the human race has had since the evil one cast Adam out from the garden and wreaked havoc on Adam's children. Because the Word's healing pedagogy occurs throughout salvation history, the mysteries of Christ can and must be seen even before his incarnation.[32]

In making his argument, Gregory runs through the Bible: Adam and the fall; the turn to idolatry; the division of languages at Babel; the flood of Noah's time; the showers of fire on Sodom and Gomorrah; the exodus from Egypt; the giving of the Law, the prophets, and kings of Israel; the miraculous birth of Christ; his obedience to the law; his Epiphany to the Magi; the call of the Gentiles to holiness to prompt the Chosen People, through envy to return to the Lord; the double gift of the Spirit and of the blood poured out for the human race; and the gift of baptism. The testaments tell the sacred story, which finds its center in the appearance of Christ in the flesh.

In this poem, Christ the King is like the father who straightens out the newly formed ankle of a child's tender foot by gradual exercises and with sweet encouragement.[33] Christ does this for the human race, which was injured by the devil's evil schemes that turned people away from God and toward the stars and idols of creatures. Christ removed the pagan idolatry, but allowed for burnt offerings for the time (in the Law). He removed those too by his own coming. When he does come, he comes as the Father's Child who received the inheritance that the Law had overseen. And what is the inheritance? Gregory says: *me.*[34]

Gregory speaks of how Christ had set a piece of heaven in the human body at the time of creation. Injured by evil, the human race needed a stronger remedy than simply little cures. He then says:

> But, emptying himself
> Of his glory as the immortal God the Father's motherless Son,
> He appeared for me himself, without a father, a strange Son;
> Yet no stranger, since from my own kind came this immortal, having being made
> Mortal by a virgin mother, so that the whole of him might save the whole of me.[35]

---

32. See *Or.* 45.13, where Gregory says that Christ was intermingled with the sacrifices of the Law.
33. See *Carm.* 1.1.9. addendum, 34–44.
34. See *Carm.* 1.1.9. addendum, 45–47.
35. *Carm. 1.1.9.39–43*, ed. Sykes and Moreschini; trans. Gilbert,.

Gregory then goes into detail about Christ's composition; Christ is God who came to be as one created later with us. One God out of both, for the human is mixed into the Godhead and, because of the Godhead, exists as Lord and Christ. Like other interpreters indebted to Paul such as Irenaeus, Gregory sees Christ as the New Adam.[36] Gregory's particular contribution is to affirm his own original identity with the old Adam, with whom the New Adam now comes to envelop in his healing:

> It is as though another, new Adam, appearing to those on earth,
> And cloaked round with a shawl, should heal the former one
> (For I could not draw close, because of my passions),
> And trip up unexpectedly the seeming-wise snake
> Who, approaching this Adam, met up with God,
> Thinking to carry him off through the force of his wickedness,
> Like the ocean that breaks on a hard and jagged rock.[37]

As Gregory does frequently, the incarnation and the cross are paired not only for their salvific value, but also more particularly for their effectiveness in saving Gregory. The blood that *Christ my God* shed was *mine,* says Gregory.[38]

Gregory concludes this poem by speaking of the common gift of baptism. He says that if he were someone invincible, he would have needed only the one commandment (given in the garden to Adam), which would have saved him and raised him to great honor. But since God did not make him a god by creation, he could go in two directions—and God was there to support him when he failed. God gave baptism, prefigured in the anointing of blood (αἵματι χριστῷ) that saved the Hebrews on the night when the firstborn of the Egyptians perished.[39] Baptism is a seal for Gregory from Christ the giver of light. Returning to the imagery of walking, Gregory says baptism was given so that he might turn his two feet back again toward life. Yet, this gift is of course not merely for Greg-

36. See Rom 5:12–21; 1 Cor 15:45–49; and *Adv. Haer.* 3.22.3–3.23.8.

37. *Carm.* 1.1.9.53–59, ed. Sykes and Moreschini; trans. Gilbert; cf. Gregory of Nyssa, *Oratio Catechetica* 26.

38. *Carm.* 1.1.9.80, ed. Sykes and Moreschini. Daley comments, "Christ's life and death, Gregory repeatedly emphasizes in this poem, is all 'for my sake.'" See Brian E. Daley, SJ, "Walking through the Word of God: Gregory of Nazianzus as a Biblical Interpreter," in *The Word Leaps the Gap: Essays on Scripture and Theology in Honor of Richard B. Hays,* edited by Ross Wagner, C. Kavin Rowe, and A. Katherine Grieb, 514–31 (Grand Rapids, Mich.: Eerdmans, 2008), 520. To support his observation, Daley refers to lines 26, 43, 69, 78–81, and 93–95.

39. *Carm.* 1.1.9.88, ed. Sykes and Moreschini.

ory himself. Just as the air, the earth, and the heaven are common, common too
is baptism given to save the human race. While Christ's life on earth is the center of the testaments, the baptismal life is the *telos,* putting into effect the story of
salvation written for all of humanity. This pastoral concern for baptism under-
girds so much of Gregory's autobiographical Christology.

The Stonings

From this basis of Gregory's life as intertwined with Christ's, we now focus on Gregory's interpretations of Christ's stoning and his own. In both cases,
Gregory ascribes greater importance to the incident than what one might initially expect. Gregory's stoning was not the only suffering or near fatality in his
life. For instance, he tells us that a man coming to murder him clung to him on
his sickbed, and cried in remorse for what he was going to do.[40] Yet that incident
does not capture Gregory's imagination as does the stoning. In an epitaph and
summary of his life, Gregory marks out ten significant aspects of his life. The last
line is: "I have been struck, tenth, by stones and even by friends."[41] Gregory similarly finds that the stoning was one of the most significant mysteries of Christ's
life. Recall that in John 8:58–59 and 10:30–39 Christ is threatened with stones
after his claim of "I am" and his statement that "the Father and I are one." These
fleeting references may be overlooked by some, who concentrate on more prominent matters concerning Christ's public ministry before his Passion in the four
Gospel accounts. But this is not so for Gregory, who finds it to be of the utmost
importance.

In *Oration* 41, *On Pentecost,* Gregory touches upon various mysteries of
Christ's life. The only mystery mentioned between Christ's tempting at the beginning of the public ministry and his betrayal at its end is the stoning. Gregory says, "stoned for our sake—by which he had to be given as a model of suffering on behalf of the word."[42] Gregory gives a similar list of Christ's actions in
Oration 38, *On the Theophany.* There he mentions the stoning as the only event
between, on one side, Christ's two actions of teaching in the Temple at the age
of twelve and driving out the moneychangers from the Temple and, on the

40. *De vita sua* 1441–74.
41. *Carm.* 2.1.93.10, trans. Abrams Rebillard, "Speaking for Salvation," 469.
42. *Or.* 41.5; trans. Harrison, 148.

THE STONING OF CHRIST

other side, Christ's appearance before Herod in the Passion. Gregory bids his listener to imitate Christ: "Be stoned, if this is what you must suffer—you will give the slip to those who cast stones at you, I am sure, and will escape through the midst of them as God did (or as a god [ὡς Θεός]); for the Word cannot be touched by stones!"[43] Notice that in both of these festal orations Gregory speaks of Christ's stoning as an example of suffering.

Christ's stoning also appears twice in the *Theological Orations*. The first time comes in *Oration* 29's long series of examples of partitive exegesis, which ascribes activities to Christ as human and activities to Christ as God. It begins, "As man he was baptized, but he absolved sins as God." Gregory later says, "he is stoned, but not hit."[44] This idea of not being hit precisely because of being God reappears at the beginning of *Oration* 31. Looking back at the previous two orations Gregory begins the last of the *Theological Orations* with "So stands the doctrine of the Son. It has passed through the midst of its adversaries unscathed by their stones. The Word cannot be stoned."[45]

Christ's stoning, seen within an explicitly doctrinal context, also appears in *Or.* 37. Gregory writes that Christ suffers stoning not only at the hands of his enemies, but even by those who seem to reverence him.[46] How so? If one speaks incorrectly of Christ, using corporeal names to describe the incorporeal, then one throws stones at the Savior. Gregory, for his part, says that he does not willingly stone him, and launches into a Christological praise that both affirms titles for Christ and exalts him above all titles. Finishing this confession to Christ, Gregory receives the abuse meant for his Lord. Gregory exclaims, "Again I set the tongues to move; again some rage against Christ, or rather against me, as I have been deemed worthy to be a herald of the Word."[47] Gregory's sufferings, including the stoning that he receives as a consequence of his preaching, are framed within his awareness of being blended with the One

43. *Or.* 38.18; trans. adapt. Daley.

44. *Or.* 29.20; trans. Wickham. For an important treatment of Gregory's emphasis on the unity of Christ with particular reference to *Or.* 29, see Christopher A. Beeley, "Gregory of Nazianzus on the Unity of Christ," in *In the Shadow of the Incarnation: Essays on Jesus Christ in the Early Church in Honor of Brian E. Daley, S.J.,* edited by Peter W. Martens, 97–120 (Notre Dame, Ind.: University of Notre Dame Press, 2008); and Beeley, *Gregory of Nazianzus on the Trinity and the Knowledge of God,* 128–43.

45. *Or.* 31.1, trans. Wickham. Gregory continues with an allusion to Exod 19:13 concerning the punishment of stoning, which he interprets to mean that unworthy arguments are the wild beasts stoned by the Word.

46. *Or.* 37.4.   47. *Or.* 37.4.

he loves. Gregory says, "For why is the Christian held in honor? Is it not that Christ is God? Even though I love him as human, I am mingled together with him by friendship (φιλίᾳ πρὸς αὐτὸν συγκεκραμένος)."[48]

Gregory's conformity to Christ in the stoning expresses itself in virtue, especially in merciful patience.[49] The longest single description of the stoning comes from Gregory's *Letter 77*, to Theodore of Tyana. Gregory gives vivid details about how he stood between the monks throwing the stones and those receiving the sacraments at the Vigil. But the point of the letter is to calm Theodore's indignation by an appeal to divine mercy. He situates the incident within a string of scriptural examples that show mercy rather than retribution to be more laudatory. He says, "Let us imitate the *philanthrōpia* of God" and highlights the example of Christ's words about how a fig tree could still bear fruit through more gardening.[50]

This Christological conformity in merciful patience through suffering appears repeatedly in Gregory's literary fashioning of his stoning. In his *Farewell to the Bishops* whose ending began this chapter, Gregory speaks of those who make war on the Godhead and says that he does not pelt his enemies with insults. Rather, "we try to show that fighting the war on Christ's behalf consists in fighting as Christ did—the meek one, the peacemaker, who sustains our weakness."[51] Both past and present are seen through a Christological lens in Gregory's account of the war he wages. Christ is not only the one who acted peacefully, but also the one who sustains Gregory's weakness in the midst of this fight fought on Christ's behalf.

In his *De vita sua*, Gregory makes light of his stoning, calling it his banquet. He says that he has only one criticism: the aim was poor.[52] Just as the Word, because he is God, cannot be stoned, it could be said that the stones cannot touch Gregory because he is deified. Gregory, in this section of the *De vita sua*, calls himself a disciple of the Word, and says that he has done no wrong. Such a remark means something other than simple self-righteousness. It can remind us of Christ's own reaction when stones are picked up to be hurled at

---

48. *Or.* 37.17.

49. See Verna E. F. Harrison, "Gregory Nazianzen's Festal Spirituality: Anamnesis and Mimesis," *Philosophy and Theology* 18 (2006): 27–51, esp. 42–43. Harrison draws attention to Gregory's understanding of Christ containing within himself the whole "circle of virtues"; see *Or.* 45.13.

50. *Ep.* 77, trans. adapt. Browne and Swallow.   51. *Or.* 42.13, trans. Daley.

52. *De vita sua* 665–67.

him. Christ says, "I have shown you many good works from my Father. For which of these are you trying to stone me?" (John 10:32). Gregory affirms that while others charged him, "there stood beside me, to defend my account, Christ—who helps those who stand up for his words."[53] Some lines later, Gregory seems to consider his position within the debate of the Antiochene episcopal schism to be as one torn between Paul and Apollos. Gregory states that they never became incarnate for us nor shed the blood of precious suffering, and asks, "Shall we call ourselves after them rather than after the Savior?"[54] As repeatedly elsewhere, Gregory here emphasizes the baptismal dignity of being named for Christ as a Christian.[55]

In his poem *Concerning Himself and the Bishops,* Gregory begins by recalling that he models himself after the commandments of him who suffered and bore with ill-use. Gregory finds, on the other hand, that he should not keep silent as Christ did, so that the wicked should not triumph. He lashes out at those he considers to be his assassins, saying such things as: "Let everyone throw at me, because long ago I have become inured to stonings."[56] The Christological connection becomes even more explicit the second time it appears in this poem. Again, Gregory professes his innocence and says that the only weakness he showed was that he "spared those evil men at whose hands I endured stoning at the very outset. When subjected to the same sufferings as Christ, it seemed the more religious thing to emulate his patience."[57]

This nonretaliatory imitation of Christ's longsuffering also appears in an acrostic poem of iambic trimeter, the first letters of whose first fifteen lines spell "Of Gregory the Priest."[58] Gregory speaks of how evil men attacked him. He says, "I was held by stones on either side, imitating the Savior, the keystone."[59] Later in this same acrostic poem he speaks directly to Christ: "Christ, I dare to say some of what is in my heart. They abuse with challenges and my stones."[60] Here, Gregory imagines himself to be the unwavering mark of truth by defending the Holy Spirit's equal divinity.

53. *De rebus suis* 673–74, trans. adapt. White.   54. *De rebus suis* 683, trans. adapt. White.
55. See, for example, *Ors.* 4.76; 14.15; and 43.21. This honor contrasts with Emperor Julian's epithet of "the Galileans" for Christians.
56. *Carm.* 2.1.12.32–33, trans. adapt. Meehan.   57. *Carm.* 2.1.12.104–6, trans. adapt. Meehan.
58. *Carm.* 2.1.14, "On Himself and against the Envious, an Acrostic."
59. *Carm.* 2.1.14.14–15, trans. Abrams Rebillard.
60. *Carm.* 1.1.14.31–32, trans. Abrams Rebillard.

Conclusion: Stoning as Image of Deification

Examples of Christ's stoning and Gregory's stoning could continue, as Gregory mentions these stonings over twenty times in his works.[61] However, I want in conclusion to draw attention to two matters. First, in Gregory's intertexuality, perhaps the centerpiece is left implicit. How so? Gregory habitually alludes to scriptural texts and offers pregnant turns of phrase. Frances Young reminds her readers that in his use of the Scriptures Gregory would have been familiar with the idea of Menander who says, "You should not ... quote the whole passage, since it is generally familiar and well known, but adapt it."[62] In mentioning Christ's stoning and his own, Gregory certainly emphasizes the significance of defending the Trinity by affirming both Christ's divinity and the Holy Spirit's. But could it be that frequent recourse to Christ's stoning alongside his own Gregory draws attention—by his silence—to the phrase in Psalm 82:6 "You are gods," quoted in John 10:34? This verse of all the Scriptures stands arguably as the most influential for the development of the teaching of deification before the fifth century.[63] Yet Gregory, who often speaks of becoming gods, never offers a direct quotation of the verse.[64] Gregory's call for people to remember his stoning identifies him with Christ, who in these Gospel passages reveals his divinity, professes his innocence, is patient and merciful, enacts what was previously written in the Scriptures, and points to the deification of others. In short, this evangelical description of Christ hints at what Gregory seeks to be in his own life.

61. See the examples of *Or.* 23.5; 29.20; 31.1; 33.1, 13; 37.4; 38.18; 41.5; and 42.27; *Ep.* 77; *Carm.* 2.1.11.665–67; 2.1.12.33, 103; 2.1.14.31–38; 2.1.15.7–12; 2.1.17.47–48; 2.1.19.13–16; 2.1.30.54–56; 2.1.30.123–28; 2.1.33.12; 2.1.59.3–7; and 2.1.93.10.

62. Menander, *Consolatory Speech, Treatise* 2.9.413.25ff, in *Menander Rhetor*, edited and translated by Donald Andrew Russell and Nigel Guy Wilson (Oxford: Clarendon: Press, 1981), 162; cf. Frances M. Young, *Biblical Exegesis and the Formation of Christian Culture* (Peabody, Mass. Hendrickson, 2002), 103.

63. For the influence of Psalm 82:6, see Carl Mosser, "The Earliest Patristic Interpretation of Psalm 82, Jewish Antecedents, and the Origins of Christian Deification," *Journal of Theological Studies*, n.s. 56 (2005): 30–74.

64. The *Biblia Patristica* references yield no quotations and only a few allusions: *Ep.* 178 and *Or.* 1.5; 14.23; 33.15; and 36.11. In his study on the Cappadocian approach to deification, Norman Russell notes that Gregory never quotes 2 Peter 1:4 (which became more popular for the theology of deification after Gregory), but Russell mentions Psalm 82:6 obliquely. Russell comments on *Or.* 7.23: "In this passage, which concludes a meditation on the Pauline theme of putting to death the 'earthly members' (Col 3:5), the Irenaean interpretation of the gods of Psalm 82:6 as those made sons of God through baptism is not far below the surface"; see Norman Russell, *The Doctrine of Deification in the Greek Patristic Tradition* (Oxford: Oxford University Press, 2004), 217.

The second point in this connection reinforces an argument made by Frederick Norris on Gregory contemplating the beautiful through both human misery and divine mystery. Norris writes:

That need for contemplation of God led to a vision of knowing and persuading through images, a demand that theology be marked by suggestive imagination rather than analytic subtlety. Or perhaps more precisely, employing analytic subtlety as the expected method in the search for the nature of God, and thus discovering its inadequacy, led to the choice of compelling images as the way to approach the unapproachable.[65]

Gregory's poetic contemplation of God's reality through biblical images can lead us from the suffering we experience to the One who comes down to be with us in our suffering. The cross is certainly the most compelling New Testament image, combining human misery and divine mystery in a call to draw us toward conformity to Christ. However, no one after Christ was recorded in the New Testament as literally crucified, and death on the cross was not a threat in Gregory's day. This differs markedly from the image of stoning, which we continue to see in the New Testament, not only for the death of Stephen the first martyr, but also in the sufferings of Paul, the Apostle "who lived in nothing other than in Christ."[66] Moreover, Gregory records in *Or.* 33 how just "yesterday" Arians greeted an old man who had just returned from exile with stones in the middle of the day and middle of the city.[67] Stonings were therefore in the Scriptures and in the news. For those familiar with biblical allusions, and even with the real threat of stoning in life, this potent image could be read to unite not only Gregory, but also Gregory's audience, to Christ.

To be sure, through Christomorphic autobiography and autobiographical Christology, Gregory commingles the life of Christ with his own for a pastoral purpose. In particular, Gregory's blend of Christ's stoning with his own may far surpass the autobiographical quality of Libanius's stoning and Liba-

65. Frederick W. Norris, "Gregory Contemplating the Beautiful: Knowing Human Misery and Divine Mystery Through and Being Persuaded by Images," in *Gregory of Nazianzus: Images and Reflections*, edited by Jostein Børtnes and Tomas Hägg, 19–35 (Copenhagen: Museum Tusculanum Press, 2006), 20–21.

66. *Or.* 32.15, trans. Vinson; cf. Acts 7:54–8:1 and 14:19; and 2 Cor 11:25.

67. *Or.* 33.5. Moreschini follows Elias of Crete and sees that this remark refers to the murder of Eusebius of Samosata. Gregory addressed *Ep.* 42; 44; 64; 65; and 66 to Eusebius, whom he highly esteemed; see Moreschini, SC 318:168–69, n2. Gregory himself immediately emphasizes how "we" forgive those who are the perpetrators, and in *Or.* 33.13 quotes Stephen's prayer from Acts 7:60.

nius's other reported sufferings. For through Gregory's life, Christian readers are invited to see the life of Christ himself and are summoned to take Gregory's side, which is the side of Christ, and be divinized like Gregory. They, too, can live out the verses of Scripture in complete baptismal conformity with the Savior. Again, in this model bishop's own closing words: "Children, for my sake 'guard what has been entrusted to you'; remember my stoning! The grace of our Lord Jesus Christ be with you all! Amen."[68]

68. *Or.* 42.27, trans. Daley. I am grateful for the assistance of Brian E. Daley, SJ, Douglas E. Finn, and Austin G. Murphy, OSB.

10. Bishops Behaving Badly

Helladius Challenges Gregory of Nazianzus and Gregory of Nyssa

Scholars have generally overlooked the interpersonal exchanges in the lives of Gregory of Nazianzus and Gregory of Nyssa, since they are tangential to the study of theological anthropology and the Trinity. Such are the "Helladius affairs," the rousing stories of Bishop Helladius' contentious behavior against Gregory of Nazianzus and Gregory of Nyssa.[1] These mundane events not only give valuable biographical information, they also isolate moments in their individual lives within the context of their social situations as powerful bishops. In the fourth century a bishop's social status was fraught with the Christian prescriptions of humility, poverty, and retreat from the world, which indeed complicated the exercise of power. Though the Gregories took these prescriptions seriously, each made his own accommodation to the exercise of power as the situation warranted. An ongoing problem is assessing Bishop Helladius' sincerity toward these Christian injunctions, since we have only the writings of the two Gregories.

As they expose his egregious behavior, the Helladius affairs are gripping and even entertaining. They also reveal much more about both Gregories in

1. For brevity and to distinguish the two Gregories, I sometimes refer to Gregory of Nazianzus as "Nazianzen" and to Gregory of Nyssa as "Nyssen," following the usage in Greek, "Nazianzenos," and "Nyssenos."

their later years. The endurance of their friendship contrasts sharply with other episcopal friendships that went awry, depending on the vagaries of the politics. Though both Gregories suffered Helladius' wrath, each handled the vexing situations differently, reflecting unique personalities and stages of life. After 381 and in his sixties, Nazianzen wanted nothing more than peace, quiet, and retreat from the public stage. By contrast, though Nyssen was only about five years younger, his career was rising. He had taken up the mantle of his elder brother Basil, earning him the respect of most people and the envy of a few, like Helladius.

The analysis of the Helladius affairs highlights the variety of styles of episcopal administration in the late fourth century, and how sensitive the power of the episcopacy was to political change. Bishops, including both Gregories, gained and lost territory with the shift of a boundary line by imperial edict; sees were awarded through private negotiations; and some bishops assumed it as their privilege to name their own successor. The events take us through some more offensive episodes of church politics.

The Helladius affairs also mark the role an individual bishop's personal gifts, such as intelligence, rhetorical skill, and spiritual discernment, played in his exercise of power. Though the episcopal office carried with it rights bestowed by consecration, we see how the laity and the imperial court alike acclaimed the personal gifts of the bishop. These were not transferable by the "laying on of hands." These accounts document wonderful adventures of episcopal intrigue and clashing personalities, with distinct winners and losers.

The Background

After Basil of Caesarea died in 379, Helladius was consecrated bishop of Caesarea. Nazianzen's letters to Helladius reveal the tenor of their friendship.[2] Helladius apparently had good relations with both Gregories through the 370s and shortly after his consecration. When Nazianzen became bishop of Constantinople in 379, Helladius assertively supported him against the Egyptian cohort that backed his rival Maximus.[3] Nazianzen wrote him three letters when he left Constantinople in 381, expressing floridly his heartfelt thanks to

2. *Ep.* 120, 127, 167, 172, 219, 220.
3. Theodoret, *H.E.*, 5.8, NPNF, 3:136.

Helladius for Easter gifts in a noticeably deferential tone.[4] The letters express Nazianzen's collegiality and respect for Helladius as his superior bishop.[5] In 381 Helladius also attended the Council of Constantinople, and it is then that Helladius' attitude to both Gregories starts to change.

Gregory of Nyssa distinguished himself at the Council of Constantinople as an eminent leader. He delivered the inaugural address at the opening of the Council; he preached at the enthronement of Nazianzen as bishop of Constantinople; and he was prominent in the theological debates against the Eunomian heresy, bringing one of his recent chapters against them in defense of his brother Basil, a treatise his brother Peter had encouraged him to write.[6] Since Basil's death in 379, Nyssen had assumed a great deal of responsibility as a vocal statesman of the church, both as a theologian battling Arians and Eunomians and as a politician supporting Flavian of Antioch.[7] Nyssen also delivered the funeral oration for Bishop Meletius of Antioch, who died during the Council.[8] Helladius perceived that though he had succeeded Nyssen's brother Basil as bishop of Caesarea, Basil's prestige and authority were not automatically his. Those charismatic gifts, deservedly, were lighting on Basil's brother Gregory.

Even worse, Helladius realized that Nyssen's outstanding accomplishments at the Council won him recognition from both the imperial court and the church.

In Edict 16.1.3, July 30, 381, Emperor Theodosius I named Gregory of Nyssa as one of the three bishops of the Diocese of Pontus to whom "all churches shall immediately be surrendered." The other two were Helladius himself and Otreius of Melitene, both orthodox Trinitarians.[9] Eight other bishops were listed, including Nazianzen's cousin, Amphilochius of Iconium. Though Helladius was recognized by the emperor, the edict blurred the lines between a small-town bishop of Nyssa and the bishop of Caesarea, the provincial capital.

Nyssen's ascendancy obviously irked Helladius. Compounding this, in 382 and 385 the imperial court chose Nyssen to deliver the funeral orations for child princess Pulcheria, and then for her mother, Empress Flacilla. A few

4. *Ep.* 120, 127, 172.   5. *Ep.* 120, 127, 172.

6. Gregory of Nyssa, *Ep.* 29 GNO (= *Ep.* 1 NPNF). See *Gregorii Nysseni Epistulae,* in *Gregorii Nysseni Opera,* vol. 8.2, edited by Georgius Pasquali (Berlin: Weidmann, 1921), 59–66.

7. For a different chronology see Gregory of Nyssa, *Lettres,* ed. Pierre Maraval, SC 178, 19–23.

8. Gregory of Nyssa, *Melet.,* NPNF, 5:513–17.   9. CTh 16.1.3.

years later Nyssen traveled to Palestine and Arabia, settling ecclesiastical disputes. Given these events, Helladius' later behavior demonstrates that he was quite sensitive to changes in the ecclesiastical landscape that mitigated his authority.

Theodosius' decisions continued to diminish Helladius' power. In 379–382, Theodosius reversed Valens' edict dividing Cappadocia. But in 382–383 he redivided Cappadocia. Until then Helladius had enjoyed episcopal jurisdiction over the entire province, including both the towns of Nyssa and Nazianzus. With the redivision, Nyssa remained under the jurisdiction of Cappadocia I under Helladius of Caesarea. But the town of Nazianzus reverted to Cappadocia II under Theodore of Tyana. Helladius' frustrations with his shrinking authority exploded first against Gregory of Nazianzus and then against Gregory of Nyssa.

Gregory of Nazianzus and Helladius

The troubles between the two bishops stemmed from Gregory's appointment of his cousin Eulalius as his successor to the see of Nazianzus in 382–383. Once Helladius discovered Nazianzen's intentions, though Gregory was no longer in his diocese, he thwarted and bullied Gregory. Helladius' subsequent vindictiveness against Nazianzen indicates that his reaction had much more to do with his desperate loss of power than Nazianzen's actions. Their friendship would not survive the redivision of Cappadocia.

Yet other bishops too had difficulties with changing diocesan boundaries. After the Council of Constantinople, tired and in poor health, Nazianzen resigned as the bishop of the capital due to infighting, rivalry, and contention over the propriety of his accession. He returned to Nazianzus and resumed the administration of his father's church. His friend Theodore had been with him in Constantinople in 379; they shared a special bond, having both been persecuted by the Arians. Safely in Nazianzus, Gregory wrote letters to Theodore that exhibit warm friendship, especially in congratulations when Theodore was consecrated bishop of Tyana in 382.[10] The sincerity between these two friends is most obvious in these letters. There is no trace of the formality a suffragen bishop would use to call upon his superior.

10. Gregory of Nazianzus, *Ep.* 77, 115, 122, 123, 124.

The good relationship would end. Two more letters to Theodore mark the intrusion of ecclesiastical politics into their friendship due to Cappadocia's redivision. No longer was Theodore his episcopal friend; he was his ecclesiastical superior. Nazianzen's formal plea to Theodore states that he must be allowed to retire due to his failing health, and consequently "this church needs a bishop."[11] The strident request suggests that his superiors had ignored his resignation. Gregory's letter lacks the former familiarity and friendship. "If the Province had any other head, it would have been my duty to cry out and protest it continually. But since Your Reverence is the Superior, it is to you I must look."[12] Significantly he mentions that he sent word to "Eulalius the Chorespisopus and Celeusius" to help him subdue some Apollinarians. Eulalius was Gregory's cousin, and his role in the Helladius affair was the central issue.

With his significant episcopal friendships sundered, Gregory sought other alliances. He wrote to Olympius, his former provincial governor, expressing his dismay at the redivision of Cappadocia. "No longer is the great Olympius with us,... we are betrayed,... we have become again the Second Cappadocia."[13] Though Nazianzen had maintained a good working relationship with the governor, Olympius had jurisdiction over Cappadocia I only. It is telling that Nazianzen rather desperately called on his former *provincial* governor, not his former *bishop,* the mercurial Helladius.

In sum, these letters capture the effects of the redivision of Cappadocia as they overflowed into Nazianzen's personal life. Unwittingly his relationships were caught in the change of administration. With power shifting from one bishop and governor to another, old friendships were tested by the obligations of bureaucratic office, and Nazianzen found himself stripped of the sustaining friendships he had long cultivated and relied upon.

In Gregory's view, his retirement from the Nazianzus church need not cause problems, because his cousin Eulalius could replace him. But his decision triggered uproar. Many bishops opposed Eulalius' appointment since, according to canon law, a bishop while still living could not appoint his suc-

---

11. Gregory of Nazianzus, *Ep.* 152. Gallay dates the letter to 383; *Lettres,* ed. Gallay, 2:43–44, 155.

12. See *Ernst Honigmann,* "Le concile de Constantinople de 394 et les auteurs du Syntagma des XIV titres," in *Trois mémoires posthumes d'histoire et de géographie de l'Orient chrétien,* by Honigmann, Subsidia Hagiographica 35 (Bruxelles: Société des Bollandistes, 1961), 28–32.

13. *Ep.* 154, trans. Browne and Swallow, NPNF 2.7:481.

cessor. Writing to Gregory of Nyssa, Nazianzen expresses genuine incredulity over the ensuing slander. He bemoans the war among the bishops, and he begs his younger, though more powerful friend to quell the gossip and to "restore the Spirit who upholds you and yours."[14] The letter reveals the slanderous versions of the situation circulating against him. "But let no one, I beg, spread false reports about me and my lords the bishops, as though they had proclaimed another bishop in my place against my will."[15]

Continuing with praise of Eulalius, who is "very dear to God," Nazianzen insists that he did not break canon law: "If any be of the opinion that it is not right to ordain another in the lifetime of a Bishop, let him know that he will not in this matter gain any hold upon us. For it is well known that I was appointed, not to Nazianzus, but to Sasima, although for a short time out of reverence for my father, I as a stranger undertook the government."[16] We have to imagine that Nyssen took up his old friend's cause.

The bishops grudgingly agreed to hold an election for Eulalius, but they purposely excluded Nazianzen from participating in the synod. They were angry that he had not ever been present *de facto* in Nazianzus as bishop.[17] In reaction Nazianzen decided to appeal to a new bishop (not Theodore) who was unacquainted with the Eulalius election. He wrote with the hope of acquainting him with the unfairness of the situation, and to ensure that his opponents did not convince him of their rectitude. There was even the outside chance that he could obtain the new bishop's aid. Their friendship ruined, he let his own superior, Bishop Theodore, alone.

Excluded from the election, Nazianzen felt slighted, especially since the new bishop (name unknown) blamed him excessively for retiring.[18] Hence the apologetic, even obsequious tone of the letter, though softened by references

14. *Ep.* 182, trans. Browne and Swallow, NPNF 2.7:461.
15. Ibid.
16. Ibid. See Honigmann, "Le concile de Constantinople de 394 et les auteurs du Syntagma des XIV titres," in *Trois mémoires*, 1–83; Paul Devos, "S. Grégoire de Nazianze et Hellade de Césarée en Cappadoce," *Analecta Bollandiana* 19 (1961): 92–101; and Devos, "S. Pierre Ier, Évêque de Sebastée, dans une lettre de S. Grégoire de Nazianze," *Analecta Bollandiana* 79 (1961): 347–60. They claim that Gregory of Nazianzus wrote the letter. I agree rather with Pierre Maraval, "L'athenticité de la lettre 1 de Grégoire de Nysse," *Analecta Bollandiana* 102 (1984): 61–70, who concludes that Nyssen is the author; but he does not think that the "Peter" is Nyssen's brother. I do; see Gregory of Nyssa, *Lettres*, ed. Maraval,84–87.
17. Gregory of Nazianzus, *Ep.* 157.
18. Gregory of Nazianzus, *Ep.* 139, is incorrectly attributed to Theodore of Tyana.

to Nazianzen's old age and poor health. He fervently wanted to air his side of the story, while not overtly directing the hierarch to take action. He hoped both to vindicate himself and to get the bishop's support, since he was "for the most part unacquainted with our history."[19]

Nazianzen's troubles continued. Helladius monitored the situation from Caesarea, across the artificial border that redivided Cappadocia, though he legally could do nothing. At the synod called to settle the Eulalius situation, Bishop Bosporius of Colonia took the lead. Helladius objected to Eulalius' election and was livid at Bosporius' role at the synod, accusing him of heresy.[20] The charges had much more to do with Helladius' loss of his suffragen bishops than Bosporius' orthodoxy.[21] At the time of Cappadocia's redivision, Colonia was part of Cappadocia II. Thus Helladius had lost Colonia and its huge contiguous area to Theodore of Tyana. Yet Helladius persisted. After bitter dissention, Helladius won; in 383 a synod tried Bosporius at Parnassus.

Helladius' calumny and malicious rumors stunned Gregory. Even though Eulalius had been elected bishop of Nazianzus, the charges against Bosporius took on a life of their own. So Nazianzus summoned more allies.[22] To one unnamed bishop he iterates that Helladius' wrong-headed positions are causing the problem: "My Lord the God-beloved Bishop Helladius must cease to waste his labour on our concerns. For it is not through spiritual earnestness, but through party zeal, that he is seeking this; and not for the sake of accurate compliance with the canons, but for the satisfaction of anger."[23] He implores the bishop to judge Bosporius fairly, so that the "novel accusation" be done away with and the "slander" cease. Helladius' anger stemmed from losing half of his diocese, not Gregory's actions.

Gregory also called on his cousin Amphilochius of Iconium. Thanks to his cousin's presence at the synod in Parnassus, Bosporius was exonerated by the ecclesiastical court.[24] Significantly Nazianzen successfully enlisted the aid

19. Gregory of Nazianzus, *Ep.* 139.
20. Gregory of Nazianzus, *Ep.* 139; see also *Ep.* 183 (NPNF 2.7.462).
21. Gallay, *Lettres,* 2:161; Jean Daniélou, "Grégoire de Nysse à travers les lettres de S. Basile et de S. Grégoire de Nazianze," *Vigiliae Christianae* 19 (1965): 31–41, here 40.
22. Gregory of Nazianzus, *Ep.* 183, 185, 184.
23. Gregory of Nazianzus, *Ep.* 183, trans. Browne and Swallow, NPNF 2.7: 474–75
24. Gregory of Nazianzus, *Ep.* 184. Parnassus was 24 miles northwest of Nyssa; see William Mitchell Ramsay, *The Historical Geography of Asia Minor,* Papers of the Royal Geographical Society 4 (Amsterdam: Adolf M. Hakkert, 1962), 298–99, and Gregory of Nazianzus, *Lettres,* ed. Gallay, 2:161.

of Nectarius, bishop of Constantinople, in order to avoid an embarrassing civil trial for Bosporius.[25]

Finally, Helladius' vengefulness emerged when Nazianzen was forced to protect the priest Sarcerdos in the mid- to late 380s. Sarcerdos, then quite old, lived in a monastic community and ministered to poor people.[26] For oblique reasons, Helladius accused him unjustly and threw him out of the community. Nazianzen refused to tolerate both Helladius' belligerence and his deliberate defamation.

Writing with the freedom that comes with old age, Nazianzen demands that Helladius gives his exhortation a just hearing.[27] He characterizes Helladius' attitude toward Sarcerdos as jaded, slanderous, and ignorant of facts. Implying Helladius' pitilessness, Nazianzen urges him to practice mercy on aged Sarcerdos, on the poor people Sarcerdos serves, and on the monastic brethren so afflicted by Sarcerdos' plight. Nazianzen thus branded Helladius as a slanderer and a mean-spirited man. He ends the letter tellingly by ordering: "forgive both Sarcerdos (and himself), say nothing unworthy about him, write nothing unworthy about him, and finally if some letter be in his possession to that effect, destroy it."[28]

Unsurprisingly Helladius did not comply. His reply to Nazianzen was so rancorous it left him at a loss for words.[29] Nazianzen was so determined to rescue Sarcerdos that he informed Helladius he was sending a monastic brother out to investigate the situation, "furnishing proof of his innocence and exposing the invented lies."

Changing politics framed the hostility between Nazianzen and Helladius. Nazianzen represented himself as one caught in the fray. His leadership style, though, never changed. He had learned episcopal management, in part, from his father, so it is no wonder he saw nothing wrong in the appointment of his cousin. He relied on the goodwill of his social network, confident in the trustworthiness of relatives, cultivating old friends and new acquaintances, and respectfully soliciting the help of his superiors.

Yet remarkably, so did Helladius! What differed between them were their

25. Gregory of Nazianzus, *Ep.* 185 (NPNF 2.7.470).

26. Gregory of Nazianzus, *Ep.* 99, 168–70, 209–21 deal with Sarcerdos, though not all on this incident.

27. Gregory of Nazianzus, *Ep.* 219.   28. Gregory of Nazianzus, *Ep.* 219.

29. Gregory of Nazianzus, Ep. 220.

methods, reactions, and personalities. Helladius took the offensive and was unscrupulous in achieving his goals. Conversely, Nazianzen used a defensive posture. Both were effective means of enacting episcopal power. Nanzianzen often expresses his hurt, disappointment, and incredulousness that such events befell him. Colloquially, one might say that he represented himself as refusing "to play the game."

But did he? Nazianzen was acutely sensitive in interpersonal relationships, as his letters reveal; he was ineffective at protecting himself from Helladius' innumerable attacks. Yet in bewailing his suffering from Helladius' intrigue, Nazianzen exposed his opponent as ridiculous and petty.

Nazianzen's leadership strengths lay in his unwavering commitment to the truth as he saw it and his exceptional intellectual abilities. Though he was unable to command others on the public stage, privately he convinced others through the power of his resoluteness and eloquence. In the Helladius situations, Nazianzen further enhanced these qualities with the freedom of old age. The contrast between his execution of episcopal leadership and Gregory of Nyssa's is distinct, yet Helladius' behavior was so atrocious that both Gregories initially react in similar ways. To Helladius and Gregory of Nyssa we now turn.

Gregory of Nyssa and Helladius

There is little agreement on the chronology of Nyssen's life; the following is a possibility. Scholars agree that after his exile, 374–377, and the death of his illustrious older siblings (Basil d. 379, Macrina d. 380), Nyssen reflected Basil's example more closely. As a powerful bishop, his counsel was widely sought out and his decisions at various councils marked his wise leadership. His outstanding abilities soon commanded the respect of Emperor Theodosius I, governors, and others bishops from all over Asia Minor and the Levant. Circumstance and Nyssen's excellence during this crucial period, 377–383, advanced his rise to power. Though Helladius remained his superior bishop in Cappadocia I, the world's demand for Nyssen's participation outside his diocese made Helladius' power over him practically nil. And as Basil's successor in Caesarea, Helladius viewed Nyssen's power as a personal affront. At each juncture of their interactions, Nyssen rises to the occasion, while Helladius descends to more desperate levels.

Regeste of Nyssen's Accomplishments, 377–394

After his return from exile in 377, Gregory was rarely in Nyssa, his own see. He attended the Council of Antioch nine months after Basil died. The agenda was to heal the Meletian schism and to quash Arianism there.[30] So outstanding was his performance that some scholars think that he was commissioned there to visit Jerusalem and Arabia. We do know that while Gregory was still in Antioch, he felt compelled to visit his dying sister, Macrina. Before her death, he arrived back in Ibora, Pontus.[31] Yet nowhere is there evidence that Nyssen was asked to visit Arabia and Jerusalem at that time. If he visited Macrina right after the Council of Antioch, insufficient travel time would have precluded such visits. Moreover, he was worried about his sister. Events in Gregory's life were so numerous between Antioch and Macrina's death that it would have been impossible for him to fit in a trip to Jerusalem.[32]

Helladius was rankled by Nyssen's growing reputation as a brilliant theologian and efficacious bishop. Soon after Macrina's death, Nyssen learned that Bishop Araxius of Ibora died. The old bishop had attended Macrina's funeral. The town clerics summoned Nyssen back to Ibora—where all his family except Basil was buried—to choose a bishop for them. Under Nyssen's direction, Pansophius was elected.[33] His influence outside the jurisdiction of Nyssa could not have pleased his superior, Helladius—even though Helladius had no authority in Pontus.

Nyssen's fame spread. Called to Sebasteia to settle an internal dispute over bishops, he endured a terrible stay in the "uncivilized" city.[34] The result of his efforts, however, was tremendous: his younger brother Peter was elected bishop of Sebasteia, home of the Forty Martyrs. Shortly thereafter the brothers planned the posthumous defense of their brother Basil against Eunomius.[35] In sum, the respect Nyssen commanded in two nearby communities fueled Helladius' resentments.

When Nyssen took his trips to the Levant is contested, but scholars agree

---

30. Karl Joseph von Hefele, *A History of the Christian Councils (to A.D. 451): From the Original Documents,* trans. William R. Clark (Edinburgh: T. and T. Clark, 1871), 2:91.

31. Gregory of Nyssa, *Life,* 39–40; and Gregory of Nyssa, *La vie de Sainte Macrine,* ed. Pierre Maraval, *SC* 178.

32. Gregory of Nyssa, *Ep.* 19.   33. Gregory of Nyssa, *Ep.* 19.

34. Gregory of Nyssa, *Ep.* 5, 19, 18, 22, and perhaps 10; *Ep.* 19.18; see Pasquali, *Epistulae,* 59–66.

35. Gregory of Nyssa, *Ep.* 29, 30 GNO (= *Ep.* 1, 2, NPNF). See Pasquali, *Epistulae,* 84–88.

that these visits were instrumental in solidifying his authority as an ecclesiastical statesman throughout Christendom. He likely made three trips to Jerusalem, one personal, taken perhaps during his exile between 374 and 378; another between Macrina's death and the Second Ecumenical Council in 381; and the third in the mid-380s.[36]

Unlike the councils of 379 and 394, the emperor called the Second Ecumenical Council. Impressed with Nyssen's leadership there, the emperor gave him imperial backing to settle disputes in Jerusalem and Arabia, despite the new canon. Nyssen probably took trips between 383 and 386. Nyssen's imperial commission, his influence, and his authority put him beyond Helladius' control. That Nyssen's younger brother Peter was bishop of Sebasteia, that he was close friends with Gregory of Nazianzus, and that he had the imperial court's benefaction made him the target of Helladius' ire.

The Situation from Helladius' Vantage Point

Helladius in the meantime was unable to rein in Nyssen. During this period he not only countered Gregory of Nazianzus whenever possible, he also consolidated his power. The strong friendship of the Gregories and their families, their excellent reputations among clergy and laity alike, and the fact that they were closer than anyone else to Helladius' predecessor, the great Basil whose amazing accomplishments Helladius could never match, all put Helladius at a great disadvantage. Yet he did not give up any of the powers of his office, as his activities illustrate.

In the mid-380s Helladius consecrated a certain Gerontius, of dubious character, to the see of Nicomedia. The earliest evidence of Gerontius' escapades comes from Sozomen.[37] It seems that Gerontius had been a deacon in Milan under Bishop Ambrose. When Ambrose heard what Gerontius was up to through his fantastic story, he put the deacon in penance, prohibiting him from liturgical duties and contact with the laity.

Gerontius reported that he had seen an *Onoscelis,* a type of demon who has a comely human body and the legs of an ass.[38] He grabbed it, decapitat-

---

36. Gregory of Nyssa, *Vita,* and *Ep.* 2, 3, 17; von Hefele, *History of the Christian Councils,* 2:291.
37. Sozomen, *H.E.* 8.8.
38. See *Testament of Solomon* 16–17; Athanasius' *Life of Anthony* 53. The gender of the *Onoskelis* Gerontius saw is unclear.

ed it, and shoved it into a gristmill, with the purpose, one imagines, of "kill-ing" it. Ambrose wisely deemed the deacon unfit for church service. Instead of obeying his bishop, Gerontius fled to Constantinople and ingratiated him-self at the imperial court. Sozomen records that Gerontius was so successful at social networking that he secured Bishop Helladius' son a "high military ap-pointment at court," in exchange for his appointment as bishop of Nicome-dia! Hence the beginning of a long and powerful friendship.

Although the correspondence is lost, Ambrose wrote to Bishop Nectari-us of Constantinople, protesting Gerontius' appointment and demanding his removal, "in order to prevent the continuance of so glaring a violation of all ecclesiastical order."[39] But Nectarius was not likely eager to obey Ambrose for significant personal reasons. When Nectarius was elected bishop of Constan-tinople in 381, after the resignation of Gregory of Nazianzus, Ambrose wrote to Emperor Theodosius, strongly protesting Nectarius' elevation to the epis-copacy, especially since Nectarius was not even baptized at the time.[40] Though it is unlikely that Nectarius ignored Ambrose's demands, he probably did not pursue the matter assiduously. Sozomen only records that Nectarius was un-successful, especially since Gerontius was so popular in Nicomedia. Geron-tius remained firmly in his position during Nyssen's lifetime. Gerontius would eventually meet his match in Nectarius' ardent successor, John Chrysostom, who would finally depose him in 399–400.

Meanwhile Helladius and Gerontius must have sustained friendly ex-changes. We next meet them as attendees listed in the official roster of the lo-cal council of Constantinople in 394, which was called by Bishop Nectarius; here Gregory is listed as "Gregory of Nyssa."[41] This is the last reference to an event in Gregory's career; he was probably in his mid-sixties then. Yet there is a discrepancy in the manuscripts regarding the correct names. Some show "Pal-ladius of Caesarea" and "Gerontius of Claudiopolis," not "Nicomedia."[42] Oth-er manuscripts and the evidence emerging from Theodore Balsamon's work reveal that these are most likely orthographic errors, but perhaps not inadver-

---

39. Sozomen, *H.E.* 8.8, trans. C. D. Hartranft, NPNF 2.2:403.

40. Ambrose of Milan, *Ep.* 13, 14.

41. The synod was to settle a dispute over episcopal accession in Arabia; see von Hefele, *History of the Christian Councils,* 2:406–7.

42. See Honigmann, *Trois Mémoires,* 35, referring to manuscripts compiled by Mansi: "'Pallade' est une fausse leçon dans le texte des actes de 394, qui ne se trouve que chez Théodore Balsamon, tandis que les meilleurs manuscrits portent 'Helladios.'"

tent.[43] The slip of the pen creating "Palladius" for "Helladius" is explainable, but "Claudiopolis" for "Nicomedia" appears deliberate. Since both are cities of Bithynia, a scribe could have substituted the less important city, Claudiopolis, for Nicomedia.[44] Even more likely, the scribe could have been so devoted to the next bishop of Constantinople, the formidable John Chrysostom, that he erased the memory of the two ignominious bishops Helladius and Gerontius. Helladius had consecrated Gerontius, and John Chrysostom succeeded finally in deposing him.

Thus it would appear that by the time of the council in 394, Helladius' reprehensible reputation extended to Milan. It is also evident that even though Helladius and Gerontius attended the council of 394, from the time of John Chrysostom's episcopacy those in ecclesiastical authority saw fit to efface the memory of these two shameful bishops. Most importantly, clearly any efforts Nectarius might have made to curtail their activities were ultimately unsuccessful. Helladius and Gerontius were too clever and popular. And this brings us to back Gregory of Nyssa. For the church in the later 380s, only someone of Nyssen's stature could have toppled these two unworthy bishops, which leads to the following evidence imbricating Nyssen and Helladius further.

It seems Bishop Nectarius attempted, albeit half-heartedly, to comply with Ambrose's protests over Gerontius' consecration as bishop of Nicomedia. Ambrose probably made his formal request sometime between 385 and 389. Gregory of Nyssa's *Letter* 17 to the church of Nicomedia appears to address the situation of a "bad" bishop. I suggest that Bishop Nectarius eventually contacted Gregory of Nyssa in the late 380s requesting his aid in ousting Gerontius. Nyssen responded affirmatively by writing the letter to the Nicomedians, though soon after felt the wrath of his provincial bishop, Helladius.[45]

In his formal letter to the Nicomedians, Gregory carefully employs Pauline echoes in order to maintain their respect, since it was a delicate matter for him to intrude in the affairs of their diocese.[46] He never mentions the problematic bishop by name. Gregory defends why he would dare encroach on the affairs of the church at Nicomedia, leaving the impression that he was both

43. Theodore Balsamon, Byzantine canonist, late twelfth century.

44. Ramsay, *Historical Geography*, 182, 318.

45. Jean Daniélou, "L'Évêque d'après une lettre de Grégoire de Nysse," *Euntes Docete* 2 (1967): 85–97, but he believes Gerontius was not appointed yet.

46. Gregory of Nyssa, *Lettres*, ed. Maraval, 216.

uncomfortable in so doing and unfamiliar with the internal politics of that diocese.

Significantly he says he was "not neglectful of the charge entrusted to us, either in time past or since the departure of Patricius of blessed memory."[47] It could be construed that the "charge" refers to the mandate Gregory received at the Second Ecumenical Council, appointing him as a "guardian of Orthodoxy."[48] In that case, Gregory was only one of eight bishops mentioned in that imperial mandate, which also included Helladius himself, equal to Nyssen as a "protector of the faith." On that basis any of those bishops could have intervened, and indeed Helladius could have used his mandate as justification for his consecrating Gerontius in the first place! On the other hand, the "charge" could be a request from Nectarius, the bishop of Constantinople, which had originated from Ambrose of Milan. The imperial mandate would have given further justification to his actions.

Nicomedia's bishop Patricius had died awhile before, since Gregory alludes both to his own busy schedule and his "advancing years."[49] References to his infirmity and old age point to a later date for the letter, probably between 389 and 391.[50] In this case, Gerontius would have had time to ensconce himself in the diocese and to aggravate other bishops; moreover Nyssen's intervention would be fresh in Helladius' mind.[51] Secondly, Nyssen's reference to his only connection to the church of Nicomedia, Bishop Euphrasius, "of blessed memory," attendee at the Second Ecumenical Council and predecessor of Patricius, would fully support a later date. Gregory used the tradition of their church to illustrate his venerable connection to their past. Finally, acknowledging that they did not ask him "by letter" to intervene, he elaborately justifies his intervention.

Asking whether Gerontius was already in power or whether Nyssen was called to influence an election in Nicomedia, especially to counter some Arian factionalism, as possible reasons for Nyssen's intervention are legitimate questions.[52] Yet Nyssen makes no mention of heresies. As the strongest voice of

47. Daniélou, "L'Évêque," 85.

48. Gregory of Nyssa, *Lettres,* ed. Maraval, 39, 216.

49. Gregory of Nyssa, *Ep.* 17, GNO (= *Ep.* 13). On Gregory's excuses, Daniélou, "L'Évêque," 87–88.

50. Gregory of Nyssa, *Lettres,* ed. Maraval, 216, gives the date of 385.

51. Daniélou, "L'Évêque," 86, 88.

52. For views that Gerontius accedes after Nyssen's letter, see Gregory of Nyssa, *Lettres,* ed. Maraval, 39; and Daniélou, "L'Évêque," 87.

Trinitarian orthodoxy since Basil's death, Nyssen would have mentioned a heretical theological party. Moreover, evidence indicating the premise that Gerontius was not yet elected is lacking. Yet there is evidence that Helladius had already appointed him. Gregory states that he is intervening in their affairs; he makes excuses that ties between the churches have been allowed to lapse since 381; and he bemoans the fact that their situation is so grave that he must try to rectify it: "either by our taking charge of you,... so as to discover a means of rectifying the disorders which have already found place,... that we were afflicted upon hearing from those who reported to us your state, that there was no return to better things."[53]

Clearly the damage had already occurred. Gerontius was their bishop. Nicomedia's existing temporarily without a bishop would not have caused such consternation. Though difficult to use as direct evidence, Sozomen's report supports the contention. He records that Helladius essentially foisted Gerontius on the church of Nicomedia in exchange for Gerontius' procuring a prominent position at court for Helladius' son. One cannot imagine that Helladius engineered such a "backroom deal" for Gerontius at a full-fledged synod of the bishops of Nicomedia. Were Gerontius not already bishop, there would have been no situation to redress; as Nyssen says, "the disorders which have already found place." Bishops all over Christendom had taken measures to stop the egregious behavior on the part of both Helladius and Gerontius. Ambrose of Milan had alerted Nectarius of Constantinople, who failed in deposing Gerontius, so Nectarius called on Gregory of Nyssa. Hence Gregory's apologetic tone comes from a kind of embarrassment for the deplorable situation.

Moreover, as Nyssen lays out the qualifications of a true bishop, he backhandedly impugns Gerontius. By highlighting the qualities of a reputable bishop, he asks the Nicomedians to oust their unworthy bishop and choose another. These oblique references to the likes of Gerontius, contrasting so well with Gregory's lucid descriptions of the qualifications of a worthy bishop, sum up his point: their present bishop is hopelessly unsuitable compared to the ecclesiastical ideal.[54] Thus he seeks to shock the Nicomedians into having the courage to oust the interloper and to choose a worthy bishop. Before launch-

---

53. Gregory of Nyssa, *Ep.* 13, trans. W. Moore and H. A. Wilson, NPNF, 2.5:535.
54. Gregory of Nyssa, *Ep.* 17.5–29.

ing into the description of an ideal bishop, he casts barbs against someone who can only be called a meddler. Most likely Nyssen is speaking about Helladius, the instigator of the problem in Nicomedia. "But as for you, you should watch your own affairs, so that a better situation come about for your church."[55] We must remember that Gerontius had escaped from Milan to Constantinople, ingratiated himself with gullible laity and clerics alike, and wrested an episcopal appointment out of Helladius.

Nyssen's apprehension that someone is now wreaking havoc on the church is obvious. "For it is disgraceful, brethren, and utterly monstrous, that while no one ever becomes a pilot unless he is skilled in navigation, he who sits at the helm of the Church *should not know how to bring the souls of those who sail with him safe into the haven of God.*"[56] The description aptly fits Gerontius as one who is hardly an example of virtue, since he had none. The Nicomedians were stuck with a bishop who likes the "trappings of outward show," has powerful friends, boasts about his achievements and large income, and "has his mind on all sides *clouded with the fumes of self-esteem!*" Gregory warns the Nicomedians to have no dealings with such a person, and to search for "one among them, who shall be a chosen vessel, a pillar of the Church."[57]

Yet Nyssen's efforts failed. Gerontius remained bishop of Nicomedia, and it is safe to presume Helladius' involvement in the matter. Nyssen had succeeded only in angering Helladius further. After Nyssen's intervention with the Nicomedians, Helladius deliberately spread lies against Gregory, and "certain people" told Nyssen. A few years passed, and sometime within 392–394, Helladius and Gregory would have a disastrous meeting in the mountainous countryside around Sebasteia.

Nyssen went to Sebasteia to celebrate the memorial of his deceased brother Peter and the feast of the Holy Martyrs. He decided to visit Helladius

---

55. Gregory of Nyssa, *Ep.* 17.8–9:51: "οὐ γάρ νόμος ἐστὶ τοῖς ἀλλοῖς πρὸς τὸ μὴ τὰ δέοντα πράσσειν τὸ παρ᾽ ἑτέροις μὴ δεόντως γινόμενον. ἀλλ᾽ ὑμᾶς χρὴ τὰ ἑαυτῶν βλέπειν, ὅπως ἂν πρός τὸ κρεῖττον γένοιτο ἡ τῆς ἐκκλησίας ἐπίδοσις." "For it is not lawful that the simple should meddle with that with which they have no concern, but which properly belongs to others. For you should each mind your own business"; trans. Moore and Wilson (NPNF, 2.5:536), who regard this passage as "unintelligible" and "incomplete." And Maraval's translation: "S'il en est d'indifférents, ou que nous-mêmes le soyons, que personne en voyant cela ne soit troublé dans sa propre conduite: ce qui est fait par les uns d'une manière qui ne convient pas n'autorise pas les autres à mettre en oeuvre ce qui ne convient pas" (Gregory of Nyssa, *Lettres,* ed. Maraval, 221).

56. Gregory of Nyssa, *Ep.* 13, trans. Moore and Wilson, NPNF, 2.5:537.

57. Gregory of Nyssa, *Ep.* 13, trans. Moore and Wilson, NPNF, 2.5:537.

quite spontaneously when he began his journey back to Cappadocia. "Finally, after having celebrated the memory of blessed Peter, who was celebrated for the first time by the inhabitants of Sebasteia, and after having commemorated with them at the same time the memory of the Holy Martyrs, whom they always celebrated, I set off for my own church."[58] Meeting face to face in the mountainous area of eastern Cappadocia at a martyr's shrine, Helladius succeeded in insulting him. Nyssen's horrible experience with Helladius so infuriated him that he felt compelled to write to his friend, Bishop Flavian of Antioch, to whom he had written before about the troublesome bishop.[59] Therein he documents the pervasive extent of Helladius' activities to exact his revenge on Gregory.

Gregory complains to Flavian that he was "not in a good way." Helladius' hatred was like a spreading fire, consuming everything, so that "piety, truth, and peace" ceased to exist. "Certain persons had informed me that the Right Reverend Helladius had unfriendly feelings towards me, and that he enlarged in conversation to everyone upon the troubles that I had brought upon him."[60] On his journey home, his entourage ran into some of Helladius' group, since they too were at a shrine in the mountains celebrating the Holy Martyrs. To dispel the growing tension and aggravating problems caused by Helladius' mounting anger, Nyssen took a detour to meet him. But it was a mistake.

Nyssen records that his group braved steep terrain in the wilds of Armenia to get to Helladius' location. The journey took them a day out of their way in the tiring heat. When they arrived, Helladius ignored Nyssen and his entourage, forcing them to wait for hours in the sun. When he finally appeared, Helladius refused to greet him properly, let alone show proper hospitality. Nyssen broke the uncomfortable silence by asking whether he should leave. Helladius responded petulantly that he was angry with Nyssen "for *all* he had

---

58. Gregory of Nyssa, *Ep.* 1, GNO 1.5–6.2: "καὶ τέλος, τὴν μνήμην τοῦ μακαριωτάτου Πέτρου παρὰ Σεβαστηνοῖς πρώτως ἀγομένην ἐπιτελέσας, καὶ τὰς συνήθως παρ᾽ αὐτῶν ἐπιτελουμένας τῶν ἁγίων μαρτύρων μνήμας κατὰ τὸν αὐτὸν χρόνον συνδιαγαγὼν ἐκείνοις, ἐπὶ τὴν ἐμαυτοῦ πάλιν ἐκκλησίαν ὑπέστρεφον."; trans. Moore and Wilson, *NPNF*, 2.5:47. Gallay's translation: "Enfin, après avoir célébré la mémoire du bienheureux Pierre que l'on fêtait pour la première fois chez les habitants de Sébaste, et après avoir du même coup passé avec eux le temps de la commémoraison des saints martyrs qu'ils ont coutume de célébrer, je reprenais le chemin de ma propre Église"; Gallay, *Lettres*, 2:140.

59. Gregory of Nyssa, *Lettres*, ed. Maraval, 39. He posits that *Ep.* 17 *probably* had something to do with Helladius' attack on Gregory for "multiple offenses," but he does not connect the letter with the *Letter to Flavian*.

60. Gregory of Nyssa, *Ep.* 13, trans. Moore and Wilson, NPNF, 2.5:546.

done against him."[61] Nyssen replied that lies have no place in the Divine Judgment, but if he had given him offence, may he never be forgiven. Helladius' reply was indignation.

At dusk the baths were readied at the martyrium and the feast prepared. But Helladius specifically asked Nyssen and his party to depart! They were exhausted, hungry, and hot, and still they were forced to leave. Incredulous at Helladius's incalculable rudeness, Nyssen nevertheless set out to his own city. Venting his frustrations, he wrote to Flavian, "for it was because his designs were not checked on *former occasions* that he has proceeded to this unmeasured display of vanity." For "he must be taught that he is human, and has no authority to insult and to disgrace those who possess the same beliefs and the same rank as himself."[62] He points out that Helladius' accusations were spurious; that no church council had convicted him nor even brought up charges. Perceptively, Nyssen attributes Helladius' anger to jealousy of his lineage, his education, his speaking ability, and probably his wealthy diocese. There is little doubt that he was correct. Yet he felt the obligation to cure Helladius' sickness of "puffed-up pride." We have no record of the resolution between the two bishops, other than a standoff. Helladius and Gerontius outwitted and outlasted both Gregory of Nyssa and Ambrose of Milan.

Changing politics again defined the parameters of the interactions between Nyssen and Helladius. Yet unlike Nazianzen, Nyssen was so occupied with countless responsibilities traveling all over the eastern Mediterranean that he spent no time second-guessing Helladius' challenges. He must have been quite aware of Helladius' anger, because he had alerted Flavian before. But Nyssen felt no need to defend his actions to other bishops, or to reassure himself of their support by means of friendly letters.

As bishop Nyssen became a strong leader. If his involvement in the church of Nicomedia is correct, it shows that he approached the Nicomedian situation with caution, and only when asked by the Bishop of Constantinople, who had been pressed by Ambrose of Milan. Because of the urgency of the situation, Nyssen was willing to invoke his imperial selection in order to sidestep the relatively new canon law prohibiting bishops from intervening in other dioceses' business. It also reveals that he took extraordinary care in delving into

61. Gregory of Nyssa, *Letter to Flavian,* trans. Moore and Wilson, NPNF, 2.5:547.
62. Gregory of Nyssa, *Letter to Flavian,* trans. Moore and Wilson, NPNF, 2.5:547.

the troubles of their diocese. His letter demonstrates that he felt compelled to intercede by virtue of their horrible bishop, but each of his suggestions is conditioned by respect for their autonomy and caution about his own intrusion. Regarding his confrontation with Helladius, we see Nyssen recovering from personal insults by writing to Flavian; but he must have let the matter alone afterward. Though we have no record of their interactions, they would have met again, finally, in 394 at the local council in Constantinople.

Conclusion

The analyses of the Helladius affairs expose various crisis points in the Gregories' lives. We see dramatic flashes of their emotions tempered by the self-assurance of their authority as they each chose their course of action. Their responses to those tenuous circumstances reveal that they utilized their elite social position and their episcopal power as statesmen quite capably.

Though evidence for the Helladius affairs is one-sided, there is little doubt that Bishop Helladius was an obnoxious fellow. But in exercising his episcopal office, his actions mirror what the Gregories themselves did, in the cases of getting their favorite candidates appointed to episcopal office, both by nepotism or favoritism and in going to great lengths to exert influence. It is these quotidian squabbles and contests for power that shape the church no less than the more elevated debates about doctrine. In this sense the fights between the two Gregories and their nemesis, Helladius, reveal a church that, for better or worse, had finally come of age.

Neil McLynn

11. The Tax Man and the Theologian

Gregory, Hellenius, and the Monks of Nazianzus

Gregory Nazianzen's poem "To Hellenius, an Exhortation Concerning the Monks," one of the small group addressed "to others," has rarely been examined as a whole.[1] The purpose of this chapter is to attempt such an examination and to suggest that the work casts a sharper light than has been realized on Gregory's position in local society in the early 370s. I shall also suggest, more controversially, that it bears directly upon Gregory's involvement in theological controversy and even upon his consecration as bishop of Sasima in 372. The sheer quantity of prosopographical information contained in the poem's 368 elegiac verses provides an immediate invitation to the social historian; the remarkably sinuous argument in which he involves his cast of characters, however, demands careful interpretation.

Gregory begins by warning Hellenius that he will not provide the master-

1. For a survey of the *Carmina ad alios,* see Demoen, "Gifts of Friendship that Will Remain for Ever: Personae, Addressed Characters and Intended Audience of Gregory Nazianzen's Epistolary Poems," *Jahrbuch der Österreichischen Byzantinistik* 47 (1997): 1–11; see also Raymond Van Dam, *Kingdom of Snow: Roman Rule and Greek Culture in Cappadocia* (Philadelphia: University of Pennsylvania Press, 2002), 87–89; McLynn, "Among the Hellenists: Gregory and the Sophists," in *Gregory of Nazianzus: Images and Reflections,* edited by J. Børtnes and T. Hägg, 229–33 (Copenhagen: Museum Tusculanum Press, 2006); and McLynn, "'Curiales into Churchmen': The Case of Gregory Nazianzen," in *Le trasformazioni delle élites in età tardoantica: atti del Convegno Internazionale, Perugia, 15–16 marzo 2004,* edited by Rita Lizzi Testa, 277–95 (Rome: "L'Erma" di Bretschneider, 2006).

piece that the latter had thought he had commissioned, but will instead give him something better: the truth (ll. 1–14); then immediately he invites Hellenius "to show benevolence to more men, not to 'the ten in need,'" whom he had "yesterday promised" to Gregory (15–18).[2] The poem thus presupposes one fiscal benefaction, just conferred, and seeks to elicit another on the strength of this. Hellenius was there to "establish just measures of *phoroi*," tribute payments (360), and Gregory sought "freedom," tax exemptions (26). Basil of Caesarea elsewhere identifies Hellenius more specifically as a *peraequator,* an "equalizer."[3] Much remains unclear about the duties of these officials, who were appointed by the central government to particular cities to adjust the census rolls.[4] Distinct from the *censitores* who compiled the registers, their name suggests that they redistributed rather than reduced the city's total quota; evidence shows them empowered to reallocate property by reassigning *agri deserti* from their owner to more energetic neighbors and to "equalize" unfair burdens by shifting loads from one taxpayer to another.[5] There are also indications that they might be authorized to reduce the overall fiscal obligation.[6] Gregory's plea, that his protégés be "freed" from their tax burden, suggests that he was requesting their removal altogether from the equation. His petition thus recalls Basil of Caesarea's attempt to secure exempt status for his clergy.[7] Gregory, however, chose to write a long poem rather than a brisk letter. Why? His reasons must be inferred from a close examination of his argument.

Moving into his most solemn register, Gregory invites Hellenius to make

2. Πλείοσιν εὐμενέειν, οὐ δέκα δευομένοις, *Carm.* 2.2.1.16. Gregory frequently uses the prose form of the participle in this sense: e.g. *Or.* 14.18: δός τι καὶ μικρὸν τῷ δεομένῳ.

3. Basil of Caesarea, *Ep.* 98.1.

4. The fullest contemporary account is Eusebius *Vita Constantini* 4.3; see André Déléage, *La capitation au Bas-Empire,* Annales de l'Est, Mémoire 14 (Mâcon: Protat frères, 1945), 34; Timothy D. Barnes, *The New Empire of Diocletian and Constantine* (Cambridge, Mass.: Harvard University Press, 1982), 236–37.

5. Arnold Hugh Martin Jones, *The Later Roman Empire* (Oxford: Blackwell, 1964), 1:448–58, at 455.

6. See Ian Tompkins, "The Relations between Theodoret of Cyrrhus and His City and Its Territory, with Particular Reference to the Letters and Historia Religiosa" (D.Phil. diss., Oxford University, 1993), 96–105.

7. Basil *Ep.* 104; Jean Bernardi, "La lettre 104 de Saint Basile: Le préfet du prétoire Domitius Modestus et le statut du clercs," in *Recherches et Tradition: Mélanges Patristiques offerts à Henri Crouzel, S.J. Professeur Honoraire à la Faculté de Théologie de l'Institut Catholique de Toulouse,* edited by André Dupleix, 7–19 (Paris: Bauchesne, 1992); Robert Pouchet, *Basile le Grand et son univers d'amis d'après sa correspondance: Une stratégie de communion.* Studia ephemeridis Augustinianum 36 (Rome: Institutum Patristicum Augustinianum, 1992), 323–25.

his distinctive contribution to God's work (19–24).[8] There are worshippers of God, says Gregory, to whom Hellenius should "provide every freedom" (26). These men, who "lead upwards the people initiated in the heavenly mysteries" (28), must be priests. They are conflated, however, with another category who deserve the same privilege: Hellenius should provide this freedom also to "all the Christ-bearers, who are above the earth, without yokes" (29–30), free from the satanic domination of possessions, free from servitude to women, not dependent on brothers or companions, not aspiring to greatness in their cities, but wholly devoted to God's service and properly trained to achieve a direct vision of Trinitarian truth (29–54). Extending the vocabulary of ascetic commitment that he had been developing in both prose and verse, Gregory ties this explicitly to the potential for divine illumination that would become the defining feature of his "theologian."[9]

Gregory then explains the different ways in which his Christ-bearers show their contempt for the world. Some live in caves, some chain themselves, some endure twenty-day fasts; some again take vows of silence; one stood in "a holy place" standing upright, while another had taken a similar stand on the Mount of Olives, refusing to relax, until his admirers built a new house for him as he was dying—a tomb, one infers (53–84). This makes explicit what an earlier reference to Nazianzus had already implied: that these practices were not local.[10] Gregory's perspectives have opened out to encompass an unequivocally devout "ascetic abroad."

But here Gregory exclaims: a shudder came over him, "that there has been created, in faithful words, this *nomos* for monks in name and lifestyle" (85–86).[11] This highly compressed couplet introduces one of the most puzzling stretches of argument in the poem. Ivano Costa's recent Italian version has the great virtue of offering an interpretation.[12] For Costa, the *nomos* is a "custom" followed by

8. Gregory claims biblical support, presumably from Exodus 35:5–6, 22–23; the central idea recalls *Or.* 1.4.

9. For earlier evocations of ascetic commitment, see *Ep.* 6.3; *Or.* 4.71, 6.2; *Carm.* 2.1.1.43–49, 608–12. For Gregory's vocabulary of divine illumination, see Beeley, *Gregory of Nazianzus on the Trinity*, 102–8.

10. For overachieving immigrants on the Mount of Olives, see Basil *Ep.* 258–59 and Palladius, *Histia Lausica* 44; cf. Edward David Hunt, *Holy Land Pilgrimage in the Later Roman Empire, AD 312–460* (Oxford: Oxford University Press,1982), 167.

11. A, φρίκος ἦλθεν ἔμοιγε· λόγοις πιστοῖσι τετύχθαι/ Τόνδε νόμον μοναχοῖς οὔνομα καὶ βίοτον. I construe the infinitive sentence as an indirect statement dependent upon the shudder, with the "faithful words" as dative of instrument referring to the law, which is made "with believing [that is, Christian] words."

12. Gregory of Nazianzus, *Poesie 2*, trans. Ivano Costa and Carmelo Crimi, Collana di testi patristici 150 (Rome: Città nuova, 1999), 223–24. The Latin versions in *PG* 37:1458–59 remain cautiously literal.

certain monks, whom "very many men know" but "a few" (correctly, it would seem) disregard, thinking them (again correctly) more reckless than prudent piety would require. When a decently pious person (the term has wholly positive connotations)[13] comes near "them" (for Costa, these excessive monks), not knowing their local "law" (that is, their excesses), at first they welcome him in their homes, show friendship, quote words "which the spirit engraved" (from the Bible),[14] and offer a splendid (for Costa, liturgical)[15] feast; but then one of them mentions their harsh custom. He asks whether it was good for religious people to die for God, which turns out to be a trick question. When the guest innocently agrees, the host at last explains what this local "custom" involves: self-inflicted death, through violence or starvation or a variety of other forms (100–5). The poor pilgrim, on this interpretation, has wandered into a suicide cult.

Although ingenious and attractive, this pushes the Greek too far. The opening statement that "very many know, but a few slight" these monks (87) is worded to imply that this minority are wrong.[16] Moreover, Costa attributes the "local" custom to the suicidal monks, but the adjective elsewhere in Gregory has a first-person force, implying close identification with the object named.[17] Most troubling of all is the abrupt shift after Gregory has introduced the leading question about the merits of death in God's name:

> But if he in his ignorance were to approve [such] an end;
> They die willingly, with many deaths,
> By themselves, under their own hand or by constraint of stomach. (99–101)

This is not a straightforward conditional sequence, but it cannot be rescued simply by ascribing the willing deaths to the interlocutor's cheerful exposition.[18] The distancing effect of the third-person plural mutes what ought to be the dramatic impact of a shocking first-person revelation and lends a descriptive character to statements to which Gregory himself cannot conceivably have subscribed, such

13. Gregory applies the term to Nonna (*Or.* 8.19), her children (8.38), and her parents (*Carm.* 2.1.45.220–21).

14. Cf. *Carm.* 2.1.1.275–76.

15. Gregory of Nazianzus, *Poesie,* trans. Costa and Crimi, 2:223n14; cf. *PG* 37:1458.

16. Gregory elsewhere signals clearly when the verb signifies justified disdain: *Or.* 4.17, *Or.* 6.5; *Carm.* 2.1.12.110.

17. For examples of Gregory's usage, see *Carm.* 2.1.17.84, 2.1.19.14.

18. Gregory of Nazianzus, *Poesie 2,* trans. Costa and Crimi, 224: "l'altro conferma che essi sono pronti a morire volontieri."

that the suicides are "martyrs of truth."[19] Nor does it lead naturally to the simile that follows, in which Gregory deprecates the erratic course taken by a headstrong pony, but does not condemn this path as fatally misdirected (106–9).[20]

On any interpretation, the argument here is complex. Much turns on our understanding of the "law" (86–87), which triggers the whole passage and recurs twice during it: the visitor knows nothing of "this law" (90) and someone then "recalls" it (95). It has been argued that the *nomos* was an actual imperial constitution, which deplored ascetic excesses in these highly colored terms.[21] However, the passage begins with an emphatic demonstrative that establishes a contrast between the reverence paid to the monk at Jerusalem and Gregory's local situation.[22] This can hardly reflect a specific piece of legislation: had the government singled out the monks of Nazianzus for such attention, Gregory's chances of obtaining fiscal relief for them would have been very slim indeed. Instead Gregory seems to evoke something less formal, an anti-ascetic norm characteristic of the conservative Christians of Nazianzus: in repeating the word he attempts a persuasive definition, crystallizing local prejudices into an (unjust) "law."[23]

Better sense can be made of the passage if those welcoming pious strangers are not ascetic extremists, but the "few" who despise the monks on the basis of alleged extremities. These are therefore conventional Christians who treat the visiting "someone" to lavish hospitality.[24] So the second "someone," who introduces the "convention" by asking the leading question, is one of these outwardly friendly people; in the puzzling lines following the innocent guest's reply, Gregory then appropriates this malicious host's voice to spell out, with heavy exaggeration, the workings of the ascetics' alleged death wish. The

---

19. *Anth. Pal.* 118.6 invokes "martyrs of truth." The Maurist editors suggested emendation: *PG* 37: 1459, at v. 103.

20. See also *Ep.* 215.4, 216.3; *Or.* 2.30, *Or.* 38.10 (=45.10), *Carm.* 2.1.17.47–48, 1.2.2.315–19. Gregory presents himself as a colt to be tamed at *Carm.* 2.1.1.559–560; cf. *De vita sua*, 123.

21. Noel Lenski, "Valens and the Monks: Cudgeling and Conscription as a Means of Social Control," *Dumbarton Oaks Papers* 58 (2004): 93–117, at 99.

22. The expression τόνδε νόμον elsewhere points to a contrast: *Carm.* 1.2.1.229, 410; 1.2.2.154; cf. 1.2.8.19.

23. Cf. *Or.* 2.7, where Gregory interrupts an appeal to those sympathetic to the ascetic vocation: "For, perhaps, I should not expect to persuade most people, for they consider the matter ridiculous, being badly disposed towards it."

24. *Carm.* 2.1.17.67–68 associates "holy feast" with birthdays, funerals, and weddings; cf. *Carm.* 2.2.3.183 (wedding), 2.2.6.63 (weddings and birthdays).

nomos here, then, is a local convention, an entrenched attitude of hostility to monks. In such a scenario the pious visitor probably represents Hellenius himself, whose mission would involve negotiations with the local elite, at whose instigation he had been appointed. In interposing his own plea Gregory thus faced the difficulty that an influential segment of local opinion would vehemently oppose concessions such as he sought.

Inspection of the catalogue of fourteen named individuals that, at some eighty lines, forms the heart of the poem explains such hostility. Having introduced, in general terms, the "light-bringing race," Gregory addresses Hellenius directly for the first time since his poem. "Look kindly on these men for me; first of all, on the gentle Cledonius" (120–21); "and after, on Eulalius, far the best among his company" (129–30); "Spare also great Nicomedes" (143). The pattern once established, the pleas become less direct: "Nor is Theognius among the last" (171); "The soul of Evander hides much treasure inside" (191–92); "Who in his senses could forget Asterius and his brothers, the saintly triad?" (193). One Philadelphius is then dealt with by paraleipsis (197); but neither is Macrobius to be forgotten (198). At least one line is missing here, as the itemized list opens out into an ascetic panorama. "Who could tell of Rheginus, walking tall, of Leontius, of Heliodorus, who possess the highest reward of the wisdom of Christ, and of [the] others, bright stars among the rustic population, although there are many on whom their light does not fall, noble among the members of Christ, seals of immortality, beauties incarnate?" (204–9). Gregory's list is thus a sample of a whole universe of *askesis*, of men uniform in their service to God (205–24).

But Gregory's names resonate. His sketches suggest considerable local prominence; for several, there is corroborating evidence. Cledonius now "lives for the poor," having dedicated everything to Christ (121–23).[25] His property, that is, was devoted to the service of the poor, the closest Gregory comes to justifying his proposed exemptions. But we should infer that Cledonius still held legal title to these possessions. Moreover, the fame he had once enjoyed in the court of the earthly king denotes the considerable status of former imperial service (127–28).[26] Eulalius was cousin to Gregory, who had previously written

25. Marie-Madeleine Hauser-Meury, *Prosopographie zu den Schriften Gregors von Nazianz,* Theophaneia 13 (Bonn: P. Hamstein, 1960), 53–55. Her Cledonius I, II, and III are probably identical.

26. *Ep.* 101–2 show him acting as Gregory's locum in the early 380s.

two letters to support him when, with his brother, he had purchased an estate
as a philosophical retreat, only for the deal to sour.[27] Now living with his
mother, he was presumably managing her property, as Gregory managed his
parents.' Nicomedes, another relative, was also a priest. He had dedicated
his two children to the holy life, and was investing his wealth in building a
church. Nicomedes had converted late in life, and although Gregory insists
that he was leaving nothing for his children, the church project to which they
were dedicated should be seen as a foundation for them to administer. A
funerary epigram duly shows Nicomedes still ruling his community from
heaven, "with your holy pair of children."[28] This was another substantial
figure, no mere subordinate.[29] The character of Nazianzus, where an unusually
undersized urban center was yoked to a large (and evidently wealthy) rural
periphery, meant that village presbyters had considerable scope for influence
and initiative independent of the cathedral.[30]

Gregory's other protégés are mostly unattested elsewhere, but the text
hints at a similar milieu. Theognius was "honey-like, sweet-voiced," epithets
that denote the fruits of rhetorical education, the badge of the elite.[31] Having
entered the ascetic "race" late in life, he had already overtaken the field; he
is also blood "of mine," another member of Gregory's extensive cousinhood.
Evander is also a white-haired old man; the reference to his treasures being
hidden might imply that he did not look like a monk. Another example,
perhaps, of asceticism as a retirement option? Asterius and his brothers shared
"life in common," possibly indicating another example of estate-based piety.[32]
With Philadelphius there is an explicit attestation of "well-born blood,"
while Macrobius was Gregory's protégé and "friend," terms that imply social
equality, and was immune from the temptation of pride, the besetting sin of
the rich. The Rheginus who bequeathed Gregory some property at Arianzus,

27. *Ep.* 14–15.

28. *Anth. Pal.* 8.141 (cf. 139); see further Hauser-Meury, *Prosopographie,* 133.

29. Gregory's epitaph for him, *Anth. Gr.* 141, induced the editor to make him a bishop; Hauser-Meury, *Prosopographie,* 133n263.

30. McLynn, "'Curiales into Churchmen,'" 277–95, for the presbyter of Borissus' conversion to the Eunomianist heresy.

31. *Anth. Pal.* 8.124.3, on Libanius' pupil (and Gregory's cousin) Euphemius; Gregory applies the same terms to his father at *Anth. Pal.* 8.12.3 and *Carm.* 2.1.1.128.

32. For a typology, see Kim Bowes, *Private Worship, Public Values, and Religious Change in Late Antiquity* (Cambridge: Cambridge University Press, 2008), 152–58.

which he disposed of in the will that he drafted in 381, is to be identified with the poem's "tall-walking Rheginus."[33] Rheginus was therefore a neighboring property owner, Arianzus being attached to Gregory's family's own holding of Karbala.[34]

There is no need to doubt the authenticity of these men's piety, but they are not obviously "men in need," the expression applied to the ten men whom Hellenius had "yesterday" promised Gregory. Basil's equivalent letter suggests that the first (and most straightforward) priority would be exemptions for the clergy serving the central cathedral on the grounds of their quasi-civic responsibilities.[35] Gregory was perhaps capitalizing on the success of such a petition and attempting a more ambitious suit. The framing of his case shows how freighted it was with potential difficulties. We have already seen that Gregory takes care to defuse a counter-argument, the local "law," before he even introduces his own clients. Nor does he follow to its conclusion the conversation that he there presents. Instead he interrupts himself to ask Christ to minimize the damage done by these devout, but misguided men: so rapidly does he shuffle his pack that it is difficult to tell whether this refers to his critics or the zealous monks whom they travestied. Instead of clarifying the issue, Gregory changes course yet again, asking why he was itemizing these details when "here" there were a few who trod the narrow path (111–14).

In concluding his catalogue, Gregory pans out from his designated candidates to a wider ascetic hinterland. Especially notable here is the way that he shifts in doing so from male to female asceticism, expanding into a memorable rhapsody over the "maiden ladies," eagerly awaiting their bridegroom (225–62).[36] Yet the emphasis on these women might seem disproportionate to their numbers, at least locally. Gregory admits to being able to count but "few" such women his own (261), and omits them from his solicitations. They nevertheless serve his purpose: Hellenius was their professed admirer, honoring them "as much as you do anyone" (229). Gregory contrives to make this a compliment to

33. J. Beaucamp, "Le testament de Grégoire de Nazianze," in *Fontes Minores* 10, edited by L. Burgmann, 54–55, Forschungen zur byzantinischen Rechtsgeschichte 22 (Frankfurt: Löwenklau, 1998).

34. Friedrich Hild and Marcell Restle, *Kappadokien: Kappadokia, Charsianon, Sebasteia und Lykandos. Tabula Imperii Byzantini 2,* Österreichische Akademie der Wissenschaften, Philosophisch-Historische Klasse 149 (Vienna: Verlag der Österreichischen Akademie der Wissenschaften, 1981), 150–51, 200–1.

35. See above, n. 7.

36. Susanna Elm, *Virgins of God: The Making of Asceticism in Late Antiquity,* Oxford Classical Monographs (Oxford: Clarendon Press, 1994), 153.

himself—"when you knew them my treasure"—but seems here to be stretching
a tenuous point.

This is just the first of the hooks Gregory baits especially for Hellenius.
During the final hundred lines he besets him with most petitionary vehemence,
attempting at least seven distinct approaches. First comes the calculus of
benefits: by this small favor Hellenius would earn a large one—rewards stored
up in heaven (281–84). The sentimental tug of the schoolroom follows, an
appeal to shared experiences as *hetairoi,* classmates, leading to a demand for
consideration for Gregory's current *hetairoi* (285–92). Enter the most special of
their mutual school friends, Basil, who stood "between" them (geographically,
between Armenia and Nazianzus) and bonded them the more tightly by their
shared desire for him. This favor for Basil would signify respect not only for his
dear fatherland (Cappadocia) and for their shared literary studies, but also for
the sacrifices that Basil now performed as bishop—in short, respect for Christ
(293–307).

Gregory then shifts from the plea circumstantial to the plea direct. "I beg,
on behalf of souls" (306), "I beg" (307); supplication becomes command, with
the monosyllabic imperative "give" reiterated four times in four lines (309–
12). Gregory now suddenly assumes his father's voice, commanding Hellenius,
in an old man's last words, to spare the flock that he had tended for so many
decades, that God might give in return a ripe old age (320–26). This oracular
voice is then capped with "a good word from our scripture," a neatly turned
versification of a Gospel sound bite, on "measures for measures" (329–32).[37]
Reflections follow upon the coincidence of Christ's incarnation with the
Augustan census, deriving from Christ's scrupulous fulfillment of his fiscal
obligations the conclusion that Hellenius should free Gregory's friends from
theirs. Further consequences, for Hellenius personally, are again indicated:
"good things" written in his register here translated into his own eventual
enrollment in the "good" register in heaven (342–43). But eschatological
perspectives yield, at the close, to more conventionally classical considerations
of reputation and reciprocity. Gregory's "fellowship" was sending the text to
Hellenius as an indestructible keepsake, on one simple condition: if he kept
the balance straight, the little *polis* of Diocaesarea would illuminate his name
before the whole world and inscribe his fame on tablets (365–68).

37. Gregory repeats the motif at *Carm.* 2.2.2.11–12.

The application of so many persuasive strategies to a single case is central to the poem's interpretation. The text is neither a generalized appeal for benevolence nor a preliminary softening up, but is designed to bear a serious load, to deliver an argument that required such framing to sustain its coherence. Its character can be best understood by contrast to Gregory's other surviving poetic plea to a *peraequator,* an elegantly banal confection of some thirty lines.[38] The convolutions of the petition to Hellenius recall instead the dossier of two letters and a sermon that constitute Gregory's response to a crisis that threatened to leave "what was once a city an empty place, recognizable only by mountains, ridges and woodlands."[39] These latter documents, significantly, indicate a drama simultaneously highly tense and carefully contrived: Gregory knew that his addressee wanted to yield, but needed cover against possible criticism for doing so too readily.[40] Collusion is likely in this case also, inasmuch as Gregory is unlikely to have committed himself to so extravagant an appeal without some confidence that it would be favorably received. But at the same time, the very contortions of his entreaty indicate that Hellenius could not afford to be seen to submit too casually. The poem arguably allows us to follow, in real time, one of those encounters characterized so vividly by Peter Brown, where a rhetor "lent momentum, through the dazzle of his words, to the slow working" of network building.[41] Through his poetry Gregory conjured a charmed circle within which the dealings between Hellenius and the monks were elevated beyond reach of any mundane carping.

We catch here the echo of a virtuoso performance. Our transmitted text probably reflects a presentation copy, a "souvenir" later "sent" to Hellenius (357–58). But behind this we can reconstruct confidently the outlines of an actual occasion. Not only does the poem presuppose a physical encounter, with Gregory introducing his protégés to Hellenius, but in the strong demonstratives that punctuate his catalogue we see him pointing them out, first as a group ("these men here": 113) and then as individuals (120). But the decisive

---

38. *Carm.* 2.2.2; see Susan R. Holman, "Taxing Nazianzus: Gregory and the Other Julian," *Studia Patristica* 37 (2001): 103–9; also Van Dam, *Kingdom of Snow,* 89–92.

39. *Ep.* 241.4.

40. McLynn, "'Curiales into Churchmen,'" 283–86.

41. Peter Brown, *Power and Persuasion in Late Antiquity: Towards a Christian Empire,* The 1988 Curti Lectures (Madison: University of Wisconsin Press, 1992), 31.

evidence is Gregory's inclusion of several men for whom he was *not* seeking fa-
vors. His "silence" over the well-born Philadelphius has been noted; still more
interesting is the announcement that although God "has given Carterius to
another," Hellenius could still make him his own by being kind to his companions (139–42). Carterius, we infer, was not on the tax register of Nazianzus.[42]
This aside, a self-contained pair of couplets, only makes sense if Carterius was
present in the audience to provide a visual cue (in contrast, Gregory would
prepare the ground very carefully when later invoking another mutual friend,
Basil). Carterius seems to have belonged to a lower social level, as Gregory's
pedagogue, a family retainer,[43] but as such he will have remembered Athens,
and probably Hellenius. The poem thus evokes a party, a convivial gathering at
which Hellenius was given the opportunity to surrender honorably to Gregory's inventive and determined siege.

But unlike the priests and deacons for whom Basil had sought exemptions, emphasizing that only the genuinely needy would be entitled to benefit, Gregory's friends were rich. Any local hostility, such as is intimated in
the poem, could moreover find authoritative sanction in the emperor Valens,
who during this period issued stern injunctions against idlers who sought to
shirk their civic responsibilities under a cloak of pious unworldliness.[44] But
there was nothing gratuitous in the exemptions that Gregory was seeking for
them. Ascetic identity was still ill-defined and contested, and those attempting to live out a commitment to the Christian God found it difficult to avoid
defiling contact with the pitch inherent in secular life. Fiscal obligations were
a particular vexation: Gregory himself complained, in an autobiographical
poem written within a year or so of this, of the fetters imposed by the "burden
of Caesar," with the hubbub of the "crowded agora" and the haughty authorities with whom he there had to deal.[45] This should be taken seriously. Self-
proclaimed ascetics were especially vulnerable to the resentments of their neighbors in a system where tax assessment was a favorite means whereby members of
the elite could conduct their feuds.[46] The 371 census, moreover, seems from con-

---

42. Hauser-Meury, *Prosopographie,* 52, and Gregory of Nazianzus, *Poesie 2,* trans. Costa and Crimi,
2:225n21, assign Carterius instead to a different monastic community.

43. McLynn, "Among the Hellenists," 231.

44. *CTh.* 12.1.63; Lenski, "Valens and the Monks," 99–100, dates this to 373.

45. *Carm.* 2.1.1.149–55; Gregory of Nazianzus, in *Poèmes personnels,* ed. Tuilier and Bady, 2:1, 1–11,
proposes a date "aux environs de 371."

46. Basil, *Ep.* 299.

temporary legislation to have been exceptionally thorough.[47] Gregory's exemptions denoted his friends as professional soldiers of Christ and so distinguished them from the mere "civilians," their Christian neighbors who followed very similar lifestyles in the countryside around Nazianzus.

Another aspect of Gregory's autobiographical poem is also of direct relevance to his dealings with Hellenius. In the concluding section he complained that he was now without "companions," having been deprived of "his sole delight": "excellent men, Christ-bearers, living on earth but above flesh."[48] Gregory here employs terms strikingly similar, and at certain points exactly identical, to those he applies to his friends when appealing to Hellenius;[49] but in this poem his friends are lost to him and "stand divided, on this side and on that" in a heated conflict about Christology.[50] It is usually assumed that these quarrels afflicted the same ascetic constituency at Nazianzus whose unity was proclaimed so forcefully to Hellenius.[51] But there is no good reason for this assumption. The studied neutrality with which Gregory regards the conflict between his companions and in particular his readiness to consign them to the same irrevocably lost past as his dead siblings suggest a much greater sense of distance.[52] Earlier in his career, moreover, Gregory had made much to audiences in Nazianzus of his intimate involvement with ascetic projects abroad.[53] The present passage is best read as announcing a definitive abjuration of this milieu: it was five years since Gregory had last visited Pontus, and he would never go again. The Pontus ascetics were not, as far as we know, quarreling more vehemently than usual about Christology in the early 370s, but little actual controversy would be needed to justify a statement that it evidently suited Gregory to make.[54] The two poems might therefore be seen as representing

47. Kyle Harper, "The Greek Census Inscriptions of Late Antiquity," *Journal of Roman Studies* 98 (2008): 83–119, here 85–89.

48. *Carm.* 2.1.1.609–10.

49. Compare *Carm.* 2.2.1.29–30, Πᾶσί τε Χριστοφόροισιν, ὅσοι χθονός εἰσιν ὕπερθεν/ Ἀζυγέες, κόσμου βαιὸν ἐφαπτόμενοι, with *Carm.* 2.1.1 609, Χριστοφόρους, ζώοντας ἐπὶ χθονὶ, σαρκὸς ὕπερθεν, and *Carm.* 2.1.1.611, Ἀζυγέας, κόσμοιο περίφρονας. *Carm.* 2.2.1.47 repeats verbatim *Carm.* 2.1.1.48 (his initial evocation of ascetic commitment in the poem): Μύσται κρυπτομένης ζωῆς Χριστοῖο ἄνακτος.

50. *Carm.* 2.1.1.612–15.

51. Costa, *Poesie 2*, trans. Costa and Crimi, 65.

52. *Carm.* 2.1.1.605–6.

53. *Or.* 6.2; see Neil McLynn, "Gregory the Peacemaker," 183–216, here 196–98.

54. Gregory's explicit note that both sides were "friends of the eternal spirit" (*Carm.* 2.1.1.611) enabled him to maintain neutrality; the Christological quarrels might refer slyly to Basil's earlier dealings, from Pontus, with the now controversial Apollinaris of Laodicaea.

a significant change of direction for him: his formal farewell to a distant ascetic community coincides interestingly with his discovery of another, much
closer to home.

Gregory's consolidation of a body of propertied ascetic supporters was of
more than local significance. His plea to Hellenius can be related to an episode of decisive importance in the shaping of ecclesiastical politics in Cappadocia and beyond. Two other sources introduce this wider context. The first
is a letter from Basil, already mentioned, which attests Hellenius as a visitor
to Caesarea on his journey to Nazianzus: he delivered an invitation from the
Armenian bishop Theodotus summoning Basil to attend the annual mid-June
feast of Phargamus.[55] The second text shows Hellenius again playing post-
man at Caesarea, this time on his homeward leg. Basil acknowledges receipt to
Gregory of the letter that had been delivered "from our most reverend brother Hellenius," and adds that Hellenius had told him "nakedly" the details of
the situation that Gregory had there described.[56] While making no secret of
his horror, Basil makes a point of replying in sorrow rather than anger. With
deliberate calm, he blames Gregory for allowing a certain "slanderer" to cause
trouble. The man in question was from Caesarea, was in some way "associated" with Basil, but knew nothing of his theology—he merely invented things
that he had never heard. And yet the "brothers" around Gregory at Nazianzus
were not only listening to him, but were becoming his disciples.

The letter from Gregory that Hellenius had delivered to Basil to cause
this dismay also survives.[57] Gregory described a symposium at Nazianzus, with
"not a few distinguished men, friends of ours," where trouble had begun even
before the wine came round. The conversation (as always) had centered upon
Basil, and had turned to Gregory's association with him—their shared philosophy, their friendship, Athens, and their harmony of spirit and mind—until a
visitor in ascetic garb interrupted this happy self-congratulation, denouncing
it as lies and flattery. The vaunted orthodox partnership was spurious, for Basil had betrayed the faith, and Gregory was an accessory. The visitor had just
come from the feast of Eupsychius at Caesarea, where Basil in an otherwise

55. Basil, *Ep.* 98, to Eusebius of Samoa.

56. Basil, *Ep.* 71. McGuckin, *Saint Gregory of Nazianzus,* 218, makes Hellenius a priest; but Basil,
Ep. 198 introduces the *peraequator* Leontius with exactly the same honorific.

57. For the preservation of the exchange, see McLynn, "Gregory Nazianzen's Basil: The Literary
Construction of a Christian Friendship," *Studia Patristica* 37 (2001): 178–93, here 185–86 and 188–89.

excellent treatment of theology had "slurred over" the question of the Spirit. And although Gregory had recently publicly proclaimed the Spirit's divinity, by tolerating Basil's stance he was abetting his treason. Gregory rehearsed in the letter the case for Basil's defense, which he had (he said) put at the party—his friend's vulnerability as the embattled bishop of a major see, surrounded by heretics looking for an excuse to remove him (in contrast to his own obscurity and consequent immunity)—but without success. The company had turned against him, insisting that it was better to uphold the truth than to ruin it, without any commensurate gains, by this so-called "economy." Gregory now asked Basil for instructions on how far he should "economize" the doctrine of the spirit.

We can confidently put Hellenius at this party, since he had provided Basil with the details on which he based his recriminations. The prominence in the conversation of student days at Athens (some fifteen years after they had graduated) is best explained by Hellenius' presence, which will have given the event the character of a reunion. The party followed shortly after the feast of Eupsychius on September 7.[58] Hellenius, his mission at Nazianzus accomplished, will have wanted to return to Armenia before the onset of winter. A further step would be to identify the guests at the party, those who eventually sided with the stranger against Gregory (or rather against Basil), as those same propertied monks whose claims are presented in the poem. The gathering described in the letter provides a plausible setting for the poem's original performance. A symposiastic context would explain such features as the introduction of the audience into the action and the sequence of characters and voices that Gregory assumed, from prejudiced householders to the Bible and his father. This would all make for a very cozy environment, rather cozier than Gregory allowed in his letter. Basil's sarcasm in response is explained if Hellenius failed to bear out Gregory's claim to have defended Basil to the bitter end of an angry confrontation.

There emerges here a crucial question of chronology. Hellenius' mission in Nazianzus is usually dated to 372 on the basis of Basil's letter to Eusebius, which (thanks to a reference to Gregory's consecration at Sasima) can be

58. For Eupsychius, see Mario Girardi, *Basilio di Cesarea e il culto dei martiri nel IV secolo: Scrittura e tradizione,* Quademi di "Vetera Christianorum" 21 (Bari: Istituto di studi classici e cristiani, Università di Bari, 1990), 179–81.

placed securely in May that year.[59] This conventional view, however, creates the problem that Hellenius would still be working on the register at Nazianzus only a few weeks before the new census—which would incorporate his adjustments—came into effect, probably in late September 372.[60] And Basil's letter points, if anything, to the previous year. His complaint to Eusebius that he had received no "reminder" from the Armenians certainly becomes much less petulant if the initial invitation (which demanded a considerable journey, since Nicopolis was as far from Caesarea as was Antioch) had given a year's notice. Since Basil was invited specifically to attend the annual festival at Phargamos in mid-June 372, the invitation might have emerged from the celebrations there in 371. This invitation was separate from the imperial mandate he received, apparently in 372, to supervise the Armenian Church.[61]

There are also difficulties in dating Gregory's exchange with Basil to the autumn of 372, when the angry recriminations following Gregory's appointment as bishop of Sasima that spring were still recent. On this view Basil would be professing, only a few months after his vehement denunciations of Gregory for abandoning his post at Sasima, that all their misunderstandings could be avoided if Gregory had "lived up to old agreements" and chosen to live beside him.[62] It is true that Gregory's "much-bruited" question about the Holy Spirit, which he had raised shortly before the symposium at "a well-attended gathering"—"How long shall we hide our lamp under the bushel?"—matches closely a statement in a sermon preached when accepting partnership in the bishopric of Nazianzus after the Sasima debacle.[63] But in the latter text the question does not announce a doctrinal initiative, but calls for the export of a position already

59. Demoen, "Gifts of Friendship," 3–4; Lenski, "Valens and the Monks," 99; Pouchet, *Basile le Grand,* 579–80; Hauser-Meury, *Prosopographie,* 97. Wolf-Dieter Hauschild dates both letter and consecration to 373, Basil of Caesarea, *Briefe,* trans. Hauschild (Stuttgart: A. Hiersemann, 1973), 1:156n3); cf. Paul Jonathan Fedwick, "A Chronology of the Life and Works of Basil of Caesarea," in *Basil of Caesarea: Christian, Humanist, Ascetic: A Sixteen-Hundredth Anniversary Symposium,* edited by Paul Jonathan Fedwick, 21–48 (Toronto: Pontifical Institute of Medieval Studies, 1981).

60. See Denis Feissel, "Notes d'epigraphie chrétienne VII," *Bullein de correspondance hellénistique* 108 (1984): 566–71.

61. Basil mentions the commission at *Ep.* 99.1, 4, reporting to the *comes* Terentius the failure both of his eventual visit to Nicopolis and of his subsequent mission to Armenia: the "summons" from Theodotus is here mentioned separately (*Ep.* 99.2).

62. *Ep.* 71.2. Basil had invited Gregory in these terms after his consecration in 370 (Gregory of Nazianzus, *Ep.* 46); Fedwick, "A Chronology," 1:13n75, notes the unlikelihood that the letter "was written after Gregory became bishop."

63. Marie-Ange Calvet-Sébasti, SC 405, 361n5, judges the two occasions "probably" identical.

well-established at Nazianzus; it might therefore be understood as the reiteration of a battle-cry that had already gained local traction.[64]

Hellenius' presence at the confrontation in Nazianzus does much to explain the vehemence of Basil's reaction. For in his letter Gregory was doing much more than reporting an unfortunate incident, or even than signaling his own disagreement with Basil.[65] He was publicizing a very sensitive question, and in a manner calculated to cause grave embarrassment for his friend. Through Hellenius he was ensuring that the controversy would spread to Hellenius' friends back in Armenia, the authors of the invitation that Basil would now spurn: Hellenius' bishop Theodotus of Nicopolis and the influential bishop Meletius of Antioch, in exile on his family estate of Getasa, outside Nicopolis.[66]

And this was the problem. Basil had immediately seen the value of Meletius, expelled from Antioch in autumn 370 at almost exactly the same time that he himself became bishop, as a focus for his "strategy of communion."[67] This involved a twin-track policy of, on the one hand, winning acceptance for Meletius by Athanasius and his Egyptians and the Nicene bishops of the West, and simultaneously on the other harnessing Meletius' already formidable Syrian coalition as a diplomatic instrument.[68] This project should be seen as a revival and extension of the Eastern anti-homoean coalition that had been assembled during the mid-360s by his old friend and mentor Eustathius, bishop of Sebaste in Armenia.[69] However, Eustathius now presented a significant difficulty. He was an inveterate enemy of Meletius, who a decade before had briefly supplanted him as bishop of Sebaste before accepting further promotion to Antioch, in both cases thanks to homoean bishops whom he had subsequently disowned as heretical.[70] Meletius' return to Armenia inevitably

---

64. *Or.* 12.6 calls for the propagation of the doctrine of the spirit's divinity 'to all cities'; the 'lamp' here is the teaching, whereas in *Ep.* 58 it seems to be the spirit.

65. McGuckin, *Saint Gregory of Nazianzus*, 216–19; Beeley, *Gregory of Nazianzus on the Trinity*, 15.

66. For the location of Getasa, see Basil of Caesarea, *Briefe*, trans. Hauschild, 2:156n18; Pouchet, *Basile le Grand*, 237, mistakenly places it near Melitene.

67. For Meletius' exile, see Hanns Christoph Brennecke, *Studien zur Geschichte der Homöer: Der Osten bis zum Ende der homöischen Reichskirche*, Beiträge zur historischen Theologie 68 (Tübingen: Mohr Siebeck, 1988), 233n64. Pouchet's argument for 371 (*Basile le Grand*, 237–38) depends on the unwarranted assumption that Meletius cannot have been in exile when Basil wrote him *Ep.* 57.

68. Pouchet, *Basile le Grand*, 237–68.

69. Brennecke, *Studien zur Geschichte der Homöer*, 126–221; Basil makes the continuity explicit at *Ep.* 67, where he invokes Eustathius' fellow-envoy Silvanus.

70. Brennecke, *Studien zur Geschichte der Homöer*, 68–77.

reignited old tensions, and other churchmen in the province took sides. Accusations of doctrinal unsoundness were duly raised against Eustathius, prompting earnest rebuttals from Basil.[71] The invitation from Theodotus that Hellenius delivered to Basil had probably been intended to force him to choose sides. Through Hellenius, Gregory was introducing into this process the question that would eventually force Basil apart from Eustathius. Nor can he have been unaware of what he was doing. He too had his reasons for wanting to force Basil to choose his friends.

Replying to Gregory, Basil appealed to the greater emergency, the danger that the imperial government might exile him—a danger that seemed real in autumn 371, as the court planned a mid-winter journey to Caesarea.[72] We have Gregory's response, gently pressing home his advantage. He had angered Basil, but had done so through simplicity, and (repeating a phrase of Basil's) blamed his own sins.[73] "But it would have been better for you to set the matter straight": politely but firmly he refuses to let the theological issue rest. Gregory then agrees graciously to come and join Basil's fight, on the condition that it really was a theological one: he would speak and contend for "the truth" under his friend's leadership. He duly set off to stand behind Basil as the emperor Valens attended a famous Epiphany service in January 372.[74] Modern scholars no longer hail this occasion as a triumph of church over state.[75] Understood in the light of the events of autumn 371, however, it takes on a new significance. Gregory agreed several months later to become bishop of Sasima. He did so, it might be suggested, because he had reason—especially after the Epiphany display—to believe that he had obtained an ascendency, and that he was in a position to recruit Basil to fight for the "truth." Basil was of course engaged in a more complex struggle on several fronts; but Gregory can legitimately claim more of the credit than is usually allowed him for helping to engineer the slow dissolution of Basil's longstanding understanding with Eustathius.

71. Basil, *Ep.* 98.2; Philip Rousseau, *Basil of Caesarea,* Transformation of the Classical Heritage 20 (Berkeley: University of California Press, 1994), 239–45, surveys the issues.

72. *Ep.* 71.2.   73. *Ep.* 59.3; cf. *Ep.* 71.2.

74. *Or.* 43.52.

75. Lenski, *Failure of Empire: Valens and the Roman State in the Fourth Century A.D.,* Transformation of the Classical Heritage 32 (Berkeley: University of California Press, 2002), 243–54; Van Dam, *Kingdom of Snow,* 115–17; McLynn, "The Transformations of Imperial Churchgoing in the Fourth Century," in *Approaching Late Antiquity: The Transformation from Early to Late Empire,* edited by Mark Edwards and Simon Swain, 235–70 (Oxford: Oxford University Press, 2004), here 253–55.

The poem to Hellenius shows why Gregory might have believed himself to be at an advantage. We easily forget how limited an infrastructure was available to the fourth-century theologians who pursued their competitively collaborative "search for the Christian doctrine of God." Bishops were unable to lay down any abiding law, either individually in their cathedrals or collectively in their councils. In such an environment, to create a coalition such as Gregory presented to Hellenius was in itself no mean achievement, and to bind such men with ties of obligation (assuming, as the poem's survival surely requires us to, that Hellenius yielded) was more significant still. A dozen loyal ascetics were as powerful a sounding board as any contemporary churchman commanded.[76] Gregory, from this perspective, should still be regarded in 371 as Basil's equal, despite the latter's eminence as bishop of Caesarea. He had coolly remained absent from the feast of Eupsychius that Basil was promoting as a focus for Cappadocian solidarity; meanwhile he enjoyed a "well-attended gathering" as a platform from which to launch his own theological agenda. It is the contention of this chapter that the ascetics introduced to Hellenius were a crucial ingredient in Gregory's confidence. If the suggestion is accepted, it has an important bearing on Gregory's decision to accept consecration at Sasima and on his response to the difficulties that he encountered there.

76. For a sense of scale, see Benoît Gain, *L'Église de Cappadoce au IVe siecle d'après la correspondance de Basile de Césarée (330–379)*, Orientalia Christiana analecta 225 (Rome: Pontifical Oriental Institute, 1985), 138–39.

PART 3   🏃   LEGACY

12. On the "Play" of Divine Providence in Gregory Nazianzen and Maximus the Confessor

Maximus the Confessor's *Ambigua ad Joannem,* addressed to Bishop John of Cyzicus (Anatolia), broaches perplexing passages in the writings of Gregory Nazianzen that Maximus clarifies in extensive expositions, often by giving Gregory's words fresh nuances. The vulnerability of Gregory to misinterpretation raises the stakes all the more, as observable in Maximus' vigorous attack on Origenists in the *Ambigua ad Joannem.*[1] But for Maximus, as bad a fate would be that Gregory's words and images would fail to register their full impact and richness.

In this chapter I will explore certain images from Gregory pertaining to divine providence that, though ostensibly ambiguous, prove to be not only adventurous or provocative, but deeply compelling from Maximus' perspective. They include the analogy of the providential "play" of the Logos and the subsidiary images of the "stable flux" of creation and the "chaos" or "flowing stream" of material existence, the very context in which, through the Logos' resourceful and strategic action, creatures find themselves in a "game" that is at once disciplinary and transformative.

The first and preeminent of these images, the Logos-at-play, is found in

---

1. See Polycarp Sherwood, *The Earlier Ambigua of St. Maximus the Confessor and His Refutation of Origenism,* Studia Anselmiana 36 (Rome: Herder, 1955).

the very last of Maximus' *Ambigua* and is the only *aporia* drawn from Nazian-zen's poetry. It comes from a passage in one of Gregory's *Poemata moralia* en-titled *Precepts for Virgins,* where Nazianzen waxes eloquent on the wonders of nature:

> Παίζει γὰρ λόγος αἰπὺς ἐν ἔιδεσι παντοδαποῖσι,
> Κίρνας, ὡς ἐθέλει, κόσμον ἐὸν ἔνθα καὶ ἔνθα.

> For the Logos on high plays in all sorts of forms,
> mingling with his world here and there as he so desires.[2]

In separate studies Hugo Rahner and Carlos Steel have tracked some of the prehistory of Nazianzen's analogy of divine play in classical sources.[3] One precedent is Plato's metaphor of humanity as a divine "plaything" (παίγνιον),[4] which doubtless also inspired Plotinus's differently nuanced reflection on hu-mans as "living toys" (ζῶντα παίγνια).[5] Gregory certainly knew this image, as it appears in one of his most somber poems.[6] Still another, much earlier prec-edent is the pre-Socratic Heraclitus' description of historical time (αἰών) itself as "a child, who plays, moving his pawns," and in so playing rules human exis-tence—though in Heraclitus' cosmology, Steel emphasizes, this is less an ex-pression of fatalism than of the Logos that "playfully" builds and destroys in the perennial flux of cosmic becoming.[7]

While Steel has furthermore observed that Gregory's line in the *Poemata moralia* is the only appearance in his corpus of the image of the Logos play-ing,[8] I would nevertheless mention a comparable, if less provocative, passage in one of his poems on providence from the *Poemata arcana:*

---

2. Gregory of Nazianzus, *Poemata theologica (moralia)* 1.2.2 (PG 37:624A–625A), quoted in Maxi-mus, *Ambigua* 71 (PG 91:1408C). Translations are mine unless noted otherwise.

3. Hugo Rahner, *Man at Play,* trans. Brian Battershaw and Edward Quinn (New York: Herder and Herder, 1972), 23–25, 41; Carlos Steel, "Le jeu du Verbe: À propos de Maxime, *Amb. ad Ioh.* LXVII [*Amb* 71]," in *Philohistôr: Miscellanea in honorem Caroli Laga septuagenarii,* edited by Antoon Schoors and Pe-ter van Deun, Orientalia Lovaniensia analecta 60, 281–93 (Leuven: Peeters, 1994).

4. *Laws* 644D–E, 803B–C.

5. *Ennead* 3.2.15 (LCL 442:90–94).

6. Gregory of Nazianzus, *Poemata theologica (moralia)* 1.2.15, *De exterioris hominis vilitate* (PG 37:776A).

7. Heraclitus, *Frag.* 22, 22B52; Steel, "Le jeu du Verbe," esp. 283–86; see also Rahner, *Man at Play,* esp. 11–25.

8. Steel, "Le jeu du Verbe," 282.

Αὐτὰρ ἐγὼ τόδε οἶδα· τάδε πάντα κυβερνᾷ,
νωμῶν ἔνθα καὶ ἔνθα θεοῦ Λόγος ὅσσα θ᾽ ὕπερθεν,
ὅσσα τ᾽ ἔνερθεν ἔθηκε νοήμασι· τοῖς μὲν ἔδωκεν
ἁρμονίην τε δρόμον τε διαρκέα ἔμπεδον αἰεί,
τοῖς δὲ βίον στρεπτόν τε καὶ εἴδεα πολλὰ φέροντα·

But this much I do know: it is God who steers the course of this universe,
the Word of God guiding here and there what his designs have placed above
and below. To the world above he has granted concord
and a fixed course lasting firm for ever. To the lower world he has
assigned a life of change which involves varied forms.[9]

The common nuance here with the passage from the *Poemata moralia* is the maneuverability of the Logos in his providential agency. The "guiding here and there" of things and the exposing of the lower world to change compare favorably with the Logos' "mingling with his world here and there" in our other text. There is, in addition, another passage from *Oration* 14 that evokes the Logos "playing" with his creatures, but I shall discuss that text later.

Steel has also identified yet another passage in Gregory's *Poemata historica* where he uses very similar phrasing—"he plays here and there" (παίζει ... ἔνθα καὶ ἔνθα)—to describe how the Devil teases monks with earthly things.[10] For Gregory, like Plato, "play" in itself is semantically pliable, capable of being rendered at one extreme as a sheer diversion typifying the stealth of the Devil and at the other extreme as evoking the sublime freedom and felicity of divine life. Maximus begins with this intriguing ambiguity, which makes in *Ambiguum* 71 for no less than four potential interpretations (θεωρίαι) of the Logos-at-play, representing plausibly latent meanings in Gregory's analogy.

The "Logos-at-Play" as a Tutorial in the Theological Language of Divine Incarnation

Maximus' first interpretation firmly sets Gregory's image in the context of the providence and wisdom manifested through God's descent in Jesus Christ. As a subtext he references a passage in the Psalms:

9. *Poemata arcana* 5 (Gregory of Nazianzus, *Poemata theologica* [*dogmatica*] 1.1.5), in Moreschini, ed., *Poemata Arcana*, 24–25.

10. Gregory of Nazianzus, *Poemata historica* 2.1.32–24 (PG 37:1454A); noted by Steel, "Le jeu du Verbe," 282–83.

> My soul was troubled at myself;
>> therefore shall *I remember you*
> *from a land of Jordan and Hermoniim,*
>> from a small mountain.
> *Deep calls to deep*
>> *at the sound of your cataracts;*
> all your surges and billows
>> passed over me.
> By day the Lord will command his mercy,
>> and at night an ode is with me,
>> a prayer to the God of my life.
>>> (Ps. 41:7–9, NETS)[11]

The "deep" (ἄβυσσος) here, says Maximus, can symbolize the contemplative mind (νοῦς) dilated in its quest to penetrate beyond sensible things to the intelligible realm, even approaching the great deep of divine wisdom itself. The "sound of your cataracts" is the relative knowledge of God's providential ways in the universe that is granted to those diligent enough to remember God "from a land of Jordan and Hermon," the *terra sancta* where the mystery of the incarnation historically unfolded.[12] This particular psalm seems a strange foray into considering the mystery of Christ's "playful" embodiment, but Maximus' figurative reading of it serves his contemplative pursuit of Gregory's deeper meaning. The image of the Logos-at-play is a mind-stretcher par excellence. It takes us into the depth of the properly *theological* (as well as soteriological) mystery that is the Incarnation. For Maximus, as for Gregory his mentor, any exploration into the divine *oikonomia* is necessarily also a venture into *theologia*.[13]

Indeed, for Maximus, Gregory's Logos-at-play offers insight into the very nature of theological language vis-à-vis divine condescension and embodiment. Like the Apostle Paul, Gregory is both an initiate (μύστης) in the divine mysteries and a teacher (μυσταγωγός) thereof.[14] Gregory's dictum about the

---

11. The italicized phrases here are those actually quoted by Maximus in *Amb.* 71 (PG 91:1409A, 1412A).

12. *Amb.* 71 (PG 91:1409A).

13. Cf. Maximus's *Expositio orationis dominicae* (CCSG 23:31–32) on the incarnate Logos being the "teacher" of *theologia,* the mystery of the Holy Trinity.

14. *Amb.* 71 (PG 91:1409A–B).

Logos-at-play is exactly matched by Paul's testimony that in the Incarnation we behold the foolishness of God that is wiser than humanity and the weakness of God that is stronger (1 Cor. 1:25). Maximus deduces that "foolishness," "weakness," and "play" are in human language *privations* (στερήσεις) respectively of wisdom, power, and prudence. But when applied to God, these privations paradoxically signify the excess (ὑπερβολή) of the positive attributes they negate, in this case the wisdom, power, and prudence of God conveyed in the Incarnation.[15]

As Steel notes, Maximus defers here to rules of apophatic language drawn from Pseudo-Dionysius the Areopagite, who had himself invoked Paul's words about divine foolishness as a sublime inversion designed to lift finite minds to an ineffable truth.[16] "It is customary in scripture," Maximus writes elsewhere, "for the unspeakable and hidden intentions of God to be represented in corporeal terms, so that we can perceive divine realities through the words and sounds that are conformable with our nature."[17] Here Maximus is specifically referencing the Areopagite's rule about the Bible's "dissimilar similitudes" (ἀνόμοιοι ὁμοιότητες), the ostensibly incongruous or offensive scriptural images paradoxically signifying spiritual beings or God himself.[18]

Thus the upshot of this initial interpretation of Gregory's Logos-at-play, viewed through the lens of Paul's teaching about the foolishness of God, is a straightforward admonition against superficial, pretentious readings of language that veils profound mysteries. Even for astute human reason, it is a matter of *conjecture* what this "foolishness," "weakness," or "play" of the Logos truly means. But a preliminary starting point is the prior observation that the "abyss" of the mind must reach out to the "abyss" of divine wisdom.[19]

"Conjecture" (στοχασμός), a scrupulous and pious guessing about a mystery within Scripture, has terminological roots in Hellenistic science and rhetoric, but appears as a hermeneutical principle in Philo[20] and more immediately in Gregory of Nyssa. For Nyssa, it is a function of his apophatic approach to

---

15. *Amb.* 71 (PG 91:1409B–C).

16. See Maximus *De divinis nominibus* 7.1 (PTS 33:193–35); also Steel, "Le jeu du Verbe," 287.

17. *Quaestiones ad Thalassium* 28 (CCSG 7:205).

18. Pseudo-Dionysius the Areopagite, *De caelesti hierarchia* 2.1–2.5 (PTS 33:9–17).

19. *Amb.* 71 (PG 91:1412A–B).

20. E.g., *De opificio mundi* 72–75, considering the use of the divine plural; cf. *De decalogo* 18; *De Josepho* 7, 104, 143; *De aeternitate mundi* 2.

scriptural symbolism, such as "perfume" as a designation for God in the Song of Songs (1:3–4), where we must adhere to the rule that God's ἐνέργειαι can be signified where his essence remains inaccessible.[21] Maximus himself, recurring to conjecture a number of times in his commentary on scriptural *aporiai* in his *Quaestiones ad Thalassium*,[22] writes:

> It is not improper, in view of that faculty in us that naturally longs for the knowledge of divine things, to undertake a conjecture (στοχασμός) about higher truths, as long as two good things from the conjecture exhibit themselves to those who possess genuine reverence for divine realities. For the one who approaches the divine realities conjecturally either attains to intelligible truth and, rejoicing, offers the "sacrifice of praise" (Ps. 49:14, 23, LXX; Heb. 13:15), thanksgiving, to the Giver of the knowledge of what was sought, or he finds that the meaning of the Scriptures alludes him and reveres the divine truths all the more by learning that the acquisition of them exceeds his own ability.[23]

In the valedictory appended to the *Ambigua,* too, Maximus reflects back on having approached "the most sublime words of our teacher Gregory … by way of conjecture, not straightforward declaration," particularly in the case of our text, *Ambiguum* 71.[24]

The "Logos-at-Play" and the Providential Strategy of Divine Incarnation

Maximus most notably uses conjecture in his second proposed θεωρία of Nazianzen's Logos-at-play.[25] It is tempting to see this pious guesswork as reciprocating the "playfulness" of the Logos who reveals himself precisely in his elusiveness. The interpreter, it would seem, must venture to play along.[26] Plotinus had called the writing of one of his treatises a kind of "playing" (παίζειν) with his own ideas, nonetheless aimed at earnest contemplation (θεωρία).[27]

21. *In Canticum Canticorum, Hom.* 1 (GNO 6:37).

22. See Blowers, *Exegesis and Spiritual Pedagogy in Maximus the Confessor: An Investigation of the Quaestiones ad Thalassium*, Christianity and Judaism in Antiquity 7 (Notre Dame, Ind.: University of Notre Dame Press, 1991), 186–88.

23. *Q. Thal.* 55 (CCSG 7:481–83).

24. *Amb.* (PG 91:1417A).

25. *Amb.* 71 (PG 91:1412B), contrasting στοχαστικῶς with ἀποφαντικῶς.

26. Twice Maximus speaks of "daring" (τολμᾶν) to put forth a particular interpretation (*Amb.* 1412A, 1412B). Pseudo-Dionysius, too, speaks of "daring" to interpret sacred revelation: e.g., *Div. nom.* 4.7 (PTS 33:152), 4.10 (PTS 33:155), 4.19 (PTS 33:163).

27. *Ennead* 3.8.1 (LCL 442:360–62).

But if, as Maximus claims, play is an inverted sign of the transcending prudence of the Logos in his Incarnation, it still carries a unique metaphorical function. After all, the most obvious privation of prudence is *imprudence*. There must be certain peculiar nuances of "play" that demand exploration. In this second exposition, Maximus wagers that the Logos' game (παίγνιον) consists in the "projecting of intermediate things, poising them equidistant between extremes on account of their flowing and pliable state."[28] These "intermediate things" are the visible created things that encase humanity and effectively constitute human life, things that the Logos has providentially poised between the "extremes" that are the reality of those *future* things yet to be manifest for humanity, things God already ordained *originally* in his ineffable purpose and plan.[29] In Maximus' more typical language, the Logos-Christ negotiates the "middle," the flow of the historical "meantime" between the beginning and end of creation as comprehended in his providential (and incarnational) purposes.[30] In an interesting twist on Ecclesiastes 1:9, Maximus suggests that Qoheleth is speaking, not of the "vanity" of historical existence, but of "first things" (τὰ πρῶτα) and "last things" (τὰ τελευταῖα), and the fact that what has been established protologically in the divine providence will eventuate eschatologically.[31]

For Maximus, then, we have in Gregory an image of the playful maneuvering of the Logos—*by virtue of his Incarnation*—in the contingencies of history to stabilize his creatures. Even though the ultimate salvific play was his historical Incarnation, the Logos has always and will always play in the precarious history of creation, the theater of his incarnate action in its eschatological fullness. Maximus further speaks in this connection of the "stable flux" (στάσιμος ῥεῦσις) of the cosmos in time and space:

This is also a paradox: that stability is seen as constantly flowing and being borne away, an ever-moving flow providentially purposed by God for the improvement of the beings governed with-

28. *Amb.* 71 (PG 91:1412B).
29. *Amb.* 71 (PG 91:1412C).
30. *Amb.* 71 (PG 91:1412C–D). Maximus sometimes affirms the Logos-Christ as himself the "beginning" (ἀρχή), "middle" (μεσότης), and "end" (τέλος) of creation within the οἰκονομία of salvation, as in *Q. Thal.* 19 (CCSG 7:119), 22 (CCSG 7:139); but he also speaks, in the register of θεολογία, of the divine nature that cannot "be" beginning, middle, and end since it transcends them all: *Cap. theol.* 1.4 (PG 90:1084A), 1.7 (PG 90:1085B).
31. *Amb.* 71 (PG 91:1412D). Steel ("Le jeu du verbe," 288) notes a parallel use of Eccl. 1:9 in *Q. Thal.* 59 (CCSG 22:63) to explain that postlapsarian humanity only knows its true ἀρχή, obscured by sin, by pursuing its eschatological τέλος.

in his economy, enabling those who are disciplined through this stable flux to be wise, to hope always for transition to a better place, and to have faith in being deified by grace as the goal of this mystery by inclining steadfastly toward God.[32]

We shall return to this theme below, as Maximus picks it up again in a later interpretation.

In Maximus' view the Logos-at-play presupposes for Nazianzen a wide chasm separating the created from the Uncreated, and he quotes one of Gregory's festal orations accordingly.[33] The Logos plays in the finite creation precisely from the standpoint of his transcendence, and in another playful image in *Ambiguum* 10 Maximus again describes how the Logos, who moved across the chasm and took flesh as the "seed of Abraham," diversified his presence while maintaining his perfect unity, "scattering himself indivisibly" (ἀμερῶς ἑαυτὸν ἐπιμερίζοντα) among all those worthy to receive him.[34] Gregory's Logos-at-play, Maximus adds, also compares favorably with Pseudo-Dionysius' equally daring image of the "ecstasy" of God, who,

in the overflow of his passionate goodness (ἐρωτικῆς ἀγαθότητος) is drawn outside himself in his provident care for everything. Beguiled, as it were, by his own goodness, love, and sheer yearning (ἔρωτι), he is enticed away from his dwelling place above and beyond all things, condescending to penetrate all things according to an ecstatic and supernatural power wherewith he can still remain within himself.[35]

Straining for a more ordinary analogy of the Logos-at-play, Maximus tenders the image of parents condescending to take part in their children's games, using nuts and dice and flowers as toys, or playing hide-and-seek, then later on training their children on the more serious matters of adulthood.[36] One hears echoes at this point of Plato's recommendation of forms of play as an honorable way of cultivating children, and in the best-case scenario as a prelude to *paideia* and philosophy.[37] Steel instead suggests that Maximus is recalling a neo-Platonic metaphor of the material world as a mere imitation of reality, as

32. *Amb.* 71 (PG 91:1412B–C).
33. *Amb.* 71 (PG 91:1413A), quoting Gregory in *Or.* 41.12 (PG 36:445B).
34. *Amb.* 10 (PG 91:1172A–C).
35. Pseudo-Dionysius *Div. nom.* 4.13 (PTS 33:158–89), in Maximus *Amb.* 71 (PG 91:1413A–B).
36. *Amb.* 71 (PG 91:1413B–C).
37. See Stephen Morris, "No Learning by Coercion: *Paidia* and *Paideia* in Platonic Philosophy," in *Play from Birth to Twelve and Beyond: Contexts, Perspectives, and Meanings,* edited by Doris Fromberg and Doris Bergen, 109–188, Garland Reference Library of Social Science 970 (New York: Garland, 1998).

when Plotinus, discussing matter as "nonbeing" and as an "unstable phantom," calls it a "fugitive plaything" (παίγνιον φεῦγον).[38] Steel qualifies this comparison by noting that Maximus places "une correction eschatologique" on the neo-Platonic juxtaposition of sensible and intelligible reality, envisioning the intelligible archetype of material creation as a *future* promise. But making the comparison with Plotinus at this particular juncture in Maximus' interpretation of the Logos' play seems premature. The whole thrust of the argument here and elsewhere in *Ambiguum* 71 is that for all its finitude and vulnerability, the sensible creation—the realm of embodiment and physical "flux"—is dignified as God's medium to intervene and resourcefully interact ("mingling here and there") with his creatures. This insight will become even more vivid in Maximus's third interpretation below.

As Maximus further avers, Nazianzen intends us to envision the Logos as condescending to guide his children up from simple amazement with phenomenal things, progressing through the vision and knowledge of them to a higher contemplation of their inherent spiritual principles (λόγοι), ultimately arriving at the mystical knowledge of *theologia*.[39] Play in this sense becomes a metaphor for the spiritual pedagogy of the Logos, a cherished theme in Maximus' engagement of the Alexandrian heritage of Christian *paideia* going back to Clement and Origen,[40] and more immediately the ascetical and contemplative theology of Evagrius Ponticus.

Divine Play and the Unstable Influx of the World

In his third attempt at interpreting Gregory's Logos-at-play, Maximus resumes the theme, partially treated in his second meditation, of the "stable flux" providentially enabling creatures to thrive amid the perilous flow of material creation.

Perhaps "play" is also the liability to change the material things in which we put our trust, things that fluctuate and mutate, and that have no secure foundation except the primary principle (λόγος) according to which they both bear up (φέρουσι) and are borne along (φέρονται)

38. Plotinus *Ennead* 3.6.7 (LCL 442:242); noted by Steel, "Le jeu du Verbe," 290–91.
39. *Amb.* 71 (PG 91:1413C–D).
40. See Adam Cooper, *The Body in St. Maximus the Confessor: Holy Flesh, Wholly Deified,* Oxford Early Christian Studies (Oxford: Oxford University Press, 2005), 48–57.

wisely and providentially. We think we have control of them, but rather than being ruled by us, they elude us, and put up with being seized by our desire for them; or rather they shake us off, as it were, completely incapable of controlling or being controlled, since the only sure definition of their own nature is flux and instability (τὸ ἀπορρεῖν καὶ μὴ ἵστασθαι). Most likely this is what our teacher [Gregory] has termed God's "play," as if to suggest that God conducts us through these very things to that which truly is and that endures ever unshakable.[41]

Maximus here appears to move the focus away from the play of the Logos proper to his incarnational condescension and to emphasize the play immanent in creation itself. In truth, however, they are of a piece, since both represent the singular strategy of divine providence in the economy of creation and redemption.[42] Elsewhere Maximus speaks of the relative "Incarnation" of the Logos in the λόγοι, or natural principles,[43] of created things—an enormous theme in his cosmology.[44]

And yet the unique feature of this third and rather brief interpretation of the Logos-at-play is the emphasis on the peculiar divine benevolence operative in the flux of material creation. The portrait painted here is far from serene and candidly descriptive of the vulnerability of the cosmos. Yet this particular angle on divine providence is hardly unprecedented in Maximus (or Gregory). At the end of *Ambiguum* 7, commenting on Gregory's depiction of human beings as "a portion of God" who have "slipped down from above,"[45] Maximus takes up the question of bodily suffering as a part of human training for deification. He quotes an especially striking section from the same *Oration* where Gregory has already called the transitory things of this world "like toy pebbles in child's play" (ὥσπερ ἐν παιδίᾳ ψήφων):

But it seems to me, for this reason none of the good things of this present life can be relied on. They are short-lived. The things we see, though made by the creative Logos and the wisdom that transcends all wisdom, are always changing, now one way and now another, borne upward and then downward. That is why it seems we are being played with (παίζεσθαι). Be-

41. *Amb.* 71 (PG 91:1416A–B).

42. *Q. Thal.* 2 (CCSG 7:51); see also Vittorio Croce and Bruno Valente, "Provvidenza e pedagogia divina nella storia," in *Maximus Confessor: Actes du Symposium sur Maxime le Confesseur, Fribourg, 2–5 septembre 1980,* edited by Felix Heinzer and Christoph Schönborn, 247–59, Paradosis 27 (Fribourg: Éditions universitaires, 1982).

43. E.g., *Amb.* 7 (PG 91:1077C–1085A), 10 (1188C–93C), 33 (1285C–88A).

44. See Torstein Theodor Tollefsen, *The Christocentric Cosmology of St. Maximus the Confessor,* Oxford Early Christian Studies (Oxford: Oxford University Press, 2008), 64–137.

45. *Or.* 14.7 (PG 35:865B–C), quoted in *Amb.* 7 (PG 91:1068Dff.).

fore something can be laid hold of it escapes our grasp. Yet there is purpose in all this, for
when we reflect on the instability and fickleness of such things, we are led to seek refuge in
the enduring things that are to come.[46]

Again in *Ambiguum* 8, Maximus expands on a similar imagery from
Gregory Nazianzen, the "chaos" and "flux" at the underbelly of creation. Specifically here he elucidates yet another passage from *Oration* 14 where, in the
context of discussing the problem of divine justice related to horrific bodily suffering, Gregory writes: "But whether their [diseased persons'] suffering
comes from God is not clear so long as matter bears with it chaos (τὸ ἄτακτον),
as in a flowing stream (ὥσπερ ἐν ῥεύματι).[47] Maximus proposes that the chaos
within the material realm was originally begotten of human sin, symptomatic
of the whole existential crisis of human liability to passions, pain, and death,
and creaturely exposure to "the instability (τὸ ἄστατον) and inequality (τὸ
ἀνώμαλον) of external and material being, and the capacity and proneness for
undergoing change."[48] But the converse side of this tragedy is the resourcefulness of the provident God who is not taken off guard, and who, having anticipated the crisis, works within the fabric of creation to seize reconciliation
and transformation from the jaws of alienation and annihilation. Either, he
says, God subjected human souls to the liabilities of bodily life punitively, at
the instant humanity lapsed—a view congenial with Paul's message about the
Creator subjecting the creation to corruption, not willingly, but with a view
to subjecting it in hope (Rom. 8:20); or else the Creator, foreknowing Adam's fall, antecedently capacitated the soul to experience the liabilities of bodily existence so as to learn its true dignity and its goal of transcending bodily
finitude.[49]

In any event, the all-wise Provider uses the "chaos" in the "flowing stream"
of material creation to reorder and redeem his fragile creation. Here, as in *Ambiguum* 71 (see the passage quoted above at note 41) and in several other texts,
Maximus employs the phrase "bearing and being borne along" (φέρουσά τε καὶ
φερουμένη) to describe the peculiar dynamic of how creatures experience the

46. *Or.* 14.20 (PG 35:884A–B), quoted in *Amb.* 7 (PG 91:1093A–B), and in *On the Cosmic Mystery
of Jesus Christ: Selected Writings from St. Maximus the Confessor*, trans. Paul Blowers and Robert Wilken,
Popular Patristic Series 25 (Crestwood, N.Y.: St. Vladimir's Seminary Press, 2003), 67.

47. *Or.* 14.30 (PG 35:897B), in *Amb.* 8 (PG 91:1101Dff).

48. *Amb.* 8 (PG 91:1104A), and *On the Cosmic Mystery*, trans. Blowers and Wilken, 76.

49. *Amb.* 8 (PG 91:1104A–B).

salutary buffeting of the stream of corporeal existence.[50] This is the deeper typological meaning of Jonah's plunge into the abyss (Jonah 1:15–2:7, LXX): the
submergence of human nature into chaos, where it both bears and is borne
along in the instability and confusion of materiality.[51] And yet the buffeting is
precisely God's means for preventing creatures from inclining in an endlessly
unnatural direction.[52] Exploiting not only Nazianzen's imagery, but also the
Bible's own rich perspective on chaos and creation, Maximus envisions chaos
as an undercurrent in the flow of historical existence that God is perpetually
taming and reorienting to his good purposes.[53] The dialectic of "bearing" and
"being borne along" reflects at the existential level the larger metaphysical dialectic of activity and passivity intrinsic to created beings.[54] In turn creatures
are called simultaneously to resign themselves to the punitive and rehabilita-
tive "flow" of creation (in which God's providential strategy and "play" are
still operative) and to put up a fierce ascetical resistance to the negative undercurrent of chaos that threatens to engulf them in material instability.[55] Here
as elsewhere in the Confessor's spiritual doctrine, the goal is healthy passibility, the submission of the passible self to the regenerative action of God who,
through the incarnate Christ, transformed human passibility.[56] Meanwhile, as
Maximus puts it bluntly, chaos (τὸ ἄστατον) and conductibility (τὸ φερόμενον)
remain the only stability and security of embodied creatures.[57] The apparent
disorder "disposes" (καθίστημι) human life in a manner actually arranged by
God's providential plan to convert creatures from the confusion of material
existence to the equanimity of spiritual goods.[58] In the life to come, however,
there will be no "bearing and being borne along."[59]

50. *Amb.* 8 (PG 91:1105B); *Amb.* 71 (PG 91:1416B).
51. *Q. Thal.* 64 (CCSG 22:191).
52. Maximus Confessor, *Ep.* 10 (PG 91:449B–C).
53. See Blowers, "Bodily Inequality, Material Chaos, and the Ethics of Equalization in Maximus the
Confessor," *Studia Patristica* 42 (2006): 52.
54. On this metaphysical dialectic see *Amb.* 7 (PG 91:1073B–77B).
55. See Blowers, "Ethics of Equalization," 54–56.
56. *Q. Thal.* 21 (CCSG 7:127–33).
57. *Amb.* 8 (PG 91:1105B).
58. Maximus Confessor, *Ep.* 10 (PG 91:449C–D).
59. *Amb.* 10 (PG 91:1172A); *Amb.* 42 (PG 91:1348D–49A).

The "Play" of Transitory Life in the World

Maximus's fourth and final "contemplation" of Nazianzen's image of the Logos-at-play is a sobering, parting reflection on the transitory nature of human life in comparison with the transformed life to come. The interpretation is simple and straightforward. We human beings, like all terrestrial animals, are born into this world and, like a fading flower, gradually wither and die, at which point we transfer to a whole new life. Our mundane existence is itself a "child's play," in Gregory's phrase, compared with "the future archetype of divine and authentic life."[60] Desiring once again to interpret Gregory with Gregory, Maximus quotes an arresting passage from his panegyric on Caesarius:

Such, brothers and sisters, is our transient life. Such is the game (παίγνιον) we play on this earth. We come into being out of nonbeing, and having existed we are dissolved. We are a dream that does not last, a fleeting apparition (Job 20:8), the passing flight of a bird (Wis. 5:11), a ship traversing the sea and leaving no waves (Wis. 5:10). We are like dust, vapor, early morning dew, a flower that blooms for a time and quickly fades.[61]

This is the same oration in which Nazianzen speaks of his brother's occupations in this world as mere child's play compared with his profession of Christianity, since they "have to do with the part we play on a stage that is rapidly put up and taken down, or perhaps more easily dismantled than constructed, as we can see from the many vicissitudes of this life and from the rise and fall of human prosperity."[62]

Steel asserts that in Maximus' interpretation and quotation of Gregory here we can detect a distant echo of Heraclitus' ancient dictum, noted earlier, about historical time being like a child who plays by moving his pawns, as if human life were a marvelous game.[63] Interestingly, in the cited eulogy for Caesarius, Gregory relishes the fact that his now glorified brother would be free from concerning himself with the Greek philosophers, including Heraclitus, among others.[64] But the comparison is still valid if we consider Maximus' de-

---

60. *Amb.* 71 (PG 91:1416C–D).

61. *Or.* 7.19, in *Amb.* 71 (PG 91:1416C–D).

62. *Or.* 7.10; cf. 7.9, where Gregory says that Caesarius used his secular career merely "as a stage, or as a mask of many transient faces for acting out the drama of this world."

63. Steel, "Le jeu du Verbe," 292.

64. *Or.* 7.20.

sire to preserve the salutary melancholia of Gregory's reflections on the fleeting play of human existence, reflections informed principally by biblical Wisdom literature and the Psalter.

Another and more compelling comparison, in my estimation, is with Plotinus' sophisticated analysis of humans as "living toys," by which he means the "external shadow of a human being" (ἔξω ἀνθρώπου σκιά) and not the inward self, the higher soul.[65] While souls should be transcending the fray of material life, the inevitable peril is that persons will forfeit their true character and be sucked into the frivolous child's play.[66] Nonetheless, this is not all without meaning teleologically. All human activity, even the most seemingly vacuous, is "artistic activity" (ἐνέργεια τεχνική) and capable of being formative.[67] Plotinus subsumes this image into a larger portrait of human existence as a grand play or drama arrayed with conflicts and struggles that can nonetheless give way to ultimate harmony through the provident Logos, the Reason Principle that radiates from the divine Mind (Νοῦς) and the World Soul.[68] The Logos comprehends order from out of the formative principles (λόγοι) of individual actors who, in their ontological remove from the Logos, are already differentiated and even contrary, and yet able through their relative freedom as actors and moral agents to move toward unity and concord.[69] Even if it is lost on the individual actors locked into the plot of the drama, there is a providence and benevolent necessity operative in the universal whole, which, though derivative of the generosity and goodness of the One, operates only through the Logos.[70]

Adequately to compare Plotinus and Maximus on the "play" of material human existence would require a detailed analysis well beyond the scope of this chapter. Certainly a crucial contrast between the two, nevertheless, is the nature of the Logos' insinuation into the play of transient human life. Unlike some of his Platonic predecessors such as Philo, Plotinus does not envision the Logos as the second divine ἀρχή, nor equate the Logos with the world of ideas. Although, as we noted above, his Logos radiates from the divine Mind, its "location" as such is properly with the World Soul.[71] In its own remove from the

65. *Enn.* 3.2.15.   66. *Enn.* 3.2.15.
67. *Enn.* 3.2.16.   68. *Enn.* 3.2.16.
69. *Enn.* 3.2.16–18.

70. On this doctrine of providence in Plotinus, see Dominic O'Meara, *Structures hiérarchiques dans la pensée de Plotin* (Leiden: Brill, 1975), 90–95.

71. See John Rist, *Plotinus: The Road to Reality* (Cambridge: Cambridge University Press, 1967), 100–102.

One, the Logos represents the world of ideas in the register of the material cosmos by comprehending all individual *logoi* of created beings, and such is its reconciling and unifying function. Maximus, too, as we briefly mentioned earlier, imagines the Logos as containing the *logoi*, or "incarnating" himself in the *logoi* of creatures, in an eschatological perspective. The profound difference with Plotinus is that the Logos for Maximus (and for Gregory) knows no ontological separation from the Father but, as the hypostasis of the coequal Son, condescends *kenotically* to bestow a deifying share of the life of the Trinity on humanity,[72] which is not only ontologically removed, but tragically alienated from the Father.

The salient contrast with Plotinus is that, for Maximus and Gregory, there is no providence and no hope amid the seemingly futile child's game of historical human existence apart from divine Incarnation. This is the true mystery of the Logos-at-play. For Maximus, that mystery, as an *incarnational* mystery, is centered in Jesus of Nazareth, but in its eschatological fullness it embraces all the "incarnations" of the Logos-Christ: in the *logoi* of the world, in the *logoi* (deep meanings) of Scripture, in the church and its sacraments, and in the virtues of the individual faithful.[73]

Conclusion

Has Maximus the Confessor done interpretive justice to Gregory Nazianzen's analogy of the Logos-at-play? Justice in this case, it seems to me, would lie in allowing Gregory's provocative image to maintain both its rhetorical and theological flair, even if it took on additional nuances in Maximus. This must have been a challenge to Maximus. Gregory was an accomplished rhetor and

---

72. Cf. *Q. Thal.* 60 (CCSG 22:79), 63 (CCSG 22:155); *Orat. dom.* (CCSG 23:31–32); on this motif in Maximus see Hans Urs von Balthasar, *Cosmic Liturgy: The Universe according to St. Maximus the Confessor*, 3rd ed., trans. Brian E. Daley (San Francisco: Ignatius Press, 2003), 103–4; and Felix Heinzer, "L'explication trinitaire de l'économie chez Maxime le Confesseur," in *Maximus Confessor: Actes du Symposium sur Maxime le Confesseur, Fribourg, 2–5 septembre 1980*, edited by Felix Heinzer and Christoph Schönborn, 160–72, Paradosis 27 (Fribourg: Éditions universitaires, 1983).

73. On these multiple "incarnations," see Irénée-Henri Dalmais, "La fonction unificatrice du Verbe incarné dans les oeuvres spirituelles de saint Maxime le Confesseur," *Sciences ecclésiastiques* 14 (1962): 445–59; von Balthasar, *Cosmic Liturgy*, 45, 120, 125–26, 278–79, 294, 355; Lars Thunberg, *Man and the Cosmos: The Vision of St. Maximus the Confessor* (Crestwood, N.Y.: St. Vladimir's Seminary Press, 1985), 75–79, 108–12, 149–73; Blowers, *Exegesis and Spiritual Pedagogy*, 117–30; and Cooper, *The Body in St. Maximus*, 36–48.

Maximus was not, such that the Confessor had to work patiently to nail down Gregory's artful rhetoric philosophically and to recontextualize his theological teaching for his own time.[74] In *Ambiguum* 71, I would contend, Maximus succeeds in providing not only a "clarification" but a kind of *sensus plenior* of Gregory's analogy of the Logos-at-play, true to the spirit—and, shall we say, "playfulness"—of the original analogy, while exploring new perspectives, as well. The upshot is a theological montage, with each of Maximus' four interpretations—some perhaps more adventurous or "conjectural" than others—supplementing and qualifying the other three.

Let us recall that the original context of Nazianzen's comment on the Logos-at-play is an excursus in his poem *Precepts for Virgins* on miraculous features of the natural world that evidence the Logos' handiwork. For Maximus Gregory is not just musing on the wonders of creation, but saying something profound about the nature of the Logos' activity in the world. To broach the subject of that activity is ipso facto to elicit the work of divine Incarnation. Exactly here begins Maximus' own "playfulness" with Gregory's image. As we have seen, Maximus in the first of his interpretative contemplations cuts to the quick, fecundating Gregory's image by recurring to Paul's paradox of divine foolishness. Rather than diluting the figure, this magnifies it all the more, dramatizing the dialectic of divine transcendence and immanence, the depth of God's condescension to creation, and the utter wisdom of the incarnational οἰκονομία.

Furthermore, in his second interpretation Maximus describes, on a breathtaking scale, the Logos' play as his maneuverability or agility in negotiating creation and history between God's appointed beginning and end. The Logos in the mystery of his Incarnation works precisely through the "stable flux" of the cosmic continuum, perpetually bringing order out of chaos and using instability as the raw material, not simply to stabilize the world, but to goad it toward God's new creation. Maximus enhances Gregory's analogy of the Logos-at-play by projecting it through the lens of Pseudo-Dionysius's equally potent image of God's "ecstasy" toward creation, his passionate outreach to the world. At this level, Maximus adds, the Logos is like a compassionate parent or pedagogue

74. Andrew Louth, "Saint Gregory the Theologian and St. Maximus the Confessor: The Shaping of Tradition," in *The Making and Remaking of Christian Doctrine: Essays in Honour of Maurice Wiles,* edited by Sarah Coakley and David Pailin (Oxford: Clarendon Press, 1993), 123–24.

stooping to his creatures' child's play in order to entice them toward the higher reaches of contemplation and deification. Indeed, the analogy of God's "reckless abandon" in pursuing his creatures, and the more serene (and traditional) image of the benevolent pedagogy of the Logos, are really of a piece.

Maximus' last two interpretations of Gregory's analogy are closely interrelated, and are concise reconsiderations of seminal motifs in his second interpretation. Their tone is decidedly more melancholy, as Maximus reflects on the deadly seriousness of the game of corporeal existence and on creation's liability to relapse into chaos. This too is very much in the spirit of Gregory. I noted earlier the passage from his poem *On the Cheapness of the Outward Man,* where Gregory invokes Plato's image of humanity being God's toy (παίγνιον).[75] It appears in a passage where Nazianzen seems to mimic Qoheleth:

> Winter again, summer again, springtime, fall, in alternation;
> days and nights, the dual perspective of our lives;
> heaven, the earth, the sea; there's nothing in this that's new to me,
> neither in what stands still, nor what keeps turning.
> Enough with them! Give me, please, another life, another world:
> Striving for this, I'll bear all sufferings gladly.
> If only I had died when wrapped in my mother's womb,
> and when the tears first came, there had been darkness!
> What is life? I've leapt from one tomb [the womb], I go to another,
> and after that tomb, I'll be buried in fire, uncared for.
> This little I breathe is a swift running river's flow,
> always receding and returning again,
> having nothing stable; it's only dust that flies into
> my eyes, so that I tumble far below God's lights,
> feeling my way about the walls, and wandering here and there.
> Let me keep my two feet out of this great life.
> I'll venture to make this true assertion: that man therefore
> is God's toy, like one of the ones they feature in the cities.[76]

Several poetic pieces in Gregory's *Poetica moralia* showcase this lamentation on the bleakness of human existence, and the stark fragility of life is poignant

---

75. See above at note 6.

76. *Carm.* 1.2.15, *De exterioris hominis vilitate* (PG 37:775A–776A), Peter Gilbert, ed., *On God and Man, 143.*

as well in his *Oration* 14—all this from the pen of one who fiercely defended God's cosmic providence and wisdom.[77]

> It is, after all, very much within the skill of the Craftsman if he should adapt the occasional disorder and unevenness of the material realm to achieve the purpose of his creation; and this will be grasped and acknowledged by all of us when we contemplate the final, perfect beauty of what he has created. But he is never lacking in the skill of his art, as we are, nor is this world ruled by disorder, even when the principle by which it is ordered is not apparent to us.[78]

The point is, for Gregory and Maximus alike, that the "child's play" of human life is eschatologically transparent to the sublime resourcefulness of the Logos who plays within the bosom of his creation to realize his perfect purposes. The Logos-at-play bespeaks the Creator's urge to cajole and "tease" the creation toward its true destiny, using all created "playthings" at his disposal. To stretch the analogy of divine gamesmanship a bit further, but congenial still with the thinking of Gregory and Maximus, the Creator "competes," not against an opposing evil principle or demiurge, but against nonbeing itself, which threatens to engulf creatures, to return them, after the fall, to nonexistence. "Play" and "chaos" together tell the tale of a *creatio continua* whereby the Logos is ever doing a new thing in providentially nurturing and transfiguring the cosmos. For Maximus the image of divine play is simply another rich metaphor for the "hidden fruitfulness" and infinite creativity of God, who reaches down from his transcendence in "ecstatic" love for the creation.[79]

That Gregory or Maximus would be so adventurous as to rework the ancient metaphor of divine playfulness is truly striking, given the adamant posturing of the patristic tradition, with few exceptions, against the culture of entertainment and amusement.[80] Frivolity and religion hardly seemed compatible, and godly delight needed to be refashioned ascetically or liturgically, as in Gregory of Nyssa's image of human nature's prelapsarian—and eschatological—dance in the presence of the Creator as Leader of the dance, a dance that can still find expression in the fallen world.[81] Maximus for his part finds

77. Cf. *Or.* 14.30–33; *Poemata arcana* 4–5; Carm. 1.1.6, *De eodem argumento* (*PG* 37:430A–38A).
78. *Or.* 14.31.
79. See von Balthasar, *Cosmic Liturgy*, 103–6.
80. Cf. Rahner, *Man at Play*, 36–105; Dirk Westerkamp, "Laughter, Catharsis, and the Patristic Conception of the Embodied Logos," in *Embodiment in Cognition and Culture*, edited by John Michael Krois, et al., 223–41, Advances in Consciousness Research 71 (Amsterdam: John Benjamins, 2007).
81. *In inscriptiones psalmorum* 2.6 (GNO 5:86), 2.2 (GNO 5:74), 2.13 (GNO 5:138); cf. *Hom. in Eccl.* 6 (GNO 5:388–89). Cf. the image of the soul's cosmic dance before God in Plotinus *Enn.* 6.9.8.

in Nazianzen's analogy of the Logos-at-play the perfect chemistry to rehearse the agony and the ecstasy, the misery and the mirth, that Christ and his creation enact in their reciprocal roles in the drama of cosmic transformation.

In closing I wish to dedicate this chapter to my former teacher, colleague, and friend of over thirty years, Fred Norris, who perhaps more than any recent scholar of Gregory Nazianzen has showcased the communicative power of his rhetorical images.[82] Fred, moreover, has combined serious scholarship with a contagious joviality and "playfulness" animating his forty-year teaching career. In a theological culture habitually liable to take itself with almost morose seriousness, and edified by all too few prophets of the playful God, Fred has demonstrated that the service of the theologian is not just dialectical prowess or rhetorical conviction, but the catching up of students in the sheer felicity of the transformative Logos-at-play.

82. See Norris, "Gregory Contemplating the Beautiful: Knowing Human Misery and Divine Mystery through and Being Persuaded by Images," in *Gregory of Nazianzus: Images and Reflections,* edited by Jostein Børtnes and Tomas Hägg, 19–35 (Copenhagen: Museum Tusculanum Press, 2006).

Andrea Sterk

13. Gregory the Theologian, Constantine the Philosopher, and Byzantine Missions to the Slavs

O Gregory, thou art a man in body but an angel in spirit.... For thy lips praise God like one of the Seraphim, and enlighten the universe with the teaching of true faith. Therefore, accept me who comes to thee with love and faith and be my teacher and enlightener.

—*Life of Constantine*

As a young pupil in Thessalonica, Constantine the Philosopher, better known as St. Cyril, apostle to the Slavs, drew the sign of the cross on his wall and penned this eulogy to his lifelong patron and mentor. Gregory Nazianzen's influence in Byzantine literature is well attested,[1] and the translation and importance of his writings in the Slavic world have also received attention.[2] Less explored and more puzzling in light of Gregory's own career, however, is the

---

1. Jacques Noret, "Grégoire de Nazianze, l'auteur le plus cité après la Bible dans la literature ecclésiastique byzantine," in *II. Symposium Nazianzenum, Louvain-la-Neuve, 25–28août 1981,* edited by Justin Mossay (Paderborn: Schöningh, 1983). For a survey of Gregory in Byzantine literature, see Simelidis, *Selected Poems.*

2. Frederick Thomson, "The Works of St. Gregory of Nazianzus in Slavonic," in *II. Symposium Nazianzenum,* ed. Mossay, 119–25, and Helmut Keipert, "Die altbulgarische Übersetzung der Predigten des Gregor von Nazianz," in *Slavistische Studien zum X. internationalen Slavistenkongress in Sofia 1988,* edited by Reinhold Olesch and Hans Rothe, Slavistische Forschunben 54 (Cologne: Böhlau, 1988).

connection in the latter half of the ninth century between Gregory and the fresh burst of missionary activity in this era. On several levels the life and writings of Gregory the Theologian served as a primary inspiration for Byzantine mission to the Slavs, especially in the ninth century's reorganization of the imperial academy and the renaissance of classical studies under Michael III and Basil I.

In this chapter I will examine evidence of Gregory's influence on mission, particularly his inspiration to Constantine the Philosopher. Two works will be central to this inquiry: the *Life of Constantine* (*LC*) and the prologue to the translation of the Gospels attributed to Constantine-Cyril. Although among the earliest works of Slavic literature, from a literary standpoint these writings represent the high point of Old Church Slavonic.[3] Though the authorship of these works is still debated, both are considered compositions of Constantine, Methodius, or a circle of their disciples and were composed before the end of ninth century. Focusing primarily on writings connected with Constantine the Philosopher, I hope to illumine some of the reasons Nazianzen held special significance for him, for other early Byzantine missionaries to the Slavs, and for the self-understanding of the newly missionized peoples in Byzantine history.

Along with the literary quality of these early Slavic writings, the historical value of the *Life of Constantine* has been well established.[4] While Constantine's mission to the Slavs of Moravia is the best-known part of the *Life*, it takes up a relatively small portion of the eighteen chapters of the text; yet the

3. Ihor Ševčenko, "Three Paradoxes of the Cyrillo-Methodian Mission," in *Ideology, Letters and Culture in the Byzantine World*, edited by Ihor Ševčenko, 220–36 (London: Variorum, 1992), here 231–35. For an introduction to Old Church Slavonic, see Alexander M. Schenker, *The Dawn of Slavic: An Introduction to Slavic Philology*, Yale Language Series (New Haven: Yale University Press, 1995).

4. Francis Dvornik, *Les legends de Constantin et de Méthode vues de Byzance*, 2nd ed., Russian Series 12 (Hattiesburg, Miss.: Academic International, 1969), disproved that the LC and LM were based on ninth- and tenth-century Byzantine legends; see Dvornik, *Byzantine Missions Among the Slavs: Ss. Constantine-Cyril and Methodius*, Rutgers Byzantine Series (New Brunswick, N.J.: Rutgers University Press, 1970). For more recent treatments, see Gilbert Dagron, Pierre Riché, and André Vauchez, *Évêques, moines et empereurs (610–1054)*, Histoire du christianisme 4 (Paris: Desclée, 1993), 217–24; Alexander Avenarius, *Die byzantinische Kultur und die Slawen: Zum Problem der Rezeption und Transformation (6. bis 12. Jahrhundert)* Veröffentlichungen des Instituts für Österreichische Geschichtsforschung 35 (Vienna: Oldenbourg, 2000), 54–90; and Sergey A. Ivanov, *Vizantiiskoe Missionerstvo: Mozhno li sdelat' iz "varvara" khristianina?* (Moscow: Institute of Slavic Culture, 2003), 149–52.

themes of mission, conversion, and disputation with various groups of nonbe-
lievers are prominent throughout Constantine's career.[5] The debt to Gregory
will be evident on several levels: as a theological mentor for Constantine, as a
paradigm for the philosopher's life, and as literary model for the saint's biographer. Franc Grivec was among the first to examine connections between the
writings of Gregory Nazianzen and the *Lives* of Constantine and Methodius.
Vladimir Vavřínek has argued that Grivec overemphasized the *Lives'* dependence on Gregory's panegyrical orations, ignoring important distinctions and
missing the biographers' creative uses of the Theologian.[6] Nevertheless, some
of the literary parallels reveal aspects of Gregory's thought that Constantine
prized and incorporated into his own teaching or that the author of his *Life*
identified with the Philosopher.

That Constantine was exposed to Nazianzen during his studies in Constantinople would not be surprising, but even before his arrival in the capital
the young Constantine had come to revere the Theologian. The son of a high-
ranking military officer, he was raised in Thessalonica, a Byzantine theme with
a large Slavic population. From boyhood he demonstrated unusual intellectual prowess, surpassing all his fellow students in learning and memory. Indeed, already as a boy Constantine had "committed to memory the writings
of St. Gregory the Theologian."[7] Though we do not know which writings the
biographer had in mind, it was not unusual for students to memorize autobiographical poetry; and given the likelihood that Nazianzen's poetry was used
in the school curriculum, it would not be surprising if his poems were memo-
rized.[8] The reference to memorizing Gregory's writings leads into the poetic
eulogy Constantine composed in Gregory's honor and wrote on the wall of

5. The *Life of Constantine* (LC) and *Life of Methodius* (LM) are edited in *Constantinus et Methodius Thessalonicenses Fontes,* edited by F. Grivec and F. Tomšič, Radovi staroslavenskog instituta 4 (Zagreb:
Radovi staroslavenskog instituta, 1960), 95–143 and 147–67; English translations in Marvin Kantor, *Medieval Slavic Lives of Saints and Princes,* Michigan Slavic Translations 5 (Ann Arbor: University of Michigan, 1983), 25–81 and 99–129.
6. Vladimir Vavřínek, "Staroslovenske Životy Konstantina a Metodeje a panegyriky Řehoře z Nazianzu," *Listy filologické* 85 (1962): 96–122, and Vavřínek, *Staroslověnské Životy Konstantina a Metoděje*
(Prague: Nakladatelství Československé Akademie věd, 1963), 50–60. Grivec and Franz Gnidovec are
cited by Vavřínek in his essay.
7. LC 4.17: *Constantinus et Methodius,* ed. Grivec and Tomšič, 97; Kantor, *Medieval Slavic
Lives,* 29.
8. See Simelidis, *Selected Poems,* chap. 2.2: "The Poems and the School Curriculum," 75–79. See
Dvornik, *Légendes,* 25–35, for comparisons of Constantine's elementary education.

his room.[9] Immediately afterward, the author describes Constantine's immersion in "numerous discourses" and in lofty ideas, yet sadness at his inability to fully comprehend their meaning.[10] Presumably these discourses refer to Nazianzen's theological writings, which eluded the young pupil, who found no one in Thessalonica able to instruct him beyond the level of grammar.[11] Unable to progress further in his native city, Constantine eagerly accepted the offer of Theoctictus, the logothete, to continue his education in Constantinople alongside the emperor Michael III.[12]

Explicit references to Gregory and allusions to his writings are most abundant in the early chapters of the *Life* concerning Constantine's upbringing and intellectual gifts. Direct borrowings are especially evident in *LC* 4, the chapter describing Constantine's studies in Constantinople, which closely parallels sections of the funeral oration on Basil (*Oration* 43).[13] In subsequent chapters direct citations are rare, but the Theologian's influence is implicit throughout, and Constantine's life and career bore many similarities to those of his famous predecessor. Like Gregory in Athens, Constantine studied in Constantinople with the leading scholars of his day. After turning down prospects of marriage, wealth, and position, and even hiding in a monastery for six months, Constantine finally acceded to the offer of an academic chair to "teach philosophy to his countrymen and foreigners"[14] A renowned scholar even at a young age, he was chosen to engage in a series of disputations

9. LC 3.18–19: *Constantinus et Methodius*, ed. Grivec and Tomšič, 97; Kantor, *Medieval Slavic Lives*, 29. For a discussion of its genre, see Antonín Dostál, "Konstantin der Philosoph und das Ausmass seiner geistigen Bildung," *Byzantinische Forschungen* 1 (1966): 80–82, and Ivan Dujčev, "Constantino Filosofo nella storia della letteratura bizantina," *Studi in onore di Ettore Lo Gatto et Giovanni Maver*, 205–22; here 209–12, Collana di "Ricerche slavistiche" 1 (Florence: Sansoni, 1962). Dujčev also attempts to reconstruct the original Greek. (212)

10. LC 3.21: *Constantinus et Methodius*, ed. Grivec and Tomšič, 98; Kantor, *Medieval Slavic Lives*, 29.

11. Franc Grivec, *Sveti Ćiril I Metod: Slavenski blagovjesnici* (Zagreb: Kršćanska sadašnjost, 1985), 14, and Dostál, "Konstantin der Philosoph," 77.

12. This detail is clearly erroneous, since Michael III could only have been six years old in 842 or 843 when Constantine arrived; Dvornik, *Byzantine Missions Among the Slavs*, 55–56.

13. Ševčenko, "Three Paradoxes," 234 and nn. 55 and 56, has praised the literary quality of the Old Church Slavonic and the skill with which the *Life*'s author has assimilated his Greek models. For side by side parallel passages of LC 4 and Gregory's *Or.* 43, see Vavřínek, "Staroslovenske Životy Konstantina," 106–7.

14. LC 4.19: *Constantinus et Methodius*, ed. Grivec and Tomšič, 100; Kantor, *Medieval Slavic Lives*, 33. Constantine is cast as one who struggled with the tumult of the world, demands of the active life over against contemplation. The real reasons for his temporary withdrawal were likely political (i.e., murder of his patron Theoctistus by Bardas); see Dvornik, *Légendes*, 112–13.

with important religious leaders of his day—iconoclasts, Muslims, and Jews in Khazaria. Indeed, discussions with the Khazars during his imperially sponsored mission form the longest single section of the *Life,* and disputations take up over half the work as a whole.[15] Describing the mission to the Khazars, the biographer explains how he was able to record in such detail the substance of the Philosopher's disputations. He condensed his account from Constantine's writings, "which our teacher Archbishop Methodius translated and divided into eight discourses."[16] This passage reminds us that in his early career Constantine wrote in Greek, and parts of his own writings were incorporated into the text of his *Life.* Although he drew broadly from patristic authors, his knowledge of Gregory was particularly influential, especially in his disputations with iconoclasts and Muslims, in which the doctrine of the Trinity was central. Constantine's metaphors also echo the Theologian's language. In his debate with the Arabs, for example, he compared God to "the breadth of the sea," recalling Gregory's comparisons of God's limitless nature with a "great sea of Being."[17] Similarly, the biographer seems to have drawn from Nazianzen regarding Constantine's defense of the Trinity in this disputation, comparing him to David, who with three stones slew the giant Goliath.[18]

Most relevant for the theology and practice of mission is the Philosopher's disputation with the Trilinguists, which is worth examining in greater detail before returning to Gregory. The story of Prince Rastislav's appeal to the Byzantine emperor for "a bishop and teacher" to explain the Christian faith to his people in their own language is well known. In response Emperor Michael III sent Constantine along with his older brother, the monk Methodius, explaining, "For you are both Thessalonians and all Thessalonians speak pure Slavic."[19] Given the tendency to idealize Byzantine universalism regard-

---

15. LC 5, 6, 9–11, and 16 are almost wholly devoted to disputations. Vavřínek, *"Staroslověnské Životy Konstantina,"* 111, affirms that 56 percent of the *Life* consists of disputations.

16. LC 10.95–96: *Constantinus et Methodius,* ed. Grivec and Tomšič, 118; Kantor, *Medieval Slavic Lives,* 57. Dujčev, "Constantino Filosofo," 214–17, praises Constantine's rhetorical skill and style. Though the Greek manuscript has been lost, this piece is confirmed by Latin and Slavic sources.

17. LC 6.17: *Constantinus et Methodius,* ed. Grivec and Tomšič, 104; Kantor, *Medieval Slavic Lives,* 37; cf. *Or.* 38.7 and 45.3; see also Vavřínek, *"Staroslověnské Životy Konstantina,"* 110. For discussion of such metaphors in Gregory, see Beeley, *Gregory of Nazianzus on the Trinity,* 95–96.

18. LC 6.6: *Constantinus et Methodius,* ed. Grivec and Tomšič, 103; Kantor, *Medieval Slavic Lives,* 35; cf. *Or.* 5.30 describing his second invective against Julian.

19. LM 5.8: *Constantinus et Methodius,* ed. Grivec and Tomšič, 155; Kantor, *Medieval Slavic Lives,* 111. For the request, the invention of an alphabet, and Michael III's response to Rastislav, see LC 14.

ing languages over against Latin intolerance, it is worth noting that Constantine faced opposition to his linguistic work already in Constantinople. His initial response to the emperor's request suggests that Byzantine opponents of the Slavic liturgy deemed such activity heretical.[20] Nevertheless, encouraged by Michael and his advisors, who recognized this undertaking as an innovation without recent historical precedent, Constantine and his associates gave themselves to prayer. God soon appeared to the Philosopher, and "he began to write the language of the Gospel, that is: 'In the beginning was the Word and the Word was with God, and the Word was God.'" In his letter accompanying Constantine's embassy, Michael described the revelation of a Slavic script as a divine intervention enabling the Moravian people to be "counted among the great nations that praise God in their own language."[21] Unfortunately, the *Life* reveals nothing specific about the Philosopher's translation work prior to setting out for Moravia. We know only that the mission was received by Rastislav "with great honor," and Constantine was given students to instruct. He taught them "Matins and the Hours, Vespers and the Compline, and the Liturgy."[22]

If opposition to Constantine's translation work was minimal in Constantinople, however, opponents of the vernacular Scriptures posed a considerable obstacle in Moravia. Frankish priests already working in this area attempted to undermine his efforts, arguing that "only three languages, Hebrew, Greek, and Latin, were chosen as appropriate for rendering glory unto God." Fighting "like David with the Philistines," the biographer explains, "Constantine defeated them with words from the Scriptures, and called them trilinguists."[23] The work of translating texts and training disciples continued successfully for forty months, then spread to Pannonia, where Constantine taught fifty students entrusted to him by the ruler Kocel. Yet opposition from the trilinguists resumed in Venice, where, before an assembly of "bishops, priests and monks

---

20. LC 14.11: *Constantinus et Methodius,* ed. Grivec and Tomšič, 129; Kantor, *Medieval Slavic Lives,* 67. Regarding diverse Byzantine perspectives on vernacular languages, see also Dimitri Obolensky, "Cyrille et Methode et la christianisation des Slaves," *Settimane di Studi del Centro Italiano di Studio sull'Alto Medioevo* 14 (1967): 587–609; here 592–93.

21. LC 14.13–18: *Constantius et Methodius,* ed. Grivec and Tomšič, 129; Kantor, *Medieval Slavic Lives,* 67.

22. LC 15.1–2: *Constantius et Methodius,* ed. Grivec and Tomšič, 131; Kantor, *Medieval Slavic Lives,* 67–69. On these earliest liturgical texts translated, see Dvornik, *Byzantine Missions Among the Slavs,* 107–9.

23. LC 15.7-9: *Constantius et Methodius,* ed. Grivec and Tomšič, 131; Kantor, *Medieval Slavic Lives,* 69.

gathered against him like ravens against a falcon," the Philosopher delivered an impassioned defense of Slavic letters.[24] Largely a concatenation of quotations from the Psalms and Gospels interspersed with Constantine's interpretive comments, the Philosopher began with the following string of questions: "Does not God's rain fall upon all equally? And does not the sun shine also upon all? And do we not all breathe air in the same way? Are you not ashamed to mention only three tongues, and to command all other nations and tribes to be blind and deaf?... We know of numerous peoples who possess writing and render glory unto God, each in its own language."[25] Not only do the passages he cited emphasize the equality of all nations and languages before God, but Constantine even modified slightly the wording of Matthew 5:45—changing "just and unjust" and "evil and good" to "equally" and "upon all"—in order to avoid any insinuation that the Slavs might be naturally inferior or less virtuous.[26] He ended with a long, almost verbatim citation of 1 Corinthians 14 on the subject of tongues and prophecy, by which he is said to have shamed his audience.

Constantine and his biographer may well have drawn from a variety of patristic sources in presenting this famous defense. Many homilies and apologetic treatises included lists of nations to which the Gospel had spread, although Constantine's list is distinctive, as well, focusing on lands around the Caucasus that were particularly relevant to imperial politics in his own day. Likewise, the defense of barbarian languages was not unknown to the Philosopher, going back to Clement of Alexandria and the sermons of John Chrysostom and Theodoret.[27] Gregory Nazianzen also affirmed the essential equality of Greeks and barbarians.[28] Indeed, Sergey Ivanov notes that, unlike Eusebius,

24. LC 16: Kantor, *Medieval Slavic Lives,* 71. Why Constantine left Pannonia for Venice is nowhere explained in the text.

25. LC 16.4–7: *Constantius et Methodius,* ed. Grivec and Tomšič, 134; Kantor, *Medieval Slavic Lives,* 71.

26. Ševčenko, "Three Paradoxes," 230. Although he sees the spirit of equality with which missionary work was conducted as one of the "three paradoxes" of the Cyrillo-Methodian mission, Ševčenko does not deny that Constantine was a cultured member of the Byzantine elite, finding no trace of condescension in Constantine's language toward missionary work among the Slavs.

27. See John Chrysostom, *Homiliae* 8, PG 63, 499–510; Theodoret of Cyrrhus, *Graecarum affectionum curatio,* V, 55–60, 66, 70–72, 74–75; and Clement of Alexandria, *Stromateis* 1.77.3 to 78.1; see also Sergey A. Ivanov, "Casting before Circe's Swine: The Byzantine View of Mission," in *Mélanges Gilbert Dagron,* edited by Gilbert Dagron and V. Déroche, 295–301; here 297–99, Travaux et Mémoires 14 (Paris: Association des amis du Centre d'Histore et Civilisation de Byzance, 2002): 295–301; here 297–99.

28. See e.g. *Or.* 7.22, and *Ep.* 136 to the (Gothic) *magister militum* Modarius. For developments in

who viewed barbarians more as enemies than as potential objects of Christianization, Gregory and Chrysostom advocated "the equality of all peoples before Christ."[29] As important as such perspectives were in shaping Constantine's views, it was probably not discussions of barbarians or lists of evangelized nations that most influenced the Philosopher in his missionary vocation, but rather Gregory's theory of language. In his lengthy paraphrase of 1 Corinthians 14, Constantine used the biblical text to redefine "barbarian" in terms that expressed the importance of speech, language, and meaning: "There are, it may be, so many kinds of voices in the world, and none of them is without signification. Therefore, if I know not the meaning of the voice, I shall be unto him that speaketh, a barbarian, and he that speaketh, shall be a barbarian unto me."[30] Like Gregory, Constantine emphasized the comprehensibility of language despite the essential incomprehensibility of God.[31]

The necessity of words, especially the words of Scripture, for salvation is a theme developed more fully in other writings attributed to Constantine, but it is evident in the *Life,* as well. It shows up clearly well before the account of the Moravian mission, while Constantine and Methodius were en route to Khazaria. Stopping with the imperial embassy in Cherson, Constantine "learned the Hebrew language and scriptures." Moreover, a certain Samaritan who came regularly to debate him once brought Samaritan Scriptures to him. Constantine took the Scriptures, locked himself in his room to pray, and was granted understanding from God so that he began to read the Scriptures in this tongue "without error." Upon hearing this, the Samaritan recognized that Christ had given him grace and the Holy Spirit, and "his son was baptized immediately and he himself was baptized after him."[32] This is the first mention in the *Life* of the Philosopher's role in conversion, and it is associated with translating and reading the words of Scripture. The connection between Scripture, language, translation, and conversion appears also in the emperor's letter to

Greek views of barbarians see Gerhard Podskalsky, "Die Sicht der Barbarenvölker in der spätgriechischen Patristik (4.–8. Jahrh.)," *Orientalia Christiana Periodica* 51 (1985): 330–51.

29. Ivanov, *Vizantiiskoe Missionerstvo,* 64–65. He places Sozomen, Cyril of Alexandria, and Theodoret in the same category, "on the side of the barbarians," before describing the opposite emphasis among later Byzantine authors.

30. LC 16.27–28: Kantor, *Medieval Slavic Lives,* 73. See also LC 6.25: Kantor, *Medieval Slavic Lives,* 37, for Constantine's affirmation that "man is distinguished from beasts by his speech and intelligence."

31. See Beeley, *Gregory of Nazianzus on the Trinity,* 95–96.

32. LC 8.11–14: *Constantinus et Methodius,* ed. Grivec and Tomšič, 109; Kantor, *Medieval Slavic Lives,* 43.

Rastislav. Introducing Constantine, Michael explained that "God, who will
have all men come unto the knowledge of the truth and raise themselves up
to a great nation ... arranged now, in our time, to fulfill your request and reveal a script for your language. Therefore, we have sent you the one to whom
God revealed this." He then affirmed the great value of this precious gift, urg-
ing the ruler to accept it and "not reject universal salvation."[33] Commenting
on the results of Constantine's translation work in a conflation of verses from
Isaiah, the biographer described how "the ears of the deaf were unstopped,
the Words of the Scripture were heard, and the tongues of stammerers spoke
clearly." Similarly affirming the power of the Scriptures, in Venice Constantine
described the trilingual heresy, with its insistence on only three tongues, as
condemning "all other nations to be blind and deaf?"[34]

These two themes, the connection between words and salvation and especially the comprehensibility of language, are more fully developed in a prose
preface to the Slavic lectionary, which appears to be the work of Constantine
himself. Although the text is badly damaged, scholars have been able to reconstruct most of this so-called *Macedonian Folio,* a one-page Slavic translation of
an original Greek document, cited by the tenth-century Bulgarian scholar John
the Exarch, in the introduction to his own translation of John of Damascus.[35]
The opening five lines are severely mutilated, but the editor suggests that they
allude to Christ's command in Mark 16:15, "Go into all the world and preach
the gospel to the whole creation," which immediately preceded his ascension,
the gift of tongues, and the related instructions in 1 Corinthians 14, which are
cited later in the preface.[36] After alluding to earlier translations of the Gospels
into diverse languages, Constantine explains his own approach to the challeng-

33. LC 14:16–19: *Constantinus et Methodius,* ed. Grivec and Tomšič, 129; Kantor, *Medieval Slavic Lives,* 67.

34. LC 15.3: *Constantinus et Methodius,* ed. Grivec and Tomšič, 131; Kantor, *Medieval Slavic Lives,* 69; cf. Isaiah 29:8, 35:5–6, and 32:4. LC 16.5: Constantine, *Constantinus et Methodius,* ed. Grivec and Tomšič, 134; Kantor, *Medieval Slavic Lives,* 71.

35. André Vaillant, "La Préface de l'Évangéliaire vieux-slave," *Revue des études slaves* 24 (1948): 5–20. Dvornik, *Byzantine Missions Among the Slavs,* 117–18, suggests that this discussion of translation was written by Constantine the Philosopher to accompany parts of the Gospel already translated into Slavic. See also Ševčenko, "Three Paradoxes," 230, and Schenker, *The Dawn of Slavic,* 195, for praise of the sophis-tication of the *Macedonian Folio* and an English translation of an excerpt. Citations here follow Vaillant's French rendering of the reconstituted Slavonic.

36. Vaillant, "La Préface," 6–7. The phrase indicating that those who received the commandments would fly "without wings" (*bez krilov*) in line 6 may draw from Gregory's oration on Pentecost (*Or.* 41.16).

es of translation. Noting that a masculine noun in Greek may at times be best translated with a feminine noun in Slavonic, he concludes, "It is not always possible to render the Greek word, but it is necessary to preserve the meaning." And again: "it is for the meaning that we translate [the teachings of the Gospel], and not only for exactness of the words."[37] The closing lines of the *Macedonian Folio* reemphasize the fruitlessness of focusing on words rather than meaning.

This emphasis on meaning over words corresponds very closely with Gregory's theory of language, emphasized especially in sections of *Oration* 31. Here Gregory described those who read the Scriptures not in a frivolous or cursory manner, but rather "with penetration so that they saw inside the written text to its inner meaning."[38] Similarly, he continued, "There really is a great deal of diversity inherent in names and things, so why are you so dreadfully servile to the letter ... following the syllables while you let the facts go? ... I should be considering meanings rather than words, and so, in the same way, if I hit upon something meant, though not mentioned, or not stated in clear terms, by Scripture, I should not be put off by your quibbling about names—I should give expression to the meaning."[39] Alongside the crucial "distinction between facts and names," Frederick Norris has explained, for Gregory, "there is a difference between 'meanings' and 'words.' The 'meanings' are what we look for."[40] The Theologian's arguments in this section of *Oration* 31 were part of his defense of the Spirit's divinity, despite an assumed lack of scriptural support. As the best recent interpreters of this sermon have emphasized, for Gregory language was only an approximation of what is real; truth lies in the realities to which the words, as signifiers, point.[41] Nazianzen's arguments in this regard did not form part of a treatise on translation, but his statements would certainly have application for translators of Scripture, particularly for those steeped in his teachings. His ideas were clearly assimilated by the author of the preface to the Slavic lectionary, and the approach to translation described here corresponds closely to the scheme the Philosopher followed in his own translation work. More-

37. Vaillant, "La Préface," 10–11.

38. *Or.* 31:21, trans. Wickham.

39. *Or.* 31:24, trans. Wickham.

40. Norris, *Faith Gives Fullness to Reasoning*, 33.

41. Norris, *Faith Gives Fullness to Reasoning*, 192; Beeley, *Gregory of Nazianzus on the Trinity*, 169 and n. 48.

over, we read in the *Folio* the same passage from 1 Corinthians 14 that Constantine cited in his Venetian speech, affirming meaning over words and the importance of comprehensible speech: "and I would rather say five words with my spirit to instruct others also than infinite words with my tongue."[42]

Like Gregory, then, Constantine recognized the limitations of language yet affirmed the comprehensibility of words and the dignity of humanity, who is given the gift of words. Tomáš Špidlík has particularly emphasized this dimension of Gregory's theology of language, especially the notion of humanity as *logikos* because the human participates in the Logos of God, as an aspect of his thought that inspired Constantine the Philosopher.[43] Gregory's ecclesiastical career and even his articulation of a theory of language seem far removed from the missionary work carried on by the earliest Byzantine missionaries in Moravia. Yet his words, whether prose or verse, clearly resonated with the Philosopher in his work of teaching and translating among the Slavs. In his passionate defense of his translation work in Venice, Constantine compared diverse languages with musical instruments, the sounds of the pipe or harp or the ring of a trumpet. Each of these has its own signification. In one of his autobiographical poems, Gregory used similar terms to describe his own vocation to praise the Word of God with language as a *hymnopolos kithare*.[44]

Gregory was no mere theoretician of language, nor concerned primarily with theological method. Even his lofty theological orations were pronounced in a liturgical setting, and his poetry expressed perhaps even more poignantly his goal of praising and proclaiming the Trinity. He was "fundamentally a confessional theologian, a preacher of the gospel,"[45] and Constantine the Philosopher seems to have recognized the Theologian as a kindred spirit in this

42. Vaillant, "La Préface," 11; cf. LC 16.36: *Constantinus et Methodius,* ed. Grivec and Tomšič, 135; Kantor, *Medieval Slavic Lives,* 73–75.

43. Tomáš Špidlík, "L'influence de Grégoire de Nazianze sur Constantine-Cyrile et Methode et sur la spiritualité slave," in *The Legacy of Saints Cyril and Methodius to Kiev and Moscow, Proceedings of the International Congress on the Millennium of the Conversion of Rus' to Christianity, Thessaloniki, November 26–28, 1988,* edited by Anthony-Emil N. Tachiaos, 39–48; here 41–43 (Thessaloniki: Hellenic Association for Slavic Studies, 1992).

44. LC 16.23–24: *Constantinus et Methodius,* ed. Grivec and Tomšič, 135; Kantor, *Medieval Slavic Lives,* 73; cf. Gregory, *Carm.* 2.1.38, v. 50–52 (PG 37:1329). These two passages are compared in Špidlík, "Gregorio Nazianzeno: Maestro e ispiratore di Constantino-Cirillo," in *Christianity Among the Slavs: The Heritage of Saints Cyril and Methodius,* edited by Edward G. Farrugia, Robert F. Taft, and Gino K. Piovesana, Orientalia Christiana Analecta 231 (Rome: Pontifical Oriental Institute, 1988), 301.

45. Norris, *Faith Gives Fullness to Reasoning,* 36.

regard. Indeed he not only drew inspiration from the poet-philosopher for his own writing, instruction, and translation work, but he equated Gregory's teachings with the work of an evangelist. Examining more closely the passage of the *Life* with which we began, we find that Constantine actually cast his mentor in the role of a missionary. In his poetic encomium to the Theologian, originally composed as a boy seeking Gregory's guidance as a teacher, he described him as "a man in body, but an angel in spirit." It was not uncommon in the Eastern tradition to equate monasticism with the "angelic life." Gregory is called an angel, however, neither for his ascetic virtues nor for his role as a philosopher but because "like one of the seraphim," his lips "praise God" and "enlighten the universe with the teaching of true faith."[46]

Another early medieval Slavic text connected with Constantine's missionary activity is the poetic preface appended to his translation of the four Gospels, generally referred to by the Slavic title *Proglas* or Prologue. Although it was long assumed to be the work of Constantine the Philosopher, most historians and literary scholars now concur with the assessment of André Vaillant that the poem was composed by Constantine of Preslav, also known as Constantine the Presbyter, a disciple of Methodius who served as a priest in Bulgaria before replacing Naum as Bishop of Preslav.[47] Like Constantine-Cyril and Methodius, Constantine of Preslav was clearly inspired by the Theologian, whose homilies, along with other important Greek patristic writings, he translated into the Slavic language. While he says that Naum, his predeces-

46. LC 3, 18–19: Kantor, *Medieval Slavic Lives,* 29. On Gregory as an earthly angel, see Avenarius, *Die Byzantinische Kultur und die Slawen,* 74 and 208, and Špidlík, "L'influence," 40. On the missionary aims of Gregory's Christian Hellenism, see John A. McGuckin, *Saint Gregory of Nazianzus,* 75–76, and Beeley, *Gregory of Nazianzus on the Trinity,* 76–79, who suggests that Nazianzen uses philosophical traditions "for Christian persuasion and conversion" (78). Beeley notes, however (79n50), that Claudio Moreschini and Susanna Elm see Gregory's aims quite differently, as an effort to promote a Platonist worldview. Constantine's own attribution of angelic status to Gregory seems much more in keeping with McGuckin's and Beeley's explanation.

47. On Constantine of Preslav, see Emil Georguiev, "Konstantin Preslavski," in *Kiril and Methodius: Founders of Slavonic Writing—A Collection of Sources and Critical Studies,* edited by Ivan Duichev, East European Monographs 172 (New York: Columbia University Press, 1985): 161–80. For the text of the *Proglas* and arguments for its attribution to Constantine of Preslav, see André Vaillant, "Une Poésie vieux-slave: La Préface de L'Évangile," *Revue des etudes slaves* 33 (1956): 7–25; also Schenker, *The Dawn of Slavic,* 198–99. On Preslav as a literary school, its prominent authors, and the development of Cyrillic in Preslav, see George C. Soulis, "The Legacy of Cyril and Methodius to the Southern Slavs," *Dumbarton Oaks Papers* 19 (1965): 19–43; and Avenarius, *Die byzantinische Kultur und die Slawen,* 161–76.

sor in Preslav, urged him to write, in his prose prologue to the "Exegetic Homilies" he cites the words of the Theologian to explain his motivation for undertaking literary pursuits.[48]

Besides his homiletic writings, Constantine of Preslav is generally considered the author of two closely related works of poetry, the *Alphabet Prayer* and the *Proglas.* Both these poems have been praised for their sophisticated adaptation of Byzantine poetic forms.[49] The former work, an alphabetic acrostic poem that formed the introduction to the *Homiliary Gospel,* not only rejoices in the Slavic people who are "flying towards baptism," but repeatedly exalts and invokes the Word, the Spirit, and "the Trinity in the deity."[50] These themes are reminiscent of the Theologian, and even the choice of an acrostic style may have been inspired by a gnomic acrostic of Gregory.[51] Whether by Constantine the Philosopher himself or Constantine of Preslav, the metrical *Proglas,* composed no later than 900, expresses the spirit of the Philosopher and the earliest Byzantine missionaries to the Slavs.[52] Extolling the creation of Slavic letters and the Slavic Scriptures, the poem begins with an allusion to Acts 2 (Pentecost): "Christ comes to gather the nations and tongues, since he is the light of the world."[53] Similarly, the *Life of Methodius* includes a letter from Pope Hadrian to the Pannonian ruler Kocel, in which he encouraged the Slavs to guard the truth they had come to hear and understand in their own language and exhorted them during the Mass to read the *Apostolos* and Gospel "first in Latin, then in Slavic, that the word of the Scripture might be fulfilled: 'Praise the Lord all yet nations,' and elsewhere, 'all the different tongues

48. Georguiev, "Konstantin Preslavski," 168.

49. Goerguiev, "Konstantin Preslavski," 166–68; Soulis, "Legacy of Cyril and Methodius," 33; and especially Roman Jakobson, "The Slavic Response to Byzantine Poetry," in *Selected Writings,* edited by Roman Jakobson, vol. 6, part 1, 240–59 (New York: Mouton, 1985). Schenker, *The Dawn of Slavic,* 218, and Ševčenko, "Three Paradoxes," 235, note that it was composed in regular Byzantine dodecasyllables, but Ševčenko judges it "hardly a masterpiece of Byzantine poetics."

50. For both a literal English translation and a metrical acrostic see *Kiril and Methodius,* ed. Duichev, 143–46.

51. Cf. *Carm.* 2.1.30 (PG 37:908–9). For this comparison see Avenarius, *Die byzantinische Kultur und die Slawen,* 162n548.

52. OCS text and French translation in Vaillant, "Une Poésie," 10–13 and 21–23 respectively; English translation in Roman Jakobson, "St. Constantine's Prologue to the Gospel," *St. Vladimir's Quarterly* 7 (1963): 16–19, preceded by Jakobson's introduction, 14–16; see also Ševčenko, "Three Paradoxes," 235, and Dvornik, *Byzantine Missions Among the Slavs,* 118.

53. Prologue, vv. 3–4: Jakobson, "Constantine's Prologue," 16.

shall claim the greatness of God as the Holy Spirit gave them utterance.'"[54] This reference to Acts 2:4 describing the descent of the Spirit on the apostles at Pentecost seems to equate the reception of the Slavic liturgy with a second Pentecost, an idea that reappears and evolves in other works of the Cyrillo-Methodian tradition.[55]

Citing the book of Isaiah, the *Proglas* expresses an emphasis similar to that of the *Life of Constantine* on the comprehensibility of words, without which people are destined to senselessness: "Since they have said, 'The blind shall see, the deaf shall hear the Word of the Book, for it is proper that God be known.'" Emphasizing the power of the Word and the comprehensibility of words in one's own language, the poet explains that the Gospels will "divide men from brutish existence and desire, so that you will not have intellect without intelligence," for "hearing the Word in a foreign tongue" is like listening to the voice of a "noisy gong." As Ševčenko has noted, the reference to bestiality from which the Gospel saves human beings was a typical Byzantine sentiment; but the comparison of "a foreign tongue," presumably Greek, to a "noisy gong," is strikingly unimperial and even unpatriotic for most Byzantines.[56]

While Špidlík was probably incorrect in attributing this work to Constantine the Philosopher, he astutely observed the dependence of the *Proglas* on the thought of Gregory the Theologian.[57] Echoing Nazianzen's enthusiasm for the Word, the poet emphasizes its role in both nourishment and enlightenment: "The Word nourishing human souls, The Word strengthening heart and mind, The Word preparing all to know God."[58] He incorporates common patristic metaphors that stress the role of the Scriptures in salvation—light to the eyes (vv.28–31), food for the body (vv. 25, 58–60, 91) sweetness to the taste (v. 39), life or death to the soul (vv. 41–42, 61–63), arms with which to fight the Adversary (vv. 80–81). There are also numerous metaphors and parallel pas-

54. LM 8.13: *Constantinus et Methodius,* ed. Grivec and Tomšič, 158; Kantor, *Medieval Slavic Lives,* 115.

55. Obolensky, "Cyrille et Méthode," 605.

56. Ševčenko, "Three Paradoxes," 231. The words *mědnъa zvona* in line 49 have been rendered "copper bell" by Jakobson, "Constantine's Prologue," 18, and "sonnerie d'airain" by Vaillant, Une Poésie," 22. That *mědnъa zvona* alludes to the χαλκὸς ἠχῶν (noisy gong) of 1 Corinthians 13:1 seems to have been overlooked by the editors.

57. Špidlík, "Gregorio Nazianzeno."

58. Prologue, vv. 25–27: Jakobson, "Constantine's Prologue," 17. See *Or.* 6.5–6 for an example of Gregory's passionate expressions of praise for the Word.

sages apparently borrowed from Nazianzen.[59] For example, Špidlík emphasizes the comprehensibility of words in Gregory's writings and finds clear echoes of this theme in the *Proglas*. The poet quotes the same passage from 1 Corinthians 14 that was cited in both the *Life of Constantine* and Constantine's prose preface to the lectionary. Tying together the emphasis on words and tongues or languages that is central to the message of the poem as a whole, he cites St. Paul: "I had rather speak five words that all the brethren will understand than ten thousand words which are incomprehensible."[60]

Celebrating the gift of Slavic letters and the life-giving power of the Word, the *Proglas* also proclaims the universal mission of the church and the role of the Slavs in the fulfillment of that mission. The opening call to "hearken, all ye Slavs" (v. 9) subtly shifts from an appeal to "Slavic people" (v. 23) to "ye men" (v. 65) to "ye nations" (v. 83), bringing us back full circle to the opening refrain.[61] There, in language that alludes to Pentecost, explicitly invoked in the *Life of Methodius,* the poet announces that "Christ comes to gather the nations and tongues." What is intimated in this verse of the *Proglas* is developed more explicitly in the Russian context. The Pentecostal miracle is not merely the descent of tongues or languages, but the triumph of unity over confusion, the abrogation of Babel by Pentecost.[62] As succinctly narrated in the Byzantine *kontakion* for Pentecost: "When the Most High went down and confused the tongues, he divided the nations: but when He distributed the tongues of fire, He called all men to unity."[63] The notion that the reuniting of languages at Pentecost overcame the confusion of tongues caused by building the Tower of Babel appeared in the writings of several early church fathers, but Gregory of Nazianzus was among its most prominent proponents.[64] He expressed the contrast between the two events in his oration for the festival of Pentecost:

But as the old Confusion of tongues was laudable, when men who were of one language in wickedness and impiety, even as some now venture to be, were building the Tower; for by the

59. See Špidlík, "Gregorio Nazianzeno," especially 300-303, and nn.7–31 for parallels and probable borrowings. On the challenge of determining Gregory's influence in later Byzantine literature see Peter Karavites, "Gregory Naizanzinos and Byzantine Hymnography," *Journal of Hellenic Studies* 113 (1993): 81–98; here 81.

60. Prologue, vv.52–53: Jakobson, "Constantine's Prologue," 18.

61. Jakobson, "Constantine's Prologue," 16.

62. On the contrast between Babel and Pentecost in the Cyrillo-Methodian tradition, see Obolensky, "The Heritage of Cyril and Methodius in Russia," *Dumbarton Oaks Papers* 19 (1965): 54–56.

63. As cited in Obolensky, "Heritage of Cyril and Methodius," 55–56.

64. Arno Borst, *Der Turmbau von Babel: Geschichte der Meinungen über Ursprung und Vielfalt der*

confusion of their language the unity of their intention was broken up, and their undertaking destroyed; so much more worthy of praise is the present miraculous one. For being poured from One Spirit upon many men, it brings them again into harmony.[65]

Although deemed less profound theologically and artistically than the preceding three orations in the Maurist ordering and less sophisticated or fully developed than his fifth theological oration on the Holy Spirit,[66] *Oration 41* became a particularly rich source for Byzantine hymns.[67] Indeed, Gregory's prose orations, with their short rhythmic sentences, were likely a greater inspiration to later Byzantine poets than his poems and "were employed almost verbatim by the great majority of Byzantine hymnographers."[68] Compared with other works in Gregory's corpus, *Oration 41* also became relatively well-known and copied in the medieval Slavic context.[69] A Byzantine churchman nourished by the Theologian's writings—whether Constantine the Philosopher or Constantine of Preslav—would have found ready inspiration in his words for their missionary work among the Slavs.

In his recent essay on Byzantine religious mission and his much fuller Russian monograph, medieval historian Sergey Ivanov has argued that the work of Constantine-Cyril and Methodius was an anomaly in Byzantine ecclesiastical history, an exceptional missionary effort that the Byzantine government ultimately failed to support or sustain.[70] The Byzantines lost inter-

---

Sprachen und Völker (Stuttgart: Anton Hiersemann, 1957), 1:227–57; especially 246 on Gregory; see also Obolensky, "Heritage of Cyril and Methodius," 56 and n. 35.

65. *Or.* 41.16; trans. Browne and Swallow, *NPNF* 2.7:384.

66. For a negative assessment of the theological value of this oration, see Moreschini's introduction, *SC* 358 .82–88. For a helpful discussion of *Or.* 41 in the context of Gregory's developing pneumatology, see Beeley, *Gregory of Nazianzus on the Trinity*, 156–74, especially 163–64 and 172–73.

67. Karavites, "Byzantine Hymnography," 81–98. For the uses of *Or.* 41 on Pentecost see 84–87, especially 87, where he discusses the passage contrasting Babel with Pentecost.

68. Karavites, "Byzantine Hymnography," 98. Celia Milanović-Barham, "Gregory of Nazianzus: *Ars Poetica* (In suos versus: Carmen 2.1.39)," *Journal of Early Christian Studies* 5, no. 4 (1997): 497–510; here 499, also affirms that Gregory's "prose orations and not his poetry served as a source of inspiration to late Byzantine poets."

69. Thomson, "Works of St. Gregory of Nazianzus in Slavonic," examines the two earliest collections of Gregory's works translated into Slavonic, and *Or.* 41 is one of eight orations included in both collections (19–20). See also Leslie Brubaker, *Vision and Meaning in Ninth-Century Byzantium: Image as Exegesis in the Homilies of Gregory of Nazianzus* (Cambridge: Cambridge University Press, 1999), 239–42, on the late ninth-century illustration of this ovation, where the connection between Gregory's words and contemporary Byzantine missions is unmistakable.

70. Sergey A. Ivanov, "Religious Missions," in *The Cambridge History of the Byzantine Empire c.*

est in the fate of their work, for they were unable to separate missionary effort from political and cultural goals, which were better served in subduing, and hence Christianizing, barbarians closer to home. As evidence of this disinterest Ivanov notes that contemporary Greek sources never mention the Moravian mission. Similarly, after mitigating the unwarranted praise of Byzantine linguistic tolerance and encouragement of national Slavic liturgy, Ihor Ševčenko admits that even the Thessalonian brothers might have originally set out on their mission with "Byzantine ideological and cultural interests" in mind. To be sure, there are hints of Byzantine cultural imperialism in the *Life of Constantine,* as there is evidence of cultural elitism in the writings of Gregory Nazianzen.[71] Ševčenko, however, presents a more dynamic picture of the Byzantine missionaries and their motives: "But in the course of years spent abroad their perspective must have changed. Men of their caliber do not voluntarily exchange lecturing at university in the Imperial City for teaching the catechism in Prince Kocel's Mudtown, or peaceful contemplation in a monastery on the Bithynian Olympus for a dungeon in a Swabian prison, merely to further Byzantine cultural imperialism."[72] Although this is not the ideal place to debate the role of mission in Byzantine discourse, to comprehend the complex phenomenon of Byzantine mission we must understand the best as well as the worst of political and theological motivations. By exposing the intellectual and vocational parallels between Constantine the Philosopher and Gregory the Theologian, I hope that I have not completely exonerated either.

Following the lead of John McGuckin, I would like to speculate in closing on how Nazianzen himself would have viewed the work of Constantine and Methodius and his own legacy among the Slavs.[73] Gregory would have been delighted to be the inspiration of a scholar, apostle, and lover of the Word such as Constantine the Philosopher. He might have been surprised to learn

---

500–1492, edited by Jonathan Shepard, 305–32 (Cambridge University Press, 2008) 316; Ivanov, *Vizantiiskoe Missionerstvo,* 159; see also Ivanov, "Casting Pearls."

71. Ševčenko, "Three Paradoxes," 230 and n. 34, cites three sentences from *Life of Constantine* that might be interpreted as expressions of Byzantine elitism—all prior to his Slavic mission. Ivanov, "Religious Missions," 317–18, attributes the failure of the Moravian mission to cultural pride and inflexibility by Methodius and his coworkers. On Nazianzen's condescension, see Norris, *Faith Gives Fullness to Reasoning,* 7–8 and 34–35.

72. Ševčenko, "Three Paradoxes," 231.

73. McGuckin, *Saint Gregory of Nazianzus,* 402, ends his biography with reflections on Gregory's probable response to his portrayal and influence in Byzantine history.

that his teachings on the Word and the Spirit had unleashed such a Babel of barbarian tongues. Ultimately, however, I suspect he would have been pleased to hear of the new Pentecostal miracle that resulted in the Slavic Scriptures and liturgy. Despite his cultural elitism, arrogance toward opponents, and apparent struggle between contemplative and active life, as Frederick Norris has so aptly reminded us, Gregory was fundamentally a "preacher of the Gospel"—as were his Byzantine heirs in their missionary work among the Slavs.

Susanna Elm

14. Emperors and Priests

Gregory's Theodosius and the Macedonians

Between 879 and 882 CE, emperor Basil I and his family were presented with an illustrated copy of Gregory of Nazianzus' *Orations.* Produced in Constantinople, this copy "is arguably the most complex and internally sophisticated illustrated manuscript ever produced in Byzantium."[1] Known as *Parisinus Graecus 510,* it is also one of the most intensely discussed manuscripts, not least because it is only one of two extant illustrated manuscripts of all of Gregory's orations (rather than of the selections known as the "liturgical sermons," of which several illustrated copies survive).[2] In addition, the manuscript represents what "the artisans, their employer, and the family for whom *Paris.gr. 510* was made" considered "visually thinkable around the year 880," after the end of iconoclasm. The family in question, that of Basil I, were the founders of the so-called Macedonian dynasty associated with a renaissance after the end of iconoclasm; it was a dynasty that from its inception prided itself for

1. Leslie Brubaker, *Vision and Meaning in Ninth-Century Byzantium: Image As Exegesis in the Homilies of Gregory of Nazianzus* (Cambridge: University of Cambridge Press, 1999), xvii, 1–13. The manuscript also includes two letters each to Cledonius and Nectarius, two poems, two texts by other authors, and the beginning of Gregory's *Life* by Gregory the Presbyter. Several leaves at the end have been lost.

2. The second one is the so-called Milan Gregory, Bibl. Ambros. Cod. E 49/50; André Grabar, *Les miniatures du Grégoire de Nazianze de l'Ambrosienne (Ambrosianus 49–50) décrites et commentées,* Ambrosiana 46–50, Orient et Byzance 9 (Paris: Vanoest, 1943). For the illustrations of the liturgical sermons, not derived from *Paris.gr.* 510, see George Galavaris, *The Illustrations of the Liturgical Homilies of Gregory Nazianzenus* (Princeton, N.J.: Princeton University Press, 1969), 9–10, 146–49.

"its triumphant orthodoxy."[3] The employer, as Leslie Brubaker has convincingly argued, was Photius, the controversial patriarch of Constantinople and well-known polymath, to whose genius as book "reviewer," evidenced in the collection known as the *Bibliotheca,* we owe a significant portion of works by authors otherwise lost.[4] According to Brubaker, Photius' signature permeates *Paris.gr. 510.* The illustrations are an exegetical commentary on selections of Gregory of Nazianzus' orations reflecting the patriarch's particular concerns (for example, some illustrations mold appropriate passages into an imperial panegyric praising Basil, whom Photius had to propitiate after his exile), and the text itself bears marks of his editing hand (the arrangement of the orations and the text itself differs from all other manuscripts).[5] Indeed, Photius, who had sponsored illustrations in other media, was associated in the mind of his supporters and detractors alike with erudition, books, and pictures.[6] Needless to say, he too, like Basil I, considered himself a tireless defender of orthodoxy, engaged in ceaseless battles against the "Arians," as which he classified his iconoclast adversaries. *Paris.gr. 510* was meant to showcase all of these patriarchal characteristics in a manner one may characterize as conspicuous expenditure.[7]

When posing the question as to "why Photius chose to get involved with a manuscript of Gregory's Homilies" for this extravagant endeavor rather than texts by other foundational fathers of the church, Brubaker's conclusions are, however, scrupulously vague.

Why Photios selected Gregory's sermons as vehicle for his various messages is an unanswerable question.... Photius linked himself with the iconophile cause throughout his career ...

3. Gilbert Dagron, *Emperor and Priest: The Imperial Office in Byzantium,* trans. Jean Birrell (Cambridge: Cambridge University Press, 2003), 194; Shaun Tougher, *The Reign of Leo VI (886–912): Politics and People,* The Medieval Mediterranean 15 (Leiden: Brill, 1997), 1–2; see also Paul Magdalino, "The Bath of Leo the Wise and the 'Macedonian Renaissance' Revisited: Topography, Iconography, Ceremonial, Ideology," *Dumbarton Oaks Papers* 42 (1988): 97–118.

4. Brubaker, *Vision and Meaning,* 236–38; Sirarpie Der Nersessian, "The Illustrations of the Homilies of Gregory of Nazianzus, Paris gr. 510," *Dumbarton Oaks Papers* 16 (1962): 197–228, see esp. 227.

5. Brubaker, *Vision and Meaning,* 147–200 for the visual panegyric to Basil I; Gregory of Nazianzus, *Discours 42–43,* ed. Jean Bernardi, SC 247:53–68 (Paris: Éditions du Cerf, 1992), and Moreschini and Gallay, SC 318:64–73, for the manuscripts and *Paris.gr.* 510's variations.

6. Brubaker, *Vision and Meaning,* 236–38 with further bibliography.

7. Cyril Mango, *The Homilies of Photius, Patriarch of Constantinople,* Dumbarton Oaks Studies 3 (Cambridge, Mass.: Harvard University Press, 1958); Glenn Peers, "Patriarchal Politics in the Paris Gregory (B.N. gr. 510)," *Jahrbuch der Österreichischen Byzantinistik* 47 (1997): 51–71.

[and] Gregory was often cited in iconophile polemic.... [But] the choice of Gregory's Homilies for the weighted miniatures they now accompany could be in part fortuitous ... we can speculate any number of things, but in the end it may not matter so much which text Photios ultimately gave.[8]

Such scrupulous avoidance of any further speculation as to why Photius chose Gregory's orations, positing in effect that no particular link existed between the illustrations and these orations rather than, say, the work of John Chrysostom or Basil, leaves me slightly puzzled. Given the enormous expense of producing such a manuscript, the collaborative effort it represented, and its extraordinary sophistication masterminded by Photius as so clearly demonstrated by Brubaker, one is encouraged to suspect that there might have been more to the choice of Gregory's orations than merely the fact that Gregory and Basil "were the patristic fathers most often quoted by Byzantines of all periods; [so that] it may simply have been Gregory's undisputed orthodoxy ... that recommended his sermons to Photios."[9]

Suspicion that Photius' selection of Gregory's orations was more deliberate than Brubaker suggests is further heightened when considering Basil I's grandson, Constantine VII Porphyrogenitus. Constantine VII had Gregory's remains transferred to the Church of the Holy Apostles and had composed and pronounced a panegyric celebrating the event on January 19, 946.[10] This act initiated a series of celebrations, including a second one commemorating Gregory's death on January 25, focusing attention on that church, itself of particular significance for the emperor, and on his accession to power. As Bernard Flusin has shown, Constantine VII's arrangements—the celebration of the transfer of Gregory's remains on January 19 followed by celebrations of the martyrdom of Timothy on January 22, of Gregory's death on the 25th, and of the translation of the remains of John Chrysostom on January 27—indicate that the emperor attributed his effective assumption of power (after the removal of the remaining Lecapeni after a dinner party on January 27, 945, that allegedly averted an attempt on his life) to the protection of these saints,

8. Brubaker, *Vision and Meaning*, 238, 413–14.

9. Brubaker, *Vision and Meaning*, 413–14. She is not alone in this vagueness; see Simelidis, *Selected Poems*, 58.

10. Bernard Flusin, "Le panégyrique de Constantin VII Pophyrogénète pour la Translation des reliques de Grégoire le Théologien BHG 728," *Revue des études byzantines* 57 (1999): 5–97, esp. 40–97; English translation is mine.

Gregory preeminently among them.[11] Indeed, the emperor stressed Gregory's miraculous intervention in his panegyric, and it is evident that he wanted to cement this link between his assumption of rule and the saint's intervention through the ceremonies henceforth associated with the Church of the Holy Apostles, the mausoleum of Constantine the Great.[12]

Again, however, the question is why Gregory? Gregory was Cappadocian, which happened to be the base of the Phocades, one of the powerful military families on whose loyal service the emperors of the Macedonian dynasty relied. Constantine appointed Bardas Phocas as domestic of the *scholai* almost immediately after his accession. Bardas' ancestor, Nicephoros Phocas, in turn, had begun his military career under Basil I. Indeed, Constantine's father, Leo VI, had been "le grand protecteur" of the Phocades, and such a link via Leo all the way back to Basil I was presumably not lost on Constantine, whose issues regarding his imperial legitimacy are well-known.[13] However, Basil of Caesarea was also a Cappadocian, so regional coincidence hardly suffices to single out Gregory of Nazianzus.

Constantine VII himself offers additional insights. In his panegyric, which he modeled at least partially after Gregory's *Orations* 42 and 43, the emperor claimed that God had wished to ascertain that the city of Constantinople was ready to accept the treasure of Gregory's remains, "having reserved the revelation [of this treasure] for appropriate times, as he often does with his judgments, setting aside the periods of ignorance, but knowing in advance those periods in which faith would rule and designated those for his revelation of his

11. See also Flusin, "L'empereur hagiographe: Remarques sur le rôle des premiers empereurs macédoniens dans le culte des saints," in *L'empereur hagiographe: Culte des saints et monarchie byzantine et post-byzantine,* edited by Petre Guran, 29–54 (Bucharest: New Europe College, 2001).

12. Synax. CP *col.* 401–25; Constantine Porphyrogenitus, *Pan. BHG* 728, 9 and 18–19; Liuprand of Cremona, *Antapodosis* (et al.) 5.22, ed. Paolo Chiesa (Tournholt: Brepols, 1998) 136–37; Flusin, "Le panégyrique de Constantin VII," 11–12. For the events see Steven Runciman, *The Emperor Romanus Lecapenus and His Reign* (1929; Repr. Cambridge: University of Cambridge Press, 1963), 231–37; Arnold Toynbee, *Constantine Porphyrogenitus and His World* (Oxford: University of Oxford Press, 1973), 10–12; Mark Whittow, *The Making of Byzantium, 600–1025* (Berkeley: University of California Press, 1996), 321–22.

13. Theophanes, *Cont.* 426, 445–46, a source favorably disposed to that family; quoted in Gilbert Dagron and Haralambie Mihăescu, *Le traité sur la guérilla (De velitatione) de l'empereur Nicéphore Phocas (963–969),* Le monde byzantin (Paris: Editions du Centre National de la Recherche Scientifique, 1986), 9, 175; Tougher, *Reign of Leo VI,* 204–7; J. C. Cheynet, *Pouvoirs et contestations à Byzance (963–1210),* Série Byzantina Sorbonensia 9 (Paris: Publications de la Sorbonne, 1990), 264, 321; Whittow, *The Making of Byzantium,* 322. Cappadocia was also the base of one other important military family favored by Leo, that of the Argyroi; see Tougher, *Reign of Leo VI,* 207–18).

unspoken secrets" (*Pan.* 18).[14] By divine design Constantine VII had been chosen to restitute Gregory's remains to their appropriate place, Constantinople.
This act, according to Constantine, placed him on a par, symbolically, with the
ruler who had first "restituted the throne" to Gregory (*Pan.* 16). This emperor
was, of course, Theodosius I, and the throne that of bishop (or patriarch) of
Constantinople. Both Constantine VII and Theodosius had thus been divinely chosen to restore to Gregory the saintly honors he so richly deserved, and I
would like to use the remainder of this chapter to suggest that the relation between Theodosius and Gregory was a considerable factor in making the latter
so attractive a candidate both for Photius, Basil I's patriarch between 879 and
882, and for Constantine, the emperor in 946.

Constantine VII and Gregory's Theodosius

Scholars overwhelmingly if not exclusively associate Constantine Porphyrogenitus and indeed the Macedonian dynasty as a whole with Constantine's namesake, "the Great."[15] The artful creation of such a dynastic link is, of
course, no scholarly invention. Constantine VII himself made it explicit on
numerous significant occasions, for example, in his eulogistic life of the dynasty's founder, Basil. According to his grandson, when Basil had come to
the gates of Constantinople he fell asleep on the door of the monastery of St.
Diomedes, which contemporary accounts considered a foundation of Constantine the Great, and the saint himself alerted the *hegoumenos* that the vag-
abond at his doorstep was "anointed by Christ to become emperor." Basil in
response "rebuilt and enlarged [the monastery], adorned it, and endowed it
with many properties." In addition, Constantine VII left no doubt that Basil's mother, who had received a vision indicating her son's glorious future, had
herself been related to Constantine the Great.[16] Further, in the panegyric on

14. Flusin, "L'empereur hagiographe," 17–21.

15. Romilly Jenkins, *Byzantium: The Imperial Centuries AD 610–1071* (London: Weidenfeld and
Nicholson, 1966), 183–210, 256–68; Athanasios Markopoulos, "Constantine the Great in Macedonian
Historiography," in *New Constantines: The Rhythm of Imperial Renewal in Byzantium, 4th–13th Centu-
ries,* edited by Paul Magadlino, 159–70 (Aldershot: Ashgate, 1994).

16. Const. Porph., V. Bas. 3, 8 and 9, in *Chronographia,* by Theophanes Continuatus, edited by
Immanuel Bekker (Bonn: Corpus Scriptorum Historiae Byzantinae, 1838), 222; Patria 3.86, in *Scriptores
originum Constantinopolitanarum,* edited by Theodorus Preger (Leipzig: Tuebner, 1901–1907), 246–47;
Dagron, *Naissance d'une capitale: Constantinople et ses institutions de 330 à 451* (Paris: Presses universita-

Gregory, Constantine VII described himself as "our new Moses," who brought with Gregory's writings, the *Theological Orations* in particular, new "tablets" to the New Jerusalem (this is also how Gregory had described the quality of his words, e.g., in *Oration* 40.45 on baptism delivered in Constantinople: "give me the tablets of your heart, I am for you Moses ... and I write in you with God's fingers a new Decalogue").[17] Constantine the Great too had been considered a new Moses.[18] *Paris.gr. 510* already reflected the same dynastic link. For example, at the beginning of the manuscript a representation of Christ Pantokrator is followed by one of the Emperor Basil receiving Constantine's standard, the *labarum,* from the prophet Elijah and the crown from the archangel Gabriel.[19] Given such consistent imperial intent, from Basil to Constantine VII, linking the dynasty to Constantine the Great, it is easy to overlook another candidate also well worth considering when establishing orthodox imperial legitimacy: namely, Theodosius I.

In other words, when asking what may have made Gregory in particular so attractive both to Byzantine patriarchal and imperial eyes, his relation to Theodosius fairly leaps to mind. The majority of Gregory's orations are situated in Constantinople (even if he later revised them in Annesi) and here—as Frederick Norris has so superbly demonstrated—Gregory's establishment of "orthodoxy" was the central task.[20] However, while he may have provided the theory defining orthodoxy and heresy, the task of actually establishing it was accomplished through the agency and in the presence of an emperor. To cite Constantine VII again, "under the effect of divine inspiration, [Gregory] came to Byzantium, [and] engaged in incessant battle against those who held adverse opinions ... [that led to] the ruin of the pneumatomachoi, the derailing of the allies of Eunomius, the vanquishing of the defenders of Apollinarius." But he did so aided by the emperor who "restituted to him his throne, the possession of his seat confirmed by a conciliar reunion" (*Pan.* 15, 16).

Indeed, Gregory established and defended "orthodoxy" in Constantino-

ires de France, 1974), 319–22; Gyula Moravcsik, "Sagen und Legenden über Kaiser Basileios I," *Dumbarton Oaks Papers* 15 (1961): 59–129; see esp. 90–93 on the St. Diomedes legends.

17. δός μοι τὰς πλάκας τῆς σῆς καρδίας· γίνομαί σοι Μωσῆς ... ἐγγράφω δακτύλῳ Θεοῦ νέαν δεκάλογον.

18. Const. Porph. *Pan.* 37, 41, cf. 20; Flusin, "L'empereur hagiographe," 31–32; Claudia Rapp, "Imperial Ideology in the Making: Eusebius of Caesarea on Constantine as 'Bishop,'" *Journal of Theological Studies,* new series 49 (1998): 685–95.

19. Brubaker, *Vision and Meaning,* 5–6; Dagron, *Emperor and Priest,* 199–201.

20. Norris, *Faith Gives Fullness to Reasoning.*

ple together with Theodosius; both ensured victory over the entrenched enemies of the faith. This, at least, is how Gregory phrased it, and how later historians recorded the events.[21] According to Gregory's *De vita sua,* Gregory and Theodosius together entered the Church of the Holy Apostles upon Gregory's accession to the bishop's seat, both miraculously illuminated by a sudden ray of light (DVS 1354–80).[22] Citing Theodosius' own words, Gregory further ascertained that "through me [i.e., Theodosius], God gives the temple to you [Gregory] and to your pains" (1311–12). Indeed, in Gregory's estimation Theodosius had not been "a bad man, in respect of faith in God" and "exceedingly overcome by the Trinity" (DVS 1282–84). Comprehending fully that persuasion (as practiced by Gregory) and not coercion were the way to deal with those of heretical opinion (1293–1301), he made "his wishes into a written law of persuasion" (1302–4). What may sound a little tepid to our ears as far as praise for a ruling emperor is concerned must have resonated quite differently once Gregory had become an established saint of the highest order—that is, once Constantine VII read those words: here was an emperor who had saved the church for orthodoxy through his laws, and whose leadership qualities had been publicly endorsed by none other than "the Theologian."

Gregory as arbiter of imperial orthodoxy was a theme also resonating in the very *Oration* 43 that Constantine VII had used when composing his panegyric.[23] This oration, after all, depicts the famous encounter between Basil of Caesarea and Emperor Valens in 372, *nota bene* as shaped by Gregory in 382. Here, the emperor and infamous Arian heretic

21. For a broader discussion of the context, see Nicanor Gómez-Villegas, *Gregorio de Nazianzo en Constantinopla: Ortodoxia, heterodoxia y régimen teodosiano en una capital cristiana,* Nueva Roma 11 (Madrid: Consejo Superior de Investigaciones Científicas, 2000), 119–42; McGuckin, *Saint Gregory of Nazianzus,* 329–31; Neil McLynn, "Moments of Truth: Gregory of Nazianzus and Theodosius I," in *From the Tetrarchs to the Theodosians: Later Roman History and Culture, 284–450 CE,* edited by Scott McGill, Cristiana Sogno, and Edward Watts, 215–39 (Cambridge: University of Cambridge Press, 2010).

22. Traditionally, Holy Apostles is the church associated with this event; see McGuckin, *Saint Gregory of Nazianzus,* 325–27. It is obvious how this would have been an attractive tradition for Constantine VII, though McLynn's argument for Holy Wisdom rather than the Holy Apostles is probably closer to the historic circumstance, here not relevant; see McLynn, "Imperial Churchgoing," 235–70, n. 80; see also Robert Ousterhout, "Reconstructing Ninth-Century Constantinople," in *Byzantium in the Ninth Century: Dead or Alive? Papers from the Thirtieth Spring Symposium of Byzantine Studies, Birmingham, March 1996,* edited by Leslie Brubaker, 115–30, Society for the Promotion of Byzantine Studies 5 (Aldershot: Ashgate, 1998).

23. Flusin, "Le panégyrique de Constantin," 18–20.

entered the holy place with his bodyguard (it was the feast of Epiphany, and crowded) and took his place among the people, thus making a token gesture of unity.... But when he came inside, he was thunderstruck by the psalm-singing that assailed his ears, and saw the ocean of people and the whole well-ordered array around the bema.[24] ... Basil stood completely still, facing his people, as Scripture says of Samuel, with no movement of his body or his eyes or in his mind, as if nothing unusual had occurred, transformed so to speak, into a *stele* dedicated to God and the *bema;* while his followers stood around him in fear and reverence.[25] When the emperor saw this spectacle and was unable to relate what he saw to any previous experience, he reacted as an ordinary man would—his vision and his mind were filled with darkness and dizziness from the shock [...] For he started trembling, and had one of those from the platform had not reached out his hand and steadied him, he would have had a fall worthy of tears. (*Or.* 43.52)[26]

Gregory's Basil, majestic and imperial in his comportment, bested a heretical emperor reduced to indecorous trembling: an encounter that showcased to perfection Gregory's capacity to adjudicate between orthodox and heretical emperors. One further point, so brilliantly evoked in that scene, is the importance of imperial ceremonial.

Gregory, Theodosius, and Ceremonies

Indeed, Gregory's entire oeuvre contains numerous detailed descriptions of how to make imperial and civic ceremonial Christian. As I have shown elsewhere, Gregory's *Orations* 4 and 5, for example, address the proper manner of honoring an emperor in public, how the emperor ought to interact with the army, how public festivals should be conducted, how emperors should construct sacred buildings, how to conduct imperial funerals, and even how to

24. Εἰς γὰρ τὸ ἱερὸν εἰσελθὼν μετὰ πάσης τῆς περὶ αὐτὸν δορυφορίας—ἦν δὲ ἡμέρα τῶν Ἐπιφανίων καὶ ἀθροίσιμος–, καὶ τοῦ λαοῦ μέρος γενόμενος, οὕτως ἀφοσιοῦται τὴν ἕνωσιν.... Ἐπειδὴ γὰρ ἔνδον ἐγένετο καὶ τὴν ἀκοὴν προσβαλλούσῃ τῇ ψαλμῳδίᾳ κατεβροντήθη, τοῦ τε λαοῦ τὸ πέλαγος εἶδε καὶ πᾶσαν τὴν εὐκοσμίαν, ὅση τε περὶ τὸ βῆμα καὶ ὅση πλησίον.

25. τὸν μὲν τοῦ λαοῦ προτεταγμένον ὄρθιον, οἷον τὸν Σαμουὴλ ὁ λόγος γράφει, ἀκλινῆ καὶ τὸ σῶμα καὶ τὴν ὄψιν καὶ τὴν διάνοιαν ὥσπερ οὐδενὸς καινοῦ γεγονότος, ἀλλ' ἐστηλωμένον, ἵν' οὕτως εἴπω, θεῷ καὶ τῷ βήματι, τοὺς δὲ περὶ αὐτὸν ἑστηκότας ἐν φόβῳ τινὶ καὶ σεβάσματι.

26. ἐπειδὴ ταῦτα εἶδε καὶ πρὸς οὐδὲν παράδειγμα ἐδύνατο θεωρεῖν τὰ ὁρώμενα, ἔπαθέ τι ἀνθρώπινον· σκότου καὶ δίνης πληροῦται τὴν ὄψιν καὶ τὴν ψυχὴν ἐκ τοῦ θάμβους [...] Περιτρέπει γὰρ καί, εἰ μή τις τῶν ἐκ τοῦ βήματος ὑποσχὼν τὴν χεῖρα τὴν περιτροπὴν ἔστησε, κἂν κατηνέχθη πτῶμα δακρύων ἄξιον; Gregory of Nazianzus, *Discours 42–43*, ed. Bernardi, SC 247, 27; McGuckin, *Saint Gregory of Nazianzus,* 372–74; and Francis Gautier, *Le retraite et le sacerdoce chez Grégoire de Nazianze,* Bibliothèque de l'École des Hautes Études, Sciences religieuses 114 (Turnhout: Brepols, 2002), 405–6 for the date and context of *Or.* 43.

honor a divinized emperor and what the categories for imperial divination ought to be.[27] As the encounter with Valens cited above proves, and as Neil McLynn has so vividly illuminated, Gregory was also the first to choreograph the manner in which the emperor ought to perform within the sacred space of the church.[28] None of this, I think, would have escaped the author of the famous tenth-century book *De cerimoniis,* of course, none other than the emperor Constantine VII.[29]

Nor would Constantine VII have remained unaware of the fact that it was the emperor Constantine the Great who had founded Constantinople, but the emperor Theodosius the Great who truly made the city into a Christian imperial residence.[30] Not only was he the first emperor who actually lived in the city for more than a few months at a time, but during the fourteen years that he resided there, Theodosius established a way of being a Christian emperor in that city that "set the pattern for generations of Byzantine emperors who succeeded him."[31] Theodosius created the blueprint for celebrating imperial births (*CTh* 2.8.19)—he fathered five children "born into the purple" in the city—an "ancient practice" of which Constantine VII certainly approved (*De caer.* 2.21), as well as that of imperial marriages. Imperial funerals, too, were sadly common during his reign. Indeed, it was Theodosius who transformed Constantine's mausoleum at the Church of the Holy Apostles into a truly imperial resting place by transferring the remains of Julian, his wife, Helena, Jovian, his wife, Charito, and those of Valentinian and his first wife there.[32] Saints' relics such as those of the apostles Andrew, Luke, and Timo-

27. Susanna Elm, "Gregory of Nazianzus's Life of Julian Revisited (Or.4 and 5): The Art of Governance by Invective," in *From the Tetrarchs to the Theodosians,* 171–82, and Elm, *Sons of Hellenism, Fathers of the Church: Emperor Juilan, Gregory of Nazianzus, and the Vision of Rome,* Transformation of the Classical Heritage 49 (Berkeley: University of California Press, 2012).

28. McLynn, "Imperial Churchgoing," 250–56.

29. Const. Porph., *De cer.* in Constantine Porphyrogenitus, *Le livre des ceremonies,* edited by Albert Vogt (Paris: Les Belles-Lettres, 1935–1940).

30. As now shown by Brian Croke in "Reinventing Constantinople: Theodosius I's Imprint on the Imperial City," in *From the Tetrarchs to the Theodosians,* 241–64.

31. Croke, "Reinventing Constantinople," 242; Steffen Diefenbach, "Zwischen Liturgie und civilitas: Konstantinopel im 5. Jhd. und die Etablierung eines städtischen Kaisertums," in *Bildlichkeit und Bildort von Liturgie: Schauplätze in Spätantike, Byzanz und Mittelalter,* edited by Rainer Warland, 21–47 (Wiesbaden: Reichert, 2002).

32. Gavin Kelly, "The New Rome and the Old: Ammianus Marcellinus' Silences on Constantinople," *Classical Quarterly* 53 (2003): 588–607; see esp. 591–94; Philip Grierson, "The Tombs and Obits of the Byzantine Emperors (337–1042)," *Dumbarton Oaks Papers* 16 (1963): 1–63; see esp. 40–42.

thy had been transferred to the Holy Apostles by Constantine and Constantius (the latter an emperor Gregory had also frequently praised as a model of orthodoxy), but Theodosius extended the custom to bishops.[33] It was he who had conveyed a bishop's remains to his resting place in the manner of an imperial *adventus* (the funeral of Meletius of Antioch as described by Gregory of Nyssa's *In Meletium*), and in 381 he had the remains of Paul of Constantinople transferred back to the city, again placing special emphasis on the *adventus* as conveying divine grace upon the city facilitated by the emperor. Theodosius carried the bishop's skull through the city, creating a ceremony that united, in Brian Croke's words, "as common suppliants the court and clergy, aristocracy and general populace." Constantine VII emulated this practice, so it seems, when transferring Gregory's remains, by carrying his reliquary in his own hands as he stood in the bow of the imperial galleon sailing toward the city, and by following it on foot to its final resting place.[34] Paul's remains were just the first in a series of translations, all establishing the prestige of Theodosius and his family as incessant defenders of orthodoxy, as Christian emperors who had united the realm after the divisions caused by Arian heretics. As seen by Constantine VII, then, Gregory had provided the sacred words in which proper Christian belief and proper Christian ceremonial and behavior had been described. He was also the saint who acknowledged a saintly emperor when he saw one, and once restituted to the see that was properly his became a defender of the kingship of the one who restituted him (*Pan.* 44–45). But, in the end, Theodosius the emperor, the "second light bringing the sun" as the second founder of Constantinople, rivaling if not surpassing Constantine the Great, had restituted Gregory's throne; the emperor had issued the appropriate laws, constructed the monuments, and had instituted the actual ceremonies during his long residence in the city. It was a relationship between emperor and priest that Constantine VII, I think, could not fail to have appreciated.[35]

---

33. Richard W. Burgess, "The Passio S. Artemii, Philostorgius, and the Dates of the Invention and Translation of the Relics of Sts. Andrew and Luke," *Analecta Bollandiana* 121 (2003): 5–36; see esp. 28–34.

34. Const. Porph. *Pan.* 25, 28.

35. Anth. *Pal.* 16.65.

Photius and Gregory's Theodosius

Gregory, however, would not have been Gregory—and hence the man so enormously influential in Byzantium—were not nearly everything I have just outlined above as describing the relation between bishop and emperor also an argument showcasing why he would have been dear to the heart of Photius—why, in short, Photius might have picked all of *his* orations to present to emperor Basil I in the most lavish manner. Constantine VII deliberately chose Gregory as his "personal saint," prostrating himself before the saint "like a slave," and then asked "the saintly men formed in the sacred sciences" to confirm his imperial will after the fact to make it clear that, while saintly bishops acknowledged orthodox emperors, such emperors also knew how to pick their saintly patriarchs—in this case a deceased patriarch in contrast to whom the living one, Constantine's brother-in-law Theopylact Lecapenus (as well as some of his immediate precursors who had declared Constantine's father's fourth marriage to his mother illegitimate) "fait aussez pauvre figure."[36] Constantine VII signaled that he was willing to adhere to a patriarch's advice and to place himself on a par with, if not indeed below, a patriarch, but only if that patriarch was a Gregory. Phrased differently, the emperor decided who his intercessory saint would be without help of the current patriarch (much like Theodosius had dismissed Demophilus in favor of Gregory).[37] But Gregory's relation to the emperor Theodosius, that is, his conceptualization of the relation between emperor and priest as expressed, for example, in his Constantinopolitan orations, could also be read to mean that *only* patriarchs could "choose" and identify truly orthodox emperors, and that orthodox emperors were orthodox and their rule therefore auspicious only because they exhibited *eusebeia* in obedience to their orthodox patriarchs—who might otherwise leave the city.

To return to Gregory's description in the *De vita sua,* the miraculously illuminated entrance of Theodosius and himself as bishop of Constantinople, side by side into the church, appears to announce the beginning of a success-

36. Const. Porph. *Pan.* 19–20; Flusin, "Le panégyrique de Constantin," 33–37; Toynbee, *Constantine Porphyrogenitus,* 11; Tougher, *Reign of Leo VI,* 155–63. For Constantine's relation to the patriarchs, including as expressed in ceremonial, see Dagron, *Emperor and Priest,* 216–19.

37. Here I differ somewhat from Dagron's assessment (cf. Dragon, *Emperor and Priest,* 218); see also the work of Flusin (see notes 10–12, 14 above).

ful partnership, destined to end heretical strife through persuasion and to create unity and harmony through *eusebeia*. However, Gregory wrote this poem after his resignation of the bishop's seat in retirement in Cappadocia.[38] Theodosius, "not a bad man, in respect of faith in God" (DVS 1282), had accepted Gregory's resignation with unflattering alacrity to appoint the not-yet baptized senator and former prefect of the city Nectarius as the new bishop (and it was together with him that he accomplished the transformation of the capital I have outlined above). Nectarius, alas, was a man entirely without the intellectual wherewithal to comprehend the nature of heresy, at least according to Gregory.[39] *De vita sua,* not surprisingly, reflects these developments to imply that Theodosius for all his orthodoxy failed to appreciate his proper role versus the city's bishop.[40] What that role should ideally have been Gregory had indicated in his inaugural oration as the new bishop of Constantinople. *Oration* 36 was the first Christian *basilikos logos* pronounced in the presence of an emperor and in a church (according to most scholars that of the Holy Apostles).[41] In keeping with the genre of an inaugural oration, Gregory devoted the entire first part of *Oration* 36 to demonstrate his readiness to assume the responsibility as bishop of Constantinople by emphasizing his extreme reluctance to accept the office offered to him by Theodosius. Gregory further stressed his suitability by showcasing his philosophical simplicity and the artlessness of his *parrhesia,* which stood in sharp contrast to his competitors, who introduced "artfulness into our simple and artless faith, and have dragged the *politike* from the *agora* to the sanctuary and from the theater to the mysteries" (*Or.* 36.2).[42] Gregory rejects such antics; he knows how to differentiate properly between marketplace and church, theater and the sacred. Though in the crowds (in Constantinople), he as true philosopher is not of the crowd, preferring retreat and the solitary life (*Or.* 36.3), so that he can remain immune

38. See Gregory of Nazianzus, *De vita sua,* ed. Christoph Jungck (Heidelberg: Winter, 1974), 3 for the date.

39. McGuckin, "Autobiography as Apologia," 160–77.

40. Gr. Naz., *DVS* 1280–1341, 1828–55, 1871–90, 1902–4; Gregory of Nazianzus, *De vita sua,* ed. Jungck, 205–9; Gómez-Villegas, *Gregorio de Nazianzo en Constantinopla,* 168–75; McGuckin, *Saint Gregory of Nazianzus,* 359–69; McLynn, "Moments of Truth," 232–39.

41. Moreschini and Gallay, SC 318:40–47. For further discussions of *Or.* 36 and 37, see Gautier, *Le retraite et le sacerdoce,* 379–83; McGuckin, *Saint Gregory of Nazianzus,* 329–36; Gómez-Villegas, *Gregorio de Nazianzo en Constantinopla,* 131–42.

42. οἱ τὴν ἁπλῆν καὶ ἄτεχνον ἡμῶν εὐσέβειαν ἔντεχνον πεποιήκασι, καὶ πολιτικῆς τι καινὸν εἶδος ἀπὸ τῆς ἀγορᾶς εἰς τὰ ἅγια μετενηνεγμένης καὶ ἀπὸ τῶν θεάτρων ἐπὶ τὴν τοῖς πολλοῖς ἀθέατον μυσταγωγίαν.

to the barbs of his critics, motivated by envy and false beliefs. As true disciple of the great defender of the Trinity (Alexander who battled Arius at the time of Constantine), he is the living embodiment of right belief and the right behavior it inspires, namely, unity and harmony. Therefore, he will hold his entire congregation to the same standard, to "a firm and solid confession of the Father, Son and Holy Spirit; adding nothing, subtracting nothing, in no way diminishing the single divinity" (*Or.* 36.10).[43]

Only at that point, well into the oration and after having solidly demonstrated the degree to which *he,* as true philosopher and true priest, defended the Trinity, did Gregory finally get around to addressing Theodosius as follows:

Emperors, respect the purple. This discourse [*logos,* which can of course also mean the *Logos*] shall give laws even to those who are law-givers.... The entire cosmos is in your hands, ruled by a small diadem and a piece of clothing. The things above are solely God's, the things below also yours. Be gods to those below you ... [but] "the heart of the emperor is in God's hands,"... There resides your might and not in your gold or in your bodyguard. (*Or.* 36.11)[44]

In *Oration* 36, Gregory created a hierarchical alignment in the presence of the emperor that makes Theodosius' alacrity in accepting his later resignation comprehensible. God is the ultimate lawgiver, the ruler of the cosmos. He will be judging the emperor, since He alone conveys imperial power. But this God, that is, the Trinity, conveys his divine will and the manner in which He ought to be comprehended and obeyed even by emperors through persons such as Gregory; it is God who placed Gregory on the Constantinopolitan throne as bishop, after all. The emperor merely executed his will. That is, the emperor ruled over those "below" as a god, but he had no discretion when it came to obey the Law (the *Logos*), since he ruled by the grace of God. That God, as Gregory had just declared, had to be explained to the emperor correctly. This could only be done by the one whom God (the *Logos*) had chosen as the proper mediator of the divine will, none other than the philosopher and priest Gregory.

It was a hierarchy Gregory had previously constructed in writing against

43. τὴν εἰς Πατέρα καὶ Υἱὸν καὶ ἅγιον Πνεῦμα ὁμολογίαν ἀκλινῆ καὶ βεβαίαν φυλάττητε, μηδὲν προστιθέντες μηδὲ ἀφαιροῦντες μηδὲ σμικρύνοντες τῆς μιᾶς θεότητος.

44. Οἱ βασιλεῖς, αἰδεῖσθε τὴν ἁλουργίδα· νομοθετήσει γὰρ καὶ νομοθέταις ὁ λόγος.... Κόσμος ὅλος ὑπὸ χεῖρα τὴν ὑμετέραν, διαδήματι μικρῷ καὶ βραχεῖ ῥακίῳ κρατούμενος. Τὰ μὲν ἄνω, μόνου θεοῦ· τὰ κάτω δὲ καὶ ὑμῶν. Θεοὶ γένεσθε τοῖς ὑφ' ὑμᾶς ... Ἑαρδία βασιλέως ἐν χειρὶ θεοῦ.... Ἐνταῦθα ἔστω τὸ κράτος ὑμῖν, ἀλλὰ μὴ τῷ χρυσῷ καὶ ταῖς φάλαγξιν.

Julian—two orations the *Paris.gr. 510* illustrated with great care—and it was a relation Gregory reemphasized in *Oration* 37, held shortly after *Oration* 36.[45] Again the emperor had to wait nearly until the end to be addressed, after Gregory had dealt with the misbehaving eunuchs of the imperial household and the "murderous" heretics against whom imperial legislation was in all likelihood already pending. Only then did Gregory finally turn to those "entrusted with rule (τοῖς ἄρχειν πεπιστευμένοις)" pleading for such legislation (*Or.* 37.23).[46] What Gregory was pleading for, to recall, was in effect "moderation in all things." He appealed to an emperor (advised by Gregory) who would choose the middle way, the "royal road" eschewing all extremes, "preferring persuasion to repression" (DVS 1412–19, 1293). Even after Theodosius had graciously accepted Gregory's resignation, Gregory praised his efforts to create harmony, blaming wrong advisors, other bishops, and never the emperor for the misstep that was the acceptance of his resignation (*DVS,* 1898–1904).[47] Gregory's relation to Theodosius, then, as he constructed it was one of trusted advisor who knew what heresy was—namely excessiveness and strife—and who would plead for unity and moderation. Alas, this did not make him immune to the attacks of his enemies, but a good emperor, an orthodox emperor, would always choose to support such an advisor, such a man as bishop of Constantinople. To do so after all guaranteed the prosperity of the realm, since it reflected divine will properly understood through Gregory's mediation between the divine and the emperor. Both then, bishop and emperor, collaborated to preserve the unity of the realm, one as lawgiver and the other as the interpreter of divine will—that is, of the content of such laws. What was not to like about that as far as Photius was concerned, another patriarch who had left his see with imperial approval (in fact by imperial command) and had been restored to the see by that very same emperor, Basil I?[48]

45. Elm, *Sons of Hellenism*; Brubaker, *Vision and Meaning,* 227–36.
46. The audience might have included Themistius, since Gregory explicitly addressed bearded philosophers; see *Or.* 36.12.
47. Gregory of Nazianzus, *De vita sua,* ed. Jungck, 228. McLynn, "Imperial Churchgoing," 258–61; McLynn, "'Genere Hispanus': Theodosius, Spain, and Nicene orthodoxy," in *Hispania in Late Antiquity: Current Perspectives,* edited and translated by Kim Bowes and Michael Kulikowski, 79–88, The Medieval and Early Modern Iberian World 24 (Boston: Brill, 2005).
48. The literature is immense; see Dagron, *Emperor and Priest,* 226–35, and Thalia Anagnostopoulos, *Object and Symbol: Greek Learning and the Aesthetics of Identity in Byzantine Iconoclasm.* (Ph.D. Diss., University of California, Berkeley, 2008), 216–20, with bibliography.

There are, of course, many features of Gregory's oeuvre that appealed to Photius, not least the fact the Theologian was a preeminent advocate of the glory of "secular" learning, including the correct use of both Aristotelian and Platonic concepts as symbol of Roman universalism (a view to which Basil I could relate).[49] Iconophiles considered love of *logoi*, of such learning, furthermore, a safeguard against heretical deviations (especially those of the "Arians," i.e., iconoclasts, and of the "Sabellians," i.e., the Latins), and Photius was an exemplary case of a patriarch as advisor to emperors who perfectly combined sacred and secular learning in aid of orthodoxy—just as Gregory had used Greek philosophy to lambast Eunomius, Photinus, and other "Arians" and "Sabellians" at Constantinople.[50] In addition, however, and again not unlike Gregory's nuanced assessment of Theodosius as persuasive and moderate, Photius was a philosopher and patriarch who advocated a measured approach to his enemies, a middle road that permitted him to praise such iconoclast Arian Origenists as Eusebius of Caesarea or Epiphanius of Salamis, both of whom had been condemned by the Seventh Ecumenical Council as iconoclast precursors.[51]

Still, Gregory's relation to Theodosius as exemplified in *Oration* 36 and 37 may have had a special appeal. Photius has been identified as the author of the preamble and the first three "titles" of the so called *Eisagoge*, the legal manual compiled between 879 and 886 to accompany the great codification undertaken by the Macedonians known as the *Basilika* (at about the same time as the production of the *Paris.gr. 510*, 879–882, and of the council rehabilitating Photius, 879–880).[52] Here, Photius explained that the Law governs all and ensures the unity of the whole cosmos as well as that of man's mixture of spiritual and corporeal.[53] This Law is God's law, written with his fingers not on

---

49. Hélène Ahrweiler, *L'idéologie politique de l'empire byzantin* (Paris: Presses universitaires de France, 1975), 37–46; Brubaker, *Vision and Meaning*, 239–80.

50. Norris, *Faith Gives Fullness to Reasoning;* Anagnostopoulos, *Object and Symbol*, 215–45; Elm, *Sons of Hellenism.*

51. Ambrosios Giakalis, *Images of the Divine: The Theology of Icons at the Seventh Ecumenical Council*, Studies in the History of Christian Thought 54 (Leiden: Brill, 1994), 44–48; Paul Lemerle, *Byzantine Humanism, the First Phase: Notes and Remarks on Education and Culture in Byzantium from Its Origins to the 10th Century*, trans. Helen Lindsay and Ann Moffatt, Byzantina Australiensia (Canberra: Australian Association for Byzantine Studies, 1986); Brubaker, *Vision and Meaning*, 201–38.

52. Dagron, *Emperor and Priest*, 229–35; Marie Theres Fögen, "Reanimation of Roman Law in the Ninth Century: Remarks on Reasons and Results," in Brubaker, *Byzantium in the Ninth Century*, 11–22.

53. In Andreas Schminck, *Studien zu mittelbyzantinischen Rechtsbüchern*, Forschungen zur byzantinischen Rechtsgeschichte 13 (Frankfurt: Löwenklau-Gesellschaft, 1986), 1–15, 62–72.

tablets of stone as in the time of Moses, but into our souls with fiery letters (a nearly literal allusion to Gregory's *Oration* 40.45). This divine law at the apex left space immediately below for the emperor as legitimate authority, as *nomos empsychos* nevertheless beholden to God's law (so that the emperor could not choose whether or not to submit to the divine law). Further, that imperial legal authority had to be informed by a second authority, that of the patriarch (or bishop of Constantinople) as "incarnate and living (*empsychos*) image of Christ, who by his words and deeds expresses the truth."[54] The emperor required the patriarch as his mediator between God and himself. The patriarch embodied truth to the emperor's law, and both needed to cooperate to preserve the unity and harmony of things "below," the realm of the Romans now once more seen as "universal," given the initial success of Basil I's rule.[55]

Photius' world, like that of Constantine VII, was, of course, very different from that of Gregory and Theodosius. But there was much in the relation between emperor and priest as constructed by Gregory in Constantinople that could be fruitfully appropriated by emperors and priests, each to further his own agenda. Here I have only scratched the surface. Detailed analysis and comparison may well reveal with greater precision why Photius and Constantine VII specifically chose Gregory of Nazianzus and his writings, why both emperor and patriarch found specific arguments beyond those mentioned that allowed them to further their own positions in their own time and place through recourse to Gregory of Nazianzus—why, in brief, so many different Byzantines were for so long so obsessed with his writings.[56]

54. *Basilica* 2.6.1–2; *Eisagoge* 2 and 3, *Jus Graecoromanum* ed. Ionnes D. Zepos (Athens: G. Fexis, 1931), 2:240–43.

55. Ahrweiler, *L'idéologie politique,* 37–46.

56. As Simelidis, *Selected Poems,* 58, points out, "the Byzantines' obsession with [Gregory] is yet to be the subject of a systematic study."

15. St. Gregory the Theologian and Byzantine Theology

In the Byzantine tradition, St. Gregory of Nazianzus was "the Theologian"; in later Byzantine tradition he appears together with St. Basil of Caesarea and St. John of Constantinople as one of the "ecumenical teachers," celebrated together on January 30, each of whom has his epithet: St. Basil the "Great," St. Gregory the "Theologian" and St. John the "Golden-mouthed" (Chrysostom, Χρυσόστομος). It seems clear that Gregory's title is derived from the five orations, *Orations* 27–31, dubbed by modern editors the "theological orations," a designation that has ancient support (though the list is not entirely stable: *Oration* 28 seems to have been inserted in its present position, probably by the Theologian himself), the group being understood to be περὶ θεολογίας, about "theology," in the sense that this word generally bears in the Greek fathers, namely the doctrine of God in himself, that is, the Trinity.[1] It was to these homilies that Fred Norris devoted his detailed commentary, published as *Faith Gives Fullness to Reasoning*.[2]

St. Gregory's title of "Theologian" therefore refers to him preeminently as an exponent of the doctrine of the Trinity. It is found relatively early—in the Acts of the Council of Chalcedon in 451[3]—and is well-established by the sixth century; the eighth-century *Vita* by Gregory the Presbyter identi-

---

1. See Paul Gallay's introduction to his edition of Gregory's *Theological Orations: SC* 250:7–10.
2. Norris, *Faith Gives Fullness to Reasoning*.
3. ACO 3:114.

fies Gregory as "the Theologian."[4] As a title it conferred authority: already in the sixth century, Gregory's words were cited as authoritative.[5] Gregory was not alone in being regarded as authoritative; he formed part of the witness of the fathers, who were to be followed in matters of theology, the emergence of which we can trace in the fifth century, especially in conjunction with the developing Christological controversy that led to the councils of Ephesos and Chalcedon.[6] But in the array of fathers, he came to be regarded as of signal importance—an authority *par excellence*.[7] Authorities need interpretation, and the extent to which this was true of Gregory the Theologian is manifest in the fact that, in Maurice Geerard's *Clavis Patrum Graecorum*, Gregory is almost unique in having listed after his works collections of *scholia,*[8] some of these major works of Byzantine theology: the *Ambigua* of St. Maximos the Confessor,[9] for example, and several of the *Opuscula* of Michael Psellos[10] (one could also include many of the *Amphilochia* of Photios, not listed by Geerard).

There were various reasons Gregory needed such commentary. Some of his sermons displayed his classical learning, not least in allusions to classical mythology, and by the sixth century these allusions had become sufficiently obscure for it to be necessary to provide an explanatory commentary. The earliest and most extensive of these is a commentary, falsely ascribed to the probably Christian poet Nonnos of Panopolis—the fifth-century author of a kind of compendium of Greek mythology called the *Dionysiaca,* as well as a paraphrase of the Fourth Gospel, both in Greek hexameters—devoted to Gregory's lengthy attack (in *Or.* 4 and 5) on Julian the Apostate and his edict forbidding Christians from teaching classical literature, in the course of which

4. Gregorius Presbyter, *Gregorii Presbyteri vita sancti Gregorii Theologii,* ed. Xavier Lequeux. CCSG 44 (Leuven:Turnhout, 2001).

5. See Caroline Macé, "Gregory of Nazianzus as the Authoritative Voice of Orthodoxy in the Sixth Century," in *Byzantine Orthodoxies: Papers from the Thirty-Sixth Spring Symposium of Byzantine Studies, University of Durham, 23–25 March 2002,* edited by Andrew Louth and Augustine Casiday, 7–34, Publications for the Society for the Promotion of Byzantine Studies 12 (Aldershot: Ashgate, 2002).

6. For the development of patristic authority, manifest in the creation of florilegia, see Aloys Grillmeier, *Christ in Christian Tradition,* vol. 1, *From the Apostolic Age to Chalcedon,* trans. John Bowden, 1–58 (Louisville: Westminster John Knox, 1975).

7. For the notion of the authority of the fathers, see Jaroslav Pelikan, *The Christian Tradition: A History of the Development of Doctrine,* vol. 2, *The Spirit of Eastern Christendom (600–1700)* (Chicago: University of Chicago Press, 1974), chap. 1.

8. *CPG,* 2:3011–31 (on the *Or.*), 3042–51 (on the *Carm.*).

9. *CPG,* 2:3020, 3041.

10. *CPG,* 2:3026.

Gregory displays his own extensive command of classical mythology, and, more briefly (though they are shorter homilies), to his homily on the Feast of Lights (Τὰ Φῶτα: Theophany or Epiphany—*Or.* 39) and his funeral homily for St. Basil (*Or.* 43).[11]

Much of the commentary Gregory needed, however, was due to the fact that by the sixth century, at the latest, the theological climate had changed from the fourth century in which Gregory had lived. The "thunder of dogmas,"[12] to give him one of his many names, sometimes seemed to be sounding with a discordant note. The sixth century was a period of Christological controversy—leading to the "Three Chapters" and the refinement of Christological orthodoxy attempted by Justinian at the Fifth Ecumenical Council in 553. Gregory's Christology was expressed in a terminology innocent of the clarifications of terminology introduced by Chalcedon; his discussions needed commentary to bring them more clearly into line with what became established terminology. Several of Maximos' *Ambigua ad Thomam,* especially, are concerned with clarifying Gregory's utterances on Christology and Trinitarian theology. Alongside the Christological controversy, and perhaps entangled with it in some way, was the continued attraction of Origen, especially in monastic circles. It was in connection with Origenism that we first find appeals to Gregory's authority. Gregory himself had been an enthusiast for Origen, and in the early 360s had drawn up, with his friend Basil of Caesarea, an anthology of passages from Origen, on subjects such as scriptural interpretation and providence and human self-determination, called the *Philokalia.* Such enthusiasm for Origen was not unusual in the fourth century, but whereas many enthusiasts, such as Basil himself and Jerome, who, as a young man, had visited Gregory in Constantinople, turned against Origen, or at least expressed critical caution, Gregory himself never seems to have publicly distanced himself from Origen. He could be and was cited by the more intellectually daring monks in support of their fondness for speculative theology—especially about the original state of the created order and its final destiny: the issues on

11. See Jennifer Nimmo Smith, ed., *Pseudo-Nonniani in IV Orationes Gregorii Nazianzeni Commentarii, CCSG,* 27 (Turnhout: Brepols, 1992), and further discussion in Smith, trans., *A Christian's Guide to Greek Culture: The Pseudo-Nonnus Commentaries on Sermons 4, 5, 39 and 43 by Gregory of Nazianzus,* with introduction and commentary, Translated Texts for Historians 37 (Liverpool: Liverpool University Press, 2001).

12. βροντὴ τῶν δογμάτων: see Macé, "Authoritative Voice," 34.

which Origen had been most controversial. For instance, in one of the letters addressed to the "Great Old Man," Barsanouphios, we read of monks who appeal to the authority of St. Gregory over the question of the preexistence of human souls:

Father, those who have these opinions on preexistence do not hesitate to say that St. Gregory the Theologian has himself held forth on preexistence in the homilies which he preached on the Feast of the Lord's Nativity and the Day of Pascha.[13] They interpret certain expressions that conform to their views and pass over what he clearly said there about the creation of the first man, body and soul, in conformity with the tradition of the Church. For this is what he said: "Wishing to manifest this, the craftsman, the Word, created man, one living being from two [elements], I mean the invisible and the visible natures; and taking the body from pre-existent matter, he inserted life from himself (which reason recognizes as the intelligent soul and the image of God)."[14]

The (non-Origenist) monk who wrote this letter clearly thinks that the Origenist appeal to Gregory is unfounded (though the variant reading—"breath" instead of "life—might have been intended to make this clear beyond a peradventure).[15] Barsanouphios, in his reply, condemns such speculation as pointless.

Cyril of Skythopolis, in his *Life of Kyriakos*, represents himself as a young man asking Abba Kyriakos about the appeal made by some monks to Gregory in support of their continued reflection on the matters such as preexistence of souls and the final restoration:

I asked him, "Father, what of the view they advocate? They themselves affirm that the doctrines of preexistence and restoration are indifferent and without danger, citing the words of Saint Gregory, 'Philosophize about the world, matter, the soul, the good and evil rational natures, the Resurrection and the Passion of Christ; for in these matters hitting on the truth is not without profit and error is without danger.'"[16]

13. That is, *Or.* 38 and 45. *Or.* 38.7–15 corresponds virtually word for word with *Or.* 45.3–9 and 26–7. The passage appealed to is: *Or.* 38.11 = *Or.* 45.7.

14. Barsanouphios and John of Gaza, *Ep.* 604, *SC,* 451: 814–16). On reading *life* rather than *breath,* see Macé, "Gregory of Nazianzus," 29 (the *Sources Chrétiennes* edition reads ζωὴν, but translates "souffle").

15. These variant readings are attested in the manuscripts both of *Or.* 38 (*SC,* 358:124) and of Barsanouphios and John (*SC,* 451:816). There is no critical edition of *Or.* 45, but Justinian's quotation from this homily, quoted by Macé from *ACO,* reads ζωὴν, instead of Migne's πνοὴν (PG 36:632B), so it is likely that these variants occur in that homily, too.

16. Cyril of Scythopolis, *Vita Cyriaci,* 229, 25–31, in *The Lives of the Monks of Palestine,* trans. R. M. Price, intro. and notes by John Binns (Kalamazoo, Mich: Cistercian, 1991), 253; quoting from Gregory Nazianzen, *Or.* 27.10.

Abba Kyriakos replies that the doctrines of preexistence and final restoration are far from being matters indifferent, and attacks what he regards as Origenist errors: errors such as the denial that Christ is one of the Holy Trinity, or that the Holy Trinity created the world, and the assertion that the resurrection body will be spherical and pass to destruction, and that at the restoration we shall be equal to Christ (views condemned as "Origenist" in 543 and at— or before—the Fifth Ecumenical Council of 553). He concludes:

> I am amazed what vain and futile labours they have expended on such harmful and laborious vanities, and how in this way they have armed their tongues against piety. Should they not rather have praised and glorified brotherly love, hospitality, virginity, care of the poor, psalmody, all-night vigils, and tears of compunction? Should they not be disciplining the body by fasts, ascending to God in prayer, making this life a rehearsal for death, rather than meditating such sophistries?[17]

As Macé points out, Abba Kyriakos is represented as quoting Gregory against Gregory, for in suggesting how they might profitably spend their time, he is paraphrasing an earlier passage in Gregory's *Or. 27*, from which the earlier quotation had come.[18] Macé also quotes a passage from the emperor Justinian's edict against Origen in which he continues the quotation from the "homily on holy Pascha" (that is, *Or. 45*) with the intent of making it clear that there is no support for the doctrine of preexistence in Gregory.[19]

The involvement of Gregory the Theologian in the Origenist controversy —cited, as we have seen, on both sides—reaches its climax (though not its end; one can still detect echoes in later writers such as Anastasios of Sinai) in the writings of St. Maximos the Confessor, especially in his *Ambigua*, devoted to the discussion of difficulties (ἀπορίαι, *ambigua*) in Gregory the Theologian (plus one difficult passage from Dionysios the Areopagite), not least those to which appeal had been made by Origenist monks. As Dom Polycarp Sherwood famously remarked, "These *Ambigua* are a refutation of Origenism, especially of the doctrine of the henad, with a full understanding and will to retain what is good in the Alexandrian's doctrine—a refutation perhaps unique

---

17. *V. Cyriaci* 230, 15–23, in *Lives of the Monks,* trans. Price, 253–54.

18. *Or.* 27.7: see Macé, "Authoritative Voice," 31.

19. For further discussion of the Palestinian monks and sixth-century Origenism, see Lorenzo Perrone, "Palestinian Monasticism, the Bible, and Theology in the Wake of the Second Origenist Controversy," in *The Sabaïte Heritage in the Orthodox Church from the Fifth Century to the Present*, Society for the Promotion of Byzantine Studies 5, edited by Joseph Patrich, 245–59 (Leuven: Peeters, 2001).

in Greek patristic literature."[20] These *Ambigua* are also something else: a way of theological reflection that takes as its starting point the difficulties found in the works of one regarded as an authority, and in that they mark an early stage in a tradition that was to continue throughout the Byzantine period. This was a form of theological reflection that takes for granted the pattern of orthodoxy and seeks to probe its depths by a form of theological meditation that relates different insights to one another and thereby attains a deeper understanding. Difficulty is seen as a spur to deeper reflection, much as difficulties and apparent contradictions in the Scriptures had been long seen as signs that the truth of the Scriptures was not something to be revealed without effort; difficulties and contradictions jolted one out of complacency and forced one to further and more considered reflection.[21]

Maximos' engagement with Gregory the Theologian is discussed elsewhere in this *Festschrift;* what I want to do in the rest of this chapter is look at the way in which the kind of theology that we find in Maximos—focusing on consideration of difficult passages in Gregory—continues in the Byzantine tradition, and especially in the works of two theologians, Photios and Michael Psellos, whose theological works, although now available in fine critical editions, have so far attracted very little attention. In those works we can, in particular, detect a thread that leads to the theological controversies of the twelfth century that became, for political reasons, a feature of the reign of the emperor Manuel Komnenos, and I shall argue that this thread leads back to Gregory himself. And then there is something else, but let us leave that until later.

Both Photios and Michael Psellos were exceptional men; in looking at them we are hardly looking at anything in any way typical. However, their fame rests less on their theological works (which are generally ignored) than on their role in history, and also the reputation both had for phenomenal learning, especially in classical literature (and, in the case of Psellos, Greek philosophy). Nonetheless, in both cases, a great deal of their writing was devoted to theological matters, more than one might suppose, given their reputation nowadays.

Both of them conform to the model of theology that we have noticed in connection with Maximos' meditations on difficulties posed by Gregory's

20. Sherwood, *An Annotated Date-List of the Works of Maximus the Confessor,* Studia Anselmiana 30 (Rome: Orbis Catholicus and Herder, 1952), 3.

21. For some consideration of the different kinds of difficulties that such an approach to theology might envisage, see Louth, "St. Maximus the Confessor," 117–30.

writings. With Photios, the parallel with Maximos is quite striking. Both of them were occasional theologians in that their theological reflection is presented as responses to questions put to them by others. The vast bulk of Maximos' writings take the form of such responses, either in letters or in responses to a series of questions, the genre known as *erotapokriseis* ("questions and answers"): there is a body of Maximos' letters, and many of the *Opuscula* are letters or extracts from letters; the *Ambigua,* the *Quaestiones ad Thalassium,* and the so-called *Quaestiones et Dubia* ("Questions and Answers," i.e., *Erotapokriseis,* would be more accurate) are all *erotapokriseis.* Photios wrote a few treatises, e.g., the *Mystagogia* (if it is indeed his), but most of his theology is found in his letters (some of which are virtual treatises, e.g., *Letter* 1, addressed to Michael/Boris, the newly converted Tsar of the Bulgarians, *Letter* 2, an encyclical letter to the Eastern patriarchs about the dangers of Latin theology, and—longer than either of these—*Letter* 284, addressed to Ašot, the Armenian sovereign, and dealing with the possible reconciliation of Byzantine and Armenian theology), many of which are responses to questions put to him by correspondents, and his collection of 329 *Amphilochia,* many of which are drawn from his correspondence.[22] The problems about the formation of the *Amphilochia* cannot be addressed here;[23] what we are now concerned with is the role of Gregory the Theologian in Photios' theology. In contrast with both Maximos and Michael Psellos (as we shall see), St. Gregory the Theologian is not a special favorite of Photios'. Only one of the *Amphilochia* (78) directly discusses difficult passages in Gregory (two, in fact), and Photios discusses no works of the Theologian in his *Bibliotheca* (though, given that we have no real evidence for the principles of inclusion in the *Bibliotheca,* nor have we for any omissions). There are, in fact, notorious omissions from the *Bibliotheca*—Plato, Aristotle, the Greek poets—though I cannot think of any other Greek theologian of note omitted other than Didymos the Blind.[24] It is not, however, that he does not know Gregory: there are plenty of references to, and quota-

22. Photius, *Epistulae et Amphilochia,* 6 vols., edited by Basil Laourdas and Leendert Gerrit Westerink (Leipzig: Tuebner, 1983–88).

23. For these, see Andrew Louth, "Photios as a Theologian," in *Byzantine Style and Civilization: In Honour of Sir Steven Runciman,* edited by Elizabeth M. Jeffreys, 206–23, esp. 210–12 (Cambridge: Cambridge University Press, 2006).

24. On the selection of writings in the *Bibliotheca,* see Nigel Guy Wilson, *Photius: The Bibliotheca* (London: Duckworth, 1994), 6–13.

tions from, Gregory in the *Bibliotheca* (in contrast with the case of Didymos), as well as in the *Letters* and *Amphilochia*. Many of these are passing allusions, suggesting that Photios knew Gregory well and recalls him easily. He also recalls important passages from the Theologian: for example, in *Amphilochia* 24, when he quotes an important passage from the last oration, the Second on Easter, on the sacrifice of Christ, which was offered neither to the devil, nor to the Father, but is rather the means by which death is overthrown and humanity rescued (here, as elsewhere, the quotation is not exact: Photios is quoting from memory, and the MSS tradition shows that later scribes supplemented the inexactness of Photios' memory); or in *Amphilochia* 36, a long discussion of the meaning of the image of God, Photios deploys Gregory's account of the formation of the human in *Oration* 45.7, to support his view that the image and "according to the image" are identical. In *Amphilochia* 78, the only one directly dealing with problems in the text of the Theologian, Photios clarifies one of Gregory's responses to a difficulty (rather than a difficulty in Gregory's text as such): the Incarnate Word is spoken of as having both God and Father, but how can the Word, as God, have a God? Photios simply repeats at greater length what Gregory had already said: that strictly speaking the Father is the Father of the Word, and God only of the human aspect of Christ ("the one seen" in Gregory, the "addition," πρόσλημμα, in Photios).

A last example from Photios is more important for what is to follow. In *Letter* 176, which reappears as *Amphilochia* 95, Photios discusses the meaning of John 14:28: "the Father is greater than I." This verse had played a major role in the Arian controversy,[25] and it is against that background that Gregory's words find their primary meaning, but in the context of the developed Trinitarian theology of later centuries, they continued to puzzle. That later Trinitarian theology owed much to Gregory, so it is no surprise that what Gregory had said about the exegesis of this verse continued to attract attention. There is no mention of Gregory in the apparatus to Westerink's text, but I think that Gregory is probably in the back of Photios' mind here. Photios makes a number of suggestions. First, perhaps the Father is greater τῷ αἰτίῳ, by virtue of being the cause, αἴτιος, of the Son. Secondly, perhaps "greater" is to be taken

---

25. On which see Manlio Simonetti, "Giovanni 14:28 nella controversia ariana," in *Kyriakon: Festschrift Johannes Quasten,* edited by Patrick Granfield and Josef A. Jungmann, 1:151–61 (Münster: Aschendorff, 1970).

κατὰ τὸ ἀνθρώπινον, as referring to Christ's humanity, that is, to τὸ πρόσλημμα, not to ὁ Λόγος. Thirdly, it might refer to Christ's "extreme self-emptying and humiliation" (ἄκρα κένωσις καὶ ταπείνωσις). Photios adds a few other suggestions: it might refer to the imperfect thoughts of the disciples, or to the Word's condescension to the human condition, his συγκατάβασις, in which state he both accommodates himself to the disciples' understanding and speaks of the Father as higher than him, one to whom he prays and gives thanks. What is striking about this list of suggestions is the way the discussion seems to follow Gregory's own discussion in *Oration* 29.15 ff. There Gregory starts by offering the suggestion that the Father is greater as being cause, partly to fend off the objection that, if cause, he must be cause by nature, and so greater than the Son by nature. Then, after dealing with the objection that "Father" designates either a nature or an activity, rather than a relationship (σχέσις), Gregory goes on to distinguish between the Son's "great and sublime names," which refer to his Godhead, and his humbler names, which refer to the compound, σύνθετον, of divine and human—the Incarnate One, among which is included what Gregory laconically lists as "greater," that is, the assertion that the Father is "greater" than the Son. Photios seems to me to be following Gregory here: first, the interpretation involving "cause," secondly, the interpretation involving the Incarnation, the πρόσλημμα. His other suggestions are variants on that starting from the Incarnation, but without the authority of the Theologian. But it is striking how closely Photios' discussion corresponds to the list of interpretations given to the Johannine verse in the theological controversy during the time of Emperor Manuel Komnenos, the results of which came to be incorporated in the *Synodikon of Orthodoxy*. In the Komnene list, the first two interpretations are approved, the third condemned, and the others either condemned or ignored.[26] It seems to me not implausible that Photios' discussion represents a stage on the way to the Komnene controversy.

Now we must turn to discuss Michael Psellos and the nature of the Theologian's influence on him. The case is rather different from Photios: whereas Photios clearly knew Gregory reasonably well, but makes little direct reference to him, in the case of Psellos, Gregory is very prominent. However, in com-

---

26. There is a good discussion of the history of the interpretation of this verse in Hilarion Alfeyev, *St. Symeon the New Theologian and Orthodox Tradition*, Oxford Early Christian Studies (Oxford: Oxford University Press, 2000), 143–50.

paring Photios and Psellos, we are comparing like with like, for both of them follow Maximos in being occasional theologians, dealing with difficulties that have been brought to their attention, using the genre of *erotapokriseis*. These theological works—the largest group in Psellos' *œuvre*[27]—are concerned to elucidate difficulties raised by passages in Scripture—what is meant by Wisdom building a house in Proverbs 9:1 (*Opusc.* 7), or what is meant by Wisdom being "created" in Proverbs 8:22 (*Opusc.* 10), difficult verses in the psalms (*Opusc.* 14, 18, 34–37, 73), on the meaning of *arche* in John 1:1 (*Opusc.* 75)—or in the fathers, especially Gregory of Nazianzus, but also Basil the Great (*Opusc.* 6) or John Klimakos (*Opusc.* 30), or in the liturgical texts—passages in John Damascene's canon on the Transfiguration and Cosmas' canon for Holy Thursday, as well as the *Kyrie eleison* (*Opusc.* 11–13)—or theological problems, for instance, why humans can change from evil to good, but angels, once fallen into sin, cannot (*Opusc.* 29). The prominence of Gregory of Nazianzus, or Gregory the Theologian, is striking. Of the 159 *Opuscula* in the new editions, 73 are explicitly on passages from Gregory's homilies; a glance at the indices reveals that there are more references to Gregory than anyone else, even Plato or Psellos' beloved Proklos. As we have seen, Gregory's prominence as "the Theologian" made the clearing up of puzzles and problems in his homilies (and also his poems, though much less so) imperative. Gregory's third *Theological Oration* (*Or.* 29) is a recurrent concern for Psellos; there is a series of problems on this homily (*Opusc.* 20–24, but also 16, 107), as is the sermon on Epiphany, *Or.* 38 (*Opusc.* 86–97, 64), but several other sermons raise problems (*Or.* 1, 21, 31, 33, 39–45). What Psellos very often does is take a problem and elucidate its philosophical background by drawing on his immense knowledge of those he calls once "the first and blessed philosophers" (*Or.* 69), by which he means Plato, Aristotle, the Orphic hymns, the Chaldaean Oracles, and the neo-Platonists, especially "the philosopher from Lycia," that is, Proklos. Sometimes it is not clear what purpose is served by this display of learning, but not infrequently it leads him to a theological discussion in which he expounds skillfully on the apophatic nature of theology, or the way in which the Incarnation of the Word of God brings about the deification of human kind.

Psellos' reverence for Gregory the Theologian is also manifest in his pan-

---

27. Michael Psellus, *Theologica* I, edited by Paul Gautier (Leipzig: Tuebner, 1989); Psellus, *Theologica* II, edited by Leendert Gerrit Westerink and John M. Duffy (Leipzig: Tuebner, 2002).

egyric on the saint.[28] Psellos' first claim for Gregory is that he is a model of all
the stylistic virtues. Whereas other orators excel at one style or another—and
here Psellos displays his learning (or perhaps pretensions to learning) by citing
various rhetors of late antiquity—Gregory excels at all. This Psellos puts down
to the divine origin of his gift; it was certainly not achieved by the usual method of imitation. Psellos explains why Gregory excels:

> For my part, every time I read him, and I often have occasion to do so, chiefly for his teach-
> ing but secondarily for his literary charm, I am filled with a beauty and grace that cannot be
> expressed. And frequently I abandon my intention, and neglecting his theological meaning
> I spend my time as it were among the spring flowers of his diction and am carried away by
> my senses. Realizing that I have been carried off I then love and take delight in my captor.
> And if I am forced away from his words back to the meaning, I regret not being carried off
> once more and lament the gain as a deprivation. The beauty of his works is not of the type
> practiced by the duller sophists, epideictic and aimed at an audience, by which one might be
> charmed at first and then at the second contact repelled—for those orators did not smooth
> the unevenness of their lips and were not afraid to rely on boldness of diction rather than
> skill. But his art is not of that kind, far from it; instead it has the harmony of music.[29]

Psellos goes on to compare Gregory's words to precious and semi-precious
stones and their various qualities, arranged by the saint with the skill of the
jeweler, and compares Gregory to various orators whom he mentions who
have the gift of selecting ordinary words and arranging them with other words
so as to bring out their beauty. Gregory does this in a way that seems not in the
least artificial: "I cannot trace the means by which his extraordinary beauty of
style is regularly achieved; I merely sense them, the experience cannot be ratio-
nally explained. But when I trace his methods and establish them as the cause
of his excellence, I see other sources from which grace flows into his writings."
These sources include sentence structure and the use of rhythm. The theological content of Gregory's sermons is never obscured; the use of rhythm prevents monotony, what he has to say ornamented by his wide reading. Psellos
returns to Gregory's ability to adapt his style, claiming for him preeminence
in the genre of panegyric, and closes by wondering why, despite the surpassing clarity of his style, Gregory seems to need explanation by commentators,
among whom Psellos numbers himself.

28. See Nigel Wilson's discussion in Wilson, *Scholars of Byzantium* (London: Duckworth, 1983),
169–72.
29. Trans. Wilson, *Scholars of Byzantium,* 169.

Psellos raises Gregory's discussion of the Johannine verse on a number of occasions. Unlike Photios—and unlike those who discussed this in the century after Psellos—Psellos finds one interpretation of the verse in Gregory, and it is this that he follows—namely, that the Father is greater than the Son in virtue of being his cause. *Opusculum* 3 develops this theme at length, citing in support of his interpretation Aristotle's logical treatises as well as Alexander of Aphrodisias. But he returns to this on several other occasions. In *Opusculum* 23, he summarizes his position as: "Therefore the Father is greater than the Son and not greater; for he is greater by cause, but equal by nature and authority. Wisely therefore the Son having become one of us said that 'the Father is greater than I'"[30] (perhaps there is a suggestion there that a further explanation of the saying is that it was uttered by the incarnate Son, but it is hardly explicit, and not related to Gregory's homily). In *Opusculum* 72, it is rather the passage in Gregory's *Oration* 40.43 that Psellos has in mind, in which Gregory expresses his reservations about saying that the Father is greater than the Son; in *Opusculum* 99, the usual position is asserted laconically.

Between Photios and Psellos, the Johannine verse was also the subject of discussion by Symeon the New Theologian, which has been well discussed by Alfeyev.[31] Symeon starts from, and rejects, the explanation of the Johannine verse in terms of causality, but there is not enough context to know to whom Symeon is referring; it is unlikely that he connected this interpretation with the Theologian. This connection, however, is quite clear with both Photios and Psellos, and suggests that whatever the occasion of the Komnene debate—Kinnamos asserts that it was a matter of a Latin view that Manuel was keen to see accepted in his court[32]—it bears witness to the long shadow cast by Gregory the Theologian in the history of Byzantine theology (which in turn suggests that the stimulus provided by Latin theology can have been no more than the occasion of the debate, which stirred up an already familiar theological controversy entirely native to Byzantium).

Whether or not it is the case that this recurrent Byzantine controversy

30. Psellos, *Opusc.* 23.128–31.

31. See n. 26 above.

32. For brief discussions, which, however, shed little theological light on the controversy, see Joan M. Hussey, *The Orthodox Church in the Byzantine Empire* (Oxford: Clarendon Press, 1986), 152–53; Magdalino, *The Empire of Manuel I Komnenos, 1143–1180* (Cambridge: Cambridge University Press, 1993), 279–90; and Michael Angold, *Church and Society in Byzantium under the Comneni, 1081–1261* (Cambridge: Cambridge University Press, 1995), 83–86.

over the interpretation of the Johannine verse is a matter of the long shadow
of Gregory, it is worth noting that Gregory's own words pass beyond the discussion of "The Father is greater than I," leading to the final paragraphs of the
homily in which he celebrates the union of opposites in Christ, a passage in
which, leaving behind the logical analysis that characterizes most of the homily, Gregory celebrates the paradox of the Incarnation; as Fred Norris put it in
his commentary, the Theologian passes from "his logical case" to his "moving
confessions."[33] For the most profound influence Gregory had on Byzantine
theology in the broadest sense—that is, not just in the relatively narrow world
of theological controversy, but in the way theological dogma was received and
expressed by believers generally—was, arguably, less through the seemingly
endless *scholia,* interpreting and justifying what he had said in his riddling language, but through the way in which his homilies, with their clashing paradoxes and intoxicating rhythmic prose, provided material for the developing
tradition of Byzantine liturgical poetry.

Already in the first part of the sixth century, we know from the *Instruc-*
tions of Dorotheos of Gaza that passages from Gregory's homilies were being turned into hymns. In *Instruction* 16, Dorotheos comments on an Easter
hymn, the text of which he gives as:

The Day of the Resurrection! Let us offer ourselves as fruits, God's most precious possession,
the one closest to him, let us restore to the image that which is according to the image, let us
recognize our worth, let us reverence the archetype, let us know the power of the mystery,
and what it was for whom Christ died.[34]

These are simply words taken from Gregory's first homily on Easter: "The Day
of Resurrection" being the opening words, and the rest the closing words of
paragraph 4. In the current Byzantine office there are two troparia that be-
gin with the words "the day of Resurrection," Ἀναστάσεως ἡμέρα: the first
troparion of the Easter canon, ascribed to St. John Damascene, which adds to
the opening words the closely following "let us be radiant" and then continues with words from Gregory's other Easter homily—"Pascha, the Lord's Pascha"—and goes on to paraphrase Gregory's explanation of "pascha" as derived
not from the verb πάσχειν, to suffer, but derived from the Hebrew *pesach,* in-

33. Norris, *Faith Gives Fullness to Reasoning,* 158.
34. Dorotheos of Gaza, *Spir. Instr.* 16 (*SC* 92: 458–72).

dicating "the passage from below to above," expressed in the words: "for from death unto life, from earth unto heaven, Christ our God has brought us over" (paraphrasing *Or.* 45.10).[35] The other troparion beginning "The Day of Resurrection," sung at Vespers, just takes its words from the rest of *Oration* 1.1: "let us be radiant for the feast, and embrace one another. Let us say to those who hate us: let us forgive all at the Resurrection" and then continues with the Easter troparion itself: "Christ has risen from the dead, by death trampling on death, and to those in the graves giving life."

The next of Dorotheos' *Instructions* gives a hymn to the martyrs, drawn from Gregory's *Oration* 33.15: "Living sacred offerings, rational holocausts, perfect sacrifices to God, sheep knowing God and known to God, whose fold is inaccessible to wolves."[36] This text also survives in the current Byzantine office, forming the basis of the *martyrikon* (troparion to the martyrs), sung at the Liturgy of the Presanctified on the Wednesday of the Third Week of Lent.[37]

This hymnic use of passages from Gregory's homilies was pursued with enthusiasm by later Byzantine hymnographers. It is striking to note, in passing, that it was Gregory's prose that was turned into verse, not the extensive verse with which he occupied his declining years, in some contrast to the bishop of the next generation, Synesios of Kyrene, whose verse seems to have been used liturgically in the Byzantine world.[38]

Many more examples could be given of the way Gregory's homilies were plundered by Byzantine hymnographers for their liturgical verse. Just two must suffice here. The *irmos* for Kosmas the Melodist's canon for the Feast of the Lord's Nativity reads:

Christ is born, glorify Him! Christ has come from heaven, go to meet Him! Christ is on earth, be exalted! Praise the Lord, all the earth, and offer him hymns with joyfulness, O people, because He has been glorified.[39]

35. For an analysis of the Easter canon, which owes a good deal to the Theologian, see Louth, *St. John Damascene: Tradition and Originality in Byzantine Theology,* Oxford Early Christian Studies (Oxford: Oxford University Press, 2002), 59–68.

36. Dorothée de Gaza, *Spir. Instr.* 17 (*SC* 92: 474–87), presumably ending with some petition to the martyrs (see 474n1).

37. I owe this identification to my colleague Dr. Krastu Banev, who recalled singing this troparion during Lent just past (2010).

38. Synesius of Cyrene, *Hymnes,* vol. 1, edited by Christian Lacombrade (Paris: Société d'édition les belles letters, 1978), 11.

39. It is interesting that Photios comments on this passage, asserting that one might have expect-

These are more or less the opening words of Gregory's *Oration* 38 on the Theophany (which then embraced the feast of the Nativity):

Christ is born, glorify Him! Christ has come from heaven, go to meet Him! Christ is on earth, be exalted! "Praise the Lord, all the earth," and bringing together both I say, "Let the heavens rejoice and let the earth be glad," on account of the one who is heavenly and then became earthly.

And, for the Feast of Pentecost, the first troparion at vespers reads:

It is Pentecost that we celebrate: the advent of the Spirit, the appointed day of the promise, and the fulfillment of hope. Such a mystery! So great and venerable! Therefore we cry out, Creator of all, Lord, glory to you!

In his homily on Pentecost (*Or.* 41.5), Gregory had exclaimed:

It is Pentecost that we celebrate: the advent of the Spirit, the appointed day of the promise, and the fulfillment of hope. Such a mystery! So great and venerable!

In this way, Gregory's exalted rhetoric entered the tradition of song of the Byzantine Church, and the words that had resounded in the Church of the Anastasia in Constantinople, celebrating the Orthodox faith with his small congregation faithful to Nicaea, came to resound throughout the Orthodox world—Byzantine, then Slav, and now further afield—in the liturgical poetry of the services.

It is rather on this note that I want to conclude. Alongside the long shadow that Gregory cast through his reputation as "the Theologian," and his popularity among later Byzantine theologians—a popularity at times as much controversial as inspiring solemn commentary—there is the way in which Gregory's rhetorical powers bequeathed to the Byzantine hymnographers sparkling encapsulations of what is celebrated in the cycle of the Feasts, that were seized on and turned into song. In that way, Gregory's influence extended beyond the study, and entered the hearts of the Orthodox faithful.

---

ed it to read Χριστὸς γεγέννηται, Christ has been born, rather than Χριστὸς γεννᾶται, Christ is born, and comments: "For he said 'Christ is born,' not because he is always being born from the Virgin, but because the present feast is the day of the Master's birth"; Photius, *Amphil.* 227, ed. Laourdas and Westerink, 6:1, 8).

PART 4   EPILOGUE

John A. McGuckin

16. St. Gregory the Comic

It was the experience of hearing Fred Norris preach, in church, a *verbatim* exposition of one of St. Gregory's homilies, that made me realize for the first time how funny he was—Gregory, that is. People laughed in all the right places, and accordingly were ready to be "touched to the heart" in all the right places, too, for laughter and weeping can indeed be gateways to the soul. Christian preachers know this, for joy is one of the unfakeable gifts of the Holy Spirit.

This was a shocking idea to classical antiquity, where weeping was considered the antithesis of the proper behavior of the sage, and where laughter, as *The Name of the Rose* reminded us, was no funny matter when it came to the virtuous life. But then again the Christian rhetoricians learned from wider sources than the standard ones available to classical antiquity. They had their Bible; and the sight of Jesus the Sage shedding tears in the Garden had already provided the necessary shock to Hellenistic *apatheia,* as too had Jesus' many good-natured jokes when alive, which are palpably better than those of the sourpuss boor Diogenes. When Jesus delivered the shock of sophistic realization of present error, it was always tempered by the possibility of greater joy to be found through reconciliation. Who but Jesus, for example, would have positioned so many kingdom illustrations around the perennial theme of "The Bishop and the Actress" (read "Pharisee" and "repentant woman"),[1] or

---

1. More on this theme in John A. McGuckin, "The Sign of the Prophet: The Significance of Meals in the Doctrine of Jesus," *Scripture Bulletin,* 16, no. 2 (1986): 35–40; and McGuckin, "Jesus' Self-Designation as a Prophet," *Scripture Bulletin* 19, no. 1 (1988): 2–11.

authored vocational literature advertising vacancies for apostles: "Only qualifications necessary: eunuch status and willingness to consider crucifixion."[2]
His summation of the career of the Great Alexander[3] also must count as even
funnier (and certainly less self-referential) than Diogenes' encounter with that
warrior dummy in the town agora.

If Fred Norris and Gregory of Nazianzus had ever met, I suspect it would
have been an encounter similar to that recorded by one of Oscar Wilde's close
friends who, having told a good joke, had all the group laughing out loud. Wilde, dabbing his eyes with a handkerchief, said: "Oh, I wish I had made up that
one"; to which his friend replied: "You will, Oscar, you will." I can imagine the
two Gregorians—one a Gregorian ontologically because it was his inescap-
able *ousia* to be the Gregory Nazianzen, the other a Gregorian *kata charin,* because it was his elected destiny to be such—carefully writing down one another's jokes, trying not be noticed while doing it, just as Gregory while delivering
the *Orations on the Lights* in the cathedral in Constantinople caught stenog-
raphers taking down his speech and shouted at them to stop plagiarizing his
best efforts. In the spirit of our common teacher who once, so memorably, said,
"Certain things should not be dwelt upon but rather passed over in silence,"
I shall not call to mind here any of the actual jokes of F. W. Norris, but I may
spend some short time, in Fred's honor, drawing some attention to the jokes of
Gregory. Many commentators have insisted on seeing him as something of a
cast-down soul as he got older and sicker, and melancholic in his poetry of the
lamentable state of the human condition. Did they somehow miss the jokes?
In one of his most solemn threnodies on the state of the fallible human body,
Gregory slips in the line: "How long shall I have to carry on as a turd-making
machine?" How do the commentators think this line went down? It was delivered well into the second bowl of the Symposium wine, I am confident to say.
Even his formal sophistic laments on the origin, state, and destiny of mortal humanity ("slime, clay, dust") are very funny. But so as not to labor humor with
much repetition—nothing is so unfunny as a treatise on humor, after all—let
me simply draw attention to some of the funnies in the first of the *Theological
Orations* (a series of lectures where he was on his best behavior)[4] and leave it as

2. Mt. 19:12; Mt. 16:24.
3. Mk. 8:36.
4. When he was not being on his best behavior Gregory could be rather naughty. Once, after he
had set off for a summer vacation on the Princes' Islands off Constantinople, the congregation called him

a challenge to future generations of post-doc scholars to produce *The Complete Gregory Book of Jokes.*

I am deliberately going to leave out the aspect of Gregory's caustic use of humor in the *Theological Orations*—that is, the element of satiric diatribe, which he uses very robustly, indeed, to put his Eunomian opponents in their place. This I do on the grounds that caustic humor is not funny, as Freud taught us, as much as it is bitterly apologetic. Gregory is here using humor as a sharp weapon. He is not ashamed of it, especially after his opponents cast more than words at him, but also availed themselves of real stones; and also given the fact that they seem to have vociferously gate-crashed his lecture hall—at least for *Oration* 27, until he got himself better security for the subsequent orations in the series—and annoyingly interrupted him as he progressed. So *Oration* 27, at least, was in the form of a real stump-sermon, dealing with hostile interlocutors with the age-old weapons of a witty orator. If we added this element of caustic humor into the account we would raise the instance of laughable moments (funny at least for those who were not the target of the wit) by a considerable percentage. But here I shall consider only the genuinely funny and non-caustic jokes.

The first of the *Theological Orations* is a very funny performance, indeed. As he progresses into the Second and Third Theologicals and onward into the discourse on the mysteries of God's love for the world and the church, Gregory's eloquence becomes more deeply lyrical, and moves more into what he said throughout the First—that theology is best honored by silence. Consummate rhetorician as he was, of course, his final silence is the silence of an audience rapt by the beauty of the vision he presents, one of the most exquisite sets of poems on the beauties of nature, on the economy of the Son, and on the harmony of the Trinitarian perichoresis that exists in all patristic literature: not the silence of the orator, but more the silencing of the orator's audience, so that they moved from listening with their ears toward understanding with their heart; for Gregory was above all a Christian priest, not a mere Hellenist.

---

back to the capital somewhat peremptorily to be the preacher at their Feast of St. Cyprian. He lets them know in the course of this 24th *Oration* that he had been having a good time on the islands before he was interrupted, then gives a lively account of the life of the blessed Cyprian. Of course the Cyprian he now expounds in amazing and lurid detail—an instance of the hilarious story of "The Magician and the Virgin"—was not their Cyprian at all. I once thought this was a simple mistake on the part of Gregory. I am now increasingly suspicious that he did it on purpose, and had his symposiasts on the Princes' Islands in tears when he came back and told them about it.

Now before this gets any further unfunny, I wish to put it back on a serious scholarly basis and number the remaining jokes, omitting the snowballs that contained rocks, and catalogue them properly. Is it the first time that Gregory's jokes have been so catalogued? If so, we ought to do it *wissenschaftliche,* and list them in terms of Jıfto, J2fto, Jısto, and so forth,[5] so that they can be accessed discretely by future generations of theologians, jokologists, and students of Greek rhetoric, much as Professor Norris himself has supplied all of us Gregorians with such a detailed commentary on the *Theological Orations.*[6]

JIFTO: *Oration 27.1*

At the very beginning of his First Theological, Gregory surveys the crowd that has gathered in the Anastasia *aula* and, seeing there some of his well-known opponents, opens the game with the following words: "For there are certain persons whose ears and tongues are itching for our words and, as I can now see for myself, in regard to some here present, even their fists are itching too." In a technical system of rating this is Quite Funny. Gregory was a funny man, a gentle soul, and he had been subject to threats so violent that he had to employ an Egyptian bodyguard and was the focus of stone-throwing and at least one assassination attempt in his time in Constantinople. In such circumstances, he had to stand back and reflect on how well his ministry was going. And now on this fine evening, when he began these historic discourses, he mentioned the "elephant on the carpet": Will it all end up in a massive brawl? Moving swiftly from "itching ears" to "itching fists," the joke probably calmed people down and elicited at least a smile. It deserves a Quite Funny classification.

J2FTO: *Oration 27.1*

And so we come to J2fto, *Or.* 27.1, where Gregory says: "I wish that they, whose tongue is so voluble and so very clever in applying itself to noble and approved language, would also pay some attention to noble deeds. For then

---

5. This ought to be self-evident, but in case there are some neophytes reading this: Jıfto standing for "Joke 1 first theological oration"; Jısto for "Joke 1 second theological oration," and so on. Grammarians and librarians are welcome to use this classification system copyright-free.

6. Norris, *Faith gives Fullness to Reasoning.*

perhaps in a little while they would become less sophistical, and less absurd as bizarre word-jugglers, if I may be allowed to use a ridiculous expression about a ridiculous subject." This is admittedly not as funny as the previous joke, but it works better in the Greek than the English: in the original, the words "word-jugglers" actually sound like a juggler, which is not all that easy a feat. It is something of a cheaper joke, because it relied for much of its effect on the venerable father Gregory making a silly noise on stage.

J3FTO: *Oration 27.2*

We come now to the third instance, J3fto, *Or.* 27.2, where the saint declares:

However, my opponents neglect the paths of righteousness, and look only to this one point, namely, which of the propositions submitted to them shall they bind or loose, like profession-al wrestlers in the theatres—you know, not that kind of wrestling match in which the victory is won according to the rules of the sport, but rather the sort that is set up to deceive the eyes of an ignorant audience and to catch applause.[7] Every market place, therefore, must buzz with their talking; and every dinner party has to be worried to death with silly chat and boredom; and every festival must be made unfestive and full of dejection, and every occasion of mourn-ing needs to be consoled by an even greater calamity—their syllogisms.

This, I think, is Very Funny. It gains in force because it goes on being Quite Funny at such length that one is increasingly moved by the ridiculous nature of the argument, until the climactic point, that even every occasion of mourn-ing is made worse ... "by their syllogisms." J3fto is also doubly funny because it is reprised, as we shall see, by J5fto below, in the image of a person laugh-ing uproariously at a funeral, which of course is one of those things you really "ought never to do." This last aspect of "Never indulge in unmeasured laughter (*gelo ametria*) at a funeral," incidentally, was rendered all the more hilarious (although Gregory sadly cannot be credited for this, since it happened post-humously) when Maximus the Confessor received a corrupted manuscript that read: "Never indulge in geometry (*geometria*) at a funeral" and spent some considerable time in his *Ambigua* trying to explain to puzzled Byzan-tines what the Theologian could have meant by the image of a man wandering round the graveyard with a protractor and pair of compasses.

---

7. It is indeed lamentable to hear from the mouth of a saint that wrestling matches in antiquity were so commonly faked. One can only be glad that such imposture is a thing of the past.

J4FTO: *Oration 27.3*

Now, since a certain lightness and deftness is the essence of humor, let us move on swiftly to our three final instances. The first is J4fto, *Or.* 27.3, where our Christian Demosthenes says:

And who are the appropriate persons [to make inquiry into divine matters]? Those to whom the subject is of real concern, and not those who make it a matter of pleasant gossip, like any other topic, a chitchat for after the races, or the theatre, or a concert, or a dinner party, not to mention still lower occupations.

Now, once again, here is the appeal to *bathos.* This one is, technically speaking, either Quite Funny or Very Funny, depending on how it is delivered.[8] It is the type of joke much favored by stand-up comics; its level of hilarity depends on what the audience supplies in the moment. The rhetor only has to adopt an innocent face (a raised eyebrow is optional, though often useful) and a pregnant pause. The force of this works on the basis of what the mind itself supplies after having a lovely rhetorical sequence of four specified examples of chitchat (after the races, after the theatre, after a concert, or after a dinner party), but then is stopped short by the single antithetical example: "Not to mention still lower occupations." By leaving the listener hanging, waiting for a balanced set of antithetical examples that never occur, the orator knows that the minds of the audience will be actively supplying examples of "still lower occupations" themselves. I leave it to the readers' imaginations to come up with suitable examples; whether cloacal or amatory, a curtain is best drawn around them. But it is certainly funny to have left one's wordy opponents pictured in this way, in such an imaginary circumstance that the orator can protest in all innocence he never even said. This, therefore, counts as the single instance in the *Theological Orations* of the "joke that never was," which compares curiously to the mystery of "the dog that never barked," which Gregory elsewhere applies to his former friend Maximus the Cynic.

J5FTO: *Oration 27.5*

Our last but one example gains force from its being a reprise of J3fto. In J5fto, *Or.* 27.5, Gregory states:

---

8. And also on the age of the hearer. My grandson, being twelve, thinks bathotic humor the height of wit.

It is not that all teaching is wrong, but only that which lacks moderation. Even in regard to sweet honey, too much and too often can make us sick. As Solomon says (and I agree with him), "There is a season for everything," and that which is good ceases to be good if it is not done in a good way; just as a flower is quite out of season in winter, and just as man's clothing does not look right on a woman, or vice versa. Just as uproarious laughter would be seriously out of place at a funeral, or bitter tears shed at a party. Shall we in the case of theology alone disregard the issue of the proper time, a matter in which, most of all, the issue of due season should be respected?

Now this is, I would say, a series of drolleries rather than being per se out-and-out laughable. But the image of laughing at a funeral, I suspect, was deliberately meant to induce a forbidden, interior laugh, both for its inappropriateness and because it reminds the listener of the previous joke about Eunomian syllogisms being "mournful"; and Gregory has buttressed his drollery with two other references to unseasonable flowers, and men and women wearing one another's clothes. This joke is more difficult to classify on the scale of funniness. Gregory was himself an obsessive rose-grower, and thus knew very well that the flower, if cultivated, could be made to last until the snows of winter in its season. He also may be making an explicit reference to Eustathian monastics present in Constantinople in 381, who had insisted on the same garb for male and female ascetics. But I suspect that he was just taking advantage of that stock-in-trade of the late-Roman pantomime where, along with a plank hitting the actors from behind, the mistaking of the genders of the players because of "wrong costume" was part and parcel of the slapstick of the day. He made a calculated guess that there must be at least one person in the audience that night who would laugh out loud at the very mention of a man looking inappropriate in woman's clothing—more along the lines of Widow Twanky in Aladdin than serious transvestism, of course. He was counting on the political incorrectness of at least one member of the congregation, and it probably paid off for him on that night. If so, we can tentatively award this last paragraph the status of Almost Quite Funny.

J6FTO: *Oration 27.9*

This leaves us with a decided preference for the award of a Very Funny to our last remaining example, J6fto, *Or.* 27.9. Here Gregory, addressing his loquacious Eunomian opponents, says: "Can't you restrain the labor pains of your mouth? Well, if that is the case you should find many other honorable subjects for discussion. Turn your disease of loquacity to these topics with some advantage. I suggest you attack the topic of Pythagorean silence, or that of the Orphic beans." Now this is funny, torn as we are between *bathos* and *pathos*. Both moments have to do with wind. The first is by the lack of it. Gregory has taken the wind from the sails of his opponents by making them truly apophatic theologians: "The best that can be said about someone who values *apophasis* is that they should shut up!"[9] The second is by the excess of it, as beans, Orphic or otherwise, are well known for their side effects. Either way, Gregory's windy opponents are "discomfited," as divines in a more elegant age were wont to say.

Conclusion

This brings me to my synopsis. I have established several things in this modest piece. First, it classifies the jokes in the first *Theological Oration* in a *wissenschaftliche* manner for the first time ever in an English-language publication. This alone is no mean feat. Second, it argues that Gregory was a funny man, especially when he was pretending not to be funny. And third, it says, on the occasion of the retirement of our dear, funny, not-so-old Professor Frederick W. Norris, thanks for all those so-illuminating laughs along the way.

9. When checked, this turned out to be an original joke of Prof. F. W. Norris.

THE WORKS OF
FREDERICK W. NORRIS
(Excluding Reviews)

Books

Single-Author

The Apostolic Faith: Protestants and Roman Catholics. Collegeville, Minn.: The Liturgical Press, 1992.

Christianity: A Short Global History. Oxford: Oneworld Publishing, 2002.

Multiple Authors

Faith Gives Fullness to Reasoning: The Five Theological Orations of Gregory Nazianzen. Introduction and commentary by Frederick W. Norris. Translation by Lionel Wickham and Frederick Williams. Supplements to Vigiliae Christianae 13. Leiden: E. J. Brill, 1991.

Multiple Editors

Encyclopedia of Early Christianity. Edited by Everett Ferguson, Michael McHugh, and Frederick W. Norris. New York: Garland Press, 1990; second edition, 2 vols., 1997.

The Early Church in Its Context: Essays in Honor of Everett Ferguson. Edited by Abraham J. Malherbe, Frederick W. Norris, and James W. Thompson. Supplements to Novum Testamentum 90. Leiden: E.J. Brill, 1998.

The Cambridge History of Christianity. Vol. 2, *Constantine to c. 600.* Edited by Augustine Casiday and Frederick W. Norris. Cambridge: Cambridge University Press, 2007.

Articles in Books and Journals, Booklets

"Hans Küng on Ministry." *Mission* (1974): 25–28.

The Spirit and the Gifts Are Ours. In *The Crucible.* Aurora, Ill.: European Evangelistic Society Publishing, 1974.

The Canon in the Church. In *The Crucible.* Aurora, Ill.: European Evangelistic Society Publishing, 1975.

"Ignatius, Polycarp and I Clement: Walter Bauer Reconsidered." *Vigiliae Christianae* 30 (1976):

23–44. Reprinted in *Studies in Early Christianity,* edited by Everett Ferguson, with David Scholer and Corby Finney, 4:237–58. New York: Garland Press, 1993.

"An Open Past." Response to Ulrich Duchrow's "The Spiritual Dimensions of the Scientific World." *Gospel in Context* 1 (1978): 16–18.

"Apostolic, Catholic and Sensible: The Consensus Fidelium." In *Essays on New Testament Christianity,* edited by Robert Wetzel, 15–29, Cincinnati: Standard Publishing, 1978.

"Authority: The New Testament as Norm, Church History as Guide." In *W. R., The Man and His Work: A Brief Account of the Life and Work of William Robinson,* edited by James Gray, 66–74. Birmingham, UK: Berean Press, 1978.

"The Social Status of Early Christianity." *Gospel in Context* 2 (1979): 4–14, 27–28.

"Social Status Revisited." *Gospel in Context* 2 (1979): 37–79.

"Asia Minor before Ignatius: Walter Bauer Reconsidered." In *Studia Evangelica VII,* edited by Elizabeth Livingstone, 355–77. Texte und Untersuchungen 126. Berlin: Akademie Verlag, 1982.

"The Fathers: Imitation Pearls among Genuine Swine." *Theological Students Fellowship Bulletin* 5 (1982): 8–10.

"Isis, Sarapis and Demeter in Antioch of Syria." *Harvard Theological Review* 75 (1982): 189–207.

"The Image of God: The Biblical Concept of Man." In *Christian Doctrine: "The Faith Once Delivered,"* edited by William Richardson, 237–63. Cincinnati: Standard Publishing, 1983.

"Strategy of Mission in the New Testament." In *Exploring Church Growth,* edited by Wilbert Shenk, 260–76. Grand Rapids, Mich.: Eerdmans, 1983.

"God and the Gods: Expect Footprints." In *Unto the Uttermost: Missions in the Christian Churches/Churches of Christ,* edited by Douglas Priest, Jr., 55–69. Pasadena, Calif.: William Carey Library, 1984.

"Mathematics, Physics and Religion: A Need for Candor and Rigor." *Scottish Journal of Theology* 37 (1984): 457–70.

"Paul of Samosata: *Procurator Ducenarius." Journal of Theological Studies,* n.s. 35 (1984): 50–70.

"Of Thorns and Roses: The Logic of Belief in Gregory Nazianzen." *Church History* 53 (1984): 455–64.

"The Authenticity of Gregory Nazianzen's Five Theological Orations." *Vigiliae Christianae* 39 (1985): 331–39.

"Gregory Nazianzen's Opponents in Oration 31." In *Arianism: Historical and Theological Reassessments: Papers from the Oxford Conference on Patristic Studies, September 5–10, 1983,* edited by Robert Gregg, 321–26. Patristic Monograph Series 11. Cambridge, Mass.: Philadelphia Patristic Foundation, 1985.

Jesus the Magician: A Response to Morton Smith. In *The Crucible.* Atlanta, Ga.: European Evangelistic Society, 1985.

"Christians Only, but Not the Only Christians: Acts 19:1–7." *Restoration Quarterly* 28 (1986): 97–105.

"Melito's Motivation." *Anglican Theological Review* 68 (1986): 16–24.

"Current Issues in Patristic Studies." In *Summary of Proceedings: Forty-Second Annual Con-*

ference of the American Theological Library Association, June 20–24, 1988, 104–18. St. Meinrad, Ind.: American Theological Library Association, 1988.

"The Tetragrammaton in Gregory Nazianzen, Or. 30.17." *Vigiliae Christianae* 41 (1989): 339–44.

"Antioch-on-the-Orontes as a Religious Center, Part I." In *Aufstieg und Niedergang der römischen Welt,* vol. 18.3, ed. Wolfgang Haase, s.v., 2322–79. Berlin: Walter de Gruyter, 1990.

"Artifacts from Antioch." In *Social History of the Matthean Community: Cross-Disciplinary Approaches,* edited by David Balch, 248–58. Minneapolis: Fortress Press, 1991.

"Wonder, Worship and Writ: Patristic Christology." *Ex Auditu* 7 (1991): 59–72.

"Eusebius on Jesus as Deceiver and Sorcerer." In *Eusebius, Christianity, and Judaism,* edited by Harold Attridge and Gohei Hatta, 523–40. Detroit: Wayne State University Press, 1992. Japanese version, Tokyo: Yamamoto Shoten, 1992.

"Fantasy and Biography." In *Journey through Fantasy Literature: A Resource Guide for Teachers,* edited by Roberta T. Herrin and Sarah K. Davis, 2:54–56. Johnson City, Tenn.: East Tennessee State University, 1992.

"Universal Salvation in Origen and Maximus." In *Universalism and the Doctrine of Hell: Papers Presented at the Fourth Edinburgh Conference in Christian Dogmatics, 1991,* edited by Nigel M. de S. Cameron, 35–72. Carlisle, UK: Paternoster Press, and Grand Rapids, Mich.: Baker Book House, 1992.

"Gregory the Theologian." *Pro Ecclesia* 2 (1993): 473–84.

"Theology as Grammar: Gregory Nazianzen and Ludwig Wittgenstein." In *Arianism after Arius,* edited by Michel Barnes and Daniel Williams, 237–49. Edinburgh: T. and T. Clark, 1993.

"Truth and Truthfulness." In *Building Up the Church: A Festschrift in Honor of Henry E. Webb,* edited by Gary E. Weadman, 101–30. Shoals, Ind.: The Old Path Tract Society, 1993.

"Black Marks on the Communities' Manuscripts." The 1994 North American Patristic Society Presidential Address. *Journal of Early Christian Studies* 2 (1994): 443–66.

"Gregory the Theologian and Other Religions." *Greek Orthodox Theological Review* 39 (1994): 131–40.

"Preaching to Pagans: Ambiguity and Clarity." In *The Gospel Unhindered: Modern Missions and the Book of Acts,* edited by Doug Priest, Jr., 131–41. Pasadena, Calif.: William Carey Library, 1994.

"The Arian Heresy?" In *Telling the Churches' Stories: Ecumenical Perspectives on Writing Christian History,* edited by Timothy J. Wengert and Charles W. Brockwell, 55–71. Grand Rapids, Mich.: Eerdmans, 1995.

"The Catholicity of Great Black Preaching." In *Sharing Heaven's Music: The Heart of Christian Preaching, Essays in Honor of James Earl Massey,* edited by Barry Callen, 137–50. Nashville: Abingdon, 1995.

"The Five-Finger Exercise." In *Faith in Practice: Studies in the Book of Acts: Festschrift for Earl and Ottie Mearl Stuckenbruck,* edited by David Fiensy and William Howden, 122–35. Atlanta, Ga.: European Evangelistic Society, 1995.

"Women Ministers in Constantinian Christianity." In *Essays on Women in Earliest Christianity,* edited by Carrol Osburn, 2:357–74. Joplin, Mo.: College Press, 1995.

"Deification: Consensual and Cogent." *Scottish Journal of Theology* 49 (1996): 411–28.

Dean E. Walker: Missiologist. Johnson City, Tenn.: Emmanuel School of Religion Press, 1997.

"Gregory Nazianzen: Constructing and Constructed by Scripture." In *The Bible in Greek Christian Late Antiquity,* edited and translated by Paul M. Blowers, 149–62. The Bible through the Ages 1. Notre Dame, Ind.: University of Notre Dame Press, 1997.

"Encyclopedia Revisited." In *The Early Church in Its Context: Essays in Honor of Everett Ferguson,* edited by Abraham J. Malherbe, Frederick W. Norris, and David M. Scholer, 256–67. Supplements to Novum Testamentum 90. Leiden: E.J. Brill, 1998.

"Mission among Christian Churches and Churches of Christ." *Discipliana* 58 (1998): 99–109.

"The Theologian and Technical Rhetoric: Gregory of Nazianzus and Hermogenes of Tarsus." In *Nova and Vetera: Patristic Studies in Honor of Thomas Patrick Halton,* edited by John Petruccione, 84–95. Washington, D.C.: The Catholic University of America Press, 1998.

"Theological Resources from Christian Churches/Churches of Christ." In *Grounds for Understanding: Ecumenical Resources for Responses to Religious Pluralism,* edited by S. Mark Heim, 107–21. Grand Rapids, Mich.: Eerdmans, 1998.

"Mission and Religious Pluralism." *Leaven* 7 (1999): 19–22.

"Origen." In *The Early Christian World,* edited by Philip F. Esler, 105–26. London: Routledge, 2000.

"Your Honor, My Reputation: St. Gregory of Nazianzus's Funeral Oration on St. Basil the Great." In *Greek Biography and Panegyric in Late Antiquity,* edited by Tomas Hägg and Philip Rousseau, 140–59. Transformation of the Classical Heritage 31. Berkeley: University of California Press, 2000.

"'Montanists' Then and Now: A Response to William Tabbernee." In *Advents of the Spirit: An Introduction to the Current Study of Pneumatology,* edited by Bradford E. Hinze and D. Lyle Dabney, 119–22. Marquette Studies in Theology 30. Milwaukee, Wisc.: Marquette University Press, 2001.

"The Returning Recognition of Religious Pluralism." *Leaven* 9 (2001): 75–79.

"'As Yourself': A Least Love." In *In Dominico Eloquio: In Lordly Eloquence: Essays on Patristic Exegesis in Honor of Robert Louis Wilken,* edited by Paul M. Blowers, Angela Russell Christman, David G. Hunter, and Robin Darling Young, 101–17. Grand Rapids, Mich.: Eerdmans, 2002.

"The Canon of Scripture in the Church." In *The Free Church and the Early Church: Bridging the Historical and Theological Divide,* edited by Daniel H. Williams, 3–25. Grand Rapids, Mich.: Eerdmans, 2002.

"3 Cheers for the Hinterland." *In Trust* 13 (2002): 14–19.

"The Transfiguration of Christ: The Transformation of the Church." In *Reading in Christian*

Communities: Essays on Interpretation in the Early Church in Honor of Rowan A. Greer, edited by Charles A. Bobertz and David Brakke. Christianity and Judaism in Antiquity 14. Notre Dame, Ind.: University of Notre Dame Press, 2002.

"Vocation in the Outback." In *The Scope of Our Art: The Vocation of the Theological Teacher,* edited by L. Gregory Jones and Stephanie Paulsell, 190–208. Grand Rapids, Mich.: Eerdmans, 2002.

"Logic and Theology: Aristotle and Gregory the Theologian." In *To Teach, to Delight and to Move: Theological Education in a Post-Christian Age,* edited by David S. Cunningham, 223–41. Eugene, Ore.: Cascade Books, 2004.

"Gregory Contemplating the Beautiful: Knowing Human Misery and Divine Mystery through and Persuaded by Images." In *Gregory of Nazianzus: Images and Reflections,* edited by Jostein Børtnes and Tomas Hägg, 19–35. Copenhagen: Museum Tusculanum Press, 2006.

"Timothy of Baghdad, *Catholicos* of the East Syrian Church, 780–823: Still a Valuable Model." *International Bulletin of Missionary Research* 30 (2006): 133–36.

"Greek Christianities." In *The Cambridge History of Christianity*. Vol. 2, *Constantine to c. 600,* edited by Augustine Casiday and Frederick W. Norris, 70–117. Cambridge: Cambridge University Press, 2007.

Encyclopedia and Dictionary Articles

"Antiochien." In *Theologische Realenzyklopädie,* edited by Gerhard Krause and Gerhard Müller, 3:99–103. Berlin: Walter de Gruyter, 1978.

Articles on all personal names in the *Ecclesiastical Histories* of Eusebius, Socrates, Sozomen, and Evagrius. In *The Lexicon of Greek Personal Names,* edited by P. M. Fraser, E. Matthews and R. M. V. Catina, 4 vols., s.v. Oxford: Clarendon Press, 1987–2005.

"Jesus of Nazareth." In *Philosophy of Education: An Encyclopedia,* edited by J. J. Chambliss, 325–28. New York: Garland Publishing, 1996.

"Adalbert," "Aidan," "Anastasius," "Anselm," "Augustine of Hippo," "Bede," "Birinus," "Clement of Ochrid," "Cuthbert," "Eligius," "Eusebius of Caesarea," "Fridolin (or Fridold)," "Gudwal (or Gurwal; Gurvalus)," "Honoratus," "Justin Martyr," "Kilian (Kyllena)," "Leander of Seville," "Lebuin," "Ninian (or Nynias; Niniavus)," "Pal, Krishna," "Paulinus of York," "Reginhar (or Renharius; Regenharius)," "Severinus," "Stephen," "Trudpert," "Ulfila (or Ulphilas; Wulfila)," "Valentinus," "Vicelin," "Virgil of Salzburg," "Wilfrid," "Willibald," "Wolfgang." In *Biographical Dictionary of Christian Missions,* edited by Gerald Anderson, s.v. New York: Macmillan Reference USA, 1997.

"Abortion," "Acacius of Caesarea," "Acts of Andrew," "Acts of John," "Aeneas of Gaza," "Alexandria," "Alogoi," "Ammonius," "Ammonius of Alexandria," "Anastasius I of Antioch," "Anastasius II of Antioch," "Anastasius Monachus," "Anastasius Sinaita," "Andrew of Caesarea," "Anianus of Celeda," "Antioch," "Aphthartodocetae," "Arnold, Gottfried," "Asia Minor," "Athanasian Creed," "Bardaisan (Bardesanes)," "Barsauma," "Basil of Caesarea," "Basilides," "Bethlehem," "Cave, William," "Chalcedon, Chalcedonian Creed," "Christ, Christology,"

"Circumcellions," "Conon," "Constantinople," "Cosmas Indicopleustes," "Cyril of Jerusalem," "Cyril of Scythopolis," "Cyrillonas," "Daniélou, Jean," "Dioscorus," "Dorotheus of Gaza," "Edessa," "Egeria, Pilgrimage of," "Epiphanius of Salamis," "Ethics," "Eulogius of Alexandria," "Eutherius of Tyana," "Evagrius of Pontus," "Evagrius Scholasticus," "Fastidius," "Fisher, George Park," "Flavian of Constantinople," "Gelasius of Caesarea," "Gelasius of Cyzicus," "George of Laodicea," "George of Pisidia," "Germanus of Constantinople," "Gregory of Nazianzus," "Gregory Thaumaturgus," "Hagia Sophia," "Harnack, Adolf von," "Hegemonius," *"Henoticon,"* "Herder, Johann Gottfried," "Hierocles," *"Homoousios,"* "Hormisdas," "Iona," "Isidore," "Isis," "Jerusalem," "John Malalas," "John Moschus," "John of Antioch," "John of Caesarea," "John of Euboea," "John of Gaza," "Jovian," "Jude," "Latourette, Kenneth Scott," "Laura (Lavra)," "Leontius of Byzantium," "Licinian," "Lightfoot, Joseph Barber," "Lucian of Antioch," "Lucian of Samosata," "Lucilla," "Malchion," "Marcia," "Marius Mercator," *"Martyrs of Palestine,"* "Melchizedek, Melchizedekians," "Menander," "Menas of Constantinople," "Methodius," "Möhler, Johann Adam," "Mosheim, Johann Lorenz von," "Neander, August," "Nectarius," "Niceta (Nicetas) of Remesiana," "Nicolaitans," "Nilus of Ancyra," "Oak, Synod of the," "Oecumenius," "Optatus of Milevis," "Orosius," "Palestine," "Palladius," "Paul of Samosata," "Peter Chrysologus," "Philostorgius," "Photinus," "Pierius," "Pneumatomachians," "Proclus of Constantinople," "Procopius of Gaza," "Rhetoric," "Sabellius," "Schaff, Phillip," "Severus of Antioch," "Shenoute of Atripe," "Socrates Scholasticus," "Sophronius," "Sozomen," "Symeon Stylites," "Synaxis," "Tatian," "Theodotus the Banker," "Theophilus of Alexandria," "Theophilus of Antioch," *"Three Chapters,"* "Timothy," "Titus of Bostra," "Walker, Williston," "Zephyrinus." In *Encyclopedia of Early Christianity,* edited by Everett Ferguson, Michael P. McHugh, and Frederick W. Norris, s.v. New York: Garland Publishing, 1990.

"Antioch of Syria." In *The Anchor Bible Dictionary,* edited by David Noel Freedman, 1:265–69. New York: Doubleday, 1992.

"Antiochien, I. Archäologie and III. Synoden und Schisma." In *Lexikon für Theologie und Kirche,* edited by Michael Buchberger, 1:768, 770. Freiburg: Herder Verlag, 1993.

"Acts of the Martyrs of Edessa," "Acts of Thomas," "Addai," "Addai and Mary, Liturgy of," "Anthony," "Apostolic Fathers," "Asterius of Amasea," "Babylas," "Basil of Cilicia," "Bauer, Walter," "Bingham, Joseph," "Columbaria," "Crete," "Cyprus," "Cyrenaica," "Diodocus of Photice," "Duchesne, Louis," "Elijah," "Flavian of Antioch," "Frumentius," "Hiereia, Council of," "John of Caesarea," "Julian of Saba," "Juvenal of Jerusalem," "Libanius," "Lietzmann, Hans," "Neochalcedonians," "Nicaea II, Council of," "Oxyrhynchus," "Patripassianism," "Paulinus of Antioch," "Peter Mongus," "Quartodecimans," "Rimini/Seleucia, Councils of," "Sardis," "Schwartz, Eduard," "Sirmium, Synods of," "Smyrna," "Suicide," "Thaddaeus," "Zosimus," and revisions of articles for the first edition; articles co-authored: "Abraham of Kaskar (Al-Wasit)," "A-lo-pen," "Asia, Central," "Asia, East," "Buddhism and Christianity," "China," "Confucianism and Christianity," "Hinduism and Christianity," "India," "Islam and Christianity," "Taoism and Christianity," "Zoroastrianism and Christianity." In *Encyclopedia of Early Christianity,* edited by Everett Ferguson, Michael P. McHugh, and Frederick W. Norris, 2nd ed., 2 vols., s.v. New York: Garland Press, 1997.

"Athanasius." In *The Encyclopedia of Christianity,* edited by Erwin Fahlbusch, Jan Milic Lochman, John Mbiti, Jaroslav Pelikan, and Lukas Vischer, 150–51. Grand Rapids, Mich.: Eerdmans, 1999.

"Gregory Nazianzen." In *Dictionary of Biblical Interpretation,* edited by John H. Hayes, 1:466. Nashville: Abingdon, 1999.

"Apollinaris," "Cappadocians." In *The Dictionary of Historical Theology,* edited by Trevor A. Hart, 18–19, 111–15. Grand Rapids, Mich.: Eerdmans, 2000.

"Gregory of Nazianzus." In *Biographical Dictionary of Christian Theologians,* edited by Patrick W. Carey and Joseph T. Lienhard, 219–21. Westport, Conn.: Greenwood Press, 2000.

"Didascalia" and [with David Bundy] "Chronicle of Seert." In *A Dictionary of Asian Christianity,* edited by Scott W. Sunquist, David Wu Chu Sin, and John Chew Hiang Chea, 241–42, 170–71. Grand Rapids, Mich.: Eerdmans, 2001.

"Apokatastasis." In *The Westminster Handbook to Origen,* edited by John Anthony McGuckin, 59–62. Westminster Handbooks to Christian Theology. Louisville: Westminster John Knox Press, 2004.

"Nestorians." In *Encyclopedia of Missions and Missionaries,* edited by Jonathan Bonk, 288–90. New York: Routledge, 2007.

"Religious Demographics and the New Diversity." In *The Oxford Handbook of Religious Diversity,* edited by Chad Meister, 201-13. Oxford: Oxford University Press, 2011.

"James Mason Neale," "Nestorians (East Syrians)," "Timothy I of Baghdad," "Andrew Walls." In *Encyclopedia of Christian Civilization,* edited by G. T. Kurian. 4 vols., s.v. Oxford: Wiley-Blackwell, 2011.

GENERAL BIBLIOGRAPHY

Gregory of Nazianzus: Texts and Translations

Orations

Or. 1–3. Ed. Jean Bernardi. SC 247. Trans. Charles Gordon Browne and James Edward Swallow. NPNF 2.7:203–29. *Or.* 1 trans. Verna E. F. Harrison. Gregory of Nazianzus, *Festal Orations.* Popular Patristics Series 36. Crestwood, N.Y.: St. Vladimir's Seminary Press, 2008, 57–60.

Or. 4–5. Ed. Jean Bernardi. SC 309. Trans. C. W. King, *Julian the Emperor, Containing Gregory Nazianzen's Two Invectives and Libanius' Monody with Julian's Extant Theosophical Works.* London: George Bell and Sons, 1888, 1–121.

Or. 6–12. Ed. Marie-Ange Calvet-Sebasti. SC 405. *Or.* 6, 9–11 trans. Martha Vinson. FC 107: 3–35. *Or.* 8 trans. Brian E. Daley, *Gregory of Nazianzus.* Early Church Fathers. London: Routledge, 2006, 63–75. *Or.* 7–8, 12 trans. Charles Gordon Browne and James Edward Swallow. NPNF 2.7:227–47.

Or. 13–19. Ed. Armand Benjamin Caillau. PG 35:852–1866. *Or.* 13–15, 17, 19 trans. Martha Vinson. FC 107:36–106. *Or.* 14 trans. Brian E. Daley, *Gregory of Nazianzus.* Early Church Fathers. London: Routledge, 2006, 75–97. *Or.* 16, 18 trans. Charles Gordon Browne and James Edward Swallow. NPNF 2.7:247–69.

Or. 20–23. Ed. Justin Mossay and Guy Lafontaine. SC 270. *Or.* 20, 22–23 trans. Martha Vinson. FC 107:107–41. *Or.* 20 trans. Brian E. Daley, *Gregory of Nazianzus.* Early Church Fathers. London: Routledge, 2006, 98–105. *Or.* 21 trans. Charles Gordon Browne and James Edward Swallow. NPNF 2.7:269–84.

Or. 24–26. Ed. Justin Mossay and Guy Lafontaine. SC 284. Trans. Martha Vinson. FC 107: 142–90. *Or.* 26 trans. Brian E. Daley, *Gregory of Nazianzus.* Early Church Fathers. London: Routledge, 2006, 105–17.

Or. 27–31 (*Theological Orations*). Ed. Paul Gallay. SC 250. Trans. Charles Gordon Browne and James Edward Swallow. NPNF 2.7:284–328; repr. with notes in Edward R. Hardy, ed., *Christology of the Later Fathers.* Library of Christian Classics 3. Philadelphia: Westminster, 1954, 128–214. Trans. Frederick Williams (*Or.* 27) and Lionel Wickham (*Or.* 28–31), in *Faith Gives Fullness to Reasoning: The Five Theological Orations of*

Gregory Nazianzen, introduction and commentary by Frederick W. Norris. Supplements to Vigiliae Christianae 13. Leiden: Brill, 1991; repr. with notes in St. Gregory of Nazianzus, *On God and Christ: The Five Theological Orations and Two Letters to Cledonius.* Popular Patristic Series 23. Crestwood, N.Y.: St. Vladimir's Seminary Press, 2002.

Or. 32–37. Ed. Claudio Moreschini. SC 318. *Or.* 32, 35–36 trans. Martha Vinson. FC 107:191–229. *Or.* 33–34, 37 trans. Charles Gordon Browne and James Edward Swallow. NPNF 2.7:328–45.

Or. 38–41. Ed. Claudio Moreschini. SC 358. Trans. Charles Gordon Browne and James Edward Swallow. NPNF 2.7:345–85. *Or.* 38–39 trans. Brian E. Daley, *Gregory of Nazianzus.* Early Church Fathers. London: Routledge, 2006, 117–38. *Or.* 38–41 trans. Verna E. F. Harrison. Gregory of Nazianzus, *Festal Orations.* Popular Patristics Series 36. Crestwood, N.Y.: St. Vladimir's Seminary Press, 2008, 61–160.

Or. 42–43. Ed. Jean Bernardi. SC 384. *Or.* 42 trans. Brian E. Daley, *Gregory of Nazianzus.* Early Church Fathers. London: Routledge, 2006, 138–54. *Or.* 42–43 trans. Charles Gordon Browne and James Edward Swallow. NPNF 2.7:385–422.

Or. 44–45. Ed. Armand Benjamin Caillau. PG 36:608–64. *Or.* 44 trans. Martha Vinson. FC 107:230–38; Brian E. Daley, *Gregory of Nazianzus.* Early Church Fathers. London: Routledge, 2006, 154–61. *Or.* 45 trans. Charles Gordon Browne and James Edward Swallow, NPNF 2.7:422–34. *Or.* 45 trans. Verna E. F. Harrison. Gregory of Nazianzus, *Festal Orations.* Popular Patristics Series 36. Crestwood, N.Y.: St. Vladimir's Seminary Press, 2008, 161–90.

Letters

Ep. 1–249. Ed. Paul Gallay. Gregory of Nazianzus, *Lettres.* Collection des universités de France. 2 vols. Paris: Les belles lettres, 1964/1967. *Ep.* 101–2, 202, repr. SC 208. *Ep.* 1–2, 4–9, 12–13, 16–19, 21–22, 25–29, 37, 39–55, 58–60, 62–66, 77, 88, 91, 93, 101–2, 104–6, 115, 121–24, 126, 131, 135, 139–46, 151–54, 157, 163, 171, 183–86, 202 trans. Charles Gordon Browne and James Edward Swallow. NPNF 2.7:437–82; trans. of *Ep.* 101–2, 202, repr. with notes in Edward R. Hardy, ed., *Christology of the Later Fathers.* Library of Christian Classics 3. Philadelphia: Westminster, 1954, 215–32.

Poems

Carm. Ed. Armand Benjamin Caillau. PG 37–38.

Carm. 1.1.1 *On First Principles;* 1.1.2 *On the Son;* 1.1.3 *On the Spirit;* 1.1.4 *On the Universe;* 1.1.5 *On Providence;* 1.1.7 *On Rational Natures;* 1.1.8 *On the Soul;* 1.1.9 *On the Testaments and the Coming of Christ (Poemata arcana).* Ed. and intro. C. Moreschini; trans. and comm. D. A. Sykes. St. Gregory of Nazianzus, *Poemata Arcana.* Oxford Theological Monographs. Oxford: Clarendon, 1997.

Carm. 1.1.1–12, 37; 1.2.1, 8, 11–18; 2.1.6, 21, 39, 45, 78; *Epit.* 119 on Basil. Trans. Peter Gilbert, *On God and Man: The Theological Poetry of St. Gregory of Nazianzus.* Popular Patristics Series 21. Crestwood, N.Y.: St. Vladimir's Seminary Press, 2001.

Carm. 1.1.2, 11, 29–33, 35; 2.1.24–25, 69–70, 76–77; *Epigr.* 3–7, 12. Trans. John McGuckin. Saint Gregory Nazianzen, *Selected Poems.* Oxford: SLG Press, 1986.

Carm. 1.1.12–38; 1.2.1–40; 2.1.1–10, 12–99; 2.2.1–8. Trans. Claudio Moreschini, Ivano Costa, Carmelo Crimi, Giovanni Laudizi. Gregory of Nazianzus, *Poesie.* 2 vols. Collana di testi patristici 115, 150. Rome: Città nuova editrice, 1994/1999.

Carm. 1.2.10. Ed. Carmelo Crimi. Gregory of Nazianzus, *Sulla virtù: Carme giambico* [*1.2.10*]. Poeti cristiani 1. Pisa: ETS, 1995.

Carm. 1.2.17; 2.1.10, 19, 32. Ed. Christos Simelidis, *Selected Poems of Gregory of Nazianzus: I.2.17; II.1.10, 19. 32: A Critical Edition with Introduction and Commentary.* Hypomnemata 177. Göttingen: Vandenhoeck & Ruprecht, 2009.

Carm. 1.2.25. Ed. Michael Oberhaus. Gregory of Nazianzus, *Gegen den Zorn (Carmen 1, 2, 25): Einleitung und Kommentar.* Forschungen zu Gregor von Nazianz 8. Paderborn: F. Schöningh, 1991.

Carm. 2.1.1–11. Ed. André Tuilier and Guillaume Bady, trans. and notes Jean Bernardi. Gregory of Nazianzus, *Oeuvres poétiques.* Vol. 1.1, *Poèmes personnels.* Collection des universités de France, Série grecque 433. Paris: Les belles lettres, 2004.

Carm. 2.1.11. Ed. Christoph Jungck. Gregory of Nazianzus, *De vita sua: Einleitung, Text, Übersetzung, Kommentar.* Wissenschaftliche Kommentare zu griechischen und lateinischen Schriftstellern. Heidelberg: C. Winter, 1974; ed. Francesco Trisoglio. Gregory of Nazianzus, *Autobiografia: Carmen de vita sua.* Collana Letteratura cristiana antica, n.s. 7. Brescia: Morcelliana, 2005.

Carm. 2.1.11 *De vita sua;* 2.1.19 *Querela de suis calamitatibus;* 2.1.34 *In silentium jejunii;* 2.1.39 *In suos versus;* 2.1.92 *Epitaph sui ipsius et compendium ipsius vitae.* Ed. and trans. Carolinne White. Gregory of Nazianzus, *Autobiographical Poems.* Cambridge Medieval Classics 6. Cambridge: Cambridge University Press, 1996.

Carm. 2.1.12. Ed. Beno Meier. Gregory of Nazianzus, *Über die Bischöfe (Carmen 2, 1, 12).* Studien zur Geschichte und Kultur des Altertums, n.F. 2. Reihe: Forschungen zu Gregor von Nazianz 7. Paderborn: F. Schöning, 1989.

Carm. 2.1.1.194–204, 210–12, 452–56 *De rebus suis;* 2.1.45.191–204, 229–69 *De animae suae calamitatibus carmen lugubre.* Trans. John A. McGuckin, *St. Gregory of Nazianzus: An Intellectual Biography.* Crestwood, N.Y.: St. Vladimir's Seminary Press, 2001, 66–69.

Carm. 2.1.1 *De rebus suis; Carm.* 2.1.11 *De vita sua;* 2.1.12 *De seipso et de episcopis.* Trans. Denis Mollaise Meehan. Saint Gregory of Nazianzus, *Three Poems.* FC 75.

Carm. 2.1.2–10, 13–99 *Poemata de seipso.* PG 37:1014–1452. Trans. Suzanne Abrams Rebillard, "Speaking for Salvation: Gregory of Nazianzus as Poet and Priest in His Autobiographical Poems." Ph.D. diss., Brown University, 2003, 229–472.

Epitaphs

Epit. PG 38:11–80. Trans. W. R. Paton. *The Greek Anthology,* Book 8. LCL 2.401–505.

Testament

Test. Exemplum Testamenti. PG 37:393. Trans. Brian E. Daley, *Gregory of Nazianzus.* Early Church Fathers. London: Routledge, 2006, 184–88.

Secondary Literature

Note: The scholarly works of Frederick W. Norris are listed in the preceding bibliography.

Abrams Rebillard, Suzanne. "Speaking for Salvation: Gregory of Nazianzus as Poet and Priest in His Autobiographical Poems." Ph.D. diss., Brown University, 2003.

———. "The Autobiographical Prosopopoeia of Gregory of Nazianzus." *Studia Patristica* 47 (2010): 123–28.

Ahrweiler, Hélène. *L'idéologie politique de l'empire byzantine.* Paris: Presses universitaires de France, 1975.

Alfeyev, Hilarion. *St. Symeon the New Theologian and Orthodox Tradition.* Oxford Early Christian Studies. Oxford: Oxford University Press, 2000.

Althaus, Heinz. *Die Heilslehre des heiligen Gregor von Nazianz.* Münsterische Beiträge zur Theologie 34. Münster: Aschendorff, 1972.

Anagnostopoulos, Thalia. *Object and Symbol: Greek Learning and the Aesthetics of Identity in Byzantine Iconoclasm.* Ph.D. diss., University of California, Berkeley, 2008.

Angold, Michael. *Church and Society in Byzantium under the Comneni, 1081–1261.* Cambridge: Cambridge University Press, 1995.

Asmus, Rudolf. "Gregorius von Nazianz und sein Verhältnis zum Kynismus." *Theologische Studien und Kritiken* 67 (1894): 314–39.

Auf der Maur, Hans Jörg, and Joop Waldram. "*Illuminatio Verbi Divini—Confessio Fidei—Gratia Baptismi:* Wort, Glaube und Sakrament in Katechumenat und Taufliturgie bei Origenes." In *Fides Sacramenti Sacramentum Fidei: Studies in Honor of Pieter Smulders,* edited by Hans Jörg auf der Maur, et al., 41–95. Assen: Van Gorcum, 1981.

Avenarius, Alexander. *Die byzantinische Kultur und die Slawen: Zum Problem der Rezeption und Transformation (6. bis 12. Jahrhundert).* Veröffentlichungen des Instituts für Österreichische Geschichtsforschung 35. Vienna: Oldenbourg, 2000.

Ayres, Lewis. *Nicaea and Its Legacy: An Approach to Fourth-Century Trinitarian Theology.* Oxford: Oxford University Press, 2004.

Bakker, Egbert. "The Making of History: Herodotus' *Historiês Apodexis,*" in *Brill's Companion to Herodotus,* edited by Egbert Bakker, Irene J. F. de Jong, and Hans van Wees, 30–31. Brill's Companions in Classical Studies. Leiden: Brill, 2002.

Balthasar, Hans Urs von. *Cosmic Liturgy: The Universe According to St. Maximus the Confessor.* 3rd ed. Translated by Brian E. Daley. San Francisco: Ignatius Press, 2003.

Baragwanath, Emily. *Motivation and Narrative in Herodotus.* Oxford Classical Monographs. Oxford: Clarendon Press, 2008.

Barnes, Michel. "One Nature, One Power: Consensus Doctrine in Pro-Nicene Polemic." *Studia Patristica* 29 (1997): 205–23.

Barnes, Timothy D. *The New Empire of Diocletian and Constantine.* Cambridge, Mass.: Harvard University Press, 1982.

Barthes, Roland. "The Discourse of History." Translated by Stephen Bann. *Comparative Criticism* 3 (1981): 7–20.

Beaucamp, J. "Le testament de Grégoire de Nazianze." In *Fontes Minores X,* edited by Ludwig Burgmann, 54–55. Forschungen zur byzantinischen Rechtsgeschichte 22. Frankfurt: Löwenklau, 1998.

Beeley, Christopher A. "Divine Causality and the Monarchy of God the Father in Gregory of Nazianzus." *Harvard Theological Review* 100 (2007): 199–214.

———. "Gregory of Nazianzus on the Unity of Christ." In *In the Shadow of the Incarnation: Essays on Jesus Christ in the Early Church in Honor of Brian E. Daley, S.J.,* edited by Peter W. Martens, 97–120. Notre Dame, Ind.: University of Notre Dame Press, 2008.

———. *Gregory of Nazianzus on the Trinity and the Knowledge of God: In Your Light We Shall See Light.* Oxford Studies in Historical Theology. Oxford and New York: Oxford University Press, 2008.

Bénin, Rolande-Michelle. "Une autobiographie romantqiue au IVe siècle: Le poème 2.1.1 de Grégoire de Nazianze. Introduction, texte critique, traduction et commentaire." Ph.D. diss., Université Paul Valery-Montpellier III, 1988.

Bernardi, Jean. "La lettre 104 de Saint Basile: Le préfet du prétoire Domitius Modestus et le statut du clercs." In *Recherches et Tradition: Mélanges Patristiques offerts à Henri Crouzel, S.J., Professeur Honoraire à la Faculté de Théologie de l'Institut Catholique de Toulouse,* edited by André Dupleix, 7–19. Théologie historique 88. Paris: Beauchesne, 1992.

Beuckmann, Ulrich. *Gregor von Nazianz, Gegen die Habsucht (carmen 1,2,28): Einleitung und Kommentar.* Forschungen zu Gregor von Nazianz 6. Paderborn: F. Schöningh, 1988.

Bianco, Maria G. "Poesia, teologia e vita in Gregorio Nazianzeno, *Carm.* 2.1.1." In *La poesia tardoantica e medievale, Atti del I convegno Internazionale di Studi, Macerata, 4–5 maggio 1998,* edited by Marcello Salvador, 217–30. Quaderni 1. Alexandria: Edizioni dell'Orso, 2001.

Billerbeck, Margarethe. "Le Cynisme idéalisé d'Epictète à Julien." In *Le Cynisme ancien et ses prolongements: Actes du Colloque International du CNRS, Paris, 22–25 juillet 1991,* edited by Marie-Odile Goulet-Cazet and Richard Goulet, 319–38. Paris: Presses universitaires de France, 1993.

Blowers, Paul M. *Exegesis and Spiritual Pedagogy in Maximus the Confessor: An Investigation of the* Quaestiones ad Thalassium. Christianity and Judaism in Antiquity 7. Notre Dam, Ind.: University of Notre Dame Press, 1991.

———. "Bodily Inequality, Material Chaos, and the Ethics of Equalization in Maximus the Confessor." *Studia Patristica* 42 (2006): 51–56.

Boedecker, Deborah. "The Two Faces of Demaratus." *Arethusa* 20 (1987): 185–201.

Borst, Arno. *Der Turmbau von Babel: Geschichte der Meinungen über Ursprung und Vielfalt der Sprachen und Völker.* 4 vols. Stuttgart: Anton Hiersemann, 1957–63.

Børtnes, Jostein and Tomas Hägg, eds. *Gregory of Nazianzus: Images and Reflections.* Copenhagen: Museum Tusculanum Press, 2006.

Bouffartigue, Jean. *L'empereur Julien et la culture de son temps.* Collection des Études augustiniennes, Série Antiquité 133. Paris: Études augustiniennes, 1992.

Bouteneff, Peter C. *Beginnings: Ancient Christian Readings of the Biblical Creation Narratives.* Grand Rapids, Mich.: Eerdmans, 2008.

Bowes, Kim. *Private Worship, Public Values, and Religious Change in Late Antiquity.* Cambridge: Cambridge University Press, 2008.

Bradshaw, Paul F. "Baptismal Practice in the Alexandrian Tradition: Eastern or Western?" In *Living Water, Sealing Spirit: Reading on Christian Initiation,* edited by Maxwell E. Johnson, 82–100. Collegeville, Minn.: Liturgical Press, 1995.

Branham, R. Bracht, and Marie-Odile Goulet-Cazé. *The Cynics: The Cynic Movement in Antiquity and Its Legacy.* Hellenistic Culture and Society 23. Berkeley: University of California Press, 1997.

Brennecke, Hanns Christoph. *Studien zur Geschichte der Homöer: Der Osten bis zum Ende der homöischen Reichskirche.* Beiträge zur historischen Theologie 68. Tübingen: Mohr Siebeck, 1988.

Brown, Peter. *Power and Persuasion in Late Antiquity: Towards a Christian Empire.* The 1988 Curti Lectures. Madison: University of Wisconsin Press, 1992.

———. *Poverty and Leadership in the Later Roman Empire.* The Menahem Stern Jerusalem Lectures. Hanover, N.H.: University Press of New England, 2002.

Brubaker, Leslie. *Vision and Meaning in Ninth-Century Byzantium: Image as Exegesis in the Homilies of Gregory of Nazianzus.* Cambridge: Cambridge University Press, 1999.

Burgess, Richard W. "The Passio S. Artemii, Philostorgius, and the Dates of the Invention and Translation of the Relics of Sts. Andrew and Luke." *Analecta Bollandiana* 121 (2003): 5–36.

Calvet-Sébasti, Marie-Ange. "L'évocation de l'affaire de Sasimes par Grégoire de Nazianze." In *L'historiographie de l'église des premiers siècles,* edited by Bernard Pouderon and Yves-Marie Duval, 481–97. Théologie historique 114. Paris: Beauchesne, 2001.

Carriker, Andrew J. *The Library of Eusebius at Caesarea.* Supplements to Vigiliae Christianae 67. Leiden: Brill, 2003.

Cheynet, Jean-Claude. *Pouvoirs et contestations à Byzance (963–1210).* Série Byzantina Sorbonensia 9. Paris: Publications de la Sorbonne, 1990.

Christ, Matthew. "Herodotean Kings and Historical Inquiry." *Classical Antiquity* 13 (1994): 167–202.

Connor, W. Robert. "The *Histor* in History." In *Nomodeiktes: Greek Studies in Honor of Martin Ostwald,* edited by Ralph M. Rosen and Joseph Farrell, 3–15. Ann Arbor: University of Michigan Press, 1993.

Cooper, Adam G. *The Body in St. Maximus the Confessor: Holy Flesh, Wholly Deified.* Oxford Early Christian Studies. Oxford: Oxford University Press, 2005.

Cribiore, Raffaella. *The School of Libanius in Late Antique Antioch.* Princeton: Princeton University Press, 2007.

Croce, Vittorio, and Bruno Valente. "Providenza e pedagogia divina nella storia." In *Maximus Confessor: Actes du Symposium sur Maxime le Confesseur, Fribourg, 2–5 septembre 1980,* edited by Felix Heinzer and Christoph Schönborn. Paradosis 27. Fribourg: Éditions universitaires, 1982.

Croke, Brian. "Reinventing Constantinople: Theodosius I's Imprint on the Imperial City." In *From the Tetrarchs to the Theodosians: Later Roman History and Culture, 284–450 CE,* edited by Scott McGill, Cristiana Sogno, and Edward Watts, 241–64. Yale Classical Studies 34. Cambridge: Cambridge University Press, 2010.

Crouzel, Henri. *Origen.* Translated by A. S. Worrall. Edinburgh: T. and T. Clark, 1989.

Cummings, John Thomas. "A Critical Edition of the Carmen *De vita sua* of St. Gregory Nazianzen." Ph.D. diss., Princeton University, 1966.

Dagron, Gilbert. *Naissance d'une capitale: Constantinople et ses institutions de 330 à 451.* Bibliotèque byzantine, Études 7. Paris: Presses universitaires de France, 1974.

———. *Emperor and Priest: The Imperial Office in Byzantium.* Translated by Jean Birrell. Cambridge: Cambridge University Press, 2003.

Dagron, Gilbert, and Haralambie Mihăescu. *Le traité sur la guérilla (De velitatione) de l'empereur Nicéphore Phocas (963–969).* Le monde byzantin. Paris: Éditions du Centre National de la Recherche Scientifique, 1986.

Dagron, Gilbert, Pierre Riché, and André Vauchez. *Évêques, moines et empereurs (610–1054).* Histoire du christianisme 4. Paris: Desclée, 1993.

Daley, Brian E. "Origen's *De Principiis*: A Guide to the Principles of Christian Scriptural Interpretation." In *Nova et Vetera: Patristic Studies in Honor of Thomas Patrick Halton,* edited by John Petruccione, 3–21. Washington, D.C.: The Catholic University of America Press, 1998.

———. "Building a New City: The Cappadocian Fathers and the Rhetoric of Philanthropy." *Journal of Early Christian Studies* 7 (1999): 431–61.

———. *Gregory of Nazianzus.* The Early Church Fathers. London: Routledge, 2006.

———. "Walking through the Word of God: Gregory of Nazianzus as a Biblical Interpreter." In *The Word Leaps the Gap: Essays on Scripture and Theology in Honor of Richard B. Hays,* edited by Ross Wagner, C. Kavin Rowe, and A. Katherine Grieb, 514–31. Grand Rapids, Mich.: Eerdmans, 2008.

Dalmais, Irénée-Henri. "La fonction unificatrice du Verbe incarné dans les oeuvres spirituelles de Saint Maxime le Confesseur." *Sciences ecclésiastiques* 14 (1962): 445–59.

Daniélou, Jean. "Circoncision et baptême." In *Theologie in Geschichte und Gegenwart: Michael Schmaus zum sechzigsten Geburtstag dargebracht von seinen Freunden und Schülern,* edited by Johann Auer and Hermann Volk, 755–76. Munich: K. Zink, 1957.

———. "Grégoire de Nysse à travers les lettres de S. Basile et de S. Grégoire de Nazianze." *Vigiliae Christianae* 19 (1965): 31–41.

———. "La chronologie des oeuvres de Grégoire de Nysse." *Studia Patristica* 7 (1966): 159–69.

———. "L'Évêque d'après une lettre de Grégoire de Nysse." *Euntes Docete* 2 (1967): 85–97.

———. "Chrismation prébaptismale et divinité de l'Esprit chez Grégoire de Nysse." *Recherches de science religieuse* 56 (1968): 177–98.

De Jong, Irene J. F. "Herodotus." In *Narrators, Narratees, and Narratives in Ancient Greek Literature: Studies in Ancient Greek Narrative,* edited by Irene J. F. De Jong, René Nünlist, and Angus Bowie, 1:102–13. Mnemosyne Supplements 257. Leiden: Brill, 2004.

Déléage, André. *La capitation du Bas-Empire.* Annales de l'Est, Mémoire 14. Mâcon: Imprimerie Protat frères, 1945.

Demoen, Kristoffel. "The Attitude Towards Greek Poetry in the Verse of Gregory Nazianzen." In *Early Christian Poetry,* edited by Jan den Boeft and Anton Hilhorst, 235–52. Supplements to Vigiliae Christianae 22. Leiden: Brill, 1993.

———. *Pagan and Biblical Exempla in Gregory Nazianzen: A Study in Rhetoric and Hermeneutics.* Corpus Christianorum Lingua Patrum 2. Turnhout: Brepols, 1996.

———. "Gifts of Friendship that Will Remain for Ever: Personae, Addressed Characters and Intended Audience of Gregory Nazianzen's Epistolary Poems." *Jahrbuch der Österreichischen Byzantinistik* 47 (1997): 1–11.

Der Nersessian, Sirarpie. "The Illustrations of the Homilies of Gregory of Nazianzus, Paris gr. 510." *Dumbarton Oaks Papers* 16 (1962): 197–228.

Deubner, Ludwig. "Kerkidas bei Gregor von Nazianz." *Hermes* 54 (1919): 438–41.

Devos, Paul. "S. Grégoire de Nazianze et Hellade de Césarée en Cappadoce." *Analecta Bollandiana* 19 (1961): 92–101.

———. "S. Pierre Ier, Évêque de Sebastée, dans une lettre de S. Grégoire de Nazianze." *Analecta Bollandiana* 79 (1961): 347–60.

Dewald, Caroline. "Narrative Surface and Authorial Voice in the *Histories.*" *Arethusa* 20 (1987): 147–70.

——— "'I Didn't Give My Own Geneaology': Herodotus and the Authorial Persona." In *Brill's Companion to Herodotus,* edited by Egbert Bakker, Irene J. F. de Jong, and Hans van Wees, 267–90. Brill's Companions in Classical Studies. Leiden: Brill, 2002.

———. "Paying Attention: History as the Development of a Secular Narrative." In *Rethinking Revolutions through Ancient Greece,* edited by Simon Goldhill and Robin Osborne, 164–82. Cambridge: Cambridge University Press, 2006.

———. "The Figured Stage: Focalizing the Initial Narratives of Herodotus and Thucydides." In *Thucydides,* edited by Jefferey S. Rusten, 128–40. Oxford Readings in Classical Studies. Oxford: Oxford University Press, 2009.

Diefenbach, Steffen. "Zwischen Liturgie und *civilitas*: Konstantinopel im 5. Jhd. und die Etablierung eines städtischen Kaisertums." In *Bildlichkeit und Bildort von Liturgie: Schauplätze in Spätantike, Byzanz und Mittelalter,* edited by Rainer Warland, 21–47. Wiesbaden: Reichert, 2002.

Dorival, Gilles. "L'image des cyniques chez les Pères grecs." In *Le Cynisme ancien et ses prolongements: Actes du Colloque International du CNRS,* edited by Marie-Odile Goulet-Cazé and Richard Goulet, 419–33. Paris: Presses universitaires de France, 1993.

Dostál, Antonín. "Konstantin der Philosoph und das Ausmass seiner geistigen Bildung." *Byzantinische Forschungen* 1 (1966): 80–82.

Drijvers, Jan Willem. *Cyril of Jerusalem: Bishop and City.* Supplements to Vigiliae Christianae 72. Leiden: Brill, 2004.

Dvornik, Francis. *Les légendes de Constantin et de Méthode vues de Byzance.* 2nd ed. Russian Series 12. Hattiesburg, Miss.: Academic International, 1969.

————. *Byzantine Missions among the Slavs: Ss. Constantine-Cyril and Methodius.* Rutgers Byzantine Series. New Brunswick, N.J.: Rutgers University Press, 1970.

Dujčev, Ivan. "Constantino Filosofo nella storia della letteratura bizantina." *Studi in onore di Ettore Lo Gatto et Giovanni Maver,* 205–22. Collana di "Ricerche slavistiche" 1. Florence: Sansoni, 1962.

Dziech, Joseph. *De Gregorio Nazianzeno diatribae quae dicitur alumno.* Poznańskie Towarzystwo Przyjacioø Nauk. Prace Komisji Filologicznej 3. Poznań, 1925.

Echle, Harry A. *The Terminology of the Sacrament of Regeneration According to Clement of Alexandria.* Studies in Sacred Theology, Second Series 30. Washington, D.C.: The Catholic University of America Press, 1949.

————. "Sacramental Initiation as a Christian Mystery Initiation according to Clement of Alexandria." In *Vom christlichen Mysterium: Gesammelte Arbeiten zum Gedächtnis von Odo Casel OSB,* edited by Anton Mayer, Johannes Quasten, and Burkhard Neunheuser, 54–65. Düsseldorf: Patmos Verlag, 1951.

Egan, Susanna. "Faith, Doubt, and Textual Identity." *Auto/Biography Studies* 23 (2008): 52–64.

Elm, Susanna. *Virgins of God: The Making of Asceticism in Late Antiquity.* Oxford Classical Monographs. Oxford: Clarendon Press, 1994.

————. "Inventing the 'Father of the Church': Gregory of Nazianzus' 'Farewell to the Bishops' (Or. 42) in Its Historical Context." In *Vita Religiosa im Mittelalter: Festschrift für Kaspar Elm zum 70. Geburtstag,* edited by Franz J. Felten and Nikolas Jaspert, 3–20. Berliner historische Studien 31. Berlin: Duncker and Humblot, 1999.

————. "The Diagnostic Gaze: Gregory of Nazianzus' Theory of Orthodox Priesthood in his Orations 6 *De Pace* and 2 *Apologia de fuga sua.*" In *Orthodoxie, Christianisme, Histoire,* edited by Susanna Elm, Éric Rebillard, and Antonella Romano, 83–100. Collection de l'École française de Rome 270. Rome: École française de Rome, 2000.

————. "Orthodoxy and the Philosophical Life: Julian and Gregory of Nazianzus." *Studia Patristica* 37 (2001): 69–85.

————. "Hellenism and Historiography: Gregory of Nazianzus and Julian in Dialogue." *Journal of Medieval and Early Modern Studies* 33 (2003): 493–515.

————. "Historiographic Identities: Julian, Gregory of Nazianzus, and the Forging of Orthodoxy." *Zeitschrift für antikes Christentum* 7 (2003): 249–66.

————. "Gregory of Nazianzus's Life of Julian Revisited (Or. 4 and 5): The Art of Governance by Invective." In *From the Tetrarchs to the Theodosians,* edited by Scott McGill, Cristiana Sogno, and Edward Watts, 171–82. Yale Classical Studies 34. Cambridge: Cambridge University Press, 2010.

————. *Sons of Hellenism, Fathers of the Church: Emperor Juilan, Gregory of Nazianzus, and the Vision of Rome.* Transformation of the Classical Heritage 49. Berkeley: University of California Press, 2012.

Fedwick, Paul Jonathan. "A Chronology of the Life and Works of Basil of Caesarea." In *Basil of Caesarea: Christian, Humanist, Ascetic: A Sixteen-Hundredth Anniversary Sympo-*

sium, edited by Paul Jonathan Fedwick, 21–48. Toronto: Pontifical Institute of Medieval Studies, 1981.

Feissel, Denis. "Notes d'épigraphic chrétienne VII." *Bulletin de correspondance hellénique* 108 (1984): 566–71.

Ferguson, Everett. "Spiritual Circumcision in Early Christianity." *Scottish Journal of Theology* 41 (1988): 485–97.

———. "Exhortations to Baptism in the Cappadocians." *Studia Patristica* 32 (1997): 121–29.

———. *Baptism in the Early Church: History, Theology, and Liturgy in the First Five Centuries.* Grand Rapids, Mich.: Eerdmans, 2009.

Flusin, Bernard. "Le panégyrique de Constantin VII Pophyrogénète pour la Translation des reliques de Grégoire le Théologien (BHG 728)." *Revue des études byzantines* 57 (1999): 5–97.

———. "L'empereur hagiographe: Remarques sur le rôle des premières empereurs macédoniens dans le culte des saints." In *L'empereur hagiographe: Culte des saints et monarchie byzantine et post-byzantine,* edited by Petre Guran, 29–54. Bucharest: New Europe College, 2001.

Fögen, Marie Theres. "Reanimation of Roman Law in the Ninth Century: Remarks on Reasons and Results." In *Byzantium in the Ninth Century: Dead or Alive? Papers from the Thirtieth Spring Symposium of Byzantine Studies, Birmingham, March 1996,* edited by Leslie Brubaker, 11–22. Publications of the Society for the Promotion of Byzantine Studies 5. Aldershot: Ashgate, 1998.

Fornara, Charles. "Studies in Ammianus Marcellinus: II: Ammianus' Knowledge and Use of Greek and Latin Literature." *Historia* 41 (1992): 420–38.

Fromberg, Doris Pronin and Doris Bergen, *Play from Birth to Twelve and Beyond: Contexts, Perspectives, and Meanings.* Garland Reference Library of Social Science 970. New York: Garland, 1998.

Gain, Benoît. *L'église de Cappadoce au IVe siècle d'après la correspondance de Basile de Césarée (330–379).* Orientalia Christiana analecta 225. Rome: Pontifical Oriental Institute, 1985.

Gallay, Paul. *La Vie de Saint Grégoire de Nazianze.* Lyons: Emmanuel Vitte, 1943.

———. "La Bible dans l'oeuvre de Grégoire de Nazianze le Théologien." In *Le monde grec ancien et la Bible.* Vol. 1. Edited by Claude Mondésert. Bible de tous les temps 1. Paris: Beauchesne, 1984.

Galavaris, George. *The Illustrations of the Liturgical Homilies of Gregory Nazianzenus.* Studies in Manuscript Illumination 6. Princeton: Princeton University Press, 1969.

Garner, Richard. *Law and Society in Classical Athens.* New York: St. Martin's, 1987.

Gautier, Francis. *Le retraite et le sacerdoce chez Grégoire de Nazianze.* Bibliothèque de l'École des Hautes Études, Sciences religieuses 114. Turnhout: Brepols, 2002.

Geffcken, Johannes. *Kynika und Verwandtes.* Heidelberg: Winter, 1909.

Georgiev, Emil. "Konstantin Preslavski." In *Kiril and Methodius: Founders of Slavonic Writing—A Collection of Sources and Critical Studies,* edited by Ivan Duichev, 161–80. East European Monographs 172. New York: Columbia University Press, 1985.

Giakalis, Ambrosios. *Images of the Divine: The Theology of Icons at the Seventh Ecumenical Council.* Studies in the History of Christian Thought 54. Leiden: Brill, 1994.

Gilbert, Peter. "Person and Nature in the Theological Poems of St. Gregory of Nazianzus." Ph.D. diss., The Catholic University of America, 1994.

Girardi, Mario. *Basilio di Cesarea e il culto dei martiri nel IV secolo: Scrittura e tradizione.* Quademi di "Vetera Christianorum" 21. Bari: Istituto di studi classici e cristiani, Università di Bari, 1990.

Golega, Joseph. *Der Homerische Psalter: Studien über die dem Apolinarios von Laodikeia zugeschriebene Psalmenparaphrase.* Studia Patristica et Byzantina 6. Ettal: Buch-Kunstverlag Ettal, 1960.

Gómez-Villegas, Nicanor. *Gregorio de Nazianzo en Constantinopla: Ortodoxia, heterodoxia y régimen teodosiano en una capital cristiana.* Nueva Roma 11. Madrid: Consejo Superior de Investigaciones Científicas, 2000.

Goulet-Cazet, Marie-Odile, and Richard Goulet, eds. *Le cynisme ancien et ses prolongements: Actes du Colloque international du CNRS, Paris 22–25 juillet 1991.* Paris: Presses universitaires de France, 1993.

Grabar, André. *Les miniatures du Grégoire de Nazianze de l'Ambrosienne (Ambrosianus 49–50) décrites et commentées.* Orient et Byzance 9. Paris: Vanoest, 1943.

Grierson, Philip. "The Tombs and Obits of the Byzantine Emperors (337–1042)." *Dumbarton Oaks Papers* 16 (1963): 1–63.

Grillmeier, Aloys. *Christ in Christian Tradition.* Vol. 1, *From the Apostolic Age to Chalcedon.* Translated by John Bowden. Louisville: Westminster John Knox, 1975.

Grivec, Franc. *Sveti Ćiril I Metod: Slavenski blagovjesnici.* Zagreb: Kršćanska sadašnjost, 1985.

Guida, Augusto. "Un nuovo testo di Gregorio Nazianzeno." *Prometheus* 2 (1976): 193–226.

Harper, Kyle. "The Greek Census Inscriptions of Late Antiquity." *Journal of Roman Studies* 98 (2008): 83–119.

Harrison, Verna E. F. "Gregory Nazianzen's Festal Spirituality: Anamnesis and Mimesis." *Philosophy and Theology* 18 (2006): 27–51.

Hauser-Meury, Marie-Madeleine. *Prosopographie zu den Schriften Gregors von Nazianz.* Theophaneia 13. Bonn: P. Hanstein, 1960.

Heath, Malcolm. *Menander: A Rhetor in Context.* Oxford: Oxford University Press, 2004.

Hedrick, Charles. "The Meaning of Material Culture: Herodotus, Thucydides, and Their Sources." In *Nomodeiktes: Greek Studies in Honor of Martin Ostwald,* edited by Ralph Rosen and Joseph Farrell, 17–38. Ann Arbor: University of Michigan Press, 1993.

Heine, Ronald E., ed. *The Montanist Oracles and Testimonia.* Patristic Monograph Series 14. Macon, Ga.: Mercer University Press, 1989.

Heinzer, Felix. "L'explication trinitaire de l'économie chez Maxime le Confesseur." In *Maximus Confessor: Actes du Symposium sur Maxime le Confesseur, Fribourg, 2–5 septembre 1980,* edited by Felix Heinzer and Christoph Schönborn, 160–72. Paradosis 27. Fribourg: Éditions Universitaires, 1983.

Hild, Friedrich, and Marcell Restle. *Kappadokien: Kappadokia, Charsianon, Sebasteia und Lykandos.* Tabula Imperi Byzantini 2. Denkschriften, Österreichische Akademie der Wissenschaften, Philosophisch-Historische Klasse 149. Vienna: Österreichischen Akademie der Wissenschaften, 1981.

Hefele, Karl Joseph von. *A History of the Christian Councils (to A.D. 451): From the Original Documents.* Translated by William R. Clark. Edinburgh: T. and T. Clark, 1871.

Hirschmann, Vera-Elisabeth. *Horrenda Secta: Untersuchungen zum frühchristlichen Montanismus und seinen Verbindungen zur paganen Religion Phrygiens.* Historia, Einzelschriften 179. Stuttgart: Steiner, 2005.

Holman, Susan R. "Taxing Nazianzus: Gregory and the Other Julian." *Studia Patristica* 37 (2001): 103–9.

Honigmann, Ernst. "Le concile de Constantinople de 394 et les auteurs du Syntagma des XIV titres." In *Trois mémoires posthumes d'histoire et de géographie de l'Orient chrétien,* edited by Ernst Honigmann, 1–83. Subsidia hagiographica 35. Bruxelles: Société des Bollandistes, 1961.

Hornblower, Simon. "Narratology and Narrative Techniques in Thucydides." In *Greek Historiography,* edited by Simon Hornblower, 54–72, 131–66. Clarendon Press: Oxford, 1994.

Hunt, Edward David. *Holy Land Pilgrimage in the Later Roman Empire, AD 312–460.* Oxford: Clarendon Press, 1982.

Hussey, Joan M. *The Orthodox Church in the Byzantine Empire.* Oxford History of the Christian Church. Oxford: Clarendon Press, 1986.

Irwin, Elizabeth, and Emily Greenwood, eds. *Reading Herodotus: A Study of the Logoi in Book 5 of Herodotus' Histories.* Cambridge: Cambridge University Press, 2007.

Ivanov, Sergey A. "Casting Pearls before Circe's Swine: The Byzantine View of Mission." In *Mélanges Gilbert Dagron,* edited by V. Déroche, et al., 295–301. Travaux et mémoires 14. Paris: Association des amis du Centre d'histore et civilisation de Byzance, 2002.

———. "Religious Missions." In *The Cambridge History of the Byzantine Empire, c. 500–1492,* edited by Jonathan Shepard, 305–32. Cambridge: Cambridge University Press, 2008.

———. *Vizantiiskoe Missionerstvo: Mozhno li sdelat' iz "varvara" khristianina?* Moscow: Institute of Slavic Culture, 2003.

Jackson, B. Darrell. "Sources of Origen's Doctrine of Freedom." *Church History* 35 (1966): 13–23. Reprinted in *Doctrines of Human Nature, Sin, and Salvation in the Early Church,* edited by Everett Ferguson, 1–11. Studies in Early Christianity 10. New York: Garland, 1993.

Jakobson, Roman. "St. Constantine's Prologue to the Gospel." *St. Vladimir's Seminary Quarterly* 7 (1963): 16–19.

———. "The Slavic Response to Byzantine Poetry." In Roman Jakobson, *Selected Writings.* Vol. 6.2, *Early Slavic Paths and Crossroads: Comparative Slavic Studies,* edited by Stephen Rudy, 240–59. Berlin: Mouton, 1985.

Jenkins, Romilly. *Byzantium: The Imperial Centuries, AD 610–1071.* London: Weidenfeld and Nicholson, 1966.

Johnson, Maxwell E., ed. *Living Water, Sealing Spirit: Readings on Christian Initiation.* Collegeville, Minn.: Liturgical Press, 1995.

Jones, Arnold Hugh Martin. *The Later Roman Empire, 284–602: A Social, Economic and Administrative Survey.* 3 vols. Oxford: Blackwell, 1964.

Karavites, Peter. "Gregory Naizanzinos and Byzantine Hymnography." *Journal of Hellenic Studies* 113 (1993): 81–98.

Keipert, Helmut. "Die altbulgarische Übersetzung der Predigten des Gregor von Nazianz." In *Slavistische Studien zum X Internationalen Slavistenkongress in Sofia 1988,* edited by Reinhold Olesch and Hans Rothe. Slavistische Forschungen 54. Cologne: Böhlau, 1988.

Kelly, Gavin. "The New Rome and the Old: Ammianus Marcellinus' Silences on Constantinople." *Classical Quarterly* 53 (2003): 588–607.

Kennedy, George A. *A History of Rhetoric.* Vol. 3, *Greek Rhetoric under Christian Emperors.* Princeton, N.J.: Princeton University Press, 1983.

Kretschmar, Georg. "Die Geschichte des Taufgottesdienstes in der alten Kirche." In *Leiturgia: Handbuch des evangelischen Gottesdienstes,* edited by Karl Ferdinand Müller and Walter F. Blankenurg, 67–169. Kassel: J. Stauda, 1970.

Krueger, Dieter. "Diogenes the Cynic among the Fourth Century Fathers." *Vigiliae Christianae* 47 (1993): 29–49.

Lampe, G. W. H. *The Seal of the Spirit: A Study in the Doctrine of Baptism and Confirmation in the New Testament and the Fathers.* 2nd ed. London: SPCK, 1967.

Lateiner, Donald. *The Historical Method of Herodotus.* Pheonix Supplement 23. Toronto: University of Toronto Press, 1989.

Lauro, Elizabeth Dively. *The Soul and Spirit of Scripture within Origen's Exegesis.* The Bible in Ancient Christianity 3. Boston: Brill, 2005.

Lemerle, Paul. *Byzantine Humanism, the First Phase: Notes and Remarks on Education and Culture in Byzantium from Its Origins to the 10th Century.* Translated by Helen Lindsay and Ann Moffatt. Byzantina Australiensia 3. Canberra: Australian Association for Byzantine Studies, 1986.

Lenski, Noel. *Failure of Empire: Valens and the Roman State in the Fourth Century A.D.* Transformation of the Classical Heritage 32. Berkeley: University of California Press, 2002.

———. "Valens and the Monks: Cudgeling and Conscription as a Means of Social Control." *Dumbarton Oaks Papers* 58 (2004): 93–117.

Lloyd, G. E. R. *Polarity and Analogy: Two Types of Argumentation in Early Greek Thought.* Cambridge: Cambridge University Press, 1966.

Lossky, Vladimir. *The Mystical Theology of the Eastern Church.* Translated by members of the Fellowship of Saint Alban and Saint Sergius. Cambridge: James Clark, 1957.

Louth, Andrew. "St. Gregory the Theologian and St. Maximus the Confessor: The Shaping of Tradition." In *The Making and Remaking of Christian Doctrine: Essays in Honour of*

Maurice Wiles, edited by Sarah Coakley and David Pailin, 117–30. Oxford: Clarendon
Press, 1993.

———. *St. John Damascene: Tradition and Originality in Byzantine Theology.* Oxford Early
Christian Studies. Oxford: Oxford University Press, 2002.

———. "Photios as a Theologian." In *Byzantine Style, Religion and Civilization: In Honour
of Sir Steven Runciman,* edited by Elizabeth Jeffreys, 206–23. Cambridge: Cambridge
University Press, 2006.

Luraghi, Nino. "Meta-historiê: Method and genre in the *Histories.*" In *The Cambridge Companion to Herodtus,* edited by Caroline Dewald and John Marincola, 76–91. Cambridge: Cambridge University Press, 2006.

Macé, Caroline. "Gregory of Nazianzus as the Authoritative Voice of Orthodoxy in the Sixth
Century." In *Byzantine Orthodoxies: Papers from the Thirty-Sixth Spring Symposium of
Byzantine Studies, University of Durham, 23–25 March 2002,* edited by Andrew Louth
and Augustine Casiday, 7–34. Publications for the Society for the Promotion of Byzantine Studies 12. Aldershot: Ashgate, 2002.

Magdalino, Paul. "The Bath of Leo the Wise and the 'Macedonian Renaissance' Revisited:
Topography, Iconography, Ceremonial, Ideology." *Dumbarton Oaks Papers* 42 (1988):
97–118.

———. *The Empire of Manuel I Komnenos, 1143–1180.* Cambridge: Cambridge University
Press, 1993.

Malingrey, Anne Marie. *"Philosophia": Étude d'un group de mots dans la littérature grecque
des Présocratiques au IVème siècle après J.-C.* Études et commentaires 40. Paris: C.
Klincksieck, 1961.

Mango, Cyril. *The Homilies of Photius, Patriarch of Constantinople.* Dumbarton Oaks Studies
3. Cambridge, Mass.: Harvard University Press, 1958.

Maraval, Pierre. "L'authenticité de la lettre 1 de Grégoire de Nysse." *Analecta Bollandiana* 102
(1984): 61–70.

Marincola, John. *Authority and Tradition in Ancient Historiography.* Cambridge: Cambridge
University Press, 1997.

———. "Genre, Convention, and Innovation in Greco-Roman Historiography." In *The
Limits of Historiography: Genre and Narrative in Ancient Historical Texts,* edited by
Christina Shuttleworth Kraus, 281–324. Mnemosyne Supplement 191. Leiden: Brill
1999.

Markopoulos, Athanasios. "Constantine the Great in Macedonian historiography." In *New
Constantines: The Rhythm of Imperial Renewal in Byzantium, 4th–13th Centuries,* edited by Paul Magdalino, 159–70. Society for the Promotion of Byzantine Studies 2. Aldershot: Ashgate, 1994.

Marsh, Herbert G. "The Use of ΜΥΣΤΗΡΙΟΝ in the Writings of Clement of Alexandria
with Special Reference to His Sacramental Doctrine." *Journal of Theological Studies* 37
(1936): 64–80.

Mathieu, Jean Marie. "Sur une correction inutile (Or. 28.8, lignes 8–9 Gallay)." In *II. Symposium Nazianzenum, Louvain-la-Neuve, 25–28 août 1981,* edited by Mossay, 52–59.

May, Gerhard. "Die Chronologie des Lebens und der Werke des Gregor von Nyssa." In *Écriture et culture philosophique dans la pensée de Grégoire de Nysse. Actes du Colloque de Chevetogne (22–26 sept. 1969). Organisé par le Centre de Recherche sur l'Hellénisme tardif de la Sorbonne,* edited by Marguerit Harl, 51–66. Leiden: Brill, 1971.

McGuckin, John A. "The Sign of the Prophet: The Significance of Meals in the Doctrine of Jesus." *Scripture Bulletin* 16 (1986): 35–40.

———. "Jesus' Self-Designation as a Prophet." *Scripture Bulletin* 19 (1988): 2–11.

———. "Perceiving Light from Light in Light (Oration 31.3): The Trinitarian Theology of St. Gregory the Theologian." *Greek Orthodox Theological Review* 39 (1994): 7–32.

———. "The Vision of God in St. Gregory Nazianzen." *Studia Patristica* 32 (1997): 145–52.

———. "Autobiography as Apologia." *Studia Patristica* 37 (2001): 160–77.

———. *Saint Gregory of Nazianzus: An Intellectual Biography.* Crestwood N.Y.: St. Vladimir's Seminary Press, 2001.

———. "Gregory: The Rhetorician as Poet." In *Gregory of Nazianzus: Images and Reflections,* edited by Børtnes and Hägg, 193–212.

McLynn, Neil. "Gregory the Peacemaker: A Study of Oration Six." *Kyoyo–Ronso* 101 (1996): 183–216.

———. "The Voice of Conscience: Gregory Nazianzen in Retirement." In *Vescovi e pastori in epoca Teodosiana: In occasione del XVI centenario della consecrazione episcopale di S. Agostino, 396–1996. XXV Incontro di studiosi dell' antichità cristiana, Roma, 8–11 Maggio 1996,* 2:299–308. Studia ephemeridis Augustinianum 58. Rome: Institutum Patristicum Augustinianum, 1997.

———. "Gregory Nazianzen's Basil: The Literary Construction of a Christian Friendship." *Studia Patristica* 37 (2001): 178–93.

———. "The Transformations of Imperial Churchgoing in the Fourth Century." In *Approaching Late Antiquity: The Transformation from Early to Late Empire,* edited by Simon Swain and Mark Edwards, 235–70. Oxford: Oxford University Press, 2004.

———. "'Genere Hispanus': Theodosius, Spain, and Nicene Orthodoxy." In *Hispania in Late Antiquity: Current Perspectives,* edited and translated by Kim Bowes and Michael Kulikowski, 79–88. The Medieval and Early Modern Iberian World 24. Boston: Brill, 2005.

———. "Among the Hellenists: Gregory and the Sophists." In *Gregory of Nazianzus: Images and Reflections,* edited by Børtnes and Hägg, 229–33.

———. "'Curiales into Churchmen': The Case of Gregory Nazianzen." In *Le trasformazioni delle élites in età tardoantica: Atti del Convegno Internazionale, Perugia, 15–16 marzo 2004,* edited by Rita Lizzi Testa, 277–95. Saggi di storia antica 28. Rome: "L'Erma" di Bretscheider, 2006.

———. "Moments of Truth: Gregory of Nazianzus and Theodosius I." In *From the Tetrarchs to the Theodosians: Later Roman History and Culture, 284–450 CE,* edited by Scott McGill, Cristiana Sogno, and Edward Watts, 215–39. Yale Classical Studies 34. Cambridge: Cambridge University Press, 2010.

Mentzou-Meimari, Konstantina. "Eparkhiaka evagé idrymata mekhri tou telous tés eikonomakhias." *Byzantina* 11 (1982): 243–308.

Milanović-Barham, Celia. "Gregory of Nazianzus: *Ars Poetica* (*In suos versus: Carmen
2.1.39*)." *Journal of Early Christian Studies* 5 (1997): 497–510.

———. "Gregory of Nazianzus's *De rebus suis* and the Tradition of Epic Didactic Poetry."
Zbornik radova Vizantoloskog instituta 45 (2008): 43–69.

Misch, Georg. *A History of Autobiography in Antiquity.* 2 vols. Translated by E. W. Dickes.
London: Routledge and Kegan Paul, 1950.

Moravcsik, Gyula. "Sagen und Legenden über Kaiser Basileios I." *Dumbarton Oaks Papers* 15
(1961): 59–129.

Moreschini, Claudio. "Dottrine ciniche ed etica cristiana nella poesia di Gregorio Nazianzeno." In *La poesia tardoantica e medieval: Atti del I Convegno Internazionale di Studi,
Macerata, 4–5 maggio 1998,* edited by Marcello Salvadore, 231–48. Quademi 1. Alexandria: Edizioni dell'Orso, 2001.

Morris, Stephen. "No Learning by Coercion: *Paidia* and *Paideia* in Platonic Philosophy." In
Play from Birth to Twelve and Beyond: Contexts, Perspectives, and Meanings, edited by
Doris Fromberg and Doris Bergen, 109–18. Garland Reference Library of Social Sci-
ence 970. New York: Garland, 1998.

Mossay, Justin, ed. *II. Symposium Nazianzenum, Louvain-la-Neuve, 25–28 août 1981: Actes
du Colloque International organisé avec le soutien du Fonds National Belge de la Recherche Scientifique et de la Görres-Gesellschaft zur Pflege der Wissenschaft.* Forschungen zu
Gregor von Nazianz 2. Paderborn: Schöningh, 1983.

Musurillo, Herbert. "The Poetry of Gregory of Nazianzus." *Thought* 45 (1970): 45–55.

Nardi, Carlo. *Il battesimo in Clemente Alessandrino: Interpretazione di Eclogae propheticae
1–26.* Studia ephemeridis Augustinianum 19. Rome: Institutum Patristicum Augustinianum, 1984.

Nasrallah, Laura S. *"An Ecstasy of Folly": Prophecy and Authority in Early Christianity.* Harvard Theological Studies 52. Cambridge, Mass.: Harvard University Press, 2003.

Noble, Thomas A. "Gregory Nazianzen's Use of Scripture in Defence of the Deity of the
Holy Spirit." *Tyndale Bulletin* 39 (1988): 101–23.

Noret, Jacques. "Grégoire de Nazianze, l'auteur le plus cité après la Bible dans la literature ecclésiastique byzantine." In *II. Symposium Nazianzenum, Louvain-la-Neuve, 25–28 août
1981,* edited by Mossay, 259–66.

Oberhaus, Michael. *Gregor von Nazianz, Gegen den Zorn (Carmen 1,2,25).* Forschungen zu
Gregor von Nazianz 8. Paderborn: F. Schöningh, 1991.

Obolensky, Dimitri. "The Heritage of Cyril and Methodius in Russia." *Dumbarton Oaks Papers* 19 (1965): 54–56.

———. "Cyrille et Methode et la christianisation des Slaves." *Settimane di Studi del Centro
Italiano di Studio sull'Alto Medioevo* 14 (1967): 587–609.

O'Meara, Dominic J. *Structures hiérarchiques dans la pensée de Plotin: Étude historique et in-
terprétative.* Philosophia antiqua 75. Leiden: Brill, 1975.

Orbe, Antonio. "Teologia bautismal de Clemente Alejandrino segun *Paed.* I, 26.3–27.2." *Gregorianum* 36 (1955): 410–48.

Ousterhout, Robert. "Reconstructing Ninth-Century Constantinople." In *Byzantium in the Ninth Century: Dead or Alive? Papers from the Thirtieth Spring Symposium of Byzantine Studies, Birmingham, March 1996,* edited by Leslie Brubaker, 115–30. Society for the Promotion of Byzantine Studies 5. Aldershot: Ashgate, 1998.

Papaioannou, Stratis. "Gregory and the Constraint of Sameness." In *Gregory of Nazianzus, Images and Reflections,* edited by Børtnes and Hägg, 59–81.

Patrich, Joseph, ed. *The Sabaïte Heritage in the Orthodox Church from the Fifth Century to the Present.* Orientalia Lovanensia analecta 98. Leuven: Peeters, 2001.

Peers, Glenn. "Patriarchal Politics in the Paris Gregory (B.N. gr. 510)." *Jahrbuch der Österreichischen Byzantinistik* 47 (1997): 51–71.

Pelikan, Jaroslav. *The Christian Tradition: A History of the Development of Doctrine.* Vol. 2, *The Spirit of Eastern Christendom (600–1700).* Chicago: University of Chicago Press, 1974.

Pelikan, Jaroslav, and Valerie Hotchkiss. *Creeds and Confessions of Faith in the Christian Tradition.* New Haven: Yale University Press, 2003.

Pelling, Chris. "Epilogue." In *The Limits of Historiography: Genre and Narrative in Ancient Texts,* edited by Christina Shuttleworth Kraus, 335–43. Mnemosune Supplements 191. Leiden: Brill, 1999.

Pépin, Jean. *Mythe et allégorie: Les origines grecques et les contestations judéo-chrétiennes.* 2nd rev. ed. Paris: Études augustiniennes, 1976.

Perrone, Lorenzo. "Palestinian Monasticism, the Bible, and Theology in the Wake of the Second Origenist Controversy." In *The Sabaïte Heritage in the Orthodox Church from the Fifth Century to the Present,* edited by Patrich, 245–59.

Podskalsky, Gerhard. "Die Sicht der Barbarenvölker in der spätgriechischen Patristik (4.–8. Jahrh.)." *Orientalia Christiana Periodica* 51 (1985): 330–51.

Pouchet, Robert. *Basile le Grand et son univers d'amis d'après sa correspondance: Une stratégie de communion.* Studia ephemeridis Augustinianum 36. Rome: Institutum Patristicum Augustinianum, 1992.

Rahner, Hugo. *Man at Play.* Translated by Brian Battershaw and Edward Quinn. New York: Herder and Herder, 1972.

Rahner, Karl. *The Trinity.* Translated by Joseph Donceel. London: Burns and Oates, 1970.

Ramsay, William Mitchell. *The Historical Geography of Asia Minor.* 8 vols. Papers of the Royal Geographical Society 4. London: John Murray, 1890; repr. Amsterdam: Adolf M. Hakert, 1962.

Rapp, Claudia. "Imperial Ideology in the Making: Eusebius of Caesarea on Constantine as 'Bishop.'" *Journal of Theological Studies,* n.s. 49 (1998): 685–95.

Ricoeur, Paul. *The Symbolism of Evil.* Translated by Emerson Buchanan. Boston: Beacon Press, 1969.

Rist, John M. *Plotinus: The Road to Reality.* Cambridge: Cambridge University Press, 1967.

Rood, Tim. "Thucydides." In *Narrators, Narratees, and Narratives in Ancient Greek Litera-*

ture, Studies in Ancient Greek Narrative, edited by Irene J. F. De Jong, Rene Nünlist, and Angus Bowie, 1:115–21. Mnemosyne Supplements 257. Leiden: Brill, 2004.

———. "Objectivity and Authority: Thucydides' Historical Method." In *Brill's Companion to Thucydides,* edited by Antonios Rengakos and Antonis Tsakmakis, 225–50. Brill's Companions in Classical Studies. Leiden: Brill, 2006.

Rousseau, Philip. *Basil of Caesarea.* Transformation of the Classical Heritage 20. Berkeley: University of California Press, 1994.

Runciman, Steven. *The Emperor Romanus Lecapenus and His Reign: A Study of Tenth-Century Byzantium.* Cambridge: Cambridge University Press, 1929.

Russell, Norman. *The Doctrine of Deification in the Greek Patristic Tradition.* Oxford Early Christian Studies. Oxford: Oxford University Press, 2004.

Saxer, Victor. *Les rites de l'initiation chrétienne du IIe au VIe siècle: Esquisse historique et signification d'après leurs principaux témoins.* Centro Italiano di Studi sull'Álto Medioevo 7. Spoleto: Centro Italiano di Studi Sull'Álto Medioevo, 1988.

Schenker, Alexander M. *The Dawn of Slavic: An Introduction to Slavic Philology.* Yale Language Series. New Haven: Yale University Press, 1995.

Schminck, Andreas. *Studien zu mittelbyzantinischen Rechtsbüchern.* Forschungen zur byzantinischen Rechtsgeschichte 13. Frankfurt: Löwenklau, 1986.

Ševčenko, Ihor. "Three Paradoxes of the Cyrillo-Methodian Mission." In *Ideology, Letters and Culture in the Byzantine World,* edited by Ihor Ševčenko, 220–36. London: Variorum, 1982.

Sherwood, Polycarp. *An Annotated Date-List of the Works of Maximus the Confessor.* Studia Anselmiana 30. Rome: Herder, 1952.

———. *The Earlier Ambigua of St. Maximus the Confessor and His Refutation of Origenism.* Studia Anselmiana 36. Rome: Herder, 1955.

Simonetti, Manlio. "Giovanni 14:28 nella controversia ariana." In *Kyriakon: Festschrift Johannes Quasten,* edited by Patrick Granfield and Josef A. Jungmann, 1:151–61. Münster: Aschendorff, 1970.

Smith, Jennifer Nimmo, ed. *Pseudo-Nonniani in IV Orationes Gregorii Nazianzeni Commentarii.* CCSG 27. Turnhout: Brepols, 1992.

———, trans. *A Christian's Guide to Greek Culture: The Pseudo-Nonnus Commentaries on Sermons 4, 5, 39 and 43 by Gregory of Nazianzus.* With introduction and commentary. Translated Texts for Historians 37. Liverpool: Liverpool University Press, 2001.

Soulis, George C. "The Legacy of Cyril and Methodius to the Southern Slavs." *Dumbarton Oaks Papers* 19 (1965): 19–43.

Špidlík, Tomáš. "Gregorio Nazianzeno—Maestro e ispiratore di Constantino-Cirillo." In *Christianity among the Slavs: The Heritage of Saints Cyril and Methodius,* edited by Edward G. Farrugia, Robert F. Taft, and Gino K. Piovesana. Orientalia Christiana analecta 231. Rome: Pontifical Oriental Institute, 1988.

———. "L'influence de Grégoire de Nazianze sur Constantine-Cyrile et Methode et sur la spiritualité slave." In *The Legacy of Saints Cyril and Methodius to Kiev and Moscow:*

Proceedings of the International Congress on the Millennium of the Conversion of Rus' to Christianity, Thessaloniki, 26–28 November 1988, edited by Anthony-Emil N. Tachiaos, 39–48. Thessaloniki: Hellenic Association for Slavic Studies, 1992.

Steel, Carlos. "Le jeu du Verbe: À propos de Maxime, *Amb. ad Ioh.* LXVII." In *Philohistôr: Miscellanea in honorem Caroli Laga septuagenarii,* edited by Antoon Schoors and Peter van Deun. Orientalia Lovaniensia analecta 60. Leuven: Peeters, 1994.

Sykes, Donald A. "The *Poemata Arcana* of St. Gregory Nazianzen." *Journal of Theological Studies,* n.s. 21 (1970): 32–42.

———. "The *Poemata Arcana* of St. Gregory Nazianzen: Some Literary Questions." *Byzantinische Zeitschrift* 72 (1979): 6–15.

Tabbernee, William. *Montanist Inscriptions and Testimonia: Epigraphic Sources Illustrating the History of Montanism.* Patristic Monograph Series 16. Macon, Ga.: Mercer University Press, 1997.

———. "Portals of the New Jerusalem: The Discovery of Pepouza and Tymion." *Journal of Early Christian Studies* 11 (2003): 87–94.

———. *Fake Prophecy and Polluted Sacraments: Ecclesiastical and Imperial Reactions to Montanism.* Supplements to Vigiliae Christianae 84. Leiden: Brill, 2007.

———. *Prophets and Gravestones: An Imaginative History of Montanists and Other Early Christians.* Peabody, Mass.: Hendrickson, 2009.

Tabbernee, William, and Peter Lampe. *Pepouza and Tymion: The Discovery and Archaeological Exploration of a Lost Ancient City and an Imperial Estate.* Berlin: Walter de Gruyter, 2008.

TeSelle, Eugene. *Augustine the Theologian.* New York: Herder and Herder, 1970.

Thomson, Frederick. "The Works of St. Gregory of Nazianzus in Slavonic." In *II. Symposium Nazianzenum, Louvain-la-Neuve, 25–28 août 1981,* edited by Mossay, 119–25.

Thunberg, Lars. *Man and the Cosmos: The Vision of St. Maximus the Confessor.* Crestwood, N.Y.: St. Vladimir's Seminary Press, 1985.

Tollefsen, Torstein Theodor. *The Christocentric Cosmology of St. Maximus the Confessor.* Oxford Early Christian Studies. Oxford: Oxford University Press, 2008.

Tompkins, Ian. "The Relations between Theodoret of Cyrrhus and His City and Its Territory, with Particular Reference to the Letters and *Historia Religiosa.*" D.Phil. diss., Oxford University, 1993.

Tougher, Shaun. *The Reign of Leo VI (886–912): Politics and People.* The Medieval Mediterranean 15. Leiden: Brill, 1997.

Toynbee, Arnold. *Constantine Porphyrogenitus and His World.* Oxford: Oxford University Press, 1973.

Trapp, Michael B. "On the Tablet of Cebes." In *Aristotle and After,* edited by Richard Sorabji, 159–80. Bulletin Supplement 68. London: Institute of Classical Studies, School of Advanced Study, University of London, 1997.

Trevett, Christine. *Montanism: Gender, Authority and the New Prophecy.* Cambridge: Cambridge University Press, 1996.

Trigg, Joseph W. "Knowing God in the *Theological Orations* of Gregory of Nazianzus." In *God in Early Christian Thought: Essays in Memory of Lloyd G. Patterson,* edited by Andrew B. McGowan, Brian E. Daley, and Timothy D. Gaden, 84–101. Supplements to Vigiliae Christianae 94. Leiden: Brill, 2009.

Vaillant, André. "La Préface de l'Évangéliaire vieux-slave." *Revue des études slaves* 24 (1948): 5–20.

———. "Une Poésie vieux-slave: La Préface de L'Évangile." *Revue des études slaves* 33 (1956): 7–25.

Van Dam, Raymond. *Kingdom of Snow: Roman Rule and Greek Culture in Cappadocia.* Philadelphia: University of Pennsylvania Press, 2002.

———. *Becoming Christian: The Conversion of Roman Cappadocia.* Philadelphia: University of Pennsylvania Press, 2003.

Van der Veen, J. E. "The Lord of the Ring: Narrative Technique in Herodotus' Story on Polycrates' Ring." *Mnemosyne* 46 (1993): 433–57.

Vavřínek, Vladimir. "Staroslovenske Životy Konstantina a Metodeje a panegyriky Řehoře z Nazianzu." *Listy filologické* 85 (1962): 96–122.

———. *Staroslověnské Životy Konstantina a Metoděje.* Prague: Nakladatelství Československé Akademie věd, 1963.

Waterfield, Robin. "On 'Fussy Authorial Nudges' in Herodotus." *Classical World* 102 (2009): 485–94.

Westerkamp, Dirk. "Laughter, Catharsis, and the Patristic Conception of the Embodied Logos." In *Embodiment in Cognition and Culture,* edited by John Michael Krois, Mats Rosengren, Angela Steidele, and Dirk Westerkamp, 223–41. Advances in Consciousness Research 71. Amsterdam: John Benjamins, 2007.

Whittow, Mark. *The Making of Byzantium, 600–1025.* Berkeley: University of California Press, 1996.

Wilson, Nigel Guy. *Scholars of Byzantium.* London: Duckworth, 1983.

———. *Photius: The Bibliotheca.* London: Duckworth, 1994.

Winslow, Donald F. *The Dynamics of Salvation: A Study in Gregory of Nazianzus.* Patristic Monograph Series 7. Cambridge, Mass.: The Philadelphia Patristic Foundation, 1979.

Wyss, Bernhard. "Zu Gregor von Nazianz." In *Phyllobolia für Peter von der Mühll zum 60. Geburtstag am. 1 August 1945,* edited by Olof Gigon, Karl Meuli, Willy Theiler, Fritz Wehrli, and Bernhard Wyss, 153–83. Basel: B. Schwabe, 1946.

———. "Gregor von Nazianz." In *Reallexikon für Antike und Christentum,* edited by Franz Joseph Dölger and Hans Lietzmann, 12:793–863. Stuttgart: Hiersemann, 1950–.

Young, Frances M. *Biblical Exegesis and the Formation of Christian Culture.* Cambridge: Cambridge University Press, 1997.

Ysebaert, Joseph. *Greek Baptismal Terminology: Its Origins and Early Development.* Graecitas Christianorum primaeva 1. Nijmegen: Dekker and Van de Vegt, 1962.

CONTRIBUTORS

Suzanne Abrams Rebillard is a visiting scholar in the Classics Department at Cornell University and has taught at the American University of Paris. She is currently working on an English translation of Gregory of Nazianzus' *Poemata de seipso*. Her article "The Speech Act of Swearing: Gregory of Nazianzus' Oath in *Poema* 2.1.2 in Context" is forthcoming.

Christopher A. Beeley is the Walter H. Gray Associate Professor of Anglican Studies and Patristics at Berkeley Divinity School at Yale and Yale Divinity School. He is the author of *Gregory of Nazianzus on the Trinity and the Knowledge of God: In Your Light We Shall See Light* (2008); and *The Unity of Christ: Continuity and Conflict in Patristic Tradition* (2012).

Paul M. Blowers is the Dean E. Walker Professor of Church History and director of the Doctor of Ministry Program at Emmanuel Christian Seminary. His works include *Exegesis and Spiritual Pedagogy in Maximus the Confessor: An Investigation of the Quaestiones ad Thalassium* (1991); and *Drama of the Divine Economy: Creator and Creation in Early Christian Theology and Piety* (2012).

Brian E. Daley, SJ is the Catherine F. Huisking Professor of Theology at the University of Notre Dame. Among his many publications on patristic theology are *The Hope of the Early Church: A Handbook of Patristic Eschatology* (1991); and *Gregory of Nazianzus* (2006).

Susanna Elm is professor of history and classics at the University of California, Berkeley. She is the author of *Virgins of God: The Making of Asceticism in Late Antiquity* (1994); and *Sons of Hellenism, Fathers of the Church: Emperor Julian, Gregory of Nazianzus, and the Vision of Rome* (2012).

Everett Ferguson is Distinguished Scholar in Residence at Abilene Christian University and a recipient of the Distinguished Service Award from the North

American Patristic Society. His most recent book is *Baptism in the Early Church: History, Theology, and Liturgy in the First Five Centuries* (2009).

Ben Fulford is lecturer in systematic theology at the University of Chester. His articles include "Divine Names and the Embodied Intellect: Imagination and Sanctification in Gregory of Nazianzus' Account of Theological Language" (2011); and "'One Commixture of Light'" (2009).

Verna E. F. Harrison is an accomplished scholar of the Cappadocian Fathers. She is the author of *Grace and Human Freedom according to St. Gregory of Nyssa* (2002); and has translated into English Gregory of Nazianzus' *Festal Orations* (2008).

Andrew Hofer, OP is a member of the Pontifical Faculty of the Immaculate Conception in Washington, D.C. His Ph.D. dissertation examined the poetry of Gregory Nazianzen, and his articles include "Origen on the Ministry of God's Word in the *Homilies on Leviticus*" (2009).

Vasiliki Limberis is professor of religion at Temple University. She is the author of "Religion as the Cipher for Identity: The Cases of Emperor Julian, Libanius, and Gregory Nazianzus" (2000); and *Architects of Piety: The Cappadocian Fathers and the Cult of the Martyrs* (2011).

Andrew Louth is professor emeritus of patristic and Byzantine studies at the University of Durham. His many publications include *The Origins of the Christian Mystical Tradition: From Plato to Denys* (1981, 2007); and *St John Damascene: Tradition and Originality in Byzantine Theology* (2002).

Brian J. Matz is assistant professor of the history of Christianity at Carroll College, Montana. He is the author of "The Kenosis as Pastoral Example in Gregory Nazianzen's *Oration 12*" (2004); and *Patristic Sources and Catholic Social Teaching: A Forgotten Dimension. A Textual, Historical, and Rhetorical Analysis of Patristic Source Citations in the Church's Social Documents* (2008).

John A. McGuckin is the Ane Marie and Bent Emil Nielsen Professor in Late Antique and Byzantine Christian History at Union Theological Seminary, New York, and professor of Byzantine Christian studies at Columbia University. Among his many publications are *St. Gregory of Nazianzus: An Intellectual Biography* (2001); and the English translation *St. Gregory Nazianzen: Selected Poems* (1986).

Neil McLynn is university lecturer and fellow in later Roman history at Oxford University. He is the author of *Christian Politics and Religious Culture in Late*

Antiquity (2009); and a number of articles on Gregory of Nazianzus, including "Among the Hellenists: Gregory and the Sophists" (2006).

Claudio Moreschini is professor of Latin literature at the University of Pisa. His numerous publications include the standard edition of Gregory Nazianzen's *Poemata arcana* (1997); and the monographs *Filosofia e letteratura in Gregorio di Nazianzo* (1997) and *I Padri Cappadoci: Storia, letteratura, teologia* (2008).

Andrea Sterk is associate professor of history at the University of Florida. She is the author of *Renouncing the World Yet Leading the Church: The Monk-Bishop in Late Antiquity* (2004); and "Mission from Below: Captive Women and Conversion on the East Roman Frontiers" (2010).

William Tabbernee is executive director of the Oklahoma Conference of Churches (Churches of Christ) and teaches at the University of Phoenix. He is the author of *Fake Prophecy and Polluted Sacraments: Ecclesiastical and Imperial Reactions to Montanism* (2007); and *Prophets and Gravestones: An Imaginative History of Montanists and Other Early Christians* (2009).

GENERAL INDEX

INDEX TO THE WORKS OF
GREGORY OF NAZIANZUS

Poems

2.1.11.1125–29: 101
2.1.11.1137–45: 101
2.1.11.1146–86: 101
2.1.11.1167–80: 101
2.1.11.1174–75: 86n7

2.1.11.1174: 101
2.1.11.1187–272: 101
2.1.11.1273: 132
2.1.11.1440–70: 99n58
2.1.11.1527: 132

2.1.12.1–10: 131
2.1.13.57–58: 131
2.1.14: 132
2.1.14.7: 132
2.1.19.38–39: 132

2.1.19.49–50: 129
2.1.34: 128, 133–41, 142
2.1.34.209–10: 130
2.1.39: 5n4
2.1.68.1–32: 131

2.2.1.1–14 (*To Hellenius*): 179
2.2.1.16: 179n2
2.2.1.19–24: 180

2.2.1.29–30: 180
2.2.1.53–84: 180
2.2.1.86–87: 182
2.2.1.100–105: 181

2.2.1.120–21: 183
2.2.1.120: 187
2.2.1.129–30: 183
2.2.1.205–24: 183

2.2.1.225–62: 185
2.2.1.281–84: 186
2.2.1.293–307: 186

Letters

6.4: 88n18
6.115: 88n18
14–15: 184n27
52–53: 93
77: 99n57, 154, 160n3, 163n10
115: 163n10

120: 160n3
122–24: 163n10
127: 160n3
139: 164n14
157: 164n18
167: 160n3
168–70: 166n26

172: 160n3
182: 164n17
183–85: 165n22
185: 166n25
202.5: 97
204: 117
209–21: 166n26

219: 160n3, 166nn27–28
220: 160n3, 166n29
241.4: 187n39

INDEX TO BIBLICAL CITATIONS